Matriarchy in Bronze Age Crete

Matriarchy in Bronze Age Crete

A Perspective from Archaeomythology and Modern Matriarchal Studies

Joan Marie Cichon

ARCHAEOPRESS ARCHAEOLOGY

ARCHAEOPRESS PUBLISHING LTD
Summertown Pavilion
18-24 Middle Way
Summertown
Oxford OX2 7LG
www.archaeopress.com

ISBN 978-1-80327-044-9
ISBN 978-1-80327-045-6 (e-Pdf)

Cover: Side panel of Ayia Triadha sarcophagus with two Goddesses being pulled by griffins. Third Temple Palace/Postpalatial period, LM IB-LM IIIB c. 1450-1350/1300 BC, sarcophagus is 0.895m in height, 1.373-1.385m in length, and 0.45m in width, limestone, found inside a tomb, Ayia Triadha, Crete. Heraklion Museum, Crete. Photograph by Dr. Mara Lynn Keller. Reprinted with permission.

This book is available direct from Archaeopress or from our website www.archaeopress.com

Contents

List of Figures

Preface

First and foremost I wish to acknowledge my beloved parents, Marie Szymanski Cichon and John Edward Cichon, now both deceased, who fostered in me a great love of learning, and the understanding that few things in life are more important than an education. It was from my father that I also acquired my love of archaeology.

I am most grateful to my mentor, Dr. Mara Lynn Keller, for her unceasing counsel, encouragement, and support over the years. Also unfailing in their support have been my family members: my husband Nikolaos Kornaros, my sister, Alexandra Cichon, and my nephew Jade Cichon-Kelly. The encouragement of all my friends has also contributed greatly to the completion of this work.

To Marija Gimbutas, Heide Goettner-Abendroth, the scholars of modern matriarchal studies, the scholars of Women's Spirituality, and Aegean archaeologists working in the field for the last one hundred years, I owe a huge debt of gratitude for laying the foundations upon which this work is built.

Finally I wish to honor my ancestors, especially the women.

Introduction

Topic and inquiry questions

In this work I look at the issue of the role of the Goddess,[1] women, and matriarchy in Bronze Age Minoan[2] society and answer the question: was Bronze Age Crete a matristic, matrilineal, matriarchal, *gylanic*, egalitarian, gender diarchic, or patriarchal society, based on the definitions of those terms by Marija Gimbutas, Riane Eisler, Peggy Reeves Sanday, Heide Goettner-Abendroth, Shanshan Du, and Gerda Lerner? I begin with the hypothesis that Minoan Crete was a matriarchal society as defined by Heide Goettner-Abendroth. However, I also consider that my investigation might prove that such was not the case, and that another form of social, economic, political, and spiritual organization might better describe Bronze Age Crete—thus my consideration of Gimbutas's, Eisler's, Sanday's, Du's and Lerner's terms and definitions.

Despite the fact that authorities acknowledge that women played an important role or roles in Minoan society, and that the preeminent Minoan deity was female, there is a gap in the scholarly literature regarding the role of women and matriarchy in Minoan Crete. The debate over whether or not Bronze Age Crete was a matriarchal society continues to be heated and unresolved, and thus it is the intention of this study to advance the discussion toward a more complex, detailed, and certain conclusion.

To answer my overarching question, was Minoan Crete a matriarchal society? I first consider several preliminary questions: Was a Mother Goddess worshipped as the preeminent deity of Bronze Age Crete, and if so, was Crete therefore a Goddess-centered society as well? Was Bronze Age Crete a woman-centered society? Finally, is there evidence for matriarchal or matrilineal/matrilocal customs in the archaeomythological record of Minoan Crete?

As the last sentence indicates, the methodology employed in this work is archaeomythology, the discipline founded by archaeologist Marija Gimbutas in the late twentieth century, and encompassing the fields of archaeology, mythology, linguistics, folklore, and history. It is described in detail in Chapter 2, Methodology.

To answer the first question that I have identified above: was a Mother Goddess the primary Cretan deity, and was Crete a Goddess-centered society?, I begin by carefully defining the term Mother Goddess. I do not limit the role of the Mother Goddess, as many do, simply to fertility,

---

[1] My explanation of the capitalization of the word Goddess is found later in this chapter. In brief, it is based on several factors: she was the primary deity of Bronze Age Crete, and my understanding that although she has many manifestations, she was one Goddess.

[2] While I have continued to use the term 'Minoan' in this work to refer to Bronze Age Cretan society, I, along with many others, would like to find an alternative appellation. The term is a misnomer. King Minos, if he did indeed exist, lived several thousand years after the foundation of the first temple-palaces on Crete, and several hundred after Bronze Age Cretan civilization had been amalgamated into the Indo-European civilization that followed it. Moreover, as shall be discussed later in this work, it can be argued that only important women are present in the archaeological and archaeomythological record. Continuing to use the term 'Minoan' predisposes our thinking and limits our understanding. A number of scholars have come forward with alternative names for 'Minoan' Crete. Of those, Ariadnian seems the most appropriate to me at this point in time. For an understanding of why I favor the designation Ariadnian for Bronze Age Crete, see Cichon 2016: 78-99.

birthing, or nursing. In my definition, the Minoan Mother Goddess also embodies power and protection within all of Nature, mediates between life, death and rebirth, between the known and unknown, and is a manifestation of all the powers of Nature and the cosmos.

A review of the archaeological and scholarly literature reveals that most authorities agree that Crete was a Goddess-centered society. It is important to underscore this agreement because, as cultural historian Riane Eisler has noted, when a male god is worshipped as the primary or sole deity, men are in charge; and, where religions are Goddess-centered, the societies tend to have a female-centered social order.

> Religions in which the most powerful or only deity is male tend to reflect a social order in which descent is patrilinear (traced through the father) and domicile is patrilocal (the wife goes to live with the family or clan of her husband). Conversely, religions in which the most powerful or sole deity is female tend to reflect a social order in which descent is matrilinear (traced through the mother) and domicile is likewise matrilocal (a husband goes to live with his wife's family or clan).[3]

Eisler's view is further substantiated by the work of anthropologist Peggy Reeves Sanday in her study of one hundred and fifty-six societies (to be discussed later in detail).[4]

While there is agreement among scholars that Crete was a Goddess-centered society, authorities differ as to whether they define the Minoan Goddess as a Mother-Goddess, and whether they believe there was one Minoan Goddess or many. The various definitions of the Minoan Goddess and the issue of whether she was one or many are dealt with at length in this work.

After defining the term Mother Goddess, I survey, analyze, discuss, and (re)interpret the archaeological artifacts, the shrines, and the religious iconography, as well as a wide range of archaeological and archaeomythological studies and interpretations, to develop in detail the criteria by which to identify a Mother Goddess, given the architecture and iconography of Minoan Crete. I then go on to discuss the methodology of archaeologists Geraldine Gesell, Marija Gimbutas, Nanno Marinatos, Marina Moss and others working in the field of Minoan religion in order to determine their criteria for recognizing the Goddess. Their views as to whether there is just one Minoan Goddess or many are presented as well. Thus Chapter 4 establishes and expounds upon the criteria by which I propose to distinguish the Minoan Mother Goddess.

Chapter 5 presents the iconographic evidence for the existence of a Mother Goddess in Crete beginning with the Neolithic and continuing through to the end of the Bronze Age. Each item—fresco, figurine, piece of pottery, seal, sealstone, or ring—is discussed in detail in order to ascertain how it fits the criteria I developed (in the previous chapter). I conclude that the Mother Goddess, as I have defined her, is primary in Minoan Crete for a period spanning some five thousand years c. 6500-1070 BC, that Minoan Crete is a Goddess-centered society, and that gods are relatively few and mostly appear late on the scene.

---

[3] Eisler 1987: 24.
[4] Sanday 1981.

As for my second question, was Minoan Crete a woman-centered society?, although most authorities will concede that Crete was a Goddess-centered society, they will not agree that it was a woman-centered one as well. Unfortunately, there is no way to empirically prove a belief system—a belief in the centrality of women; or to prove beyond a shadow of a doubt that matriarchy existed in Minoan Crete. I believe I have constructed a case that is plausible and well substantiated.

Since the written language for this time period has not been definitively deciphered, and such written records as exist are small in number, the evidence for a woman-centered society consists primarily of archaeological evidence, artifacts, and architecture: artistic representations such as frescoes, figurines, seals and rings, alongside the remains of temple-palaces, towns, tombs, and residences. Mythology and history provide clues as well. I examine this evidence in Chapter 6, and conclude that a plausible and highly probable case for a central role for women in Minoan Crete can be made. Chapter 7 reinforces the argument that women were central by looking at the paucity of male ruler images in Bronze Age Crete; it examines those images that have been pointed to by authorities as possible candidates for such a role; and deconstructs the arguments for male rulership.

Regarding my third question: is there evidence for matriarchal or matrilineal/matrilocal customs in Minoan Crete, Chapter 8 provides extensive archaeological evidence as well as mythological and historical data for just such customs. Having answered in the affirmative to my three query questions, I conclude in Chapter 8 that based on the evidence presented in that chapter and the previous four chapters, a plausible, and compelling case can be made for declaring that Minoan Crete was a matriarchal society based on Heide Goettner-Abendroth's and modern matriarchal studies' definitions of the term.

Personal relationship to topic

I have long had a fascination with Bronze Age Crete. It stems from my first trip to Crete in 1987 when I spent a week visiting sites as a student in the six-week summer program of the American School of Classical Studies in Athens. Listening to archaeologists lecturing on the sites we were visiting, I kept asking myself, yes, but what was the life of the people of that society really like? Such questions came to me, I believe, as part of my previous training as an historian of social history. Indeed that was the reason why I was attracted to the new field of social history. It sought to answer the questions I was asking: how were the people living; not just the kings and aristocrats, but everyone and most especially the women. Unfortunately, the archaeologists I studied with that summer of 1987 could not or would not explore the issues of women and men, gender relations, religion, and social life in Minoan Crete. So I was left to wonder.

For the last thirty years I have wondered and studied and read. I also had the opportunity of participating in an archaeological survey on Crete. Thus this work arises out of my studies, my inquiry, my work with archaeologist Barbara Hayden at the Vrokastro (Iron Age) site of eastern Crete, my repeated visits to Cretan sites and museums, and the many months I have spent visiting and exploring the island. It also arises out of my long-standing feminism and my immersion in the Women's Spirituality movement for the last twenty-five years. Finally, it is a product of my interest in and study of Goettner-Abendroth's work and the work of other scholars in the field of modern matriarchal studies.

Scope and limitations of the study

This investigation focuses on Minoan Crete in the Bronze Age. While there is some discussion of the Neolithic period in Crete, and Cretan Neolithic artifacts, my consideration of the Neolithic is not nearly as comprehensive as that of the Bronze Age. Even though concentrating on the Bronze Age, this is not a comprehensive discussion of all the images and artifacts of that era. While I am well-versed in the vast array of archaeological artifacts and imagery across Crete from the Neolithic to the Classical Greek era, and have highlighted many of the key images that represent the major attributes of the Goddess(es) and the key social-spiritual roles of women in Bronze Age Crete, I have not included all of them.

I myself have not excavated in Crete, but as much as is possible I have worked with the site reports of those who have conducted the excavations. I have, moreover, visited most, if not all, of the sites discussed in this work, and viewed the artifacts examined in this study in the museums of Crete.

I have considered, but have not treated in a comprehensive way, Minoan gods or royalty. In my view, there is a small amount of evidence for a youthful god from the Neolithic onward. However, the imagery of gods in Minoan Crete is a small fraction compared to the imagery of the Goddess. Thus I chose not to focus on gods nor do a comprehensive discussion of them. As for Minoan royalty, I do not believe that Minoan Crete had kings or queens or an aristocracy. My Chapter 7 addresses the issue of the lack of ruler iconography in Crete, especially iconography of a priest-king. Nor does my research lead me to believe that there was a Minoan queen. Rather, I find evidence for councils of consensus facilitated by women elders of the society. The works of Marina Moss and Nanno Marinatos can provide those interested with an extensive treatment of Minoan gods and royalty.[5]

Although a part of archaeomythology, linguistics does not figure prominently in this study. This is partially because I myself am not a linguist, and partially because the written records such as we have for Minoan Crete are small in number, and there is as yet no agreement on their decipherment. I do however reference a small amount of linguistic information in this work.

Related to this issue of the lack of written records and the lack of consensus over how they are to be deciphered is the issue of social relations. There is little evidence regarding social relations in Minoan Crete because there are no written records. Thus we must learn what we can about this extremely important topic from the archaeological artifacts alone, especially the iconography, which of course is subject to interpretation.

I realize this work would be enhanced by the inclusion of more illustrations, and I would have liked to illustrate it extensively. However, I am limited by the photographs I myself was able to take (or borrow) given the difficulty of obtaining permission to publish photographs from those who hold the copyright.

---

[5] Moss 2005; Marinatos 2010.

The state of the art of archaeology in Crete is yet another limitation of this study. I have carefully addressed the complexity of the scholarly debate, but in many cases that debate is unsettled. For example, as I detail in my Methodology Chapter and elsewhere in this work, scholars are not agreed about the date of the Thera eruption, nor are they agreed as to how or when Greeks from the mainland, the Mycenaeans, arrived in Crete.

Related to this issue of the unsettled nature of the scholarly debate is the understanding that our knowledge about Minoan Crete is limited. We have access to only a fraction of what once existed, and new information, through chance finds or new excavations, could change what we know at any moment.

Within these limitations I have tried to present a well-balanced picture of Minoan Crete in the Bronze Age, and address both the pro's and con's of issues—not just the side which supports my own view. I believe I have been thoughtful and reasonable.

Finally, what I see as strengths, some might view as limitations: feminism, woman-centeredness, ecofeminism, an interest in the Goddess traditions of the world, my partiality to the theories and worldview of Marija Gimbutas, my use of the discipline of archaeomythology as my methodology, and my decision to use the term matriarchy, a term that is often misunderstood, and the definition of matriarchy as given by modern matriarchal studies.

Key definitions

I turn now to the definitions and key terms as used in this study. In this work I shall be considering several definitions of matriarchy, that of anthropologist Peggy Reeves Sanday and of philosopher Heide Goettner-Abendroth, as they might be applied to Minoan Crete; as well as archaeomythologist Marija Gimbutas's definition of the terms matristic and matrilineal; cultural historian Riane Eisler's definitions of *gylany* and partnership society; and anthropologist Shanshan Du's definitions of gender equalitarian societies. These are discussed in detail in the following pages. I will also consider again Gerda Lerner's definition of patriarchy. It may be that one or a combination of these definitions best fits Bronze Age Cretan society.

In a paper presented at the Sixteenth Congress of the Indo-Pacific Prehistory Association in 1998 entitled 'Matriarchy as a Sociocultural Form: An Old Debate in a New Light,' Sanday, specifically using the word matriarchy, argues that it is a construct 'based on gendered divisions in the sociocultural and *cosmological orders*. [emphasis added]'[6] Rejecting the usual definition of matriarchy as the opposite of patriarchy, Sanday asserts that matriarchy 'has never been theorized in and of itself.'[7] She goes on to explain:

> I suggest that the term matriarchy is relevant in societies where the cosmological and the social are linked by a primordial founding ancestress, mother goddess, or archetypal queen . . . the archetypal qualities of feminine symbols do not exist solely in the symbolic realm but are manifested in social practices that influence the lives of both sexes, not just women. These practices involve women (usually in their roles as mothers) in activities that authenticate and regenerate . . . , that nurture the social

---

[6] Sanday 1998: 1.
[7] Sanday 1998: 1.

order. By this definition, the ethnographic context of matriarchy does not reflect female power over subjects ... but female power ... *to conjugate*—to knit and regenerate social ties in the here-and-now and in the hereafter.[8]

Sanday concludes:

> In a strongly tradition-based society ultimate authority does not rest in political roles but in a cosmological order. If this cosmological order pivots around female oriented symbols and if this order is upheld by ritual acts coordinated by women whose social salience is also grounded in this order we can speak of matriarchy.[9]

Sanday says that in order to determine whether or not a society is a matriarchy we must also ask the following questions:

> Which sex bears the symbolic and social burden for conjugating the social universe? Which sex is imbued naturally or socially with the reproductive powers that recharge the sources of supernatural fecundity? What is the gender of the dominant symbols tying the archetypal to the social? How do males and females complement one another in the political arena and how is this arena tied to the cosmological order?[10]

In addition to her definitions of matriarchy and patriarchy, Sanday also defines the notion of *diarchy* as 'a complementary relation between the sexes;' here she uses Janet Hoskins's definition, one 'of shared powers and oscillations in control, structured by a doctrine of interdependence and mutuality.'[11] However, Sanday rejects the term diarchy as appropriate for the Minangkabau people of Western Sumatra (about whom she has conducted extensive field research), and she ends her article by noting that: 'Considerations of matriarchy, patriarchy, or diarchy should not be about which sex rules but how gender is represented in archetypal scenarios and reflected in social practices.'[12]

Since 1998 Sanday has reiterated and further elaborated her definition of matriarchy in two different publications: *Women at the Center: Life in a Modern Matriarchy*, published in 2002, and an article 'Matriarchal Values and World Peace: the Case of the Minangkabau,' in the 2009 anthology *Societies of Peace*, edited by Heide Goettner-Abendroth. In these works, Sanday, who has spent twenty years studying the matriarchal society of the Minangkabau of Western Sumatra, declares that we must abandon our idea that matriarchy means women's control of political power and substitute for it the understanding that matriarchy emphasizes 'the role of maternal symbols in webs of cultural significance.'[13] She proposes that matriarchy be redefined in terms of '*cultural symbols and practices associating the maternal with the origin and center of the growth processes necessary for social and individual life.*[emphasis in original]'[14]

---

[8] Sanday 1998: 1.
[9] Sanday 1998: 7.
[10] Sanday 1998: 7.
[11] Sanday 1998: 7.
[12] Sanday 1998: 7.
[13] Sanday 2003: 236.
[14] Sanday 2003: 236.

Sanday reserves the term matriarchy for 'structures highlighting maternal symbols and meanings.'[15] She believes that the maternal symbols and meanings of the Minangkabau (described below) evolve from the fact that the Minangkabau people are guided by the proverb 'Growth in nature is our teacher.'[16] In nature, all that is born in the world comes from the mother. Moreover, the growth of all living beings, from rice to children, must be nurtured; thus nurturance, by both females and males in Minangkabau society, is key.

Minangkabau society is matrilineal and matrilocal. Sanday maintains that, 'Maternal symbols related to origin and center ramify through the Minangkabau social universe.'[17] Bundo Kanduang, the mythical queen mother, is at the center of the Minangkabau world and that title, Bundo Kanduang, is also applied to senior Minangkabau women in their ceremonial roles. In Minangkabau society women oversee access rights to ancestral property, and all families trace their origins to a founding ancestress. Senior women are equated with the central pillar of the house which is considered its origin, navel, and ritual center. In *adat* (meaning local custom or tradition) ceremonies, which are at the crux of village social life, women are more involved than men. It is the women who fulfill *adat*. It is their ceremonial activities, and their devoted commitment to raising children according to *adat*, that ensures the stability of tradition. Minangkabau villages are known as 'mother,' and the cultural focus on maternal origin and center is even evident in songs which place the mother at the center of emotions.

Although women are at the center, Sanday stresses that there is balance in male and female relations and both must be nurturers for society to remain stable and for growth to continue. As she writes in 'Matriarchal Values and World Peace':

> matriarchal values grow out of a social philosophy in which the emphasis is on cooperation . . . matriarchy is not about 'female rule,' but about social principles and values rooted in maternal meanings in which both sexes work together to promote human well-being.[18]

In contrast to Goettner-Abendroth (the next theorist to be discussed) Sanday calls her approach 'particularistic'—she is not a believer in evolutionary stages, rather she holds that institutions such as matriarchy are the consequence of the blending and interaction of complex structures within cultures.[19]

German philosopher and feminist Heide Goettner-Abendroth, who has spearheaded the modern matriarchal studies movement, has also resurrected and redefined the term matriarchy—independently of Sanday. Goettner-Abendroth has spent her lifetime studying matriarchies both in their socio-cultural and historical contexts. Pointing out, as does Sanday, that the Greek word *arché* has a double meaning, 'beginning' as well as 'domination,' Goettner-Abendroth argues that matriarchy should be translated as 'the mothers from the beginning.'[20] Her 'explication' of matriarchy is more than a simple definition, for her goal is to set out the deep structure of matriarchal society; provide a structural definition that can form the

---

[15] Sanday 2003: 236.
[16] Sanday 2003: 236.
[17] Sanday 2003: 237.
[18] Sanday 2009: 217.
[19] Sanday 2008: 3:194.
[20] Goettner-Abendroth 2009: 17.

basis of a comprehensive theory on matriarchal societies to be used and developed by other researchers in the field of matriarchal studies; and to provide a hybrid methodology that is multidisciplinary. Indeed, Goettner-Abendroth has created a new paradigm which she calls the 'matriarchy paradigm.' 'The central tenet of this paradigm is that women have not only created society and culture over long periods of human history, but that all subsequent cultural developments originated there and are based on these societies.'[21]

What Goettner-Abendroth calls the deep structure of matriarchal societies refers to four levels of society: the economic, social, political, and cultural (including worldview and spirituality). At the level of economics, matriarchal societies, which are usually, but not always, agricultural societies,

> practice a subsistence economy that achieves local and regional self-reliance. Land and houses belong to the clan in the sense of usage rights, while private ownership of property and territorial claims are unknown concepts. There is a vivid circulation of goods along the lines of kinship and marriage customs. The system of circulation prevents the accumulation of goods by one individual or clan, as the ideal is distribution rather than accumulation. . . . In economic terms, matriarchies are known for their perfectly balanced reciprocity. For that reason I define them **as societies of economic reciprocity**. [emphasis in original][22]

At the social level, matriarchal societies are founded on motherhood and are based on the clan.

> People live together in large kinship groups that follow the principle of matriliny, that is, relatedness based on the mother's line. The name of the clan, and all social honours and political titles, are inherited from the mothers. A matri-clan consists of at least three generations of women, plus the directly related men.[23]

Such societies are also matrilocal, with women remaining in the maternal home permanently and husbands moving there. Marriage between clans is either achieved through en mass marriages between clans or individual choice. What is important is that 'in this way, a society without hierarchies is shaped, one that sees itself as an extended clan. Therefore, I define matriarchies as **non-hierarchical, horizontal societies of matrilineal kinship**. [emphasis in original]'[24]

At the level of politics, the process of decision making is also organized along kinship lines.

> In matriarchal societies, political practice follows the principle of consensus which means *unanimity* for each decision. Matriarchal societies are well-organized to actualize this principle, and practice it along the lines of matriarchal kinship. . . . The source of all the politics are the clan house where the people live, and in this way, a true 'grassroots democracy' is put into practice. The foundation for this political system is an economy of reciprocity, based on gift-giving and the 'big family' of a society of matrilineal kinship.[25]

---

[21] Goettner-Abendroth 2009: 19.
[22] Goettner-Abendroth 2007: 3-4.
[23] Goettner-Abendroth 2007: 4.
[24] Goettner-Abendroth 2007: 4.
[25] Goettner-Abendroth 2009: 23.

Goettner-Abendroth calls matriarchies 'egalitarian societies of consensus.'

Finally on the cultural level, matriarchies are **'sacred societies as cultures of the Goddess or Divine Feminine**. [emphasis in original]'[26] In matriarchy, divinity is immanent and feminine, and everything is sacred.

In their works, both Sanday and Goettner-Abendroth have stressed the non-hierarchical, reciprocal, egalitarian nature of the relationship between men and women in matriarchal societies. Riane Eisler, scholar, futurist and activist, offers a similar vision, but without using the term matriarchy—which she believes has a negative connotation. Eisler has developed her 'cultural transformation theory' which proposes that underlying the great surface diversity of human culture are two basic models of society: the dominator model, in which one half of humanity (male) is ranked over the other (female); and the partnership model in which social relations are primarily based on the principle of linking rather than ranking. In this partnership model, diversity is not equated with either inferiority or superiority.[27] Eisler has also coined a term for this more egalitarian relationship: *gylany*.

> *Gy* derives from the Greek root word *gyne,* or 'woman.' *An* derives from *andros,* or 'man.' The letter *l* between the two has a double meaning. In English, it stands for the linking of both halves of humanity, rather than, as in androcracy, their ranking. In Greek, it derives from the verb *lyein* or *lyo,* which in turn has a double meaning: to solve or resolve . . . and to dissolve or set free. . . . In this sense the letter *l* stands for the resolution of our problems through the freeing of both halves of humanity from stultifying and distorting rigidity of roles imposed by the domination hierarchies inherent in androcractic systems.[28]

In Eisler's perspective, seemingly irrational historical events can be understood as 'the tension between organized challenges to traditions of domination . . . and enormous dominator resistance.'[29] Her research also illustrates the pivotal importance of the fact that how a culture structures the most fundamental of human relations, the relations between the female and male halves of society, structures everything else about the society.[30] In Eisler's model a dominator system is characterized by top-down authoritarianism in both the family and state; the subordination of the female half of humanity to the male half; and a high level of fear and institutionalized violence. The partnership system, on the other hand, exhibits the following configuration: a more democratic organization in both the family and state or tribe; the equal valuation of men and women, and of stereotypically feminine values (such as caring and nonviolence) whether they are embodied in women or men; and a less violent or nonviolent way of life, as violence will not be needed to maintain hierarchies.[31]

Lithuanian-American archaeologist, and founder of the discipline of archaeomythology, Marija Gimbutas, adopts Eisler's term *gylany* in her work with the pre-Indo-European societies of Old Europe/Anatolia and she employs the terms matrilineal and matristic as well.

---

[26] Goettner-Abendroth 2007: 6.
[27] Eisler 1987: xvii.
[28] Eisler 1987:105.
[29] Eisler 2008: 44.
[30] Eisler 2008: 44.
[31] Eisler 2008: 44-45.

Gimbutas was a pioneer in the study of the symbolic imagery of the earliest farming peoples of Europe. Examining thousands of sculptures, vessels, and pieces of cult equipment from the cultures of Old Europe, southeast Europe and Anatolia, *c.* 6500-3500 BC, as well as settlement patterns, social structures, and burial evidence; and using other component disciplines of archaeomythology: linguistics, mythology, and historical research, Gimbutas developed a worldview which is made up of four parts. The first is an understanding that the sacred source of life in Old Europe was venerated as a female, a Goddess, who was one with Nature, and manifesting in three aspects: as Life-Giver, Life-Taker, and Regeneratrix; the second, the deciphering of a complex system of symbols related to Her worship in Her three aspects, the 'language of the Goddess'; the third, a reinterpretation of Neolithic Europe and Anatolia as peaceful, egalitarian, matrilineal, and artistic, as 'a true civilization in the best meaning of the word'; [32] and the fourth, an explanation of how and why the civilization of the Goddess was amalgamated into the patriarchal civilizations that 'conquered' it. The third point above speaks to Gimbutas's view of the social structure of Old Europe/Anatolia (which includes Bronze Age Crete), which she believed mirrored sacred beliefs.[33]

Gimbutas defined matrilineal as 'A social structure in which ancestral descent and inheritance is traced through the female line.'[34] She called this social system 'matristic,' and defined matristic as 'a matrilineal "partnership" society in which women are honored but do not subjugate men.'[35] Explaining her use of these terms rather than the term matriarchy, she writes:

> The difficulty with the term matriarchy in 20th century anthropological scholarship is that it is assumed to represent a complete mirror image of patriarchy or androcracy. . . . We do not find in Old Europe, nor in all of the Old World, a system of autocratic rule by women with an equivalent suppression of men. . . . I use the term matristic simply to avoid the term matriarchy with the understanding that it incorporates matriliny.[36]

Gimbutas died in 1994. If she were still alive today, I believe she would revise her stance on the term matriarchy. Indeed, although she never used the term, her description of the societies of Old Europe/Anatolia closely resembles the definitions of matriarchy proposed by Sanday and Goettner-Abendroth.

Several other definitions I shall consider, as they might apply to Bronze Age Cretan society, are those developed by Shanshan Du in her works *Chopsticks Only Work in Pairs*, published in 2002, and 'Frameworks for Societies in Balance: A Cross-Cultural Perspective on Gender Equality,' published in 2009. In her earlier work Du, as a result of her anthropological field research with the Lahu people in southwestern China, identifies three types of gender equal societies. A gender equalitarian society is 'one whose dominant ideology, institutions and social practices

---

[32] Gimbutas 1991: viii.
[33] While the term 'Old Europe' is generally understood to encompass the Neolithic period 6500-3500 BC, Gimbutas did include Bronze Age Crete in the term. In the *The Civilization of The Goddess* she writes, 'Old European culture continued on the island of Crete for several millennia longer than on the mainland' (Gimbutas 1991: 344). In *The Living Goddesses* she says, 'Minoan culture had deep roots in Old Europe and Old Anatolia' (149). She adds, 'Minoans continued the Neolithic artistic and goddess-centered cultures. . . . With the fall of the Minoan culture (1450 BCE), the last of the Old-European-The old Anatolian civilizations disappeared' (Gimbutas 1999: 150).
[34] Gimbutas 1991: 433.
[35] Gimbutas 1991: 433.
[36] Gimbutas 1991: 324.

value its male and female members equally, regardless of the roles they play.'[37] The three types are: dyadic, or gender similarity (in a later article, discussed below, Du changes this term to gender unity); gender complementarity; and gender triviality (differences without significance). In 'Frameworks for Societies in Balance: A Cross-Cultural Perspective on Gender Equality,' Du adds a fourth type: maternal centrality.

This fourth type of gender equal society, maternal centrality, 'greatly overlaps'[38] with matriarchy as defined by Sanday and Goettner-Abendroth. Du defines it as follows:

> Typically associated with societies that are characterized by matrilineal descendant rule and matrilocal residence pattern, the socio-cultural framework of maternal centrality tends to highlight gender difference . . . the symbolism of this model tends to elevate the female principle over its male counterpart. . . . The principle value of this framework is placed on the characteristics that are commonly associated with maternity, such as life-giving, nurturance, connection, and harmony.[39]

Du stresses that despite the fact that in such a system the mother is favored, it does not mean that the male is subordinate.

Gender complementarity is the perception of the two sexes as 'different-but-equal.'[40] Du believes that the framework of gender complementarity generates equality between men and women by promoting symmetrical reciprocity of the two sexes. She finds it similar to maternal centrality because it symbolically highlights the differences between the sexes and institutionalizes gender separation in social and economic spheres. In contrast to maternal centrality, however, gender complementarity does not favor female gender symbolism over male.

Gender triviality is the third type of 'egalitarian framework.' In this framework, men and women are equal because of 'the gender-blind attitudes of the dominant ideologies and institutions.'[41] Neither sex is judged more significant than the other, and 'gender itself is ignored.'[42] Du has found that gender trivial societies highly value individual autonomy and collective cooperation.

The final type of egalitarian framework is gender-unity, what Du had previously called dyadic or gender-similarity. Such societies 'minimize the symbolic and social significance of sex differences.'[43] Du's research and fieldwork have focused on just such a society, the Lahu people of southwest China. The worldview of the Lahu highlights similarity and harmony between males and females. This is apparent not only in daily activities, such as childcare, domestic chores, subsistence work, and leadership, but in their cosmology as well where the supreme godhead is a male/female dyad.

---

[37] Du 2002: 9.
[38] Du 2009: 257.
[39] Du 2009: 257.
[40] Du 2009: 258.
[41] Du 2009: 260.
[42] Du 2009: 259.
[43] Du 2009: 260.

I will consider whether Minoan Crete might better fit into one of Du's categories than into the categories of matriarchy, or *gylany*, or matrilocal/matrilineal/matristic. I will also consider if her investigations might prove fruitful for understanding the status of women in Minoan Crete.

Finally, I want to define patriarchy. As has already been stated several times, patriarchy is generally understood as male power over—male political, social, and economic power over women and children. Sanday defines it as 'father-right'; 'a code word for male tribal leadership';[44] exclusive male rule.[45] Eisler refers to patriarchy as 'a social system ruled through force or the threat of force by men.'[46] Patriarchy is an example of Eisler's dominator society or model. These generally agree with the view of cultural historian Gerda Lerner, who defines patriarchy as:

> the manifestation and institutionalization of male dominance over women and children in the family and the extension of male dominance over women in society in general. It implies that men hold power in all the important institutions of society and that women are deprived of access to such power.[47]

For the purposes of this study, I will be using Lerner's definition of patriarchy. In this investigation I shall be re-evaluating whether ancient Crete is to be considered a Goddess-centered society that is also a male-dominated society, as interpreted by the majority of archaeologists at this point in time. Their views I will consider more closely in Chapter 8.

To summarize, I will be examining five different definitions to see which might best apply to Bronze Age Crete: Sanday's and Goettner-Abenroth's definitions of matriarchy, Gimbutas's definitions of matrilineality, matrilocality and matristic, Eisler's partnership society or *gylany*, Du's gender equal society; or Sanday's, Eisler's, or Lerner's definition of patriarchy. I anticipate my research will show that one of the definitions of matriarchy; matrilineality, matrilocality and matristic; *gylany*; or gender equal rather than patriarchy, best describes Crete from the Neolithic until at least *c.* 1450 BC.

Explanation of capitalization of Goddess

I would like to explain my capitalization of the word Goddess(es) and the use of lower case for the word god(s). In Minoan Crete, the Goddess was the primary deity. Thus, I believe that capitalizing the word Goddess(es) reflects the Goddess's central significance in Bronze Age Crete where the male deities were of secondary importance. Moreover, my studies have led me to conclude that in Bronze Age Crete one Goddess in many manifestations was worshipped. Since I understand the Minoan Goddess as one Goddess, I believe the term should be capitalized. I am aware that there is disagreement among Aegeanists on the issue of whether there was one Goddess or many Goddesses. Some of those who are of the opinion that the ancient Cretans worshipped one Goddess, capitalize the term Goddess, while others do not. Among those authorities who see Crete as worshipping many Goddesses, the term is not capitalized.

---

[44] Sanday 1998: 1.
[45] Sanday 1998: 1.
[46] Eisler 1987: 105.
[47] Lerner 1986: 239.

Of course the larger context in which the issue of a single Cretan Goddess or many Goddesses is held, is that of the controversy that ranges across numerous disciplines, as to whether or not a single Goddess in her various manifestations was worshiped in the Neolithic. I am a proponent of the argument that such was the case. I am especially persuaded by the theories of Gimbutas whose work demonstrating a Goddess-centered culture in Neolithic Old Europe, including Crete, has already been and will be discussed in detail in this work. This is an added reason that factors into my decision to capitalize the word Goddess.

Finally, my personal beliefs enter into my choice to capitalize the word Goddess. In my spiritual practice it is a Divine Female that I envision and it is a Divine Female that I pray to and commune with. While I do not claim that the Divine Feminine is superior to or more important than the sacred masculine, it is the Divine Feminine that is of the uppermost importance in my life and for this reason also I capitalize the word Goddess.

Significance of the study: academic, social, personal, and spiritual

Academic significance

The academic significance of this work is to be found in several areas. First of all, I believe this research has advanced the debate over whether or not Bronze Age Crete was a matriarchal society, a debate that has been heated and unresolved, toward a more complex, detailed, and certain conclusion. Advancing that debate was one of the stated intentions of this study.

This work also provides a very different perspective of Bronze Age Crete than that usually found in academic writings on Minoan Crete. It contributes not only to a better understanding of Minoan society, but adds to our knowledge of ancient women-centered, Goddess-centered societies in general.

Additionally, this investigation is of significance academically because it combines two relatively new fields of academic study, archaeomythology and modern matriarchal studies, to examine an issue that is of interest across the disciplines of archaeology, mythology, history of religion, anthropology, Women's Spirituality and women's studies. It is illustrative of the way in which the two fields can be used in combination to address issues of interest to scholars.

This work is also of academic significance because it advances the field of archaeomythology, illustrating how archaeomythology's use as a methodology can expand the academy's knowledge of both the spiritual and material aspects of ancient societies.

Another contribution is my construction of a set of characteristics for identifying a Mother Goddess in the iconography of ancient Crete. This is detailed in Chapter 4.

Finally, this study contributes to the field of modern matriarchal studies because it provides a picture of a woman-based culture in pre-patriarchal Europe--Minoan Crete--that is based on rigorous academic scholarship, not on fantasy; adds a voice to those who would argue that one can make a plausible case for the existence of pre-historical matriarchal societies; and familiarizes scholars and non-academics alike with the field of modern matriarchal studies, Sanday's and Goettner-Abendroth's definitions of matriarchy, and a more complex understanding of how matriarchy is not simply the reverse of patriarchy.

Social significance

I believe this work provides evidence for scholars and the general public alike that will enable them to understand that the theory of the existence of ancient matriarchy is not simply a fanciful concept, but has a basis in reality. Such knowledge may help people to envision and perhaps work, in a more hopeful way, toward a different sort of world than now exists, one that exhibits equality between the sexes, a balanced economy, peacefulness, and puts the spiritual rather than the material at the center of human concern. Gerda Lerner noted, 'The system of patriarchy is a historical construct; it had a beginning and it will have an end.'[48] This work gives some notion of what history might have been like before the historical construct of patriarchy, and of what society's goals and values might be once it comes to an end.

Personal and spiritual significance

On a personal level, researching, writing, and refining this work has allowed me to further ground my own belief in a Divine Female in material reality. It is important to my own spirituality that I can find evidence for the existence and centrality of a Female Divine in Old Europe for that is the area of the world from which my ancestors came and where my roots are.

It is also personally significant to me that I am able to ground in academic scholarship the understanding that at least one matriarchal society existed in the past. As a woman and feminist, I am heartened by the knowledge that human history sustained a balanced, egalitarian, peaceful, woman-centered, sacred society for several thousand years.

Conclusion

This introductory chapter has set forth the issue I look at in this study: the role of the Goddess, women, and matriarchy in Bronze Age Crete; stated my relationship to the topic; defined the key terms to be used; and addressed the limitations and significance of this work. The question I set out to answer was: Is Bronze Age Crete a matriarchal, matrilineal/matrilocal/matristic, *gylanic*, gender equal, or patriarchal society? I detailed the lines of approach I will follow to answer that question.

The conclusions I have drawn as a result of my research are presented in Chapter 8. Chapters 4, 5, 6, and 7 present the bulk of the evidence in support of my conclusions; Chapter 2 describes the methodology utilized to analyze the data and arrive at my conclusions; and Chapter 3 gives the historical background to the more than century-old matriarchy/patriarchy debates. Chapter 1 will now review the literature of Women's Spirituality, modern matriarchal studies, archaeomythology, and Aegean, particularly Minoan, archaeology.

---

[48] Lerner 1986: 198.

Chapter 1

Literature Review

Having given some background as to my interest in the subject, stated the questions to be answered, discussed the most important definitions to be used in this study, and highlighted the significance of this study, I will now turn to the literature review. The literature to be reviewed is divided into four sections: Women's Spirituality and the Study of Ancient Mediterranean Cultures; Anthropological, Archaeological and Historical Evidence for Matriarchy; Archaeological and Mythological Evidence for Bronze Age Crete as a Goddess-Centered Society; and Archaeological, Archaeomythological and Historical Evidence for Bronze Age Crete as a Woman-Centered Society. I begin with the relevant literature in the field of Women's Spirituality.

Women's Spirituality

My life and work have been shaped and informed by the Women's Spirituality movement. I have read extensively in the literature of Women's Spirituality and been influenced by many, if not all, of the works I have read. The first work that profoundly impacted me was Carol P. Christ's 1987 publication *The Laughter of Aphrodite.* In that work Christ recounts her spiritual journey and her discovery of the Divine Feminine. I realized while reading that book that the Divine Feminine was the missing piece that I too had been searching for. Finding her, I finally felt whole.

Most important among the works of Women's Spirituality, as regards this work, have been the books of archaeomythologist Marija Gimbutas, *The Language of the Goddess* published in 1989, *The Civilization of the Goddess*, published in 1991, and *The Living Goddesses*, published in 1999. Her theories will be elaborated upon more fully in the methodology section.

Carol Christ's 1995 work *Odyssey with the Goddess*, in which she details her further spiritual transformation while researching and traveling to sites sacred to the Goddess in Crete and then leading groups of women pilgrims there, is also germinal to this study. It was after reading that book and then making a pilgrimage to Crete with Christ and fifteen other women, that I integrated the Female Divine into my life, came to know and appreciate the work of Marija Gimbutas, and began my own serious archaeomythological research by authoring a brief article entitled 'The Octopus as a Symbol of the Goddess in Minoan Crete.'

Dr. Mara Lynn Keller's 1998 article 'Crete of the Mother Goddess: Communal Rituals and Sacred Art,' that details with art, archaeological, mythological, and historical examples the Goddess culture that once existed on that island and that one still feels when one visits Crete, has also been of great importance to me in my understanding of Minoan Crete. The art of ancient Crete, the dance, the religious symbols, the birth/death and rebirth rituals, are all discussed by Keller to illustrate how the ancient Cretans lived 'in harmony with the universal stream of life.'[1]

Susan Evasdaughter's 1996 book *Crete Reclaimed: A Feminist Exploration of Bronze Age Crete* is yet another work that has served to inspire me in my own research. Evasdaughter brings out in her work a rich evocation of the everyday life of the ancient Cretans, something I had been looking for on my trip to Crete twenty years earlier, and she details, as the subtitle suggests, the important role of women in that ancient society.

Other Women's Spirituality works pertaining to ancient Crete which have been inspirational to me include those of Elinor Gadon, *The Once and Future Goddess* published in 1989, and Anne Baring and Jules Cashford, *The Myth of the Goddess: Evolution of an Image* published in 1991.

Anthropological, archaeological, and historical evidence for matriarchy

My review of relevant anthropological, archaeological, and historical texts will begin with the historical background to the debates over matriarchy, which have raged for over one hundred years. In these debates, Johann Jakob Bachofen's 1861 publication *Das Mutterrecht*, John McLennan's 1865 work *Primitive Marriage*, and Friedrich Engels' *The Origins of the Family, Private Property and the State*, published in 1884, are important as early works that argued for matriarchy as an evolutionary predecessor to patriarchy. It was Bachofen's work that first put forth the theory of original matriarchy arguing that hetaerism, a period of complete male promiscuity, was followed by matriarchy, which was characterized by monogamy, the supremacy of mothers, and the tracing of descent through the motherline. Matriarchy was then followed, according to Bachofen, by patriarchy, a superior stage of human development in which society moved from an 'acceptance of nature to a transcending of nature.'[2] Both McLennan's and Engles' work, which built on Bachofen's, though with different results, are discussed later in this study.

Classicist Jane Ellen Harrison's works: *Prolegomena to the Study of Greek Religion*, published in 1903, and *Themis: A Study of the Social Origins of Greek Religion*, published in 1913, are also reviewed in this investigation. Harrison, who built on the works of these early 'matriarchal theorists,' is important as an early proponent of a pre-Hellenic, woman-centered, Goddess-centered and matriarchal society. A classics scholar who used mythology and archaeology extensively, Harrison, like so many of her era, was influenced by Frazer's *Golden Bough*, a compilation of anthropological data and a monumental study in comparative folklore, magic, and religion.

With the demise of the evolutionary paradigm in the early twentieth century, the term matriarchy fell into disuse. Peggy Sanday notes that it was revived in the early 1970s by feminist activists. The 1970 work of Kate Millet, *Sexual Politics*, and Adrienne Rich's 1976 publication *Of Woman Born* are discussed in this regard; at that time they were denounced by male as well as female anthropologists who argued that there was no archaeological or ethnographic evidence for the existence of matriarchy.[3] The work of some of these anthropologists: Louise Lamphere, Michelle Rosaldo, and Joan Bamburg, is collected in a 1974 book edited by Lamphere

---

[1] Keller 1998: 15.
[2] Bachofen 1967: 111.
[3] Sanday 1998: 5-6.

and Rosaldo entitled *Women, Culture and Society* and is reviewed in this study. We will see this same argument used over and over again by archaeologists and classicists in connection with Minoan Crete, for example in Peter J. Ucko's 1968 book *Anthropomorphic Figurines* and, more recently, in Ronald Hutton's 1997 article, 'Neolithic Great Goddess', and Ruth Tringham and Margaret Conkey's 1998 essay 'Rethinking Figurines' discussed below.

It is Sanday and her 2003 book *Women at the Center: Life in a Modern Matriarchy*, who, along with Goettner-Abendroth and her work, the latest of which is the 2012 book entitled *Matriarchal Societies: Studies on Indigenous Cultures Across the Globe*, who are currently reviving the term matriarchy with the very precise definitions that we saw in the Introduction. Sanday's earlier work, *Female Power, Male Dominance*, published in 1987, which explores correlations between natural and social environments, psychological orientations, male and female deity worship, the gendered distribution of roles and social power, and the amount of violence in a society, is also very important for my study.

Although she does not use the term matriarchy, Riane Eisler, in her 1987 book *The Chalice and the Blade* (also discussed in the Introduction), stresses an egalitarian relationship between the male and female halves of society and proposes her 'partnership model' as an alternative to the 'dominator model' of patriarchy. In Eisler's view, Minoan Crete was such a partnership model or *gylany*.

Marija Gimbutas, whose methodology of archaeomythology figures very prominently in this present work, in her books *The Language of the Goddess* (1987), *The Civilization of the Goddess* (1991), and *The Living Goddesses* (1999), used Eisler's term *gylany* as well as the terms matristic and matrilineal to describe the societies of Old Europe/Anatolia of which Minoan Crete was a part. Her work is vitally important to any discussion of gender relations in Bronze Age Europe.

Finally, anthropologist Shanshan Du, who is also working in this new field of modern matriarchal studies, adds an important dimension with her 2002 study of the Lahu people of China, in *Chopsticks Only Work in Pairs*, and her elaboration of four different types of gender equal societies. Her work was reviewed in the Introduction.

Another anthropologist who concluded from her study of the available evidence that Crete was a matriarchy is Ruby Rohrlich-Leavitt, whose article 'Women in Transition: Crete and Sumer,' published in 1977 in the anthology, *Becoming Visible: Women in European History*, contrasted the matriarchy of early Crete with the rise of patriarchy in Sumer.

Finally, it must be noted that the new field of modern matriarchal studies is not without its critics. Perhaps the most vocal has been historian of religion Cynthia Eller and her work, *The Myth of Matriarchal Prehistory*, published in 2000. Eller's book is discussed and critiqued in Chapter 3.

Archaeological and mythological evidence for Bronze Age Crete as a Goddess-centered society

In the first part of the twentieth century, archaeology was closely associated with mythology, and in fact, a number of the key figures to be discussed here worked as archaeologists who relied heavily on the works of ancient mythology. These include Sir Arthur Evans, Martin P. Nilsson, and Jacquetta Hawkes, among others. While this combination of interests was eschewed by the 'new archaeologists' following World War II, the combination of interest in archaeology and mythology has been pioneered in the Post World War II era, to a great extent, by archaeologist and mythologer Marija Gimbutas. All these scholars have made contributions to an understanding of Bronze Age Crete as a Goddess-centered society.

Any evidence for Minoan Crete as a Goddess-centered society must begin with the work of archaeologist Sir Arthur Evans, the man who excavated Knossos and 'discovered' Minoan civilization. In his monumental work, *The Palace of Minos*, published between 1921-1926, Evans sets forth the view that the Minoans worshipped a Goddess, in many different manifestations, as the primary deity in Minoan Crete.

> Clearly, the Goddess was supreme, whether we are to regard her as substantially one being of varied aspects, celestial, terrestrial or infernal, or whether we have to deal with separate, or partly differentiated divine entities. As a working hypothesis the former view has been here preferred, and it has been assumed that the same Great Goddess is represented. [4]

In his 1949 work *The Minoan-Mycenaean Religion and its Survival in Greek Religion*, classical archaeologist and historian Martin P. Nilsson argues, as the title of his work indicates, that Greek religion of the Classical Age was a blending of Greek and Minoan religion. Nilsson, like Evans before him and many scholars to follow, believed that female deities were the more prominent in Minoan religion. Unlike Evans, he saw many Goddesses, not one all-embracing Goddess, at the center of the Minoan pantheon. In accordance with Evans, however, Nilsson did note that 'male gods are surprisingly rare.'[5]

Archaeologist Jacquetta Hawkes writing in her 1968 work *The Dawn of the Gods*, reaffirmed Evans's view: 'In the scenes from the seal-stones, not only is the Goddess always the central figure, being served and honored in a variety of ways; she is sometimes shown seated on a throne.'[6] Hawkes goes on to note that 'the Cretans saw the supreme divine power in terms of the feminine principle, and incarnate in a woman whom they portrayed exactly as one of themselves.'[7] For Hawkes, it is the Goddess, in her many manifestations, who rules supreme in Minoan Crete and who retains her ascendancy 'for a time even under the Mycenaeans.'[8] 'The attributes of the Cretan goddess help to reveal her as both the one and the many.'[9]

Eminent Greek archaeologist Nicholas Platon, discoverer of the palace of Zakros, and former chief curator of the Heraklion Museum, writing in 1966 about religion in Minoan Crete says:

> Goddesses, as the productive deities, were considered the most important. In art they are portrayed in their various aspects as the Queen of the Wild Beasts, *Kourotrophos*

---

[4] Evans 1964: 3:457-458.
[5] Nilsson 1949: 396.
[6] Hawkes 1968: 154.
[7] Hawkes 1968: 131.
[8] Hawkes 1968: 133.
[9] Hawkes 1968: 137.

(Nursing Mother of Youths), Mother and Daughter, the Goddess of the Serpents, and the Goddess of the Doves.[10]

As for a male god, Platon believes that the fact that one is generally missing from the artifacts and iconography, in addition to the fact that the bull symbol seems to have played an important role for the Minoans, indicates that 'the bull symbolized the male creative force and that the god was worshipped in this form.'[11] If this interpretation is correct, the question remains as to why the sacred masculine principle was not imaged anthropomorphically.

The 1985 book of archaeologist Geraldine C. Gesell, *Town, Palace and House Cult in Minoan Crete*, presents her findings that all the known Minoan figurines which may represent a divinity are female. She adds that it is not understood whether the various attributes represented on the Minoan Goddess represent one Goddess or many.[12] Gesell finds no evidence of a preeminent male divinity until the Geometric period (c. 810 BC).[13]

Archaeologist Nanno Marinatos in her 1993 work *Minoan Religion* also takes up the issue of polytheism versus monotheism. She concludes that Evans was correct: 'There is an essential unity in the symbolism which connects the goddess with nature in all its manifestations.'[14] For Marinatos, the essence of the Minoan Goddess is 'a nurturing goddess of nature.'[15] As for gods, Marinatos disagrees with Nilsson that gods are rare: 'Despite the indisputable predominance of goddesses, male gods are neither rare nor unimportant.'[16] She believes that Minoan gods were not just simply the consort of the Goddess, but that their domain included both the wilderness and urban settings. She finds no 'creator or god of wisdom,' nor does she find martial deities, 'the armed god seems rather to be a hunter.'[17] However, in a more recent work of 2010, *Minoan Kingship and the Solar Goddess*, Marinatos reverses some of her thinking and argues that the Minoan god is the 'bright star in the constellation of Minoan deities.'[18] This work is discussed and critiqued in Chapter 7.

Archaeologist Marija Gimbutas discusses Minoan Crete in several of her works, including *The Living Goddesses*, published in 1999. Calling Bronze Age Crete an Old European/Anatolian society, one of the hallmarks of which is a Goddess-centered religion, Gimbutas feels there is no question that the iconography of ancient Crete preserves the Goddess of Old Europe/Anatolia in her triple aspect as Birth-Giver, Death-Wielder, and Regeneratrix, and she details that iconography in her chapter on Crete: the pillar crypts, the horns of consecration, the double ax, the tree of life, the faience Snake Goddesses, spirals, breasts, rosettes, marine life, lilies, and bulls' horns. Calling the palaces 'religious-administrative-economic complexes' (as does author Rodney Castleden and archaeologist Nanno Marinatos), Gimbutas interprets them as temples of rebirth and regeneration and notes that they are 'embellished with ubiquitous scenes of goddess worship' and 'embrace an entirely female-oriented symbolic system.'[19]

---

[10] Platon 1966: 182.
[11] Platon 1966: 183.
[12] Gesell 1985: 64.
[13] Gesell 1985: 67.
[14] Marinatos 1993: 165.
[15] Marinatos 1993: 165.
[16] Marinatos 1993: 166.
[17] Marinatos 1993: 167.
[18] Marinatos 2010: 167.
[19] Gimbutas 1999: 135.

Archaeologist Adonis Vasilakis, author of a comprehensive guide to Minoan Crete, *Minoan Crete from Myth to History*, published in 1999, also posits a 'woman-centered' religion.[20]

> The main deities of Minoan religion were nature, worshipped as the Great Mother, and vegetation, personified by the young god who dies and is reborn. Another deity who dies is the young goddess Kore. The relationship between the first two of these is both maternal and erotic, while that between the two young gods is that of brother and sister. . . . The fertility goddess was called Great Mother, Mountain Mother, Mistress of the Animals, Kourotrophos, Idaean Mother, and Cybele-Hera.[21]

Archaeologist Marina L. Moss's 2005 work *The Minoan Pantheon: Towards an Understanding of its Nature and Extent* attempts to identify the types of deities worshipped in Minoan Crete and to assess the nature of overseas influence on Minoan religion. She concludes that the Minoans worshipped a pantheon of Goddesses and gods, with Goddesses predominating. As for the nature of overseas influence on the Minoans, she determines that Egypt was the primary region of influence and that the Minoans adopted both Egyptian iconography and its meaning, perhaps along with some of the deities themselves.

All the authorities cited above from Evans to Moss recognize a Goddess or Goddesses as the central figure(s) in Minoan religion, even when such authorities also point to gods in the 'Minoan pantheon.' But despite this long history of scholarship which articulates the worship of a Goddess as the preeminent deity in Minoan Crete, there are a few scholars who do not agree.

Archaeologist Peter J. Ucko is the first critic who must be discussed in this regard. In his widely influential 1968 publication, *Anthropomorphic Figurines of Predynastic Egypt and Neolithic Crete with Comparative Material from the Prehistoric Near East and Mainland Greece*, Ucko charged that 'the general Mother Goddess interpretation fails to cover all the known facts.'[22] At this point in time Marija Gimbutas had not written her works on Old Europe; the first, *The Gods and Goddesses of Old Europe* was published in 1974; the scholars Ucko is referring to include Jacquetta Hawkes and Jane Ellen Harrison.

For his study Ucko examined the Neolithic figurines of Crete known up to that point in time, and compared them with those of pre-dynastic Egypt and other, roughly contemporaneous non-literate agricultural societies. His conclusions are detailed later in this work. In summary, Ucko proposed that the figurines, rather than being Goddesses, were possibly dolls, initiation figures, or figurines to be used for sympathetic magic.

Of course, as Ucko is only looking at Neolithic figurines, his findings do not necessarily apply to those artifacts found in Minoan Crete that date to the post-Neolithic—which are the majority upon which a Goddess-centered religion is hypothesized. Nevertheless, modern day critics of a Goddess-centered religion continually cite Ucko's work and use it, in my opinion, as an argument to discredit all discussion of a Goddess-centered society—in Crete or anywhere else, during the Bronze Age as well as the Neolithic.

---

[20] Vasilakis 2001: 128.
[21] Vasilakis 2001: 181.
[22] Ucko 1968: 38.

One such critic is Ronald Hutton in his 1997 article 'The Neolithic Great Goddess: A Study in Modern Tradition.' Much of Hutton's article is a personal attack on Marija Gimbutas and her work, although he attacks Hawkes and Harrison as well. Hutton accuses all three of them of being profoundly reactionary and hints that Hawkes and Gimbutas turned to popular audiences because archaeologists (the experts) ignored their theories—they had been discredited by Ucko's work. Hutton saves his worst attack for Gimbutas, accusing her, among other things, of trying to conform to 'evolving feminist opinion.'[23]

A slightly less harsh critique of Gimbutas's work can be found in feminist archaeologists Ruth Tringham and Margaret Conkey's 1998 article 'Rethinking Figurines: A Critical View from Archaeology of Gimbutas, the "Goddess" and Popular Culture.' In this essay they categorize Gimbutas as an 'essentialist,' one who 'reduce[s] a complex idea/object to simplistic characteristics, thereby denying diversity and multiple meanings and interpretations.'[24] They also accuse her of being authoritarian: 'The narrative is presented in [a] way in which the process of inference from artifact to interpretations is mystified and ambiguities of the archaeological record are hidden.'[25] While they admit that Gimbutas's interpretations 'can be considered plausible within the constraints of the material evidence,' they believe many other interpretations are plausible as well. Thus they conclude by suggesting that 'the interpretation of figurines should be presented in relation to, not in exclusion of, alternative interpretive narratives.'[26]

'Beyond the Great Mother: The Sacred World of the Minoans' by archaeologists Lucy Goodison and Christine Morris, published in 1998, does not focus on Gimbutas and a critique of her work, but rather attempts 'to emphasize that within the rich tapestry of the Minoan sacred world there is still much to discover.'[27] In attempting to discover more of the Minoans' sacred world, the authors use Ucko's arguments in discussing the Neolithic Cretan figurines and come to the same conclusions he does: they could just as well be dolls, initiation figurines, and so forth. When they come to the later Minoan periods, they do not so much argue against the Minoan worship of a Goddess, as argue for the idea that she probably symbolized more than just fertility. However, I do not think any of the scholars I have reviewed meant that the Minoan Goddess was only a fertility Goddess, in the strictest sense of the word fertility. Goodison and Morris also argue that there was more than one Goddess and that they were accompanied by male gods as well. Their argument for the existence of numerous male gods is not well developed.

Theologian Rosemary Radford Ruether's 2005 book *Goddesses and the Divine Feminine* also attempts to discredit Gimbutas's 'religion of the goddess' and her thesis that ancient peoples of Old Europe/Anatolia had a unified understanding of the Goddess as Birth-Giver, Death-Wielder, and Regeneratrix. 'Much of Gimbutas's reconstruction of the Goddess religion seems eisegesis—that is, it involves reading into ancient artifacts a predetermined worldview in which she already has come to believe.'[28] Ruether is also critical of Gimbutas's theories of matriliny and matrilocality and faults her for glorifying the role of women and ignoring or

---

[23] Hutton 1997: 6.
[24] Tringham and Conkey 1998: 22.
[25] Tringham and Conkey 1998: 24.
[26] Tringham and Conkey 1998: 45.
[27] Goodison and Morris 1998: 132.
[28] Ruether 2005: 24.

minimizing the role of men in the Old European societies she studied.[29] Ruether suggests that Ucko's hypothesis for alternative uses for figurines may well be correct, or at least worth considering, and she wonders if ancient peoples even had a concept of Goddesses and gods. She sees Gimbutas's 'overall interpretative framework as lacking credibility.'[30] In a footnote she faults Gimbutas for illustrating her works with only three mother/child artifacts, as if only such artifacts would indicate the worship of a Mother Goddess.[31] As I shall attempt to show in this study, a Mother Goddess or Goddess does not have to be shown with a child to signify her divinity or role as creatrix.

Archaeological, archaeomythological, and historical evidence for Bronze Age Crete as a woman-centered society

In order to eventually make the argument that Crete was a matriarchal, or matristic/matrilocal/ matrilineal society, it must also be shown that in all probability Minoan Crete was a woman-centered society. This is not a conclusion that all authorities will necessarily agree to. However, I believe that when one surveys the archaeological, and archaeomythological evidence, the argument that Bronze Age Crete was a woman-centered society becomes entirely plausible.

Bull-leaping

I will begin my review of women in Minoan society with what might seem like an unlikely subject: the acrobatic feat of bull-leaping. I start with bull-leaping because it illustrates the dichotomy that exists between authorities on the subject of the role of women in Minoan Crete.

Why is the role of women in bull-leaping important enough to be a topic of controversy? Bull-leaping was an extremely dangerous, demanding 'sport,' or ritual activity, the sort of activity that women most probably would not participate in, in a patriarchal society. The women bull-leapers are especially prominent on a very famous fresco (which Evans named the 'Taureador Fresco') and on two fresco fragments.[32] Considered in conjunction with other representations of women, the artistic representations of women bull-leaping impart the idea that women were equal to the men not only in the bull arena, but in all facets of Bronze Age life.

Some authorities, like archaeologists Nanno Marinatos[33] and Silvia Damini Indelicato,[34] argue that women did not participate in the sport or ritual. Marinatos believes that bull-leaping was a rite of passage, reserved for men, and that the so-called women in the bull-leaper fresco are actually men, who are painted white to denote their status rather than gender. Damini Indelicato supports Marinatos in some of her conclusions and adds one of her own: the color white in this case is not being used to indicate a woman (as was typical in Minoan as well as Egyptian art), but rather to convey a mental picture of movement.

---

[29] Ruether 2005: 35.
[30] Ruether 2005: 35.
[31] Ruether 2005: 314.
[32] Immerwahr 1990: 91.
[33] Marinatos 1989 and 1993.
[34] Damini Indelicato 1988.

Others, including Sir Arthur Evans,[35] the archaeologist who discovered and excavated Minoan society, archaeologist John G. Younger,[36] and Marija Gimbutas[37] present persuasive evidence that women did participate in the bull-games. Evans was the first to identify the two white-skinned leapers in the Toreador Fresco as women, based on several facts, one of which is that Aegean painting, like Egyptian, reserves the color white for the portrayal of women. Thus Evans writes:

> Here, beside the male performer, of the usual ruddy hue, . . . are two female taureadors, distinguished not only by their white skin but by their more ornamental attire. Their loin-cloth and girdle is identical with that of the man but of more variegated hue, . . . They wear bands round their wrists and double necklaces—one of them beaded—and . . . blue and red ribbons round their brows. But perhaps their most distinctive feature is the symmetrical arrangement of short curls over their foreheads and temples, already noticed in the case of the female 'cow-boy' of the Vapheio cup.[38]

Gimbutas refers to the women bull-leapers in *The Living Goddesses* as athletes participating in ritual bull-games and as examples of the place of honor women held in Minoan society. Younger, like Gimbutas and Evans, believes the white color of the leapers signifies women: 'white painted people should always be female in the Aegean,' and he argues that the bull-games were a rite of passage for both men and women.[39]

Although he does not involve himself in the controversy surrounding female bull-leapers, archaeologist and archaeological artist M. A. S. Cameron has a distinctive understanding of the bull-leaping fresco that sheds further light on the role of women in Minoan Crete and that dovetails into another important area for consideration: the portrayal of women (and of the Goddess) in Minoan frescos. I focus next on the images of women and/or Goddesses in the artworks of Crete, beginning with the interpretation of the bull-leaping frescoes by Cameron.

Women and/or the Goddess in frescoes, statues, and seals

In 'The "Palatial" Thematic System in the Knossos Murals: Last Notes on the Knossos Frescoes' published in 1984, Cameron argued that 'all the frescos [at Knossos] centered around one idea: a festival of birth/regeneration with the "great goddess" in the center,'[40] and that 'the significance of the bull-leaping rituals [was] the shedding of blood in connection with the fertility festival.'[41]

The frescos of the new palace at Knossos represented, for Cameron, the different stages of the festival (or series of festivals) in honor of the Great Goddess. As part of the festival(s), Cameron believed a woman/priestess, a 'goddess impersonator,' was chosen; she then entered into a *hieros gamos* (perhaps with a male priest?); and eventually bore a divine child.

---

[35] Evans 1964.
[36] Younger 1995.
[37] Gimbutas 1999.
[38] Evans 1964: 3:212.
[39] Younger 1995: 535.
[40] Cameron 1987: 323.
[41] Cameron 1987: 325.

The Minoan frescoes point not only to the importance of women as representatives of the Goddess and her attendants, and thus women's supreme role in the religious sphere, as the summary of Cameron's work makes clear, but to women's major role in all aspects of Minoan society as well. The frescoes are important for illustrating the role of women in Minoan society because they 'provide the fullest picture of Minoan life'[42] that we have.

Archaeologist C. G. Thomas, in her 1973 article entitled 'Matriarchy in Early Greece: The Bronze and Dark Ages,' looked at, among other things, the question of whether or not women enjoyed 'privileged social status' in Minoan Crete. On the basis of 'all categories of artifacts [including, of course, frescoes] with the exception of painted pottery,'[43] and on the basis of architecture, Thomas answered in the affirmative. According to Thomas, the frescos show women present at ceremonial and religious occasions, attending public performances, and in the bull-leaping fresco, performing physical feats of bravery like men. Moreover, in all the frescos they are more fully represented than the men. The architecture of the palaces shows that women were not secluded. The religious artifacts: seals, rings and small statues, illustrate the major role women played in Minoan religion.

I would add here that painted pottery also illustrates the important role played by the Goddess and the major role women played in Minoan religion. The most important example that comes to mind is the famous MM I, *c.* 2100-1900 BC, bowl found at the temple-palace of Phaistos in south-central Crete. It shows two women dancing around the Snake Goddess and a flower growing up from the earth. This piece and a companion piece are discussed in more detail in Chapter 5.

Writing in 1974, in an article entitled 'Priests-kings?', archaeologist Helen Waterhouse also looks to portrayals of Minoan women in art to make her case regarding women's preeminence in Minoan society. She concludes, 'There is massive pictorial evidence, from the miniature frescoes onwards, for the predominant position of women in such scenes and in Minoan culture as a whole.'[44]

Aegean archaeologist and fresco expert Sara A. Immerwahr, in her 1983 article 'The People in the Frescoes,' suggests that based on the frescoes, Minoan society can be said to exhibit a 'female bias.'[45] Immerwahr further notes in her classic 1990 work, *Aegean Painting in the Bronze Age*, that male figures in the frescoes seem subordinate to the females.[46]

Gimbutas also elaborated upon the privileged status of women in Minoan Crete. Discussing the frescoes she notes, in *The Civilization of the Goddess*, that women are portrayed as bull-leapers, and chariot drivers, and they are shown intermingling with men at festivals. The Theran frescoes depict women overseeing naval festivals as well as processions of men leading animals to sacrifice.[47] In this same work and in a later work, *The Living Goddesses*, Gimbutas goes on to call this society which featured 'outstanding women' in its great works of art, and priestesses and Goddesses in its religious iconography, a matrilineal and matristic society. She writes, 'a

---

[42] Thomas 1973: 175.
[43] Thomas 1973: 173.
[44] Waterhouse 1974: 153.
[45] Immerwahr 1983: 237.
[46] Immerwahr 1990: 53.
[47] Gimbutas 1991: 346.

vast amount of religious art, architecture, and sepulchral evidence of Minoan culture attests to the importance of the female and the matrilineal inheritance patterns of the culture.'[48] Gimbutas finds affirmation of matrilineal inheritance patterns of the culture in the marriage laws preserved in the fifth century BC Law Code of Gortyn (Crete).

Approaching the issue of the role of women in Minoan society through the lens of motherhood, archaeologist Barbara A. Olsen finds that rather than 'idealizing women as mothers,'[49] Minoan art associates women with power and status. Olsen's 1998 article 'Women, Children and the Family in the Late Aegean Bronze Age: Differences in Minoan and Mycenaean Constructions of Gender,' argues that as far as the iconography is concerned, the social and public rather than the private roles of Minoan women are emphasized.

Looking at frescoes, seals, and rings, archaeologist Doniert Evely concludes his 1999 work *Fresco: A Passport into the Past: Minoan Crete through the Eyes of Mark Cameron*, with the observation that 'women played a prominent part in the workings of the high levels of Minoan culture and society.'[50] The British archaeologist J. Lesley Fitton expresses the idea current in much of the archaeological literature when she writes in her 2002 book *The Minoans* that 'the importance of women in Minoan iconography cannot be denied.'[51] Finally, archaeologists John Younger and Paul Rehak, studying both seals and frescoes, have argued in their 2008 essay that 'The prominence of females in Neopalatial art, important mortal women and goddesses . . . , makes it possible to imagine that women dominated Neopalatial society, perhaps even politics.'[52] In 2016 writing about 'Minoan Women' in a chapter of the work *Women in Antiquity*, Younger further theorized that 'important and powerful women' might well have been the catalyst for the LM IB destructions and the subsequent establishment of the Mycenaeans in Crete.[53]

Women's legal rights in marriage, divorce, and property

As indicated above, one of the most important pieces of evidence for matrilineal customs in ancient Crete is the Law Code of Gortyn which is dated to the fifth century BC. The Law Code of Gortyn, transmitted orally for hundreds of years, was eventually written down in c. 480-460 BC—engraved on the stone walls of the law court of the city of Gortyn in south-central Crete. It is accepted by experts that the Code contains traces of much older laws. Within the Code are provisions for women to own and dispose of property, to divorce 'at their pleasure,' and for a woman's brother to be engaged in the raising of her children. The Law Code of Gortyn is discussed at length in Chapter 6 of this work.

Archaeologists divided on Crete as a matriarchy

Sir Arthur Evans was the first to use the term matriarchy in describing Crete. In discussing the supremacy of the Goddess in the 1920s, he wrote: 'The Religion itself is of an unitary type,

---

[48] Gimbutas 1999: 121.
[49] Olsen 1998: 390.
[50] Evely 1999: 88-89.
[51] Fitton 2002: 178.
[52] Younger and Rehak 2008: 180.
[53] Younger 2016: 588.

revolving round a central theme and, being itself the outcome of what seems to have been largely a matriarchal society.'[54]

However, as archaeologist Lucia Nixon,[55] and classicist Marymay Downing[56] have pointed out, Evans was not consistent in his views and assigned larger rooms in the palaces and the throne room at Knossos to a 'priest-king.'

Despite Evans's inconsistencies, anthropologist Ruby Rohrlich-Leavitt notes:

> A number of scholars are convinced that Crete was matriarchal, a theocracy ruled by a queen-priestess. The absence of portrayals of an all-powerful male ruler, so widespread in the Bronze Age, backs them up; so does the religious prominence of women.[57]

She concludes from her study of the available evidence in 1977, that Crete was a matriarchy.

R. F. Willetts, translator and commentator of the Law Code of Gortyn, makes a similar point:

> We have noticed some evidence [frescoes] suggesting the freedom enjoyed by women in Minoan society. This evidence, supported by later customs and traditions, has led some scholars to the conclusion that the Minoan civilization could have been based upon matriarchal institutions.[58]

But for any scholar who might call Crete a matrilineal or matriarchal society, there is another who would argue this is not the case. Archaeologist Nanno Marinatos, while recognizing the importance of the female deity in Crete, does not believe that such primacy correspondingly means political/social importance for women. She observes that although the Virgin Mary is highly venerated in the contemporary Catholic societies of South America and the southern Mediterranean, male dominance in those countries is the rule.[59]

Archaeologist Margaret Ehrenberg argues against the matriarchal interpretation in her 1989 book *Women in Prehistory* when she writes,

> As regards matriarchy, . . . I have tried to show not only how little evidence there is in any living or documented society, but also how difficult it would be to prove from archaeological data. Even if we may hypothesize that women . . . may have had a better deal in Minoan Crete than in many other later societies, it is impossible to argue that they actually held power. Equally, however, as in most other prehistoric societies, there is no evidence that men held power at the expense of women.[60]

Ehrenberg further cautions:

---

[54] Evans 1964: 2, pt.1:277.
[55] Nixon 1994.
[56] Downing 1985.
[57] Rohrlich-Leavitt 1977: 49.
[58] Willetts 1969: 139.
[59] Marinatos 1993: 192.
[60] Ehrenberg 1989: 118.

Archaeological evidence in itself tells us little. It needs to be interpreted. All archaeologists would agree with that, but how far that interpretation can go and on what basis it should be made, is the subject of considerable controversy.[61]

In other words, the artifacts generally permit a limited range of interpretations. All archaeologists provide interpretations which are influenced by multiple personal and social factors, including available finds, technology, and cultural context as well as personal values, preconceptions, and predispositions.

Generally, the archaeologists who insist that Crete was not a matriarchy never define the term. I believe they are so critical of matriarchy because they assume it means simply the reverse of patriarchy: the rule, by force, of women over men. However, also important is that the argument they put forward against considering Minoan Crete a matriarchy, that matriarchy has never existed and does not now exist, is unfounded and untrue. Sanday has documented a matriarchal society among the present day Minangkabau of Indonesia, and Goettner-Abendroth has done the same with the Mosuo of China.[62] The Hopi as well as the Iroquois and other North American Indian societies also consider themselves as matriarchal, and numerous works have been written about them.[63]

One archaeologist who does define the term matriarchy and then goes on to designate Crete as a matriarchal society is C. G. Thomas whose 1973 article entitled 'Matriarchy in Early Greece: The Bronze and Dark Ages' was discussed above in conjunction with the portrayal of women in the frescoes. In her article Thomas defined a matriarchal society as one in which 'women enjoy recognizable economic, social and religious privileges which . . . give them greater authority than men.'[64]

Thomas looked at three factors: 'one, can and do women possess the right of ownership of property; second, do women play a major role in the religious worldview of the society; third, do women enjoy a privileged social status?'[65] On the basis of 'all categories of artifacts with the exception of painted pottery,' and on the basis of architecture, Thomas answered a definite 'yes' to conditions two and three for matriarchy in Minoan Crete. As for condition number one, 'can and do women possess the right of ownership of property?'[66] on the basis of the Law Code of Gortyn, Thomas answered a probable 'yes' to that 'condition' for Minoan Crete as well.

Of course, there has been criticism of Thomas's work. Shelia Dickinson, writing in 1976, cites the standard arguments advanced against matriarchy, that no historical or contemporary evidence exists for the rule of women, and calls Thomas's definition of matriarchy 'vague and broad.'[67] Dickinson also faults Thomas for confusing an emphasis on women in religion with the assertion that women thus also had social or political powers. Marinatos advances that same argument, as we saw above.

---

[61] Ehrenberg 1989: 13.
[62] Sanday 2003; Göttner-Abendroth 1999. See also Yang Erche Namu and Christine Mathieu 2003.
[63] Mann 2000; Allen 1992.
[64] Thomas 1973: 173.
[65] Thomas 1973: 174.
[66] Thomas 1973: 174.
[67] Dickinson, 1976: 9.

Like Dickinson, classicist and feminist Sarah Pomeroy, also writing in 1976, believes that Minoan women were 'dominant in the religious sphere.'[68] However, in another work, written in 1973, she says: 'There is, to be sure, a dearth of evidence establishing matriarchy, but there is equally . . . a lack of conclusive evidence proving the existence of patriarchy in Crete.'[69]

Thomas's study leaves open the question of what understanding of the social and religious roles of women can be garnered from a study of painted pottery. I indicated above that I believe pottery can provide us with some understanding of at least the religious roles played by women in Minoan Crete. I return to that question in Chapter 6.

Evidence for male rulership?

Ever since the days of Sir Arthur Evans, it has been assumed that a king or priest-king ruled Crete. This view is still upheld by various scholars, although very few important images of males, I would contend, have ever been found. As Waterhouse notes, 'Though scenes of ceremony are common in Minoan art, no kingly figure takes part in or presides over any of them.'[70] Indeed it was Waterhouse who, some thirty years ago, in one of those rare exceptions in mainstream literature, put aside androcentric assumptions and critically looked at Evans's priest-king in her 1974 article 'Priest-kings?' Her conclusion was that ancient Crete was a theacracy, that is, a society under the rulership of a Goddess.

In 1995 Ellen N. Davis also addressed the lack of a priest-king figure in Minoan iconography in 'Art and Politics in the Aegean: The Missing Ruler.' Davis, like Waterhouse and other scholars, finds no images to which to attach the title of king. She discusses each of the five images in Minoan iconography that she believes are possible candidates for the priest-king title. (I consider those images in Chapter 7). She then quite convincingly argues that none of the iconography that has yet been discovered in Crete could represent a priest-king. However, despite her quite convincing arguments, Davis tells the reader she still finds it difficult to imagine a Bronze Age society in the Mediterranean without a male ruler(s),[71] and concludes scholars have yet to understand the unique society that is Minoan Crete.[72]

Archaeologist Robert Koehl attempts to come to an understanding of this unique society in his 1995 work, 'The Nature of Minoan Kingship,' although I think he reveals his bias right from the start in the title of his article. Reviewing the iconography, he will concede only that women were important in the religious sphere.[73] While he begins his article seemingly in agreement with the conclusions of Helen Waterhouse, Koehl soon qualifies his support,[74] and sides with Pomeroy's conclusions: ancient Crete was neither a matriarchy nor a patriarchy.[75] He theorizes that Crete was governed through 'shared rulership;' his shared system of power includes a male and a female, with the male, a priest-king-shaman, being the more important of the two.

---

[68] Pomeroy 1976: 223.
[69] Pomeroy 1973: 134.
[70] Waterhouse 1974: 153.
[71] Davis 1995: 18.
[72] Davis 1995: 19.
[73] Koehl 1995: 25.
[74] Koehl 1995: 26.
[75] Koehl 1995: 26.

Shared rulership is also the theme of Marinatos's 1995 article 'Divine Kingship in Minoan Crete.' She finds evidence for shared female/male rulership in iconographical sources,[76] especially the miniature wall paintings of Thera which illustrate what Marinatos interprets as an example of shared rulership between a male and female with both exhibiting religious and political authority.[77] She perceives hints of matriliny in the iconography as well.[78]

Regarding Crete, Marinatos argues that we lack much ruler iconography because Crete was a 'theocracy,' and so rulers and deities were interchangeable. Although she speaks of the 'duality' of Minoan rulership, Marinatos, like Koehl, emphasizes the male element and so she titles her article 'Divine Kingship,' thus indicating her male-oriented bias. That bias is evident as well in her recent work on male rulership in Minoan Crete, *Minoan Kingship and the Solar Goddess: A Near Eastern Koine* (2010), discussed below.

Despite Davis's 1995 article arguing there were no reliable candidates in Minoan iconography for the title of 'priest-king,' the debate did not end with her work. In 2004 in an article entitled 'The "Priest-King" Fresco from Knossos: Man, Woman, Priest, King, or Someone Else?', archaeologist and fresco expert Maria Shaw argued that Evans's reconstruction of the 'Priest-King' fresco was indeed an accurate restoration and quite possibly represented the priest-king ruler of Crete. Shaw's arguments regarding the accuracy of Evans's restoration and the identity of the figure are discussed and critiqued in Chapter 7.

Yet another candidate for the role of priest-king that is still often cited is the male figure on the sealing known as the 'Master-Impression' from western Crete and dated to Late Minoan IB, *c.* 1480-1390 BC. While some have argued that this figure represents a god, Davis among them, others have seen him as Evans's missing king. An alternative view of the figure is provided by archaeologists Günter Kopcke and Eleni Drakaki in their 1999 article 'Male Iconography on Some Late Minoan Signets,' who argue that the 'Master' represents not a Minoan king, but a Mycenaean interloper. These ideas are discussed in detail in Chapter 7.

Evidence for male rulership in Minoan Crete is addressed at length in Marinatos's 2010 book *Minoan Kingship and the Solar Goddess.* There she argues more forcibly than in any of her other works that in Minoan iconography the god and the king are interchangeable. In this book, which utilizes Near Eastern iconography and mythology, and the assumption that a shared pool of religious concepts and beliefs operated across the ancient Near East, Marinatos hypothesizes that Minoan Crete was once ruled by a king in his role as storm god and son of the solar Goddess. This work is reviewed in Chapter 7.

Aegeanists seem to find it nearly impossible to give up the notion of a king or priest-king ruling in Bronze Age Crete; perhaps for the reason that they fear they will then have to admit that Crete was a matriarchy. Castleden believes the reluctance to give up the notion of a priest-king can be found in the fact that the Mycenaeans had a king, thus the Minoans must have also; the Minoans must have begun the tradition.[79] However, as Younger has pointed out, Linear B evidence, with its tantalizing references to the *Potnia* ruling in conjunction with the *Wanax*,

---

[76] Marinatos 1995: 47.
[77] Marinatos 1995: 40.
[78] Marinatos 1995: 46.
[79] Castleden 1990: 117.

lends itself to the understanding that the Mycenaeans had both a female and male ruler.[80] Thus perhaps instead of looking for a priest-king, all along experts should have been searching for the priestess-queen who, even after the amalgamation of Minoan society into Mycenaean society was, for a time at least, still visible within the Mycenaean's system of shared rulership.

Conclusion

To conclude the literature review, it is my hope that this work will fill a gap in the scholarly literature and contribute to some resolution of the lively debate over the role of women and the existence of matriarchy in Minoan Crete. I believe that by carefully defining terms such as matriarchy, as well as the term Mother Goddess; and by skillfully analyzing the archaeological material, as well as the archaeological and archaeomythological literature, including linguistics, mythology, anthropology and the history of religion as they pertain to Minoan Crete, I can advance the discussion to a more complex, current, and certain conclusion.

---

[80] J. G. Younger to Aegeanet mailing list, March 11, 1996, http://umich.edu/classics/archives/aegeanet/ aegeanet.960311.02. No longer accessible.

Chapter 2

Methodology

I now turn to the subject of how I answered the question that I am investigating in this study: Was Bronze Age Crete a matriarchal society? The previous two chapters have already indicated the steps I followed. My work is both theoretical and scientific. Using the available evidence of archaeology and mythology, in conjunction with linguistics and the special study of Greek religion, I develop my thesis and draw the plausible and probable conclusions.

To reiterate: First, I show that a strong case can be made for the preeminence of the Goddess in Minoan society. I accomplish that through an examination of the relevant archaeological and archaeomythological literature, as indicated in the literature review. In addition, I have viewed and have re-examined most of the key artifacts by visiting the archaeological museums of Crete, Athens, and Thera. I also address the issues of whether this primary deity can be called a Mother Goddess or not, and also whether to consider her as one or many, or perhaps both.

I then proceed to demonstrate that a strong case can also be made for the preeminence of women in Bronze Age Cretan society. I examine the archaeological evidence regarding women and their economic, social, political, and religious roles in Minoan society. I use archaeological artifacts and interpret them through the lens of archaeomythology as well as Women's Spirituality and the history of religion. Finally, I apply the definitions of Sanday, Goettner-Abendroth, Gimbutas, Eisler, Du, and Lerner regarding matriarchy, patriarchy, matristic cultures, and egalitarian cultures to the empirically-grounded sketch of cultural history which I develop, to determine if the society I have uncovered fits the definitions of any or perhaps all of the first five of these theorists, or if it might rather be closer to the definition of patriarchy given by Lerner.

I begin with a statement of my own values, for I know that they have influenced my work. My biases include feminism, woman-centeredness, eco-feminism (the belief that a historic, symbolic, and political relationship exists between the denigration of nature and the denigration of the female in Western cultures), and an interest in the Goddess traditions of the world.

Because my degree is in Philosophy and Religion with an emphasis in Women's Spirituality, which is defined here as 'the spiritual experiences, expressions, and contributions of women across time and around the world,'[1] I include myself in my work, having come to know myself through many years of 'alternative ways of knowing': meditation, psychotherapy, and ritual practice. Making my own values clear at the outset is part of 'standpoint feminism' in Women's Studies; and the conscious, reflective inclusion of oneself as researcher (open to transformation by the study) is part of heuristic inquiry in psychology as well as in Women's Spirituality.

---

[1] Keller, 'Here I Stand—In This Place, This Time, This Body: The Situated Self, Womanist-Feminist Standpoint, and Agency and Advocacy in Women's Spiritual Research,' 4. (This is a revision of a panel at CIIS for the School of Consciousness and Transformation March 30, 2006, Faculty Development Retreat, 'On the Positionality of the Self in Research.')

The methodologies I have chosen are congruent with my beliefs and worldviews. Like Mara Lynn Keller, Professor of Philosophy, Religion, and Women's Spirituality at the California Institute of Integral Studies, I too

> draw upon the findings of each discipline, and then seek patterns and interconnections to create a more complete understanding of my particular subject. These findings, associations and insights converge within the framework of my own nature-based, woman-affirming spirituality.[2]

Archaeomythology

Marija Gimbutas, the originator of archaeomythology, defined her methodology as: 'A combination of fields—archaeology, mythology, linguistics and historical data—[which] provide the possibility for apprehending both the material and spiritual realities of prehistoric cultures.'[3] Gimbutas's great contribution to the field, which is voluminously documented by four of her major texts: *The Gods and Goddesses of Old Europe* (1974), *The Language of the Goddess* (1989), *The Civilization of the Goddess* (1991), and *The Living Goddesses* (1999), as well as in numerous scholarly articles, may be outlined in the following four points: First, an understanding of the Goddess as one with Nature and as manifesting in three aspects: Life-Giver, Death Wielder and Regeneratrix; secondly, a reinterpretation of the Neolithic or 'Old Europe' as a 'true civilization in the best meaning of the word,'[4] an egalitarian, matrilineal, peaceful and artistic one; thirdly, the deciphering of a complex symbolic system formulated around the worship of the Goddess in her various aspects; and finally, an explanation as to how and why the civilization of the Goddess was amalgamated into the patriarchal, sky-god worshipping civilization that overtook it. These are views to which I am partial. I understand that her unorthodox views remain controversial. After extensive study of the details and patterns of her work, I find her interpretations of Old European artifacts to be persuasive and compelling. Gimbutas included Crete in her discussion, but not in as much detail as I am able to do at this point some twenty years after the publication of her last two texts.

In further trying to understand or elaborate upon the method of archaeomythology and Gimbutas's contribution as the mother of the discipline, it is helpful to see the discipline, as Keller suggests, 'as a bridge between archaeology and mythology, which is to say between science and religion.'[5] Keller continues, 'She was endeavoring to discover with scientific empirical methods the spiritual beliefs of the ancient Old Europeans.'[6]

As Gimbutas did not elaborate upon her methodology, I find it helpful to review what Keller wrote in her 1997 article: 'The Interface of Archaeology and Mythology: A Philosophical Examination of the Gimbutas Paradigm':

> Gimbutas' archaeomythology scientifically analyzes the material database for Old Europe and draws possible and probable inferences from these analyses, mediated

---

[2] Keller n.d.: 32.
[3] Gimbutas 1991: x.
[4] Gimbutas 1991: viii.
[5] Keller, pers. comm.
[6] Keller, pers. comm.

by the application of her knowledge of mythology, folklore, history of religion and linguistics, to reconstruct the symbolic, religious ideology of Old Europe.[7]

Keller goes on to say that unlike the cognitive archaeologists, 'Gimbutas grapples with the possible and probable reality of an immanent and transcendent goddess mythology and its implications for gendered social relations in Neolithic Old Europe.'[8]

Like Gimbutas, this is what I have attempted to accomplish in my work: using archaeology and the database archaeologists have created for Bronze Age Crete, to draw possible and probable inferences, mediated by the application of mythology, folklore, history of religion, and linguistics, and then grapple with the possible and probable reality of an immanent and transcendent Goddess mythology and its implications for a possibly matriarchal society in Bronze Age Crete.

Components of archaeomythology: archaeology

It is obvious from my literature review that archaeology plays an extremely important role in my own (and in everyone else's) understanding of Bronze Age Minoan society. Were it not for archaeologist Sir Arthur Evans, Minoan Crete might not have been 'discovered,' and thus we owe him and all the other pioneers in the field a huge debt of gratitude.

But archaeology has changed greatly since the late nineteenth century when Evans first arrived in Crete. So in addition to defining the field in the paragraphs below, I also describe how it has evolved since its inception, with an emphasis here on the changing developments in archaeological methodologies.

British archaeologists Colin Renfrew and Paul Bahn, leading authorities in the field today, write that archaeology is the study of past societies through their material remains and that, as one of three branches of anthropology (the other two being biological/physical and cultural anthropology), it is concerned in the broadest sense with the study of humanity.[9] Archaeology can also be thought of as history, and as Renfrew and Bahn make clear, if we mean history to include the whole history of humankind that began three million years ago, archaeology 'is the only [other than physical anthropology] significant source of information, . . . for the many thousands of years of "prehistory."'[10]

Archaeology is also an interpretive science, for the objects themselves cannot tell us much, it is the archaeologist who must interpret them based on data, experimentation, the development of the hypothesis, and testing of the hypothesis against further data. Archaeology as well as being a science is an endlessly fascinating discipline and one that has undergone tremendous change since its inception. In the twentieth century its focus has shifted from being more humanistic, then to the more positivist scientific study of the sequencing of material artifacts, to once again developing a more humanistic focus concerned with interpretation in order to discover the way humans have lived from the most remote human origins to the present.

---

[7] Keller 1997: 391.
[8] Keller 1997: 391.
[9] Renfrew and Bahn 1996: 11.
[10] Renfrew and Bahn 1996: 12.

In its infancy in the nineteenth century, and well into the first half of the twentieth century, the aim of archaeology was to describe material artifacts and to date them. Interpretations were made, usually with reference to legends and myths. Indeed archaeology only became established as a discipline when the concepts of the great antiquity of humanity, Darwin's principle of evolution, and the Three Age System for dating material culture (Stone Age, Bronze Age, and Iron Age) were accepted.

After the Second World War major changes took place within the discipline, spurred on in particular by new scientific techniques, especially for the dating of artifacts. These new dating techniques included radiocarbon dating, dendrochronology, optical dating, and thermoluminescent dating, among others.

By the 1960s, the goal of the 'New Archaeology,' also known as functional-processual or processual archaeology, was to explain as well as to describe material artifacts. Renfrew and Bahn list six key points that distinguish the New Archaeology from the old. First, archaeology's role was to explain how change took place, not just describe ancient societies. Second, archaeology would now make generalizations and 'think in terms of culture process'[11]-- referring to changes in economic and social systems. Third, 'appropriate procedure was now seen as formulating hypotheses, constructing models, and deducing their consequences.'[12] Fourth, conclusions could not be based on the authority or the reputation of the researcher, but on the testing of hypotheses. Fifth, 'research should be designed to answer specific questions.'[13] Finally, the quantitative approach was to be preferred.

During the 1980s and 1990s, the functional-processual phase of the New Archaeology was followed by a cognitive archaeology phase which focused on 'the study of past ways of thought and symbolic structures from material remains.'[14] More recently, a cognitive-processual phase 'which seeks more actively to include the consideration of symbolic and cognitive aspects of societies into the program of research'[15] has become a trend in archaeology.

Since the 1980s a 'diversity of theoretical approaches, often grouped under the label postprocessual, highlighted the variety of possible interpretations and the sensitivity of their political implications.'[16] This new approach is exemplified in the following excerpts from archaeologist Ian Hodder, one of the early proponents of this postprocessualism. Hodder is the leader of a large team that has been excavating the important Neolithic site of Çatal Hüyük, Turkey. Begun in the early 1990s, the excavations ended with the 2017 season. One of Hodder's expressed aims in re-opening the Çatal Hüyük excavation (which was originally excavated by British archaeologist James Mellaart in the 1960s, whose excavations indicated that the primary deity for most of the site's history was a Mother Goddess) is to test out the postprocessual approach to archaeology. Because 'the site of Çatalhöyük and its imagery seem to exist in a whirlwind of competing and conflicting special interests,'[17] Hodder believes the archaeological data collection techniques employed here must be as free from bias as possible.

---

[11] Renfrew and Bahn 2004: 39.
[12] Renfrew and Bahn 2004: 39.
[13] Renfrew and Bahn 2004: 39.
[14] Renfrew and Bahn 2004: 580.
[15] Renfrew and Bahn 2004: 42.
[16] Renfrew and Bahn 2004: 48.
[17] Hodder 1997: 693.

According to Hodder, archaeologists have always made interpretations 'at the trowel's edge' (the trowel's edge meaning excavation method, data collection, and data recording), yet claimed objectivity. The time has come, says Hodder, to employ a 'reflexive methodology,' a methodology that will admit that archaeologists make interpretations already at the trowel's edge as well as subsequently, and that 'the public role of the archaeologist in a global and diverse fragmented world is increasingly to cooperate and to integrate.'[18]

Thus Hodder introduced at Çatal Hüyük a post-processual methodology that seeks to be

> critical of assumptions and taken for granteds, . . . reflexive about the effect of archaeological assumptions and work on the different communities within the public domain, . . . [and is] relational or contextual. . . . Everything depends on everything else. So to interpret involves creating a circuitry between participants in the project and between the different types of data. One implication is that conclusions are always momentary, fluid and flexible as new relations are considered. . . . interactive in the sense of providing information that can be questioned and approached from different angles . . . multivocal, plural, open or transparent so that a diversity of people can participate in the discourse about the archaeological process.[19]

For Hodder these themes of post-processual archaeology: critical, reflexive, interactive, multivocal, fluid, changeable, and changing are central aspects of high or late post-Modernism which is linked to globalism.

So what are the practical steps being taken at Çatal Hüyük to be interactive, reflexive, relational, and multivocal in a post-colonial world? Hodder lists eight. One, have non-field project specialists (faunal, lithic, archaeobotanical) present in excavation trenches and taking part in the interpretive process as it goes on in the trenches. Two, get information back to the excavator as soon as possible through the use of a local on-site computer network, and a full-time on-site data analyst. Three, construct a database which allows for easy evaluation of and comparison between artifacts and contexts. Four, cross reference the database to interpretive data such as excavation diaries. Five, use video documentation to highlight the discussion and interpretation that takes place in the excavation trenches. Six, have an anthropologist present in the field who exposes unexamined assumptions and contradictions, and proposes alternative interpretations of the data. Seven, develop a website within which the entire raw database is included. In this way information is available to the public at large prior to formal publication. Eight, employ virtual reality as a way for people to understand the site.[20]

Has Hodder's approach been successful? He admits there have been a lot of problems and tensions. But he believes the effort is necessary, as he explains:

> In a postcolonial world, every aspect of our work and all our assumptions as archaeologists need to be open to critique and evaluation by a wide range of different communities in different ways. We cannot assume an authority, we have to argue for it. We cannot simply police the boundaries of the academy and the discipline against

---

[18] Hodder 1997: 694.
[19] Hodder 1997: 694.
[20] Hodder 1997: 695-699.

particularist world views. We have increasingly to argue our case in the temporal flow of a diverse global community.[21]

Postprocessual archaeology is becoming more multi-dimensional and complex, with new attention brought to bear not only on the interpretive process of the discovery of artifacts, but also on the interpretive process of the presentation of findings.

Having given this introduction to the discipline of archaeology, I want to note that many archaeologists (with the exception of Evans, Nilsson, Hawkes, Platon, Vasilakis, Gimbutas, and Marinatos) are hesitant to speculate about Minoan religion. Although archaeologist Timothy Insoll has written that 'Archaeological approaches to religion have been remarkably naïve and it has frequently been thought of as a relatively simple area of investigation,'[22] my experience with Aegean archaeology has not been that the authors are naïve or simplistic, but that they are reluctant to draw conclusions about the essential spiritual concerns of the human condition as expressed in a culture's religion. I think archaeologist Nanno Marinatos put it very well when she noted that the practitioners of the New Archaeology tend to marginalize religion because they view it as 'elusive,' and believe that speculation on mental processes is likely to produce fantasy rather than solid academic scholarship.[23] However, like Gimbutas, Marinatos believes that 'no ancient culture can be understood without its religion.'[24]

For Marinatos, what is important is not just presenting all the data, but exploring ways it can be interpreted. In her exploration of how the data can be interpreted, she overlaps with those who call themselves archaeomythologists. It seems to me she also overlaps with or shares common ground with the field of Women's Spirituality when she writes, referencing German scholar of Greek religion, Walter Burkert, that some of our behavior as humans goes back to our very origins as a species. Focusing on the level of ritual, and noting that much of human ritual—weddings, funerals, initiations, sacrifices—is similar across time and cultures, Marinatos argues that there is a biological explanation for this. 'The common factor must be human nature itself.'[25]

In the above quote I am reminded of Carol Christ's 'embodied thinking' and her observation that 'Thealogy begins in experience.'[26] Affirming the Women's Spirituality community and their sharing of rituals is an important part of Christ's methodology. Experience and community are an important part of Women's Spirituality's approach to its studies. Experience and community appear to be important to Marinatos's approach to Minoan religion as well.

In order to explore the ways Minoan religion can be interpreted, Marinatos looks to isolate 'those patterns which recur in many societies,' and 'from which we can create a basis for understanding the mechanisms, purpose and function of religion.'[27] This, in combination with the archaeological data and comparison with other cultures, allows her to approach Minoan religion as a whole.

---

[21] Hodder 1998: 217.
[22] Insoll 2004: 1.
[23] Marinatos 1993: 10.
[24] Marinatos 1993: 10
[25] Marinatos 1993: 11.
[26] Christ 1997b: Chapter 1.
[27] Marinatos 1993: 11.

Marinatos admits in her work, *Art and Religion in Thera*, published in 1984, that when studying the religion of an era without written records,

> it is impossible to avoid speculation if any interpretation.... of rituals is to be attempted at all. But if speculation is based on a well-defined method some progress can perhaps be made towards understanding the elusive Therans.[28]

For this study, Marinatos used a methodology that combined archaeology with comparative religion and semiotics.

In this work my hope is that, because my speculation is based on the carefully-defined method of archaeomythology, some progress can be made toward an understanding of the role of the Goddess and women in Minoan Crete, and a plausible and highly probable determination made of whether or not matriarchy existed in ancient Crete.

Before concluding this section, one final aspect of the discipline of archaeology which is important to this study must be briefly discussed: a subfield of post-processual archaeology known as 'archaeology of cult.' According to Anna Lucia D'Agata, the editor of a volume entitled *Archaeologies of Cult*, the archaeology of cult has brought into the field of Aegean archaeology 'a shift toward an archaeology concerned with reconstructing ritual and the human actions underlying cult activity, and a gradual retreat from reconstruction of beliefs and the definition of religion.'[29] She goes on to say that 'The evidence connected to ritual and cults is increasingly resistant to monolithically unitary perspectives inspired by ideas of historical development and divorced from the relevant historical context.'[30] Archaeology of cult is an area in which there are no comprehensive works available. Moreover, there is disagreement among experts on definitions and no fully developed theory. The field is hampered by the fact that, for the Bronze Age, few sanctuaries have been the subject of definitive publication and 'a comprehensive view of the processes behind the creation and control of ritual practices in the Bronze Age is lacking.'[31]

It was Renfrew who, in 1985, introduced a more complex approach to the subject of religion in Aegean archaeology than had previously been undertaken. At that time (and since), Renfrew has argued that religion is 'Action or conduct indicating a belief in, or reverence for, and desire to please, a divine ruling power.... the essence of religion is some framework of beliefs.'[32] Religion is also, according to Renfrew and Bahn, a social institution.[33] They agree with anthropologist Ray Rappaport that 'through ritual religion helps regulate the social and economic processes of society.'[34] Unfortunately for the archaeologist, belief systems are not always given precise or unambiguous expression in material culture; for example, the Minoans left no written records that have yet been deciphered definitively. Even when belief systems are given expression in the material culture, in what Renfrew and Bahn also call the 'archaeology of cult,' and which they define as 'the system of patterned actions in response to religious beliefs,' there is the

---

[28] Marinatos 1984: 10.
[29] D'Agata 2009: 1.
[30] D'Agata 2009: 1.
[31] D'Agata 2009: 2.
[32] Renfrew 1985: 11-12.
[33] Renfrew and Bahn 2000: 412. Renfrew has written at length on this subject previously in *Archaeology of Cult*.
[34] Renfrew and Bahn 2000: 412.

problem, according to the authors, that 'such actions are not always clearly separated from the other actions of everyday life.'[35] In other words, religious activity may be very difficult to distinguish archaeologically from the non-religious activities of daily life.

To help establish the distinguishing features of religion from other activities, Renfrew and Bahn argue that one must 'not lose sight of the transcendent, or supernatural object of the cult activity.'[36] According to the authors, religious ritual 'involves the performance of expressive acts of worship toward the deity or transcendent being. In this there are generally at least four main components.'[37]

> *Focusing of attention*, including . . . use of a sacred location, architecture, . . . light, sounds and smell to ensure that all eyes are directed to the crucial ritual acts;

> *Boundary zones between this world and the next.* The focus of ritual activity is the boundary area between this world and the Other World. It is a special and mysterious region with hidden danger . . . in which ritual washing and cleanliness are . . . emphasized;

> *Presence of the deity.* For effective ritual, the deity or transcendent force must in some sense be present, . . . this may be a cult image or merely a very simple symbol of the deity;

> *Participation and offerings.* Worship makes demands of the celebrant. These include . . . words, gestures, prayer, . . . movement, perhaps eating, and drinking. Frequently, it involves also the offering of material things to the deity, both by sacrifice and gift.[38]

How is one to determine the components of religious ritual archaeologically? Renfrew and Bahn elaborate on each of the components. For an archaeologist to determine the 'focusing of attention' component, s/he must identify a cave, a grove of trees, a spring, a mountaintop, temple, or church. Attention focusing devices can be part of the architecture as well, thus one looks for: altars, benches or hearths; or for moveable equipment: ritual vessels, bells, or gongs. Moreover, 'The sacred area is likely to be rich in repeated symbols.'[39]

As for the 'Boundary zone between this world and the next' component, the authors remark that 'Ritual may involve both conspicuous public display . . . and hidden exclusive mysteries.'[40] They note that the concepts of purity and pollution will be reflected in facilities such as pools or basins of water.

Component number three, 'Presence of the deity,' is relatively straightforward. There may be a cult image or a representation in abstract form. The archaeologist is aided in identifying this component by the fact that 'The ritualistic symbols will often relate iconographically to the deities worshipped and to their associated myth.'[41] In this work I have identified the

[35] Renfrew and Bahn 2000: 412.
[36] Renfrew and Bahn 2000: 412.
[37] Renfrew and Bahn 2000: 412.
[38] Renfrew and Bahn 2000: 412.
[39] Renfrew and Bahn 2000: 413.
[40] Renfrew and Bahn 2000: 413.
[41] Renfrew and Bahn 2000: 413.

'presence of the deity', in this case the Mother Goddess (in contrast to a human woman), using the methods Renfrew and Bahn have indicated. Thus in addition to what archaeologists have called attributes, cult symbols, and cult equipment (the three categories, which overlap and are discussed in detail in Chapter 4, include: horns of consecration, double axes, rhyta or libation vessels, offering tables, snake tubes, incurved altars, bulls, birds, snakes, agrimia, sacral knots, sun disks and moon crescents among others), I have observed the following ways in which the Minoan Mother Goddess may be identified in iconography. Position, size, gesture, clothing, human and animal attendants, and mythological or supernatural creatures (such as the griffin or sphinx) are all important factors in determining whether or not the Minoan Mother Goddess is present (in contrast to a human woman). When the female figure in a fresco or sealing is seated on a platform, or a rock, or under a tree, especially if she is also more elaborately dressed, or larger in size than the other figures in the composition, or occupies the central or focal area of the work, and has female or fantastic, or heraldic animal attendants, it is very likely that she is a representation of the Mother Goddess. I discuss my methods for identifying the Mother Goddess in contrast to a human woman in Minoan iconography in greater detail in Chapters 4 and 5.

Finally, as for 'Participation and offering,' Renfrew and Bahn advise that the art or iconography will reflect prayer and special movements such as gestures of adoration; the ritual may employ dance, music, drugs, or other devices for inducing religious experience; the sacrifice of humans or animals may take place; food and drink may be brought and consumed as offerings, or burned and poured away; other material objects, votives, may be brought and offered; the act of offering may entail breakage or hiding or discarding; and great investment of wealth may be reflected in the structure itself, its facilities, its equipment and offerings.[42]

The authors state that in practice, 'only a few of these criteria will be fulfilled in any single archaeological context.'[43] They give as an example Renfrew's own excavations at the Sanctuary at Phylakopi on the Aegean island of Melos, dated to *c.* 1400-1120 BC. There several of the criteria listed above were found: a 'focusing of attention' devise—a structure consisting of two rooms, with platforms, that probably functioned as altars; 'Presence of the deity' via a 'rich symbolic assemblage including some human representations;' and 'Participation and offering' via votive offerings. Because his arguments did not seem completely conclusive, Renfrew compared Phylakopi with

> some sites in Crete that shared similar features. The Cretan sites could be recognized as shrines precisely because there were several of them. One such occurrence might have been attributable to special factors, but the discovery of several with closely comparable features suggested a repeated pattern for which the explanation of religious ritual seemed the only plausible one.[44]

This last comment brings up a perhaps obvious, but important point: the observation of repeated patterns is crucial in stating one's case and determining whether or not one has found evidence of religious ritual.

---

[42] Renfrew and Bahn 2000: 413.
[43] Renfrew and Bahn 2000: 413.
[44] Renfrew and Bahn 2000: 413.

Renfrew and Bahn admit that religious ritual can more easily be proven when literacy and literary evidence are available; however, they note that the absence of such need not be a deterrent. In such cases, one must look for 'developed iconography . . . in which individual deities are distinguished.'[45]

Renfrew's work on the archaeology of cult has not only led archaeologists, in the years since its publication, 'to adopt precise criteria for evaluating cult evidence'[46] but has also created a new climate in Aegean archaeology which emphasizes the reconstruction of ritual and human actions underlying cult activity over reconstruction of beliefs.[47] While I find Renfrew and Bahn's criterion useful in pinpointing and understanding religious ritual activity, I feel such understanding should be used to elucidate rather than shy away from ancient religious beliefs.

Unlike archaeologist D'Agata, who sees the study of cult as allowing archaeologists to retreat from the reconstruction of beliefs and definitions of religion (as though this were something archaeologists are not able to discuss empirically and cogently), I believe studying ritual and cult can be extremely helpful in discerning the beliefs and religion of the Bronze Age Minoans. Like Renfrew and Bahn, I further believe that such understanding can also lead to a better comprehension of the social and economic processes of Minoan society. I apply their criteria to representations of ritual in Minoan iconography to aid me in my understanding of Minoan ritual and religious beliefs.

In concluding this section, I wish to discuss my personal experience with the archaeology of Bronze Age Crete and how I use archaeology's various methods for my own work. In my years of studying Bronze Age Crete, I have read hundreds of books and essays written by Aegean archaeologists describing the work they have done: sites they have surveyed or excavated, artifacts they have unearthed and preserved, and interpretations they have made. I have also been a subscriber to AegeaNet, the listserve for archaeologists working in the Aegean, since its inception twenty-eight years ago. It is an invaluable source for keeping up-to-date on discoveries, publications, research, and controversies in the field of Aegean archaeology.

Because I was a member of the American School of Classical Studies in Athens Summer Program in Crete, 1989, and have 'hands-on' experience, having worked for University of Pennsylvania archaeologist Dr. Barbara Hayden in east Crete surveying the Iron Age site of Vrokastro, 1990, and have visited the island every year for the past thirty years, I am familiar with the surveys and excavations taking place in Crete and with many of the archaeologists who lead them. I continue to keep current with new excavations. I also continue to revisit the archaeological museums in Crete: Heraklion, Agios Nikolaos, Siteia, Rethymnon, Chania, and the folkloric museums, especially that of Vori. I find that with each visit to the museum I 'see' something with new eyes. Of course, my visits most recently have been with an eye toward the iconography of Goddesses, especially Mother Goddesses, women, and the relationship of women to men, and the ritual relationships of women and of men to the Goddess(es) and gods. I also continue to revisit the major and not so major archaeological sites of Crete: Knossos, Malia, Kato Zakros, Phaistos, Chania, Arkhanes, Palaikastro, Mochlos, Amnisos, Nirou Hani, Ayia Triadha, Gournia, Vasiliki, Myrtos, Kavousi, Chamezi, Mt. Jouktas, The Caves of Psychro,

---

[45] Renfrew and Bahn 2000: 415.
[46] D'Agata 2009: 5.
[47] D'Agata 2009: 5.

Trapaza, Skotenio, Eileithyia, and the Idaian Cave. I have visited all of these sites on one or numerous occasions either as a student of the American School, the guest of an archaeologist, or the leader of a tour. Since 2001, I have taken five different groups of Americans to visit the archaeological sites and museums of Minoan Crete.

It is due mainly to the archaeologists working in Crete since even before the days of Sir Arthur Evans that we are aware of the existence of ancient Minoan civilization and have a sophisticated understanding of it. I am grateful to them for the information they have made available and for the methodologies they have developed over the last one hundred years.

The methodology of archaeology informs my work in multiple ways. Like those of the school of New Archaeology, I am concerned with how changes in the social system (of Bronze Age Crete) take place. I too want to base my conclusions on the testing of hypotheses, and design my research to answer specific questions—in my case was the Goddess preeminent, was she a Mother Goddess (perhaps among other roles), and was Bronze Age Crete a matriarchy? Like the post-processualists, I wish to be honest about my biases, I too understand that conclusions can change when new data is unearthed, and perhaps most importantly, that the interpretation of artifacts and sites involves creating a 'circuitry' among the participants and the data. I appreciate their caution in interpreting religion.

What I do not appreciate in some of the archaeological work I have studied are the unacknowledged biases. Nor do I appreciate the fact that in nearly all the work I am familiar with there are very few who will consider the hypothesis that the centrality of a Mother Goddess in Minoan religion points to the centrality of women in Minoan society and perhaps even to matriarchy. Two of those few are John G. Younger and Paul Rehak, who, in their 2008 article 'Minoan Culture: Religion, Burial Customs and Administration' in *The Cambridge Companion to the Aegean Bronze Age*, write:

> The prominence of females in Neopalatial art, important mortal women and goddesses . . . make it possible to imagine that women dominated Neopalatial society, perhaps even politics. All human societies, however, ancient and modern, have been patriarchies with men in positions of authority; no matriarchy has ever been documented. But Neopalatial Crete offers the best candidate for a matriarchy so far.[48]

Renfrew and Bahn have written that 'archaeology has an important role to play in achieving a balanced view of our present world, which is inescapably the product of the worlds which have preceded it.'[49] It is my hope that my work will contribute to archaeology's goal of achieving a 'balanced view of our present world,' by presenting a more balanced view of the Goddess's and women's role in the ancient society of Crete.

---

[48] Younger and Rehak 2008: 180.
[49] Renfrew and Bahn 1996: 49.

Components of archaeomythology: mythology

Although in modern day society the term myth has come to mean something that is not true, I prefer the view of Professor of Religion Donald E. Miller: 'in religious terms a myth is any powerful and evocative story that dramatically reveals something about the underlying meaning and purpose of creation, nature or history'; as well as his observation that: 'myths are the oldest forms of religious reflection, usually passed on orally from generation to generation, and providing the central themes for a culture's self-understanding and self-definition.'[50] I also appreciate Miller's statement that sacred myths 'involve recounting the moments and places where people believe they have glimpsed . . . something of the fundamental nature of reality.'[51] The well-known mythographer Alan Dundes has defined myth as 'a sacred narrative explaining how the world and man came to be in their present form.'[52] He has noted that 'myth may constitute the highest form of truth, albeit, in metaphorical guise.'[53] The renowned theorist of myth, Mircea Eliade, in his essay 'Towards a Definition of Myth,' gives a six-part definition. He writes:

> In general one may say:
>
> -----that myth, such as it is lived by archaic societies, constitutes the story of the deeds of Supernatural Beings;
>
> -----that the story is considered absolutely *true* . . . and *sacred;*
>
> ------that myth always concerns a 'creation'; it tells how something has come into existence, or how a way of behaving, an institution, a way of working, were established; this is why myths constitute paradigms for every meaningful human act;
>
> -----that in knowing the myth one knows the 'origins' of things and is thus able to master things and manipulate them at will; this is . . . a knowledge that one 'lives' ritually, either by reciting the myths ceremonially, or by carrying out the ritual for which it serves as justification;
>
> -----that in one way or another one 'lives' the myth, gripped by the sacred, exalting power of the events one is rememorializing and reactualizing.
>
> In sum, myths reveal that the world, man and life have a supernatural origin and history, and that this history is meaningful, precious and exemplary.[54]

It is evident from the above, that not even the scholars who value myth as a bearer of significant cultural and spiritual visions and values, all agree upon the definition of myth. Where there is the greatest disagreement, however, is not over the definition but over how myth is to be interpreted or what its essential function is. Theories of interpretation tend to fall into two main categories, what Classicist Elizabeth Vandiver has called 'what and why is

---

[50] Miller 1992: 7.
[51] Miller 1992: 7.
[52] Dundes 1984: 1.
[53] Dundes 1984: 1.
[54] Eliade 1992: 5.

myth.'[55] Within the 'what' category, which 'attempt[s] to explain myth by identifying it as a subcategory, derivative, or forerunner of something else,'[56] one finds Andrew Lang's myths as primitive science; Frazer's myths as an explanation for ritual; and Malinowski's myths as 'charters' providing validation for the social institutions they describe. The 'why' category 'assumes that myths reflect the same underlying human realities in all cultures and . . . are somehow cross-cultural or transcultural.'[57] This category includes Freud's theory that myth reflects psychological forces present in the individual; Jung's view that myths reflect the collective unconscious; the structuralists, among them Claude Levi-Strauss, who see myth as mediating contradictions in the human condition; Walter Burkert, who believes that myth is rooted in pre-cultural biological realities; and Joseph Campbell's metaphysical approach to myth which sees myth as the medium which connects the human plane of existence with the supernatural or divine realms. Finally there are the current day mythologists, who fall into neither of these camps, who reject any grand unified theories, and are attempting to strike a balance between focus on method and an exclusive focus on area studies.[58] Several of these, influenced by deconstructionism, see ancient myth, and also the contemporary theories and interpretations of myth, as ideologies.[59]

Used in conjunction with the other disciplines of archaeomythology, I believe myths can give us important clues to events and to the cultural and social institutions of ancient societies. Like Mycenologist Thomas G. Palaima, who argues that the Homeric poems 'may be more useful in preserving some form of authentic memories of Bronze Age religion than it is now fashionable to accept,'[60] in that same vein, I would suggest that Greek myths may preserve more about Minoan religion and society than is commonly acknowledged. Like archaeomythologist Susan Carter, I believe that 'continued analysis and / or new interpretations of . . . myths are needed,'[61] based, as she emphasizes, on an understanding of the history and culture of the society that produced the myths and on the history and culture of the societies that transmitted and altered them.

In my interpretation of myths, I follow a feminist hermeneutical approach. That is, I follow Elisabeth Schüssler-Fiorenza's four-part method in which she utilizes a 'hermeneutics of suspicion,' a 'hermeneutics of remembrance,' a 'hermeneutics of evaluation and proclamation,' and a 'hermeneutics of creative actualization.'[62] Beginning with a 'hermeneutics of suspicion,' I start with the understanding that, like the biblical texts that Schüssler-Fiorenza analyzes, some myths and their interpretation are 'androcentric and serve patriarchal functions.'[63] I also understand that a feminist 'hermeneutics of suspicion' requires that I question 'the underlying presuppositions, androcentric models, and unarticulated interests of contemporary [mythological] interpretation.'[64] Utilizing a 'hermeneutics of remembrance,' I keep in mind that myths might well preserve a pre-patriarchal element, and that patriarchy was not

---

[55] Vandiver 2000: 8.
[56] Vandiver 2000: 9.
[57] Vandiver 2000: 12.
[58] See the essays in Patton and Doniger 1996.
[59] See Lincoln 1999; Csapo 2005.
[60] Palaima 2008: 355.
[61] Carter 2001: 53.
[62] Schüssler-Fiorenza 1984: 15-22.
[63] Schüssler-Fiorenza 1984: 15.
[64] Schüssler-Fiorenza 1984: 16.

necessarily an inherent ingredient of Minoan society. As Schüssler-Fiorenza explains it: 'Rather than understand the texts as an adequate reflection of the reality about which they speak, we must search for rhetorical clues and allusions that indicate the reality about which the texts are silent.'[65] A 'hermeneutics of evaluation and proclamation' requires that one analyze those myths that are related to Minoan Crete and identify those elements that are sexist and patriarchal as well as recognize those that 'transcend their patriarchal contexts.'[66] Finally a 'hermeneutics of creative actualization' seeks to retell myth from a feminist perspective; and, as Schüssler-Fiorenza puts it, 'to create narrative amplifications of the feminist remnants that have survived in patriarchal texts.'[67]

When looked at in light of the above observations and definitions, it becomes apparent that one can learn a great deal about the ancient culture of Crete, its Goddess(es), and the role of women in Minoan Crete, by studying the ancient mythology. Minoan mythology is buried, however, under layers of Mycenaean and classical Greek mythology. Fortunately, a number of scholars, including Nilsson, Willetts, Gimbutas, Vasilakis, and others have dug down through the layers and brought to light various strands of Minoan sacred myths. The work of these scholars, and the examples of myth discussed in Chapters 4, 5, and 7, illustrate the important part mythology can play in arguing for the preeminence of the Goddess and women and matriarchy in Minoan Crete. This is so because the mythology left to us by the Classical Greeks contains much that is in all probability pre-Mycenaean, as indicated in part by linguistic analysis. As Gimbutas explained, the Minoans not only gave the Mycenaeans the names of many of the Goddesses and gods they venerated in the Linear B tablets, the Minoans also gave the Mycenaeans many elements of their culture. The Mycenaeans represent, according to Gimbutas, 'an important transitional phase between Old European gynocentric culture and the classical Greek culture.'[68]

Eventually the Mycenaeans themselves fell to other Indo-European invaders and for a period of about three hundred and fifty years (c. 1110-750 BC), Greece fell into a Dark Age. In spite of the cultural decay, Gimbutas notes that Mycenaean elements 'shifted to later Greek culture in several ways.'[69] Among those ways were language and religious activity. The Greek culture that arose at the end of the Dark Ages was vastly different from the Mycenaean and yet, strong Goddesses remained.

> By examining the written texts depicting Greek goddesses, we can gain valuable insight into the Old European forebears, since archaeology alone does not preserve details comparable to the comments of ancient writers. Some of the deities were clearly continuous with Neolithic and Minoan times. We should remember that the amalgamation of Indo-European and Old European culture, . . . engendered the goddesses and gods of classical Greek religion.[70]

As Gimbutas indicates, it is the mythology, as well as the archaeological artifacts, that one must use to understand Minoan religion and society. In interpreting myth, I take into account the interpretations of Nilsson, Willetts, Hawkes, Gimbutas, Vasilakis, and others. I also look at how

---

[65] Schüssler-Fiorenza 1984: 112.
[66] Schüssler-Fiorenza 1984: 19.
[67] Schüssler-Fiorenza 1984: 21.
[68] Gimbutas 1999: 152.
[69] Gimbutas 1999: 153.
[70] Gimbutas 1999: 154.

my and their interpretations of myth can be corroborated by shrines, frescos, and artifacts used in religious ritual. I look for consistencies and congruencies, as well as incongruencies, between myths, artifacts, and linguistics.

At the root of my interpretation is the understanding that the myths must be interpreted in the context of the symbol system of ancient Crete, a system we can derive from the archaeological artifacts and sites. Minoan Crete was, as archaeologist Lucy Goodison has pointed out, 'a society very different from our own. It was differently organized; women held different status; and the symbols attached to women were very different.'[71] My interpretation also takes into account the controversial idea that was brought to my attention by archaeologist Nanno Marinatos, that cultures of all ages and all times and places share striking similarities on the level of ritual.[72] If that is so, then I may expect to be able to have some understanding and draw some conclusions about Minoan myth based on the simple fact that I too am a human being and a woman who engages in ritual. And if, as Marinatos and other theorists further believe, there is a level of human behavior that goes back to our origins as a human species, then I might expect to find in Minoan myth a veneration of the Great Mother expressive not only of the natural bond between human mothers and their children, but also of the deep understanding that we are all children of a Great Mother, the mother of all humankind.

Components of archaeomythology: linguistics

In order to draw conclusions about the preeminence of the Goddess, and women in Minoan society, the discipline of linguistics is an important component. As I am not myself a linguist, I draw on the work of experts in the field: Marija Gimbutas, Michael Ventris and John Chadwick, Gareth Owens, Thomas G. Palaima, Harald Haarmann, and others.

One way in which Aegean archaeologists attempt to understand Minoan society and culture is to draw inferences from Mycenaean to Minoan times using Linear B script. Thus in arguing that Minoan Crete very possibly had a joint female/male ruler, Younger looks to the Linear B tablets.

> What has not . . . been sufficiently stressed for the Late Bronze Age is the role of the female entitled 'po-ti-ni-ja' in Linear B—since she appears in texts that also mention divinities, Potnia is almost always considered to be a goddess. But in several texts, she also appears alongside the Wanax, and in a couple of brief but illuminating texts, she is paired with the Wanax.[73]

I use linguistic studies for words and phrases which serve to illuminate both the social status of women and the prominence of the Goddess in Minoan Crete.

Linguistics is problematic because the earlier pre-Mycenaean script, Linear A, has not been definitively deciphered; and because Linear B, while it might very well include elements of Linear A, and if linguists like Haarmann are correct, Old European script as well, is still a

---

[71] Goodison 1990: 326.
[72] Marinatos 1993: 11.
[73] J.G. Younger, email to Aegeanet mailing list March 11, 1996, http://umich.edu/classics/archives/aegeanet/aegeanet.960311.02. No longer accessible.

product of the interface of patriarchal Mycenaean Greece with pre-Mycenaean Crete, and thus its use as a tool in helping us learn about women and the Goddess in Minoan society is limited. Moreover, the purpose of the Linear B tablets, which were written by anonymous scribes, was primarily to keep track of economic information related to the operation of the Mycenaean palatial centers, rather than to describe aspects of Minoan-Mycenaean religion, although offerings to deities such as Eileithyia or Potnia are noted also. Nevertheless, if one keeps these problems in mind, one can cautiously use Linear B texts, along with the other disciplines that comprise the work of archaeomythology, and especially with archaeological, iconographical, and artifactual data, to reconstruct a fuller understanding of Minoan religion and society, and the Goddesses' and women's place in it.

Dating system used within this work

Before concluding this chapter some comments must be made regarding the dates used within this study. In this work several ranges of dates are given for the artifacts and time periods discussed. I have included dates according to Sir Arthur Evans's chronology, and dates based on the catalog of the Archaeological Museum of Heraklion authored by Greek archaeologist Nota Dimopoulou-Rethemiotakis.[74] The latter corresponds to Evans's dates, but is derived from the work of archaeologists Peter Warren and Vronwy Hankey.[75] Both chronologies are termed by experts 'low chronology,' and are arrived at through traditional archaeological techniques of cross-dating. There is also a 'high chronology' with somewhat differing dates. This chronology is based upon scientific methods of dating archaeological artifacts, and its most well-known proponent is archaeologist Sturt W. Manning.[76] An explanation of what the terms low and high chronology mean in the context of Minoan Crete is in order.

It was Sir Arthur Evans who, during his excavations at Knossos in the early 1900s, produced a chronology for Minoan Crete. Evans based his chronology on Minoan relations with Egypt, and thus he divided Minoan history into Early, Middle and Late Minoan corresponding to the Old, Middle and New Kingdoms of ancient Egypt. Each of these periods he further subdivided in three, for example, Early Minoan I, II, III, with these categories subdivided into A, B, and C. These were further divided into 1 and 2.

To devise his chronology Evans used Minoan imports in Egypt, Egyptian exports found in Crete, and 'Egyptian influence on Minoan glyptic work and painting.'[77] Egypt was used because it was a culture for which written records exist for the Bronze Age. Evans's divisions are based on Minoan pottery styles and do not correspond to the major destructions of the temple-palaces nor to their building phases (as do the divisions in Platon's chronology[78]). Neither do Evans's divisions take into account regional differences in Minoan pottery styles. Nevertheless, as J. Lesley Fitton so elegantly put it:

---

[74] Dimopoulou-Rethemiotakis 2005.
[75] Warren and Hankey 1989.
[76] For example see Manning 2010: 11-28.
[77] Gesell 1985: 4.
[78] Greek archaeologist Nicholas Platon, in his 1966 work *Crete*, developed a dating system that uses four major divisions based on temple-palace architecture: Prepalatial, Protopalatial or First Palace Period, Neopalatial or Second Palace Period, and Postpalatial or Third Palace Period.

> The relative chronology of Minoan civilization—the chronology dependent on changes in material culture within the island and expressed in archaeological phases—is quite well understood. A broad consensus exists.[79]

The consensus exists and Evans's chronology continues to be used by many scholars today, often in modified form, because it has been elaborated upon and refined since Evans's time. A major study by Peter Warren and Vronwy Hankey, *Aegean Bronze Age Chronology,* is particularly important in this regard. Warren and Hankey reviewed the links between Minoan Crete and the Near East that had 'potential chronological significance,'[80] and attempted to impartially determine how reliable each supposed link was. Their conclusions are widely accepted within the field of archaeology.

Because, as I related above, Evans's dating system does not take into account destruction horizons, building phases, nor regional differences in pottery, in recent years science-based dating techniques have been challenging dates arrived at by Evans's method of cross-dating Minoan and Egyptian artifacts and time periods.[81] The greatest point of disagreement has arisen over the date of the Late Bronze Age eruption of the island of Thera. The date of the Theran eruption is important because it 'provides a peg for the absolute chronology of Crete';[82] that is, a chronology based not on internal cultural sequences (relative chronology), but on actual calendar dates.

At this point in time there is approximately one hundred years difference between the dating of the Theran eruption based on traditional archaeological methods of cross-dating, or low chronology, and dating arrived at by scientific methods like radiocarbon dating corrected through the use of dendrochronology and Greenland ice-core testing, or high chronology. Unfortunately, the scientific evidence is not conclusive either. Scientific methods support a date of 1628 BC for the eruption of Thera, but also concede the possibility of a date in the mid-sixteenth century BC. This is close to, but is still earlier than the date proposed by the proponents of low chronology of 1520 BC.

The new and old chronologies, or high and low chronologies, are most out of step for the Middle Minoan III to Late Minoan IIIA1 period, *c.* 1700-1400 BC. In the succeeding periods they reconverge.

> In particular the 1628 BC date poses very real problems for archaeologists studying the material culture of Crete during LM IB and LM II. The finds suggest that neither period was very long and that together they spanned no more than about 100 years. The new dating for Thera, however, would make these periods stretch some two hundred years and, at the same time, shorten preceding periods dramatically, squeezing earlier developments into an improbably short time frame.[83]

---

[79] Fitton 2002: 27.
[80] Fitton 2002: 31.
[81] Fitton 2002: 31.
[82] Fitton 2002: 33.
[83] Fitton 2002: 35-36.

Since science has not yet come up with an indisputable date, and because 'archaeologically derived synchronisms still carry much conviction,'[84] a compromise has been reached with most archaeologists taking the date 1530-1520 BC for the Theran eruption. It is 'the latest possible date allowed for by scientific methods, and one that does not greatly upset traditional synchronisms.'[85]

Many of the archaeologists cited in this work use Evans's dates or a 'compromise early chronology' which derives from Warren and Hankey. A few, most notably Marina Moss,[86] favor the high chronology. I favor the low chronology for the reasons discussed by Fitton in the above quote. When dates for artifacts are given by authors or excavators, their dates, whether low or high chronology, are used and denoted. When such dates are not provided, I have added Evans's divisions, and the dates based on the low chronology of the Heraklion Museum catalog.

Conclusion

In this chapter I have outlined in some detail the methodology that is used in this work. It includes archaeomythology and its component parts: archaeology, mythology, linguistics, and the history of religion; and to this I also add some of the methods of the academic field of Women's Spirituality, including the use of feminist standpoint and feminist hermeneutics.

I defined Women's Spirituality, and gave a statement of my values and worldview. I then discussed each of the components of archaeomythology that I focus on here. As regards archaeology, I traced its historical development as a discipline, noted its current concerns, especially as regards the study of ancient religion, discussed my own archaeological experience in Crete, and how the methodologies of archaeology inform my own work.

As for the second component of archaeomythology, mythology, I defined it, briefly surveyed the various theories of how myths can be interpreted, and expressed my belief that myths can give scholars important clues to events and to the cultural and social institutions of ancient societies. I also defined and discussed a feminist hermeneutics approach to the interpretation of myth, and named some of those scholars who have dug down through the layers of Greek and Mycenaean myth to bring to light the strands of Minoan mythology.

As regards linguistics, I noted that scholars frequently draw inferences backwards in time from Mycenaean to Minoan times using Linear B script, and that cautious use of the current decipherments of Linear A can allow us to trace back some of the Greek Goddesses to their possible Minoan predecessors, thus perhaps adding to the evidence in support of the preeminence of the Mother Goddess. I addressed the problems revolving around the relative and absolute chronologies of Minoan Crete and explained why I shall be giving two sets of dates for the artifacts and time periods discussed in this work.

Applying my methodology to the available shrines, architecture, artifacts, religious iconography, existing texts, and mythology, in the following chapters I argue that a strong case can be made for the preeminence of the Goddess in Minoan society and for the preeminence

---

[84] Fitton 2002: 36.
[85] Fitton 2002: 36.
[86] Moss 2005.

of women in Bronze Age Cretan society. Having developed an empirically grounded sketch of Minoan cultural history, I determine whether or not the society I have uncovered fits the definition of matriarchy offered by Goettner-Abendroth.

Chapter 3

Theoretical Context: Matriarchy / Patriarchy Debates

Before beginning to answer the question: was Bronze Age Crete a matriarchal society?—I would like to look at the historical background to the debates over matriarchy that have raged for over one hundred years. An understanding of those debates will help place this study in its proper context as a work that contributes not only, I hope, to a better understanding of Minoan society, but that adds to our knowledge of pre-historical, woman-centered, Goddess-centered societies in general; and adds a voice to those who would argue that one can make a plausible case for the existence of pre-historical matriarchal societies. In these debates the 1861 work of Johann Jakob Bachofen's *Das Mutterrecht*, John McLennan's *Primitive Marriage*, published in 1865, and Friedrich Engles' 1884 publication, *The Origins of the Family, Private Property and the State* are important as early nineteenth century works that argued for matriarchy as an evolutionary predecessor to patriarchy.

Historical background to the debates over matriarchy

It was Bachofen's work that first put forth the theory of original matriarchy. Belonging 'to the progressive, idealistic, European tradition of evolutionary theory of the 18th and 19th centuries . . . *Mother Right* was one of three seminal works of evolutionary theory published within a period of eight years,'[1] the others being Darwin's *Origin of the Species* and Marx's *Capital*.

Citing numerous cases from classical literature, myths, legends, folklore, and legal documents, Bachofen, a legal scholar and a judge as well as a classicist, argued that in human history, what he called or postulated as 'hetaerism,' a period of complete male promiscuity, which characterized the hunter-gatherer stage, was followed by matriarchy. He wrote:

> There is no doubt that Matriarchy everywhere grew out of woman's conscious, continued resistance to the debasing state of hetaerism. Defenseless against abuse by men, . . . woman was the first to feel the need for regulated conditions and a purer ethic, while men, conscious of their superior physical strength, accepted the new constraint only unwillingly.[2]

Matriarchy, which coincides with the introduction of agriculture, according to Bachofen, triumphed because women and religion were closely linked in ancient societies: 'This religious primacy of motherhood leads to a primacy of the mortal woman.'[3] In Bachofen's view, the stage of matriarchy was characterized by monogamy, the supremacy of mothers, and the tracing of descent through the motherline. But Bachofen not only viewed matriarchy as the domination of the family by women, but the domination of the state by women as well.[4]

---

[1] Partenheimer 2003: iii.
[2] Bachofen 1967: 94.
[3] Bachofen 1967: 87.
[4] Bachofen 1967:107.

Matriarchy was ultimately followed, according to Bachofen, by patriarchy, a superior stage of human development in which society moved from an 'acceptance of nature to a transcending of nature.'[5] As one of Bachofen's translators describes this stage, paraphrasing Bachofen:

> The spiritual aspect of man transcends the muck and mire of the material world. Both in the heavens and on earth, the father and son rule through their intellect, reason, and creative imagination. They reveal and offer to humanity a celestial world beyond time, space, and suffering.[6]

Appearing only four years after the publication of Bachofen's work, John F. McLennan's *Primitive Marriage* added to this new scholarship by synthesizing current anthropological data and concurring with Bachofen (contrary to what most scholars of the time thought), that marriage as it existed in 1865, did not exist in ancient times. McLennan argued that since group marriage or polyandry was the norm then, and since there was no way to determine paternity, ancient societies must have traced their ancestry through female kinship. He referred to this tracing of one's descent through the motherline as 'the most ancient system of kinship.'[7] In McLennan's own words:

> The indigenous customs of most early communities—whether of the Indo-European, Tuaranian, or Semitic race—exhibit peculiarities intelligible only on the supposition that kinship and succession through females were the rule before the rise of agnation [related on the male or father's side]. Further we have seen that wherever non-advancing communities are to be found—isolated in islands or maintaining their savage liberties in mountain fastnesses—there to this day exists the system of kinship through females only. . . . But at a yet older date we must conclude that neither the state, nor the family properly speaking existed. And at that earlier time the unnamed species of kinship—the counterpart and complement of agnation—was the chief determinant of social phenomena.[8]

McLennan believed that once paternity became certain,

> a system of kinship through males would arise with the growth of property, and a practice of sons succeeding, as heirs direct, to the estates of fathers; and as the system of kinship through males arose, that through females would—and chiefly under the influence of property—die away.[9]

Before continuing I must note that Peggy Reeves Sanday has pointed out that neither Bachofen nor McLennan ever used the word matriarchy in their works. In Bachofen's case only the terms *mutterrecht* (mother right) and gynecocracy (rule by women) appear. Sanday speculates that Bachofen's English translator used the word matriarchy rather than gynecocracy because, in 1967 'popular usage made matriarchy a synonym of gynecocracy.'[10] In McLennan's case only phrases like 'system of kinship through females' appear. Nevertheless, notes Sanday,

---

[5] Bachofen 1967: 111.
[6] Bachofen 2003: v.
[7] McLennan 1865: 160.
[8] McLennan 1865: 229.
[9] McLennan 1865: 246.
[10] Sanday 1998: 4.

Bachofen's and McLennan's works paved the way for matriarchy being defined as the mirror image of patriarchy and thus for the negative connotation the word now has.

Neither does Friedrich Engels use the term matriarchy in his work *The Origins of the Family, Private Property and the State*. Drawing on the works of both Bachofen and McLennan, as well as the great anthropologist Lewis Henry Morgan, Engels posits that originally all people of antiquity, because of their sexual practices, reckoned their descent through the female line only; and that because only the mother (and not the father) of the younger generation was known with certainty, she was accorded a high status. It was this high status which led to a rule of women (gynecocracy).[11] Women's rule continued, according to Engels, even as people moved from 'group marriage' to 'the pairing family' characterized by the union being easily dissolved by either partner, and the children belonging to the mother alone upon the dissolution of the pairing.[12] It was not until the introduction of herding and slavery that the balance tipped in favor of men. According to Engels, when herding and slavery were introduced, men became the owners of the instruments of labor—the cattle and the slaves. Simultaneously paternity was becoming better understood. As wealth increased, the man's position in the family became more important than the woman's. His increased wealth and importance made him all the more anxious to 'overthrow, in favor of his children, the traditional order of inheritance.'[13] In this case the traditional order of inheritance is not the paternal children, but the maternal lineage on the mother's side.

Engels says we will never know exactly how the transition to father right in prehistoric times was accomplished. However, he says of this transition: 'The overthrow of mother right was the world historical defeat of the female sex.'[14]

Another early proponent of a pre-Hellenic, woman-centered, and, in this case, Goddess-centered, matriarchal society was classicist Jane Ellen Harrison. While some might feel she belongs more appropriately in a section on the history of Greek religion, she is included here because, like so many of her era, Harrison was influenced by Frazer's *Golden Bough*, a compilation of anthropological data and a monumental study in comparative folklore, magic, and religion. Harrison was also well aware of the works of Bachofen, McLennan, Engels, and E. B. Tylor.[15] Like her fellow classicist Bachofen, Harrison draws upon her vast knowledge of ancient literary sources and artifacts to uncover the matriarchal underpinnings of Greek society.

Her monumental 1903 *Prolegomena to the Study of Greek Religion* gives numerous examples of the matriarchal nature of pre-Hellenic society that can be discovered in the works of classical authors and archaeological artifacts. A few examples follow. Writing of the Greek festival of the Thesmophoria, Harrison notes that in Isaeus' oration, *About the Estate of Pyrrhos*, the question comes up: 'Was Pyrrhos lawfully married?' Isaeus asks, 'If he were married, would he not have been obliged, on behalf of his lawful wife, to feast the women at the Thesmophoria?'[16]

---

[11] Engels (1942) 1972: 77.
[12] Engels (1942) 1972: 110.
[13] Engels (1942) 1972: 119.
[14] Engels (1942) 1972: 120.
[15] Harrison writes in *Prolegomena*, 261n3: 'The clearest and most scientific statement of the facts as to this difficult subject known to me is to be found in an article by Dr. E. B. Tylor, *'The Matriarchal family system,' Nineteen Century*, July 1896.'
[16] Harrison (1903) 1991: 130-131.

Harrison observes that men 'may have had to make peace with the community by paying the expenses of the Thesmophoria feast.'[17] She is probably referring here to the fact that prior to the introduction of patriarchy, women had more than one established partner. It seems she agrees that the evolution of patriarchal forms of marriage introduced exclusive rights over one woman, thus violating 'the old matriarchal usages,'[18] hence men's need to pay for the feast—to pay for the exclusive right to the woman.

Inscriptions also give Harrison the clues she is searching for. Thus, one from the third century BC in Gambreion (in Asia Minor) shows that 'mourning laws of the ancients bore harder on women than on men.'[19] According to the law Harrison is referring to, the dress worn by women at funerals should be dark, and it should not be torn. Men are not required to wear dark colors. Moreover, men's mourning period is shorter than that of the women. Women who broke these mourning laws are to be punished by the *gynaikonomoi* with exclusion from the state festival of the Thesmophoria and from sacrifice to any god for a period of ten years. Men do not appear to have received any such punishment for infractions of mourning laws. Harrison believes that this stiff punishment meted out to women can be explained

> not by the general lugubriousness of women, nor even by their supposed keener sense of convention, but by those early matriarchal conditions which relationship naturally counted through the mother rather than the father.[20]

Some of Harrison's most convincing reasons for describing pre-Hellenic Greece as a matriarchy come in her discussion of the local cults that preceded Olympian Greek religion. 'When we come to examine local cults we find that, if these mirror the civilization of the worshippers, this civilization is quite other than patriarchal.'[21] Citing Hera reigning alone at Argos, Demeter and Persephone supreme at Eleusis, Athena in Athens, and Themis, Phoebe, and Gaia preceding Apollo at Delphi, Harrison tells us that these 'primitive goddesses' reflect 'another condition of things, a relationship traced through the mother, the state of society known by the awkward term matriarchal.'[22] Even in various of the cults of local heroes Harrison finds that the goddesses are supreme. Not only does each local hero descend from a local earth-nymph or mother, but when he accompanies 'these early matriarchal, husbandless goddesses,'[23] he is chosen by the Goddesses not to be their lovers, but so they can protect him and inspire him on to great deeds. 'With the coming of patriarchal conditions this high companionship ends. The women goddesses are sequestered to a servile domesticity, they become abject and amorous.'[24]

Because their cults were long established before the advent of patriarchy, Goddesses like Hera, Demeter, and Persephone continued to be worshipped, albeit in a diminished form, even in historical times. At least one of the ancient Great Goddesses did not make it into the patriarchal pantheon. Pandora 'is in ritual and matriarchal theology the earth as Kore, but in

---

[17] Harrison (1903) 1991: 131.
[18] Harrison (1903) 1991: 131.
[19] Harrison (1903) 1991: 143.
[20] Harrison (1903) 1991: 143.
[21] Harrison (1903) 1991: 260.
[22] Harrison (1903) 1991: 261.
[23] Harrison (1903) 1991: 273.
[24] Harrison (1903) 1991: 273.

the patriarchal mythology of Hesiod her great figure is strangely changed and minished [*sic*].'[25] Quoting from Hesiod's *Works and Days*, Harrison describes how Zeus orders that Pandora be fashioned out of clay, and given the gifts of tricks, flattery, and thievery. Harrison concludes:

> Zeus the Father will have no great Earth-goddess, Mother and Maid in one, in his man-fashioned Olympus, but her figure *is* from the beginning, so he re-makes it; woman who was the inspirer, becomes the temptress; she who made all things, gods and mortals alike is become their plaything, their slave, dowered only with physical beauty, and with a slave's tricks and blandishments.[26]

Other local goddesses, whose cults were newer, never made it to the great patriarchal pantheon and remain known to us today only vaguely or as appendages of the Olympian Goddesses. Thus Callisto is subsumed by Artemis, and Callisto's ancient sanctuary in Arcadia is known as the sanctuary of Artemis Calliste—the last letter of Callisto changed and added to the name of Artemis to mean Artemis the Fairest or most beautiful.[27]

The twentieth century debates over matriarchy

Harrison may have been one of the last scholars to subscribe to this evolutionary paradigm, for by the early twentieth century it was in its demise and the term matriarchy fell into disuse. Sanday notes that the term was revived again in the early1970s by feminist activists, and at this time it was denounced by male as well as female anthropologists who argued that there was no archaeological or ethnographic evidence for the existence of matriarchy.[28] We see this argument used over and over again by archaeologists and classicists in connection with Minoan Crete. In order to understand the argument put forward by the anthropologists, an examination of some of their essays on the subject is helpful, most notably those by Louise Lamphere, Michelle Rosaldo, and Joan Bamberger in a 1974 collection entitled *Woman, Culture, and Society*. The works of those who revived the matriarchy argument in the 1970s and 1980s are then reviewed.

Rosaldo and Lamphere wrote the preface and introduction to the collection of early feminist anthropological essays, and in that preface they note that: 'The anthropological literature tells us relatively little about women, and provides almost no theoretical apparatus for understanding or describing culture from a woman's point of view.'[29] They address the question of matriarchy in the first pages of their introduction and tell us immediately that 'most academic anthropologists have dismissed it [matriarchy] out of hand.'[30] Why? No anthropologist has observed a society

> in which women have publicly recognized power and authority surpassing that of men. . . . All contemporary societies are to some extent male-dominated, . . . sexual asymmetry is presently a universal fact of life.[31]

---

[25] Harrison (1903) 1991: 284.
[26] Harrison (1903) 1991: 285.
[27] Harrison (1903) 1991: 325.
[28] Sanday 1998: 5-6.
[29] Rosaldo and Lamphere 1974b: vi.
[30] Rosaldo and Lamphere 1974a: 2.
[31] Rosaldo and Lamphere 1974a: 3.

This statement, according to Sanday, was later retracted,[32] but the retraction was not always noted. What of ancient societies? The authors look askance at archaeological data, calling it 'problematic.' 'Elaborate female burials might, for example, indicate a world in which women were the rulers; but they could equally be the remains of wives, mistresses, concubines of male elites.'[33]

Joan Bamberger in her essay 'The Myth of Matriarchy' begins with some of the same comments with which Rosaldo and Lamphere begin their introduction to the volume. 'Because no matriarchies persist anywhere at the present time, and because primary sources recounting them are totally lacking,' their existence and constitution can only be 'surmised.'[34] Bamberger criticizes Bachofen for his use of 'dubious historical sources,' and for his confusion of myth for history. She proposes to look at the 'myths of matriarchy' as 'social charters,' that is, not verbatim histories, but as ways for a society to 'reorder its social experiences.'[35] Bamberger focuses her attention on 'myths of matriarchy' in two areas of South America that have been studied by anthropologists since the early twentieth century: Tierra del Fuego and the forests of northwest Amazon and central Brazil. Bamberger herself has worked in central Brazil. In the myths of both peoples, Bamberger found the same theme: from the time of creation women ruled, keeping men in subjugation through impersonation of evil spirits, or through black magic. Finally, however, the men of the tribe discovered the ruse and decided to wrench power from the women. In the ensuing battle the women lost and the 'catastrophic alternative' of a society dominated by women ended.[36]

Bamberger cautions that these South American myths 'constantly reiterate that women did not know how to handle power when they had it,' and they harken 'back to a past darkened by repeated failures.'[37] In Bamberger's view the myths of matriarchy of South America reduce women to the status of a child, while Bachofen's elevate her to the status of a deity. Both are unrealistic and dangerous and keep woman 'bound to her place. To free her we need to destroy the myth.'[38]

One anthropologist who feels no need to destroy the 'myth of matriarchy' is Ruby Rohrlich-Leavitt, whose article 'Women in Transition: Crete and Sumer,' was published in the 1977 anthology, *Becoming Visible: Women in European History.* Rohrlich-Leavitt starts off her contribution to the anthology by immediately offering a completely different point of view from those of her anthropological colleagues.

> Minoan Crete, the first European civilization, was a matriarchy. This term emphasizes the political role of women in society but also includes economic, social, and religious privileges that give them greater authority than men. Minoan Crete fulfills these criteria for a matriarchal society.[39]

---

[32] Sanday 1998: 6.
[33] Rosaldo and Lamphere 1974a: 3.
[34] Bamberger 1974: 263.
[35] Bamberger 1974: 268.
[36] Bamberger 1974: 279.
[37] Bamberger 1974: 280.
[38] Bamberger 1974: 280.
[39] Rohrlich-Leavitt 1977: 38.

She is quick to point out that the Cretan matriarchy was not a mirror image of existing Near East patriarchies. Rather she sees matriarchal Crete as evolving from Neolithic gynocentric institutions brought to the island by its Anatolian settlers. Drawing evidence from the archaeological site of Çatal Hüyük in Anatolia, Rohrlich-Leavitt finds that from its foundation in the Neolithic *c.* 7000-3000 BC, Crete, because it was settled by people like those at Çatal Hüyük, enjoyed an economy based on well-developed agricultural practices, occupational specialization with little social stratification, and egalitarian, democratic and peaceful communal clan-based structures. Rohrlich-Leavitt also believes that the evidence shows in Anatolia, and also in Crete, that women played important political and economic roles and that they clearly enjoyed social preeminence. Moreover, in religion women also predominated. 'Not only was the goddess the principal object of worship. . . it was women who ministered to her cult.'[40]

By 3,000 BC, Crete, like other areas in the Bronze Age, began to undergo a transformation. However, unlike the others, 'the Minoan state was not a strong centralized entity, warfare was absent, and the status of women apparently became even higher than it had been during the Neolithic era.'[41] Examining the archaeological artifacts, particularly frescos, seals, rings, statues, sarcophagi, and gold cups, Rohrlich-Leavitt finds women portrayed as merchants and navigators, farmers, priestesses performing rituals, hunters, and bull-leapers. She says: 'Women were the central subjects, ... And they are shown mainly in the public sphere.'[42] Most importantly women predominated in religion, 'the institution that integrated Bronze Age life.'[43] 'By 2000 B.C., . . . , the Minoan goddess had become pervasive, and she or her priestesses or votaries were pictured in almost every aspect of the natural and social ambience of Crete.'[44] Based on this preeminence of women in religion, and the 'absence of portrayals of an all-powerful male ruler,'[45] Rohrlich-Leavitt believes it is quite possible that a 'queen-priestess' occupied the throne at Knossos and she endorses the view that Minoan Crete was matriarchal and a theocracy.

Another work that offers an alternative to some of the views expressed by Rosaldo, Lamphere, and Bamberger in *Woman, Culture, and Society* is Peggy Reeves Sanday's 1981 publication *Female Power and Male Dominance: On the Origins of Sexual Inequality* which examines the correlates of female/male roles and social forms in one hundred and fifty-six bands and tribes studied by modern anthropologists.

Sanday makes the argument that contrary to what Lamphere, Rosaldo, and Bamberger have suggested, male dominance is not universal. Rather, she argues, their point of view betrays a bias which equates dominance with public leadership. 'By defining dominance differently, one can show that in many societies male leadership is balanced by female authority.'[46] Women can hold a great deal of authority, as, for example, in the right of Ashanti, Iroquois, and Dahomean women to veto men's actions. They are just not as visible as men in external public affairs. Sanday notes that it is not authority but focal leadership roles that women rarely hold. 'Women

---

[40] Rohrlich-Leavitt 1977: 40.
[41] Rohrlich-Leavitt 1977: 42.
[42] Rohrlich-Leavitt 1977: 46.
[43] Rohrlich-Leavitt 1977: 48.
[44] Rohrlich-Leavitt 1977: 49.
[45] Rohrlich-Leavitt 1977: 49.
[46] Sanday 1981.

either delegate leadership positions to the men they select or such positions are assigned by men alone. In those cases where women delegate such authority, they retain the power to veto the actions of those they have selected.'[47] Why do women choose to delegate leadership rather than exercise the authority themselves? Sanday believes the answer lies in women's reproductive roles. 'Since women are the potential bearers of new additions to the population, it would scarcely be expedient to place them on the front line at the hunt and in warfare.'[48]

In making her argument against universal male dominance, Sanday is also careful to make a distinction between real male dominance and 'mythical' male dominance: situations in which 'females have political and economic power but men act as if males were the dominant sex.'[49] When such distinctions are made, 'sexual asymmetry is not as widespread as some anthropologists have argued.'[50]

One of the most important conclusions that Sanday draws, in regard to this study, is that 'male dominance is a response to pressures that are most likely to have been present relatively late in human history.'[51] Interestingly, Sanday found a correlation between the gender of a people's creator Goddess or god, their orientation to the creative forces of nature, and secular expressions of male and female power. 'When the female creative principle dominates or works in conjunction with the male principle, the sexes are either integrated and equal in everyday life . . . , or they are separate and equal.'[52] When god is defined in only masculine terms, one almost always finds a male-dominated society.

Sanday found that the environment molds not only people's creator and creation stories, but determines the sexual division of labor. When the environment itself is perceived as a 'partner,' the sexes mingle in most activities. 'But when the environment is defined in hostile terms, the sexes tend to separate from each other.'[53] When they are separate, due to the condition of a hostile environment, one usually then encounters male dominance. Sanday finds a causal relationship between 'depleting resources, cultural disruption, migration and the oppression of women.'[54]

One of Sanday's conclusions that is most interesting and relevant for this study is her observation that, 'If there is a basic difference between the sexes, other than the differences associated with human reproduction, it is that women as a group have not willingly faced death in violent conflict. This fact, perhaps more than any other, explains why men have sometimes become the dominating sex.'[55] As will become apparent in this study, Minoan Crete has long been considered a peaceful society. Might it be because Neolithic and Early and Middle Bronze Age Crete lacks a history of warfare and thus had no need for its male population to be willing to die in violent conflict, that Crete did not become a male-dominated society until the Late Bronze Age?

---

[47] Sanday 1981: 115.
[48] Sanday 1981: 115.
[49] Sanday 1981: 8.
[50] Sanday 1981: 8.
[51] Sanday 1981: 4.
[52] Sanday 1981: 33.
[53] Sanday 1981: 7.
[54] Sanday 1981: 8.
[55] Sanday 1981: 211.

Before continuing on with more recent works in anthropology and the new emerging field of modern matriarchal studies, Peggy Reeves Sandy's work as well as Heide Goettner-Abendroth's and others, I will now turn to some of the literature which revived the issue of matriarchy in the 1970s and 1980s. As I noted above, it was in the 1970s that feminist activists began to bring back the term matriarchy and those that did so were denounced by anthropologists who argued that there was no anthropological nor archaeological evidence for the existence of matriarchy.

One of those activists to revive the term matriarchy was Kate Millet, considered one of the leading theorists of the feminist movement in the second half of the twentieth century. Millett's 1970 book *Sexual Politics* puts forth her definition and theoretical understanding of 'sexual politics,' or the rule of men over women in 'patriarchy.' She discusses, among other subjects, the historical background of patriarchy and the challenges to it of the nineteenth and early twentieth centuries. Millett notes that while 'no matriarchal societies are known to exist at present,'[56] it is possible (although very difficult to prove) that a period preceding patriarchy included a social order in which there was equality of the sexes.[57] Such an argument is based, Millett believes, on the fact that in this hypothetical pre-patriarchal period, human fertility and the female were venerated, 'and linked analogically with the growth of the earth's vegetation.'[58]

Millett discusses some of the early patriarchal and matriarchal theorists. She is, as would be expected, critical of those patriarchalists 'who take the patriarchal family to be the primordial form of human social organization,'[59] and who argue that the physical superiority of the male, the woman's role as child-bearer and nurturer of children, and the needs of a hunting society all logically led to the subordination of women. Millett objects:

> There are several weaknesses in this theory making its hypotheses insufficient to constitute *necessary* cause: social and political institutions are rarely based on physical strength but are generally upheld by value systems in conjunction with other forms of social and technical force; hunting culture was generally succeeded by agricultural society which brought different environmental circumstances and needs; pregnancy and childbirth may be socially arranged so that they are very far from debilitating events or the cause of physical inferiority. . . . And finally, since patriarchy is a social and political form, it is well here, as with other human institutions, to look outside nature for its origins.[60]

Millett finds the main value of the matriarchal theorists (most of whom are discussed above) to reside in the fact that 'They see patriarchy as but one era of human history and therefore, theoretically as capable of dissolution as it was of institution.'[61] She believes that the debate over whether or not matriarchy preceded patriarchy seems 'incapable of resolution since the information from prehistory which might settle it is inaccessible.'[62] In a footnote she elaborates:

[56] Millett 1970: 25.
[57] Millett 1970: 28.
[58] Millett 1970: 28.
[59] Millett 1970: 108.
[60] Millett 1970: 109.
[61] Millett 1970: 110.
[62] Millett 1970: 110.

'Of the social organization in prehistory there is simply insufficient evidence to judge and the social organization of contemporary preliterate peoples does not provide a reliable guide to the social conditions of pre-historical peoples.'[63]

Millett is an admirer of Engels' work, for it was Engels' *Origins of the Family, Private Property and the State* that 'provided the most comprehensive account of patriarchal history and economy—and the most radical, for Engels alone among the theorists attacked the problem of patriarchal family organization.'[64] Where Engels failed in his theorizing, says Millett, was in his attempt to come to terms with the origins of patriarchy, which he located in the movement from communal sexual life to pairing and then monogamy. What makes Engels' work so valuable in Millett's eyes is that not only did he attempt to prove that patriarchy was not 'an eternal feature of life,'[65] something which the other matriarchal theorists had done as well, but also that he attempted to show that revolutionary social reorganization was possible. I think for Millett, those two points are key: if we can understand that patriarchy is not 'an eternal feature of life,' then another future can be envisioned. For Millett that future will not include patriarchy.

Another feminist activist who revived the term matriarchy is the poet and scholar Adrienne Rich. In her influential and landmark book from 1976, *Of Woman Born*, Rich spends several chapters examining the history of matriarchy. Preferring the word *'gynocentric'* to the word matriarchy, Rich is using this term

> when speaking of periods of human culture which have shared certain kinds of woman-centered beliefs and woman-centered social organization. Throughout most of the world, there is archeological evidence of a period when Woman was venerated in several aspects, the primal one being maternal; when Goddess-worship prevailed and when myths depicted strong and revered female figures. In the earliest artifacts we know, we encounter the female as primal power.[66]

Drawing on the works of Robert Briffault, who will be discussed below, Bachofen, and Harrison, as well as feminist writers like Elizabeth Gould Davis, and others, Rich writes about prehistory as a time in which women exercised organic control: 'rather than one in which the woman establishes and maintains domination and control over the man, as the man over the woman in patriarchy.'[67] For Rich this organic control arose as a result of woman's role as a transformer. She transformed menstrual blood into the child, and into the breast milk with which to feed it; the clay into the pot, and thus the means to store food as well as change it from raw to cooked; the plant fiber into woven cloth. Her transforming extended to the invention of agriculture, of community, and even of language. It was because of woman's inherent transformative powers that 'prepatriarchal religion acknowledged the female presence in every part of the cosmos.'[68] Because she was the great transformer, 'spiritualized into a divine being,'[69] woman in pre-patriarchal society was placed at the center of its religious and social life.

---

[63] Millett 1970: 110.
[64] Millett 1970: 110.
[65] Millett 1970: 120.
[66] Rich 1976: 93.
[67] Rich 1976: 60.
[68] Rich 1976: 107.
[69] Rich 1976: 100.

It seems appropriate to briefly discuss Briffault's 1927 book, *The Mothers*, at this point, as his writing influenced Rich's work and the works of other contemporary authors as well. *The Mothers* falls into the same category as the works of Bachofen, McLennan, and Engels, in that it presents a picture of cultural evolution. Amassing a very large amount of anthropological data as well as drawing upon classical literature (his work is in three volumes), Briffault, like several of his predecessors in the cultural evolution field, attempts to prove that matriarchy universally preceded patriarchy, and that this move from matriarchy to patriarchy was associated with the move to agricultural production and the emergence of private property. While he generally seems to define matriarchy as women's social preeminence, as Rich has pointed out, he sometimes uses terms like matriarchy, gynocracy, and mother-right imprecisely.[70]

While not a feminist activist, cultural historian William Irwin Thompson also envisions a future that does not include patriarchy. In his 1981 work *The Time Falling Bodies Take to Light: Mythology, Sexuality and the Origins of Culture*, Thompson argues that matriarchy is a historical fact, and cites Neolithic, Anatolian Çatal Hüyük as a prime example of a matriarchal society. Thompson puts forth a definition of matriarchy which he develops in contra-distinction to patriarchy:

> Where patriarchy establishes law, matriarchy establishes custom; where patriarchy establishes military power, matriarchy establishes religious authority; where patriarchy encourages the *aresteia* of the individual warrior, matriarchy encourages the tradition-bound cohesion of the collective. . . . Custom, the collective, and a religion of some twenty thousand years of tradition is the force that holds Çatal Hüyük together. It . . . is a question of feminine cultural authority.[71]

Like many other scholars both before and after him, Thompson believes the 'Great Goddess' is central to the development of matriarchal society and he calls the worship of the Great Goddess the 'first universal religion.'[72]

Thompson traces the demise of matriarchy to the development of agriculture, the expansion of trade, the rise of cities, and the accumulation of wealth, which caused warfare to become 'more common.'[73] Agricultural surplus allowed men to turn from hunting to trade and warfare. The growth of cities made the rule of custom and maternal authority obsolete; trade caused new specializations like metallurgy to develop; and as wealth accumulated with the growth of those new specializations, a military class grew. There followed, says Thompson, a period in which the emphasis shifted from agriculture to herding and raiding, which in turn was followed by the growth of larger and more defensive settlements. 'From the implosive force of such concentrations of people, culture itself began to change.'[74] From a combination of irrigation farming, specialization and literacy, civilization arose, and with it the dispossession of the Goddess and women. Recounting the Mesopotamian myth of the male god Enki trying to give birth, Thompson concludes: 'The effort to displace the female seems to be the archetypal foundation for civilization.'[75]

---

[70] Rich 1976: 59.
[71] Thompson 1981: 149.
[72] Thompson 1981: 153.
[73] Thompson 1981: 154.
[74] Thompson 1981: 161.
[75] Thompson 1981: 163.

Historian Gerda Lerner's contribution to the matriarchy debate is found in her ground-breaking 1986 work *The Creation of Patriarchy*. Lerner's book speaks to all the works discussed above. She both disagrees with them, and also has much in common with them. Like Thompson and Rohrlich-Leavitt, early in her work Lerner discusses Çatal Hüyük. Unlike the other two authors, she does not believe Çatal Hüyük was a matriarchal society, although she does find evidence of matrilocality as well as 'goddess worship' there. What Lerner believes is important about Çatal Hüyük is that it offers 'some sort of alternate model to that of patriarchy.'[76]

Addressing some of the claims of Rosaldo, Lamphere, and Bamberger, Lerner points out, contrary to their argument, that 'we can assert that female subordination is not universal.'[77] Yet she seems to echo them somewhat when she says, 'The creation of compensatory myths of the distant past of women will not emancipate women in the present and the future.'[78]

Lerner does not equate Goddess worship with matriarchy, and cites the historical evidence for the coexistence of symbolic idolatry of women and their actual low status,[79] for example, in the adoration of the Virgin Mary in Medieval Christian Europe. She is critical of Bachofen and Engels, saying that such evidence as they provide argues only for matrilocality and matriliny.

In Lerner's opinion, matriarchy has never existed because, in her definition, matriarchy is the mirror image of patriarchy: 'I think that one can truly speak of matriarchy only when women hold power over men, not alongside them, when that power includes the public domain and foreign relations and when women make essential decisions not only for their kinfolk but for the community.'[80] What Lerner does have in common with Bachofen, McLennan, Engels, Harrison, Briffault, and the other 'matriarchalists' is her belief that patriarchy is not the original condition of humankind. For Lerner, gaining an understanding of the origins of patriarchy is absolutely essential if we are to stop treating it as 'ahistorical, eternal, invisible and unchanging.'[81] Human beings created patriarchy at a certain time in history. It is a social construct and as such it can be replaced by something else. Lerner defines patriarchy as 'the manifestation and institutionalization of male dominance over women and children in the family and the extension of male dominance over women in society in general.'[82]

The Creation of Patriarchy presents a complex explanation of the establishment of patriarchy, which Lerner says was a process spanning 2,500 years (3100 to 600 BC). She dates its beginning to sometime during the agricultural revolution, for 'in the course of the agricultural revolution the exploitation of human labor and the sexual exploitation of women become inextricably linked'.[83] Lerner believes that women's sexual and reproductive functions were appropriated by men prior to the formation of private property and classes. At some point during the agricultural revolution, relatively egalitarian societies, which were often matrilineal and matrilocal, with a sexual division of labor based on biological necessity, were replaced by more highly structured societies 'in which both private property and the exchange of women

---

[76] Lerner 1986: 35.
[77] Lerner 1986: 35.
[78] Lerner 1986: 35.
[79] Lerner 1986: 29.
[80] Lerner 1986: 31.
[81] Lerner 1986: 37.
[82] Lerner 1986: 239.
[83] Lerner 1986: 52.

based on incest taboos and exogamy were common.'[84] With changes in ecological and cultural conditions, the archaic state took shape; temple-towns emerged first, then city-states grew up and eventually nation states developed. In this process the society changed from a kin-based to a class-based society and one in which males were dominant in public life and external relations. In this shift, women were the great losers, for as Lerner shows, they became utterly dependent upon men.[85] With the institution of slavery, women lost further ground. Indeed, as Lerner points out, it was women that men first enslaved. Weaker and more physically vulnerable, female war captives (and their children) were less of a threat in captivity than were enemy males. Historians are generally agreed that it was women who were first enslaved, but 'they have passed over it without giving it much significance.'[86] Lerner believes slavery in the ancient world was possible mainly because men already had the model of subordination of women of their own tribes and clans. She concludes that the raping of conquered women and their sexual enslavement 'is a practice built into and essential to the structure of patriarchal institutions and inseparable from them.'[87]

Tracing the development of Mesopotamian and Biblical law for a thousand year period, 1750-700 BC, Lerner finds that during that time the control of women's sexuality passed from the hands of individual husbands to the state. Analyzing a Middle Assyrian law (referred to as MAL sec. 40 and dating to 1250 BC), representative of Mesopotamian law codes that proscribed which women should or should not be veiled in public, and the punishment for failing to adhere to the law, Lerner observes that this law seems to mark the beginning of women being legally classified according to their sexual activities. Women under the protection of one man and sexually serving one man are designated as respectable and must be veiled, 'women not under one man's protection and sexual control are designated as "public women", and hence unveiled.'[88]

Beyond the legal classification, the law also specified punishment for the women violators: a punishment that included beating, being stripped naked, having one's head covered with tar, and being paraded in the street. 'Here, what began as a minor, seemingly petty regulation of morality [the failure to wear a veil in public] is suddenly regarded as a major offense against the state.'[89]

Lerner believes this law not only institutionalized a ranking order for women, with the married woman and her daughter at the top, and the prostitute and slave woman at the bottom, but it also provided the visible means needed to distinguish those belonging to different classes. As Lerner notes, class formation demands such a distinction. This law, perhaps the earliest historians have for such a practice, is illustrative of the way in which class distinctions were institutionalized for women. 'For women, from MAL [sec.] 40 forward, class distinctions are based on their relationship—or absence of such—to a man who protects them, and on their sexual activities.'[90] Based on her analysis, presented above, Lerner further concludes that the

---

[84] Lerner 1986: 53.
[85] Lerner 1986: 74.
[86] Lerner 1986: 79.
[87] Lerner 1986: 80.
[88] Lerner 1986: 135.
[89] Lerner 1986: 135.
[90] Lerner 1986: 139.

sexual regulation of women 'underlies the formation of class.'[91] Moreover, since hierarchy and class privilege are essential and 'organic' to the functioning of the state, she also concludes that the sexual regulation of women 'is one of the foundations upon which the state rests'[92] as well.

Yet even when it took control of women's sexuality, the archaic state ultimately was dependent upon the patriarchal family and 'equated the family's orderly functioning with order in the public domain.'[93] The patriarchal family for its part mirrored the state in its mixture of paternalism and unquestioned authority.[94]

Turning to the religion of ancient societies, Lerner finds that the dethroning of the Mother Goddess, worshipped at least since the Neolithic, did not keep pace with the subordination of women economically, educationally, and legally. The Near Eastern Goddesses continued to remain independent and dominant even as human women's position declined. On the other hand, even though women lost tremendous ground—and with them, finally, the Mother Goddess as well, as she changed from sole symbol of fertility to watered-down, domesticated consort to an all-powerful storm-god—human women's 'essential equality as human beings remained un-assailed.'[95] They continued to play important roles as priestesses, healers, and diviners. Lerner argues that women's 'essential equality as human beings' was ended by the Hebrew Book of Genesis which defined women as essentially different from men; redefined

> their sexuality as beneficial and redemptive only within the boundaries of patriarchal dominance; and . . . excluded [them] from directly being able to represent the divine principle. . . . Here is the historic moment of the death of the Mother-Goddess and her replacement by God-the-Father . . . under patriarchy. [96]

However, other feminist scholars, notably Carol P. Christ, and Judith Plaskow, have argued that it is inaccurate to blame 'the death of the Goddess' singularly on Hebrew religion rather than seeing it as a general cultural shift in the ancient world due to the rise of chronic warfare.[97]

Lerner's great contribution with this work is many layered and multifaceted, but most importantly for this study I think it lies in her statement that 'The system of patriarchy is a historic construct; it has a beginning; it will have an end.'[98] One cannot begin to consider Minoan Crete a matriarchal (or even equalitarian) society if one cannot imagine a past without patriarchy.

The late twentieth century/early twenty-first century debates over matriarchy

The criticism against matriarchy did not end with Rosaldo, Lamphere, and Bamberger in 1974. Critics of the matriarchy thesis in the late twentieth and beginning of the twenty-first

---

[91] Lerner 1986: 140.
[92] Lerner 1986: 140.
[93] Lerner 1986: 121.
[94] Lerner 1986: 121.
[95] Lerner 1986: 160.
[96] Lerner 1986: 198.
[97] Christ 1987: 83-92; Plaskow 1980: 12-14.
[98] Lerner 1986: 228.

centuries differ from Rosaldo, Lamphere, and Bamberger, however, in that they are part of a backlash against the women's movement which has attempted to discredit any interpretation of prehistory as woman centered, peaceful, and Goddess worshipping. As Riane Eisler has noted, this backlash is part of a larger cultural backlash and has occurred at the same time that fundamentalist religious leaders have mounted an anti-feminist crusade and the wealth of the world has been re-concentrated in the hands of multinational corporations and a new class of billionaires.[99] Two examples of the new critics are discussed below.

One is Ronald Hutton whose article 'The Neolithic Great Goddess: A Study in Modern Tradition' was published in *Antiquity* in 1997. Hutton, who was associated with the Çatal Hüyük archaeological team at the time, originally presented the article at an archaeology conference.

Hutton begins his work by noting that until the mid-nineteenth century, the Goddesses of the ancient classical world were thought of simply as allegorical representations of civilization. Under the influence of (especially German) Romanticism, the suggestion was advanced that behind them all was a single Great Goddess venerated before history. According to Hutton, as the century wore on, this idea was adopted by some classicists and Near Eastern archaeologists who began to interpret the female figurines being uncovered in Anatolia and Mesopotamia at the time as the Great Goddess. Hutton claims that Sir Arthur Evans, the discoverer of Minoan civilization, was one of the early archaeologists to adopt the idea whole-heartedly. As we have seen already, during the latter half of the nineteenth century, at the same time that the idea of a Great Goddess was being adopted by classicists and archaeologists, Bachofen, McLennan, and Engels were proposing their anthropological or economic theories about original matriarchies.

According to Hutton, this image of prehistoric Europe worshipping one Great Goddess was combined with the image of matriarchy offered by Bachofen and others, as in the work of Jane Ellen Harrison, whose *Prolegomena to the Study of Greek Religion* was discussed above. He asserts of her work that it

> posited the previous existence of a peaceful and intensely creative womancentred civilization, in which humans, living in harmony with nature and their own emotions, worshipped a single female deity. . . . In Harrison's vision, male deities existed only as sons and consorts of the Great Goddess. This happy state of affairs, she proposed, had been destroyed before the opening of history by patriarchal invaders from the north, bringing dominant male deities and war-like ways. [100]

Following Harrison, 'the idea of a matristic early Europe' which venerated a Great Goddess was developed by 'amateur scholars' Robert Briffault (in 1927) and Robert Graves (in 1946).[101] Between 1920 and 1940, 'acceptance of the concept of the single prehistoric goddess continued to grow among experts in the prehistory of Greece, the Balkans and the Near East.'[102] Although scholars 'in the emerging fields of western European prehistory'[103] exercised caution and declined to speak of a great Goddess, non-academic writers continued to popularize the idea.

---

[99] Eisler 2009: 274.
[100] Hutton 1997: 3.
[101] Hutton 1997: 3.
[102] Hutton 1997: 3.
[103] Hutton 1997: 3.

By the 1950s even archaeologists like Jacquetta Hawkes (whose work is discussed elsewhere in this study), Gordon Childe, and O. G. S. Crawford:

> declared their belief in the veneration of a single female deity by Neolithic cultures from the Atlantic littoral to the Near East. . . . . Works on the history of art absorbed the same idea, and it governed the initial interpretation of fresh excavations in the Near East, such as those of James Mellaart at Çatal Hüyük.[104]

By the late 1970s, the 'Great Goddess theory,' as Hutton calls it, had filtered down to the general public. Hutton argues that those who believed the one Great Goddess theory were driven by a hatred of modernity.

As his critique reaches the 1970s, Hutton turns his attentions to the work of archaeologist Marija Gimbutas, whose theories play an important part in this study. The rest of his article is a vindictive attack on her work. He belittles her accomplishments and her scholarship, while showing little understanding of her theories. These views were repeated and repackaged in his book *The Triumph of the Moon: A History of Modern Pagan Witchcraft,* published in 1999 by Oxford University Press.[105]

Before leaving Hutton's work, a brief discussion of archaeologist Peter J. Ucko's article 'The Interpretation of Prehistoric Anthropomorphic Figurines,' published in 1962 is in order.[106] It is appropriate to discuss Ucko's article here, for Hutton's attack on Gimbutas relies upon Ucko's analysis and because Hutton states that Ucko's essay 'rocked the foundation of the whole structure of [Great Goddess] theory,'[107] and caused most archaeologists to abandon it. Although Ucko's essay was written more than fifty years ago, and published before the publication of Gimbutas's research, it is still cited by critics of the Mother Goddess theory and the matriarchy theory as proof that those theories are invalid.

In 'The Interpretation of Prehistoric Anthropomorphic Figurines,' Ucko argues that 'the general Mother Goddess interpretation fails to cover all the known facts.'[108] Specifically he points out that few, if any, of the proponents of the Mother Goddess theory have done a comprehensive examination of the figurines themselves or considered the archaeological context in which they were found, and he asserts that absolutely no one has considered 'relevant anthropological data.'[109]

Ucko's article is his attempt to correct the situation. For his study he examines the Neolithic figurines of Crete and compares them with those from 'pre-dynastic Egypt and other roughly contemporaneous non-literate agricultural societies.'[110] He takes his comparison no further because he believes that archaeologists must exercise extreme caution in applying conclusions derived from one country to another region.

---

[104] Hutton 1997: 5.
[105] Hutton 1999: 356-359.
[106] Ucko 1962: 38-54. In 1968, Ucko published *Anthropomorphic Figurines,* elaborating and expanding upon the ideas discussed in his earlier article.
[107] Hutton 1997: 5.
[108] Ucko 1962: 38.
[109] Ucko 1962: 38.
[110] Ucko 1962: 38.

Ucko's detailed examination of the Cretan figurines and of the archaeological context in which they were found indicated to him that 'several peculiar features are left unexplained by the Mother Goddess interpretation.'[111] In the first place the 'Mother Goddess proponents' have failed to explain the existence of 'sexless' (having no breasts or a penis) figurines. (In the case of Neolithic Crete, Ucko found 44 out of 102 figurines he examined to be sexless, 33 female, 5 male, the remaining 20 animals). According to Ucko the 'Mother Goddess proponents' have also failed to explain why most were made of clay, 'a cheap material;' or why the figurines 'showed marked differences in quality, [and] in artistic merit.'[112] Finally the 'Mother Goddess proponents' have failed to explain how they can identify the figurines as Goddesses when 'no figurines from Crete come from any building which might be considered a shrine.'[113]

How then to interpret the figurines? To find an answer, Ucko, an anthropologist, turns to anthropological evidence. On the basis of comparisons with twentieth century non-literate tribes, Ucko concludes:

> it is possible that the figurine material . . . may include figurines made for the following categories of reasons: those made by, and for, children to play with [in other words they are dolls]; others as some sort of initiation figures used as teaching devices to accompany songs or tales, and thrown away after use; still others as vehicles for sympathetic magic, carried and cared for by mothers desirous of offspring and kept in the house until the birth of a child.[114]

In evaluating Ucko's work we must remember that this article was written over fifty years ago. It should also be remembered that it appeared twelve years before the publication of Marija Gimbutas's 1974 ground-breaking book *The Gods and Goddesses of Old Europe*. Gimbutas was well aware of the article's existence, and that the majority of the archaeological world sided with Ucko. This points to the tremendous courage Gimbutas exhibited when she challenged the prevailing view as elucidated by Ucko, and more recently Hutton, and pursued her work in the face of archaeology's virtually united front against the 'Mother Goddess interpretation.'

The criticism Ucko leveled against the 'Mother Goddess proponents' in 1962 fails to stand up when leveled against Gimbutas's work. In twenty years of work with Neolithic material, Gimbutas examined thousands of artifacts and led five major excavations. Analyzing the symbols and images, Gimbutas discovered an 'intrinsic order' and thus the main themes of the Old European ideology—the worship of the Goddess in her triple aspects. What appeared to Ucko to be 'sexless' figurines, because he examined only several hundred, ignored the symbolism of them and on them (he called the markings 'tattoo marks'), and refused to compare them with figurines from other countries (except for Egypt); Gimbutas referred to as images of the Feminine Divine. She could do so because she looked at the larger context—thousands of figurines and symbols across time and cultures, and because she was thus able to decipher a 'meta-language' of which the figurines were 'the grammar and syntax' and 'by which an entire constellation of meanings is established.'[115]

---

[111] Ucko 1962: 45.
[112] Ucko 1962: 41.
[113] Ucko 1962: 41.
[114] Ucko 1962: 47.
[115] Gimbutas 1989: xv.

The males and animal figurines also fit into the picture. Gimbutas's research demonstrated that throughout her long history, the Goddess often had a male consort, and that male gods were metaphors for rising and dying vegetation. Gimbutas's decipherment of the 'meta-language' of Old Europe also illustrated that the Goddess was often represented as an animal: a bear, bird, deer, snake, and sow, to name a few examples. Even Ucko's conclusion that some of the Neolithic Cretan figurines might have been dolls can be reframed within the context of archaeomythology. Dolls need not be thought of as inconsequential items. To the Hopi Indians Kachina dolls are supernatural and sacred. Even as a child's toy an ordinary doll can be thought of as magical.[116]

Ucko asserted that the Cretan figurines could not be called Goddesses because none of them came from any building which might be considered a shrine. Marija Gimbutas's research indicated to her that the meaning of the word 'shrine' needed to be expanded from the narrow one of 'cult building' to a definition that would include grain bins, ovens, the interiors of caves, and other common, ordinary places. The evidence indicated to Gimbutas that the people of Old Europe, like the Native Indians of North America, did not separate life into sacred and profane. All of life was sacred. Therefore the Goddess and her images were not confined to a 'cult building.'

Gimbutas was aware that many of the previous studies of the Mother Goddess, the ones Ucko so roundly criticized, were 'simplistic and presented without the benefit of background studies.'[117] She was also well aware that she could not casually make sweeping generalizations and draw indiscriminately on analogies from around the world. Thus she focused her research only on European evidence, tracing symbols from the Neolithic up through to the historical period and back again to their origins in the Paleolithic.

Where Ucko advocates the use of anthropological data to understand what the Cretan figurines symbolized and what they were used for, Gimbutas urges archaeologists to expand their vision or interpretive horizons by incorporating not only anthropology but comparative mythology, folklore, linguistics, and other disciplines into their research as well. She urges them to engage in the work of archaeomythology.

Hutton is not the only critic of the theory that matriarchal societies prevailed in the Paleolithic, Neolithic, and even some Bronze Age societies. Perhaps the most well-known is Cynthia Eller who has devoted a whole book, *The Myth of Matriarchal Prehistory*, published in 2000, to the topic. She bases her argument that matriarchal prehistory is a myth on the belief that

> what evidence we do have from prehistory cannot support the weight laid upon it by the matriarchal thesis. . . . Nothing offered up in support of the matriarchal thesis is especially persuasive.[118]

Eller has written this book because she believes:

---

[116] Joan Marler, e-mail message to author, March 31, 1999.
[117] Gimbutas 1989: xvi.
[118] Eller 2000: 6.

Relying on matriarchal myth in the face of the evidence that challenges its veracity leaves feminists open to charges of vacuousness and irrelevance that we cannot afford to court. And the gendered stereotypes upon which matriarchal myth rests persistently work to flatten out differences among women; to exaggerate the differences between women and men; and to hand women an identity that is symbolic, timeless, and archetypal, instead of giving them the freedom to craft identities.[119]

Eller defines matriarchy as 'a shorthand description for any society in which women's power is equal or superior to men's and in which the culture centers around values and life events described as "feminine."'[120] She sees the 'myth of matriarchal prehistory' as having been invented to meet needs that grew out of the women's liberation movement of the 1960s. For many, says Eller, that movement did not go far enough. Thus, borrowing from the cultural feminists and radical feminists, the feminist matriarchalists crafted a myth that combined a belief 'that the values and dispositions associated with women . . . need to play a key role in reforming society,'[121] along with 'a lively concern with . . . sexual harassment and violence toward women.'[122] The central function of the 'myth of matriarchal prehistory,' according to Eller, is that:

> It takes a situation that invites despair . . . and transforms it into a surpassing optimism: patriarchy is recent and fallible, it was preceded by something much better and it can be overthrown in the near future.[123]

Eller traces the history of the 'myth of matriarchal prehistory' up to the 1970s citing, with little comment, the works of Bachofen, McLennan, Engels, and others. Eller reserves her criticism for the 'myth' as it emerged in the early 1970s 'as second-wave feminists began to take it over in earnest, engineering a decisive shift in its meaning in the process.'[124] Where previous theorists deemed the change from matriarchy to patriarchy a sign of progress, or if not progress, at least as a change that was unavoidable and necessary for civilization, by the 1970s 'the myth of matriarchal prehistory' had become 'the myth of paradise lost.'[125]

The contemporary version of the myth, Eller says, has been shaped by three main factors: '(1) the steadfast rejection of matriarchal myth by most feminist anthropologists; (2) a burgeoning feminist spirituality movement intent on placing goddess worship in prehistory; and (3) the pioneering archaeological work of Marija Gimbutas.'[126] As anthropologists rejected a matriarchal prehistory, she continues, the Women's Spirituality movement took the idea of a matriarchal prehistory as foundational. Eller believes that it is the 'myth of matriarchal prehistory' that holds the movement together. According to Eller, spiritual feminists adopted the one Great Goddess theory of archaeologists and 'drew new conclusions from ancient goddess worship,'[127] arguing that ancient Goddess worship had been enormously beneficial to

---

[119] Eller 2000: 8.
[120] Eller 2000: 13.
[121] Eller 2000: 16.
[122] Eller 2000: 17.
[123] Eller 2000: 18.
[124] Eller 2000: 34.
[125] Eller 2000: 34.
[126] Eller 2000: 34.
[127] Eller 2000: 36.

women; that Goddesses had been worshipped to the near exclusion of gods; and claimed that one of the surest signs of patriarchy's triumph had been the banishment of the Goddess.[128] All the 'myth' lacked, says Eller, was credibility. That was provided, she says, by archaeologist Marija Gimbutas who 'loaned her impressive archaeological credentials to the myth at a time when other academic archaeologists were steadfastly unwilling to do so.'[129]

What do feminist matriarchalists believe, as Eller sees it? She describes it this way: feminist matriarchalists date the beginnings of matriarchy to the Paleolithic and earlier, but believe it reached its height in the Neolithic in southeastern Europe, the Mediterranean, and the Near East. They draw a picture of a society characterized by Goddess worship, harmony between human beings and nature, communal property, and no distinction between the sacred and the profane. The political organization of matriarchal societies is centered around mothers. Finally, men are given lesser or greater roles depending on who is writing about the 'myth.'[130]

Eller asserts that the feminist matriarchalists offer two basic reasons, which she calls internal and external, for the end of matriarchy and the transition to patriarchy. Among the internal causes are the change from horticulture to agriculture and herding, and the discovery of the male role in human reproduction. The external cause is explained by Marija Gimbutas's 'Kurgan hypothesis,' first developed in 1956 and refined over decades, which posits invasion by patriarchal tribes from the steppes of southern Russia. Eller endeavors to belittle the Kurgan hypothesis. It is important to note here that one of the most well-known critics of Gimbutas's Kurgan hypothesis, archaeologist Colin Renfrew, recently gave a public lecture at which he announced that recent genomic studies reveal that Gimbutas was correct in positing a steppe origin for Indo-European culture.[131]

Eller spends the last two-thirds of the book attempting to refute the 'myth of matriarchal prehistory.' While it is not the purpose of this work to thoroughly critique her work (it has been done by others),[132] I will offer some observations on Eller's criticisms and their validity or non-validity, as the case may be.

Eller explains that one of the major ways to prove that prehistoric societies were or were not matriarchal is by drawing equivalencies with living or historical peoples through the ethnographic record. The other way is through archaeology. She remarks that since anthropologists acknowledge that reconstructing the prehistoric past through analogy with ethnographic data is tricky (nevertheless they still do it) and 'gendered archaeology' is still in its infancy, the problem is difficult. She does note that both '*au courant*' anthropologists and archaeologists who practice 'gender archaeology' are much less interested in general theories than the feminist matriarchalists, and more interested in variety, particularity, and the ambiguities of gendered relationships.[133]

---

[128] Eller 2000: 36.
[129] Eller 2000: 39.
[130] See Eller 2000: Chapter 3.
[131] Colin Renfrew, 'Marija *Rediviva* DNA and European Origins,' First Marija Gimbutas Memorial Lecture, Oriental Institute, Chicago, Illinois, November 8, 2017.
[132] See especially Marler 2006: 163-187; Max Dashu 2000; Holmström 2000: 43-47; Griffin 2000: 43, 48-52.
[133] See Eller 2000: Chapter 5.

Eller then goes on to try to disprove, using anthropological and archaeological data, some of what she considers to be the major tenets of the feminist matriarchalists: 'men's ignorance of their role in conception, the correlation between goddess worship and women's social status, women's invention of agriculture, and the peacefulness of prehistoric societies.'[134]

Two of Eller's arguments are discussed here: first, that the anthropological and archaeological data do not uphold the feminist matriarchalist belief that there is a one-to-one relationship between Goddess worship and high status for women. Eller claims that as part of this belief, feminist matriarchalists posit Goddess monotheism for prehistory. Eller says that there is no evidence for that. In making such a claim she ignores the work not only of Marija Gimbutas, but of many other highly regarded archaeologists as well. If she were familiar with the archaeological literature of Minoan Crete, she would know that many Aegeanists believe the Minoans worshipped one Goddess in various aspects. Rather than look at the archaeological literature of the Bronze Age period under her review, Eller looks to the Greeks of the Classical Age, a period over a thousand years later, and argues that the classical Greeks did not worship a unitary Goddess.[135]

In her next example, which is to prove that Goddesses were not always the benevolent beings feminist matriarchialists believe them to be (somehow she finds this related to her argument that there is no one-to-one relationship between Goddess worship and high status for women), Eller again makes the mistake of mixing her historical periods. This time she draws an example from Ugarit *c.* 1400 BC, a period well into the time when patriarchy was in its ascendancy.[136]

Discussing the issue of whether or not prehistoric human societies were peaceful, Eller claims that the ethnographic and archaeological evidence shows that they were not. One of her examples comes from Minoan Crete. Eller claims that the archaeological record does not show that the Minoans were warlike because they carried on their warlike activities on the sea and thus left no record.[137] Here Eller is making the assumption that it is human nature to be aggressive and warlike. She cannot imagine a society without warfare, even when the evidence is inconclusive. Moreover, in making such a statement Eller leaves out entirely a discussion of the debate within the field of Aegean archaeology regarding the peacefulness of Minoan society—thus leading her reader to believe that her view is the only accepted one. On the contrary, there is much debate among Aegeanists regarding the *Pax Minoica*. The issue is far from being resolved.

Turning from anthropology and archaeology to prehistoric art and symbols as indicators of how people of prehistory viewed themselves, Eller argues that 'when images are divorced from most other markers of culture (such as language and behavior), as they are for prehistoric societies, accurate interpretation becomes extremely difficult.'[138] Again using Crete as one of her examples, Eller attempts to discredit interpretations of female figurines as Goddesses by claiming that most representations of the Goddess in Minoan Crete were found in 'garbage heaps.'[139] In making such a claim, Eller betrays her ignorance of the archaeological evidence

---

[134] Eller 2000: 93.
[135] Eller 2000: 103.
[136] Eller 2000: 104.
[137] Eller 2000: 114.
[138] Eller 2000: 116.
[139] Eller 2000: 153.

which shows that the majority of representations of the Goddess in Minoan Crete were found at sites that have been identified by experts as sacred: town and house shrines, tombs, and rooms within the temple-palaces of Minoan Crete.[140] Her accusation is certainly not true of the two representations of the Goddess, the Knossos Snake Goddesses, which Eller devotes two pages to discussing. They were found not in garbage heaps, but in the Temple Repositories —which were storage places for ritual equipment, and part of the Throne Room complex, and the Central Palace Sanctuary of Knossos.[141]

What Eller fails to tell her readers is that Aegean archaeologists are generally agreed that a Feminine Divine was worshipped by the Minoans; what they disagree about is whether she represented the One or the Many.[142] But even when she admits that 'scholars are generally agreed that many of the female images in Minoan sealstones and statuary represent goddesses,' she attempts to minimize their conclusion by adding that such a conclusion is probably due to the fact that 'they are reading back from classical times when this was a common meaning of female images.'[143]

I think I can best sum up my criticism of Eller's work by pointing out that she does in her book exactly what she accuses the feminist matriarchialists of doing: citing only the evidence that supports her story. Moreover, she does not draw her evidence from the relevant chronological eras, for example, she often projects from the Classical Greek era backwards into the Minoan Crete era; and she makes generalizations for which there is insufficient evidence or no evidence at all. In addition, she ignores obvious evidence that leads to a different conclusion, as with the example of the Snake Goddesses from the Temple Repositories at Knossos. The evidence she does not cite tells another story.

I believe the evidence I provide in the body of this study will give a number of examples to prove that Eller is wrong when she says that 'there is nothing in the archaeological record that is at odds with an image of prehistoric life as nasty, brutish, short and male dominated.'[144] In attempting to provide a different picture of Minoan Crete than that proposed by Eller, I turn now to the evidence for the worship of the Minoan Mother Goddess. I will carefully define the term Mother Goddess, determine whether she was worshipped as the one or the many, and, using key archaeological characteristics for deciphering which female images are likely human and which are more likely divine, detail how the presence of a Mother Goddess can be recognized in the archaeological record of Bronze Age Crete.

---

[140] See my Chapter 5 for a detailed discussion of the find spots of many of the most well-known representations of the Minoan Goddess.
[141] See Panagiotaki 1999 and my discussion of the find spots of the Knossos Snake Goddesses in Chapter 5.
[142] See my detailed discussion of this issue in Chapter 4.
[143] Eller 2000: 153.
[144] Eller 2000: 181.

Chapter 4

The Mother Goddess of Crete: Interpreting the Archaeological Record, Iconography, and Sacred Sites, Using Cultural Context, Mythology, and Historical Correlates

In this chapter I attempt to show that there is substantial evidence to argue that the original settlers of Bronze Age Crete came to the island from Anatolia during the Neolithic Age, bringing the worship of the Mother Goddess with them, and that her worship in Neolithic Crete was characterized by female [imagery or] iconography. I discuss the chief attributes of the Anatolian Mother Goddess, the lion and raptor, because by the Bronze Age, as we shall see, those attributes belonged to the Minoan Mother Goddess as well. In this context I look at the work of Lynn Roller, archaeologist of ancient Anatolia, who studied representations of the deity, cult monuments, votive offerings, sacred spaces, and inscriptions (which for her time period of study, the ninth century BC to the fourth century AD, are plentiful) to come to her understanding of the Phrygian Mother Goddess. I also discuss Mellaart's work at Çatal Hüyük, since there is Neolithic evidence of the worship of a Mother Goddess there; and because some of the earliest settlers to Knossos in the Neolithic came from the region of Çatal Hüyük. I offer my understanding of what constitutes a Mother Goddess for the Minoans.

I then go on to discuss the methodology of some of the most prominent archaeologists working in the field of Minoan religion and the Goddess in order to determine not only how they view the Goddess—as one or many—but primarily how they propose to recognize her. I particularly consider the work of Gesell, Gimbutas, Marinatos, Moss, and Renfrew.

The Mother Goddess of Anatolia

In order to understand and interpret the iconography of the Goddess of Minoan Crete, it is helpful to begin by looking back to the civilizations that preceded Minoan society, especially that of ancient Anadolu—Land of Mothers.[1] Anatolia is important for understanding the Mother Goddess in Crete not only because she appeared earlier there, but also because current genetic evidence indicates that Crete was originally settled by immigrants from Anatolia. A 2008 article from the *Annals of Human Genetics* reports the results of a study that attempts to address several issues of importance to archaeologists, historians, geneticists, and linguists. The first and most important question addressed is whether farmers in mainland Greece and Crete, sites of the earliest Neolithic settlements in Europe (*c.* 7000 BC), originated in neighboring Anatolia. The researchers also asked if population movements account for the rise of Minoan civilization in the 3rd and 2nd millennia BC; and whether 'the earliest farmers to Greece arrive via terrestrial or maritime colonization routes.'[2]

---

[1] Ergener 1988: 8.
[2] King et al. 2008: 205-214.

The researchers collected 171 saliva samples from long-term inhabitants near the areas of three early Neolithic sites in Greece, and 193 samples from long-term inhabitants near Knossos in Crete. 'An analysis of Y-chromosome haplogroups determined that the samples from the Greek Neolithic sites showed strong affinity to Balkan data, while Crete shows affinity with central/Mediterranean Anatolia.'[3] Based on their samples and analysis, the researchers are further able to draw the conclusion, extremely important for the current discussion, that the first settlers from Anatolia to Crete came from the areas of the well-known Neolithic sites of Asikh Höyük, Çatal Hüyük, Hacilar, Mersin/Yumktepe, and Tarsus.[4] As the authors note, these findings support the long-held theory, first proposed by Sir Arthur Evans, that Crete was settled by colonists from Anatolia.[5]

The Y-chromosome research also allows the authors to propose that there was a second migration from Anatolia to Crete, approximately 3100 BC, this time from the regions of west and northwest Anatolia. They note that 'the implications of these data are tantalizing.'

> A date of 3100 BC is a highly significant one for Aegean prehistorians, as it marks approximately the boundary between the Neolithic and Bronze Age Crete, . . . a period associated with a series of major changes in settlement patterns, demography, material culture, technology, iconography and burial practices. Many scholars have suggested that new influxes of populations were responsible for triggering these changes. [6]

These scientists further suggest that the first farmers of Greece and the Balkans probably arrived via maritime colonization routes from Anatolia. And they cautiously agree with those linguists who suggest that 'Anatolian related languages . . . may be reflected in the un-deciphered scripts . . . Cretan hieroglyphic and Linear A.'[7]

My discussion of the Goddess of ancient Anatolia will start with Çatal Hüyük, a large Neolithic mound located in central Turkey. Continuously inhabited for about 1,400 years, between 7400 and 6000 BC, it was first excavated in the 1960s by British archaeologist James Mellaart and reopened in 1993 under the direction of Ian Hodder with excavations finishing two years ago. Only a small portion of the extensive site has been excavated and it is still 'imperfectly understood.'[8]

What has been revealed thus far is a large Neolithic settlement which consists of a series of contiguous houses with shared walls, entered through openings in the roof. 'There is no evidence of large-scale public buildings or houses that might signify social stratification by rank.'[9] Because new homes were built directly on top of destroyed or abandoned ones, the Neolithic material is extremely well-preserved. The extensive state of preservation has allowed the archaeological community to learn about the social and religious life of the settlement.

---

[3] King et al. 2008: 205.
[4] King et al. 2008: 211.
[5] The findings of King et al. receive support in a 2013 article in *Nature Communications*. In that article Hughey *et al.* report the results of their research into the question of the origins of the Minoans. Having analyzed mtDNA polymorphisms in skeletal materials from two Minoan populations, they conclude that 'the most likely origin of the Cretan Neolithic settlers was Anatolia and the Middle East.' Hughey *et al.* 2013: 3.
[6] King et al. 2008: 212.
[7] King et al. 2008: 212
[8] Roller 1999: 28.
[9] Roller 1999: 28.

'Çatal Hüyük is remarkable for the frequent occurrence, at all twelve excavated levels of habitation, of individual rooms with wall paintings, plaster reliefs on walls and benches, and a variety of objects, including several unusual figurine types, all suggesting that the rooms had been used for a ritual purpose.'[10]

The wall paintings at Çatal Hüyük exhibit human, animal, and abstract imagery including human hands; a landscape which depicts a nearby volcano, Hasan Dag, erupting; scenes of men hunting wild animals; and vultures denuding human corpses of their flesh. Plaster reliefs include leopards, human beings, and especially interesting for purposes of this study, several figures which look like women giving birth, and various representations of human breasts. The figurines, found in different contexts, include female, male, animal, and 'schematic' ones.[11] Some of the female figurines have 'exaggerated breasts, hips, buttocks, and abdomens of a type found widely throughout the Mediterranean Neolithic.'[12] Included among the figurines is one that archaeologists have identified as a mother and child. And finally, 'probably the most widely illustrated figure is that of a female seated on a throne supported by two felines: she appears to be shown in the act of giving birth, with the child's head appearing between her legs.'[13] Called by Gimbutas the 'enthroned Goddess'[14] and by others as the Great Mother of Çatal Hüyük, she is dated to about 6000/6500 BC.

British archaeologist James Mellaart, who excavated one acre of the eastern mound of Çatal Hüyük from 1961-1965, discovered not only the contiguous houses, but also the shrines, which he identified on the basis of their elaborate wall-paintings, reliefs in plaster, animal heads, stylized bucrania, and cult figures, all of which were mentioned above. It was from this material that Mellaart reconstructed the religious beliefs of the people of Çatal Hüyük.

Describing the art and religion of Çatal Hüyük Mellaart noted that scenes concerned with life were generally found on the west wall of shrines, the color red was usually associated with them, and they often portrayed the Goddess giving birth to an animal figure, frequently a bull or ram. Scenes concerned with death were located on the east walls of shrines, and were associated with the color black. In several instances death was symbolized as a vulture attacking headless human corpses. However, Mellaart also observed that in most cases, death was expressed by the people of Çatal Hüyük in less obvious ways, for instance,

> representations of women's breasts . . . , which are of course symbolic of life, contained such items as the skulls of vultures, the lower jaws of wild boars and the heads of foxes and weasels—all scavengers and devourers of corpses.[15]

Elaborating upon some of the other figures and symbols he found in the shrines and their meaning, Mellaart interpreted the numerous figures carved out of stalactites as suggesting a link with humankind's 'first refuge and sanctuary,' caves.[16] A wall-painting with what he interpreted as 'a honeycomb with eggs or chrysalises on boughs, and with bees, or butterflies'

---

[10] Roller 1999: 29.
[11] Roller 1999: 30.
[12] Roller 1999: 30.
[13] Roller 1999: 30.
[14] Gimbutas 1989: 107.
[15] Mellaart 1964: 103.
[16] Mellaart 1964: 103.

framed by hand-prints in red and black and pink, Mellaart suggested might 'perhaps symbolize the souls of the dead.'[17] Paintings with net patterns (sometimes framed with hands, sometimes appearing without hands), symbols of horns, and symbols of crosses, Mellaart interpreted as fertility symbols. 'Rosettes and the double ax (or butterfly) are in the same category.'[18] As we shall see later, many of the symbols Mellaart found at Çatal Hüyük, such as breasts, rosettes, and double axes or butterflies, are found in Minoan religion as well, either as attributes of the Goddess or in her cult equipment.

About fifty figurines were discovered by Mellaart at Çatal Hüyük. He notes, 'it is evident that statues of a female deity far outnumber those of the male deity, who moreover, does not appear to be represented at all after Level VI.'[19] The figurines also prove to Mellaart that the 'deities' were conceived of in human form and that they were 'endowed with supernatural power over their attributes and symbols taken from the familiar animal world.'[20] The Goddess was often shown with wild animals, and Mellaart believes this reflects her ancient role as provider of game for a hunting population. She was also shown with domesticated animals and 'her power over plant life and hence agriculture is clear not only from the numerous representations of floral and vegetable patterns, painted on her figure or in her shrines, but also from the association of her statuettes in heaps of grain.'[21] On the basis of the textile designs found in her shrines, Mellaart also thinks she was the patroness of weaving.

The Goddess who was worshipped at Çatal Hüyük was not only the Goddess of life, she appears as the Goddess of death as well:

> As a probable goddess of death, she is accompanied by a bird of prey, possibly a vulture and her grim expression suggests old age, the crone of later mythology. Her symbols of death, vultures, are frequently represented in early shrines, and an elaborate symbolism, foreshadowing the words 'in the midst of life there is death,' finds plastic expression in mother's breasts which incorporate skulls of vultures, fox and weasel or the lower jaws of boars with enormous tusks, eminently symbolic of the scavengers which thrive on death. A firm belief in afterlife is well attested by the burial customs. . . . The care of the dead suggests the idea of resurrection, the denial of death, the tenet of all religion. The stalactite goddess probably also stresses the idea of chthonic power and the underworld.[22]

Noting the lack of 'sexual vulgarity and eroticism' in the figurines, statuettes, plaster reliefs, and wall paintings,[23] Mellaart postulates that 'Neolithic woman was the creator of Neolithic religion,'[24] and that it was mainly women who administered the Goddess's cult.

Archaeologist Lynn Roller—whose 1999 book *In Search of God the Mother* traces the development of the Mother Goddess of the ancient Mediterranean world from her 'provincial origins' as the

---

[17] Mellaart 1964: 103.
[18] Mellaart 1964: 103.
[19] Mellaart 1967: 181.
[20] Mellaart 1967: 181.
[21] Mellaart 1967: 183.
[22] Mellaart 1967: 183-184.
[23] Mellaart 1964: 101.
[24] Mellaart 1964: 101.

Phrygian Mother, to a deity known to the Greeks as Meter and to the Romans as Magna Mater with a wide following throughout the empire[25]—concedes that Çatal Hüyük 'has produced abundant material that can directly be connected with a belief in a mother goddess.'[26] She posits that if one is looking for the ancestress of the Phrygian Mother Goddess (the Mother Goddess whose worship begins about 900 BC in Phrygian Anatolia and who forms the basis for the Meter of the Greeks and Magna Mater of the Romans), 'one must look for some indication in the Neolithic cult materials of images that were especially enduring.'[27] Roller finds such enduring images in felines and raptors—the prominent symbolism of Çatal Hüyük associated with the birthing mother/Goddess images.[28]

The Phrygian Mother Goddess of Anatolia is separated by several thousand years from Çatal Hüyük in the Neolithic Age. Thus, in addition to the images at Çatal Hüyük, and its contemporary neighbor, Haçilar, Roller looks for antecedents to the iconography of the Phrygian Mother Goddess in the intervening cultures: the Hittites, the dominant culture in Anatolia in the Middle and Late Bronze Age, contemporaries of the Minoans; and the Neo-Hittites and Urtarian cultures of the early Anatolian Iron Age.

From the Hittites (although it is usually a god not a Goddess that the Hittites portray on the sacred mountain), Roller finds that the Phrygians adopted the imagery of the sacred mountain; and also the Goddess with a bird of prey. A stamp seal impression from Bogazköy illustrates a seated Goddess holding a bird of prey and a bowl.[29] With the Urtarians, who associated the Goddess with the mountain, the Phrygians found the Goddess/mountain imagery reinforced; while with the Neo-Hittites, who pictured their Goddess Kubaba with lions, the iconography of the Goddess with felines was affirmed.

What has this to do with the Minoans? As we shall see, one of the most well-known images of the Goddess in ancient Crete is that of the Mother of the Mountains, or Mountain Mother as she is called. A sealing from Knossos, dated to LM IIIA1, *c.* 1400 BC, portraying the Goddess in a pose of authority on top of a mountain, shows her flanked on either side by lions. Is the Mountain Mother of Crete an adaptation of the Neolithic 'enthroned Goddesses' of Çatal Hüyük, influenced as well by the wall painting of the mountain/volcano landscape, and of the Hittite images of the sacred mountain in association with the divinity? Roller does not make these connections. What she does say is that the Minoans (and the Mycenaeans who were heavily influenced by Minoan religious iconography) 'probably had a significant effect in forming the visual image and character of the Greek Meter' of the Classical period.[30] Here she is referring especially to the image of the Mountain Mother I just described above.

Building on the evidence Roller has provided, it is possible to argue (although she does not) that aspects of Minoan Goddess iconography evolved from the Neolithic symbols of the Goddess that early settlers brought with them from Anatolia to Crete. Furthermore, Minoan Goddess iconography may have also been influenced by, and in its turn influenced, Hittite iconography. As Nanno Marinatos points out, 'Anatolia, Syria, the Levant, Minoan Crete, Mycenaean Greece

[25] Roller 1999: 345.
[26] Roller 1999: 30.
[27] Roller 1999: 39.
[28] Roller 1999: 39.
[29] Roller 1999: 43.
[30] Roller 1999: 134.

and Egypt were interconnected on a semiotic level.'[31] And finally by the classical period, when the Phrygian Mother Goddess's cult spread to Greece as Greek Meter, the Goddess's images and character were influenced by the memory of the Minoan Goddess, the Mountain Mother. As Roller puts it, in the 5th century BC there are frequent references to close links between Meter and Crete, 'and this link may well derive from memory of cult practice on Crete.'[32]

One aspect of the religion of Meter that may derive from Crete is Meter's conflation with the Goddess Rhea, and association with ecstatic dance. To understand this connection, one must be familiar with a myth regarding the birth of the Greek god Zeus. In the mythology surrounding the birth of Zeus it is said that his mother, the Goddess Rhea, hid him in a cave in Crete so he would not be devoured by his father, the god Kronos. Hidden in the Cretan cave, Zeus survived on milk fed to him by the goat Amaltheia, while his cries were drowned out by the noise made by the Kouretes, youths who clashed their shields, beat drums, shouted and danced wildly so Kronos would not know of Zeus's existence.

> Just as the baby Zeus had been cared for on Crete by the Kouretes, who sang and danced and clashed their shields, so the followers of Rhea/Meter would also sing and dance and make raucous noises during their rites, in imitation of the Kouretic attendants of her son Zeus.[33]

The second aspect of Meter's cult that may derive from Crete is found in the kindly, helpful qualities that are attributed to Meter in Sicily. That aspect of Meter is especially reflected in her worship in the Sicilian town of Engyion, settled by people from Crete.

> This town . . . had an important shrine to the Mothers, honoring the goddesses who saved Zeus on Crete from his father, Kronos. These goddesses and their helpers, the Kouretes, were honored also for their useful skills, which they taught to human beings; such skills including metallurgy, the domestication of animals, the technique of hunting, and also political and social harmony.[34]

Ultimately, however, the most important link between Meter and Crete is the very ancient, Minoan one, the Mountain Mother:

> the figure of a standing female deity flanked by lions, found on seals and sealings. This deity is often shown standing on mountaintops, suggesting that her power derives from control over the untamed mountain environment, as symbolized by her lion attendants.[35]

Before leaving the Mountain Mother imagery, it is important to point out that Minoan religious practice, especially in the Early and Middle Minoan Periods, c. 3200/3000/2600-1580 BC, involved worship at peak sanctuaries, religious sanctuaries on the peaks of mountains, and in caves as well. This reinforces the link between the symbol of the mountain and the Goddess. Worship on mountain tops and in caves also reinforces the relationship of the people to the

---

[31] Marinatos 2010: 139.
[32] Roller 1999: 135.
[33] Roller 1999: 172.
[34] Roller 1999: 174.
[35] Roller 1999: 135.

natural environment, something that Roller believes is vitally important to understand, for it is her power within all nature that is one of the hallmarks of the Mother Goddess. Roller asserts that the people of mountainous Anatolia created their definition of divinity using the symbols of the natural landscape.[36]

In addition to tracing the iconography that is used in connection with the Mother Goddess of Anatolia over millennia, and the probable links between that iconography and the iconography of Minoan Crete, what I also find so important about Roller's work is her understanding of the role of the Phrygian Mother Goddess. I believe it is similar to the role of the Minoan Mother Goddess, and must be considered in addition to her role as birth-giver and nurturer. Roller describes it thusly:

> Finally I want to touch on one crucial question about this goddess—namely of what was she the mother? . . . The Mother does not fit into the conventional female roles of reproduction and nurturing. . . . In Phrygian texts and monuments, the most prominent aspect of the Mother Goddess is her association with mountains, hollows and wild spaces. The awesome character of the mountainous Anatolian landscape and the sense of sacred space in the natural environment clearly were key factors in defining her divinity. We seem to see a goddess whose position of power over the natural environment, rather than any specifically maternal function, was the chief factor that gave her the status of a Mother.[37]

I believe that in addition to understanding their Mother Goddess as a birth-giver and nurturer, the Minoans shared the Anatolians' view of the Mother Goddess as described by Roller above. It was the Goddess's 'power over the natural environment . . . that gave her the status of a Mother.'

At another point in her book Roller again emphasizes that the Mother Goddess was not limited to fertility and nurturing, 'but was . . . a figure of power and protection, able to touch on many aspects of life and mediate between the boundaries of the known and unknown.'[38] Those last words, 'mediate between the boundaries of the known and unknown,' could refer to death and rebirth, and I believe that the Minoan Mother Goddess was also a powerful protector of life and mediator between life, death, and rebirth as well.

Earlier I discussed the Neolithic connection between the Goddess and raptors. As for the meaning of the association of the Goddess with birds of prey, Roller says:

> They do not give the goddess a frightening image, but rather one of strength and control over the natural environment. The goddess becomes the Mother of the natural world and her human worshipers approach her to gain her help in obtaining a measure of control over the natural environment for themselves.[39]

My study shows that such a role is also applicable to the Minoan Goddess.

---

[36] Roller 1999: 62.
[37] Roller 1999: 6.
[38] Roller 1999: 113.
[39] Roller 1999: 114.

Attributes and iconographic forms of the Minoan Mother Goddess

Because Roller is concerned in her book primarily with the Phrygian Mother Goddess and her evolution into the Greek Meter and Roman Magna Mater, and is thus dealing with time periods for which there are decipherable languages, Phrygian, Greek, and Latin, much of her evidence is based on literary and epigraphical sources. Nevertheless, Roller also uses a methodology which includes archaeological material: representations of deity, cult monuments, votive offerings, and sacred spaces. Roller finds a number of attributes and iconographic forms (which change in emphasis according to the culture and the time period) that denote the Mother Goddess: mountains, springs and shrines located near springs, predator and raptor imagery, nature symbolism, niches imitating the façade of buildings, natural settings, tympanum, and enthronement. Roller can be sure of her identification of the Goddess because the inscriptions on her representations, monuments, offerings, and sacred spaces, specifically address and name her. Scholars of Minoan Crete have no such assurances, for the languages and writing systems used by the Minoans have not been definitively deciphered. As previously discussed, the main methodological tool used in this project is archaeomythology. To recapitulate, archaeomythology is a discipline comprised of multiple aspects: archaeology, mythology, linguistics, and history, which 'provide the possibility for apprehending both the material and spiritual realities of prehistoric cultures.'[40] The great contributions that the founder of archaeomythology, Marija Gimbutas, made to the emerging field can be summarized in the following four points: an understanding of the Goddess as one with Nature and as manifesting in three aspects: Life-Giver, Death-Wielder and Regeneratrix; a reinterpretation of Neolithic 'Old Europe' as a 'true civilization in the best meaning of the word:'[41] an egalitarian, matrilineal, peaceful and artistic one; the deciphering of a complex symbolic system formulated around the worship of the Goddess in her various aspects; and an explanation as to when, how and why the Old European 'Civilization of the Goddess' was amalgamated into the patriarchal, sky-god worshipping civilization that overtook it.

Gimbutas emphasizes that the iconography of the Goddess always contains several types of symbols that indicate her roles as Life-Giver, Death-Wielder, and Regeneratrix. The three aspects of the Goddess are closely inter-twined and 'stem from a holistic perception of the world.'[42]

It is to the third point I want to turn now, for it is that aspect of Gimbutas's work that is most pertinent to identify the Mother Goddess in Crete: the deciphering of a complex symbolic system formulated around the worship of the Goddess in her various aspects. Point three is most fully addressed by Gimbutas in her 1989 work *The Language of the Goddess*. In that work Gimbutas presents her analysis of the signs and symbolism of Old Europe and how they reflect the Old European belief in a Goddess as Giver, Taker, and Renewer of Life. Although her focus in that work is on the Neolithic (6500-3500 BC) in southeastern and western Europe, Gimbutas traces the symbolic 'language of the Goddess' back to the Paleolithic and then forward into the Bronze Age civilizations of Crete, Cyprus, Thera, Sardinia, and Malta,—where it received its fullest expression.

---

[40] Gimbutas 1991: x.
[41] Gimbutas 1991: viii.
[42] Gimbutas 1991: viii.

Gimbutas likened her work of studying, analyzing, and questioning the meaning of the signs and patterns that appeared on cult objects and painted pottery throughout the Neolithic in Old Europe (and in Crete in the Bronze Age) and finally discovering their 'intrinsic order,' to putting together a giant jigsaw puzzle.

> As I worked at its completion, the main themes of Old European ideology emerged. . . . They [the symbols and images] represent the grammar and syntax of a kind of meta-language by which an entire constellation of meanings is transmitted. They reveal the basic world-view of Old European (pre-Indo-European) culture.[43]

What are the grammar and syntax of this meta-language which presents to us the pictorial 'script' for the religion of the Old European Goddess? Gimbutas classifies the symbols she uncovered into four groups: Life-Giving, Renewing and Eternal Earth, Death and Regeneration, and Energy and Unfolding (the last one supports and amplifies the first three). Below is a list of some of the symbols she associates with each. These specific symbols can be found on Cretan artifacts of the Bronze Age. In the discussion of the individual artifacts which follows, Gimbutas's analysis is used to point out the various symbols of the Goddess present on Minoan artifacts. I accept Gimbutas's conclusions that when these symbols in their various combinations are present on pottery and cult objects, these objects represent the Goddess and a culture in which the Feminine Divine was worshipped in her three aspects of Life-Giver, Death-Wielder, and Regeneratrix.

In her two categories of symbols which represent the Goddess as Life-Giver and as Renewing and Eternal Earth, Gimbutas begins with symbols from the aquatic world: streams, chevrons, zig-zags, wavy and serpentine bands, net and checkerboard patterns, waterfowl, and bird women. She explains that these symbols originated in the Paleolithic. To the Goddess in her aspect as Birth-Giver, Gimbutas connects images of the vulva, primeval mothers in animal form, snakes and snake coils.

Gimbutas emphasizes that 'images of death do not overshadow those of life: they are combined with symbols of regeneration.'[44] Images which Gimbutas interprets as symbolizing the Goddess in her Death and Regeneration aspect include: vulture heads within breasts; owls with labyrinths on their bodies which contain a vulva in the center; the uterus shaped like a bucranium; 'analogous animal forms—fish, frog, toad, hedgehog, turtle',[45] graves in the shape of an egg, vagina or uterus, or the whole female body; and stiff nudes with pubic triangles.

Finally, in the category associated with all three of the previous categories, what Gimbutas calls 'energy and unfolding and motion and twisting,' she lists spirals, horns, crescents, U-shapes, whirls, crosses, various four-cornered designs, and ithyphallic men. 'All are symbols of the dynamism in nature which secures the birth of life and turns the wheel of cyclic time from death to life, so that life is perpetuated.'[46]

---

[43] Gimbutas 1989: xv.
[44] Gimbutas 1989: xxii.
[45] Gimbutas 1989: xxiii.
[46] Gimbutas 1989: xxiii.

Archaeologist Geraldine Gesell approaches the understanding of Minoan religion in the absence of deciphered texts through a focus on the chronological development of Minoan 'cult,' as she calls it, 'from its beginnings in the Early Bronze Age to its assimilation into early Greek cult [3000-600 BC].'[47] Limiting herself to sanctuaries and domestic shrines in towns and palaces (and thus omitting caves, peak shrines, and most open air sanctuaries, except those on the edge of settlements), Gesell 'determines the earliest use of the individual types of sanctuaries and cult objects,' and then traces their development or modification 'until each drops out of use or is assimilated into Greek cult.'[48]

Gesell's work, *Town, Palace and House Cult in Minoan Crete,* published in 1985, is rich in its detailed explanation of cult objects: representations of the Goddess, ritual equipment and votive offerings; cult symbols: including the double axe, horns of consecration, bulls, birds, snakes, agrimia (the long-horned wild goat of Crete), sacral knots, sun disks, and moon crescents; sacred architecture, including bench sanctuaries, lustral basins, and pillar crypts; and cult equipment, including offering tables, rhyta, pottery, and chalices. When studied in combination, and in context, cult objects, cult symbols, sacred architecture, and cult equipment allow Gesell to identify the deity worshipped, in this case the Minoan Goddess, and to get a glimpse into how she was understood by the Minoans, and how her worship might have changed over time.

Gesell also provides a thorough discussion of the attributes of the Goddess. In the Prepalatial period, *c.* 2600 to 2100 BC, vases in the shape of women with their hands under their breasts with open nipples (to allow the pouring of liquids) indicate to Gesell the worship of a fertility or birth Goddess. The Goddess of Myrtos, whose unique bell shape and prominent pubic triangle are suggestive of pregnancy and fertility, implies to Gesell that the Goddess of Prepalatial Crete was also a 'general protectress of women and women's affairs.'[49]

In the Protopalatial Period, *c.* 2100-1700 BC, Gesell believes that two vases, a bowl and a fruit stand (a shallow bowl on a stand) found at the Palace of Phaistos, 'may depict an epiphany of the goddess in different aspects.'[50] She identifies the central figures in these objects as Goddesses because they are the central figures, and because they are surrounded by adorants or dancers. Specifically, on the Phaistos bowl, the Goddess has loops down the sides of her robe indicating to Gesell she is a Snake Goddess. Because the central figure surrounded by dancers on the fruit stand is holding flowers in her upraised hands, Gesell identifies her as Goddess of the Lilies. Based on the fact that the Bench Sanctuary complex at Phaistos had images of birds on stone libation tables and a triton shell (used to summon the Goddess, she thinks), Gesell posits that a Sky Goddess was also worshipped during this period.

In the Neopalatial Period, *c.* 1700-1450 BC, the Snake Goddesses from the Temple Repositories at Knossos, since they were found with 'a large variety of marine and animal life,' symbolize for Gesell 'the universal Mother or Earth Goddess.'[51] This period also sees the appearance of a chthonic Goddess. According to Gesell, the Neopalatial period witnessed something new in sacred architecture—the Pillar Crypt-Upper Column Room Complexes with their symbols of

---

[47] Gesell 1985: 1.
[48] Gesell 1985: 2.
[49] Gesell 1985: 64.
[50] Gesell 1985: 17.
[51] Gesell 1985: 65.

bull and double axe. Gesell proposes that because the bull and double axe are found with the Goddesses 'with upraised hands,' as she calls them, in the Postpalatial period, c. 1400-1070 BC, a connection between the Goddess and the bull and double axe in the earlier period is likely. She believes the bull and double axe symbolize the Goddess who held sway over earthquakes and the dead.

In Postpalatial times, c.1400-1070 BC, based on the stone concretions from the Little Palace at Knossos, among which are a mother and child pair, Gesell finds a continuation of the fertility and birth Goddess worship which began in the Prepalatial era. In the Goddesses 'with upraised hands' that are unique to this and the Postminoan period c. 1070-1000 BC, she finds the Goddess of the Earth and the Sky once again represented, symbolized by the birds and snakes adorning those Goddesses.[52] The appearance of both the bird and the snake on the Kannia Goddess with Upraised Arms (from southern Crete near Gortyn) signals to Gesell that in this Goddess with Upraised Arms we see the union of the two aspects of snake and bird, Earth and Sky Goddess.[53]

In the Postminoan period, c. 1070-1000 BC, the Goddess 'with upraised hands,' or Goddess with Upraised Arms, survives and continues to be venerated until at least the Protogeometric period, c. 1000-810 BC, and perhaps later. Indeed, Gesell sees traces of Minoan cult extending all the way to the Orientalizing period, c. 700-600 BC, as evidenced in such objects as the cult bench, offering table, Goddess with Upraised Hands, parturient female figurine, hut urn, relief plaque, kernos, and triton shell.[54]

Gesell's work provides a rich elaboration of and catalog of Minoan cult objects, cult equipment, cult symbols, and attributes of the Goddess, all of which are extremely important if one is to have an understanding of Minoan religion and the place of the Goddess within that religion. Her work makes an important contribution to the history of Minoan religion, and her phase-by-phase analysis of sanctuaries, cult objects, equipment symbols, and the Goddess's attributes brings into relief the significant iconographic transformations that occurred over the two thousand year period covered by her book.

Archaeologist Nanno Marinatos also tackles the problem of understanding Minoan religion and identifying the Goddess's place in it. She uses a methodology which combines structuralism, semiotics, anthropology of religion, and cultural anthropology with archaeological data, as well as 'comparative material from other cultures.'[55] Marinatos's detailed discussion of the attributes and iconography of the Goddess further brings to light the numerous ways in which we can recognize her.

In her introduction to *Minoan Religion*, published in 1993, Marinatos lists Minoan cult equipment which can be thought of as symbols of Minoan religion: horns of consecration; double axes; rhyta or libation vessels; libation tables; incurved altars, used as thrones or platforms on which the Goddess sat; offering tables including stone altars; sacrificial tables, used in animal sacrifice; conical cups; stone maces; *kernoi*, vessels used for multiple offerings; and snake tubes, stands with snake motifs used to hold offering bowls. When any of these are present, they can

---

[52] Gesell 1985: 65.
[53] Gesell 1985: 65.
[54] Gesell 1985: 65.
[55] Marinatos 1993: 11.

help with the identification of shrines and sanctuaries and indicate where ritual has taken place. When female or male figures are found with these symbols, depending upon the size and gestures and costumes of the figures, a determination can be made about the divinity or humanity of the figure.

The attributes of the Minoan Goddess are taken up in Marinatos's chapter on 'Goddesses and Gods.' In the Prepalatial Period, c. 2600 to 2100 BC 'goddess vessels,' which portray a mother holding a jug like a baby (and which were often found in burial contexts), show that 'the Minoans connected the goddess with sustenance through her ability to supply life-giving liquid.'[56] Bird and animal figurines, also found in burials, indicate to Marinatos that the Goddess 'was a protectress of nature already in the PrePalatial period.'[57]

Artifacts from the Old Palace Period, c. 2100-1700 BC, connect the Goddess (who is a female, and larger in size than any of the other humans depicted on the artifact) with lilies, and thus, according to Marinatos, with 'vegetation and a seasonal cycle.'[58]

In the New Palace Period, c. 1700-1450 BC, the Goddess of Crete continues to be connected with flowers and plants as evidenced in frescoes from Ayia Triadha and Thera. In this period, the Goddess's association with lilies occurs again—lilies are the subjects of frescoes and occur in the necklace of the Goddess—and Marinatos concludes that the lily 'was not just a decorative motif, but that it had a symbolic content and was closely related to the goddess.'[59] To underline the symbolic importance of the lily, Marinatos compares it to the religious function of the papyrus and lotus in Egypt.

The Goddess is also shown with trees and has an unusual relationship with the animal world—for she is portrayed with goats, deer, and lions, as well as the more mythical griffins. One particularly powerful image illustrating her unique relationship with animals is the impressive seal (described above) called 'Mother of the Mountains.' Birds are also shown with the Goddess and are sometimes shown alone, 'sacred in their own right.'[60] Occasionally the Goddess is portrayed with a bird head and wings. Marinatos believes that the 'Bird Goddess' is 'the merging of the goddess and her attribute as in Egypt.'[61] Marine life is also sacred to the Goddess, for she appears on seals with dolphins, and representations of marine life are found on the floors of her sanctuaries. The two Snake Goddesses from the Temple Repositories at Knossos present yet another attribute of the Goddess—the snake—representing for Marinatos the underworld and thus completing the association of the Goddess with all of the realms of nature: earth, air, and sea.

Even after 1450 BC and the fall of the palaces, the Goddesses appear with many of the attributes attested in the Palatial Period, c. 1700-1450 BC: birds, flowers, and snakes, indicating to Marinatos that there is continuity of religious belief with the preceding period, and that

---

[56] Marinatos 1993: 142.
[57] Marinatos 1993: 147.
[58] Marinatos 1993: 149.
[59] Marinatos 1993: 152.
[60] Marinatos 1993: 155.
[61] Marinatos 1993: 156.

the figurines do represent Goddesses.[62] For Marinatos it is the Goddess of Nature who has flourished throughout the Minoan period.

Archaeologist Marina Moss attempts to come to terms with ancient religious beliefs in her work *The Minoan Pantheon: Toward an Understanding of its Nature and Extent,* published in 2005. As her title suggests, her thesis is that many Goddesses were worshipped on Crete, and that gods were worshipped as well.

Adopting the cognitive archaeology approach, 'the study of pathways of thought from material remains,'[63] Moss examines archaeological material found 'in what appear to be religious contexts.'[64] Looking at the time period of the Middle Minoan to Late Minoan, 2000-1000 BC, Moss chooses a selection of excavated sites in Crete that have 'adequate published evidence for . . . use for apparently religious purposes and . . . make a contribution towards an understanding of the types of deities worshipped there.'[65] These she divides into five categories: settlements, palaces, sanctuaries on hills, caves, and rural settlements. For each site Moss presents: a description of architecture; reference to significant features in the landscape; the context of the archaeological finds and their association with each other; a description and discussion of the finds; and an iconographic analysis which includes comparisons with similar evidence from a number of cultures in the east Mediterranean region.[66]

Like Gesell and Marinatos, Moss draws up a list of the type of archaeological material she will be considering: frescoes, mason's marks, and finds such as pottery, altars, offering tables, snake tubes, horns of consecration, double axes, and figurines of people, animals, and other creatures.

After each site has been described according to the categories listed above, 'conclusions are drawn as to the nature of the deities worshipped at each site based on an analysis of the iconography of the finds and of other significant features of the area described.'[67] Moss admits that interpreting the information, that is, drawing conclusions as to the nature of the deities worshiped, 'based on an analysis of the iconography of the finds,' is very difficult and that interpretations of iconography will differ from scholar to scholar. She intimates that comparisons with other cultures may be of help, but certainly cannot provide the final word. The best we can do, she concludes, is determine what kind of Goddess or god may have been worshipped at a particular place and time. Her hope is that by 'naming' the Goddesses and gods, based on their attributes and the symbolism associated with them, 'we can propose possible areas of responsibility they may have had to the people who venerated them in the Bronze Age on Crete.'[68]

While I do not agree with Moss's conclusion that many Goddesses were worshipped on Crete, rather than one, I find her meticulous compilation of data admirable and of great help for my own work. I appreciate her knowledge of eastern Mediterranean cultures contemporary

---

[62] Marinatos 1993: 227.
[63] Moss 2005: 3.
[64] Moss 2005: 3.
[65] Moss 2005: 3.
[66] Moss 2005: 3.
[67] Moss 2005: 3.
[68] Moss 2005: 5.

with the Minoans and her ability to make comparisons with, and draw conclusions from them. And finally, I find her acknowledgement of the difficulty of interpreting iconography and her admission that there are many possible interpretations very refreshing.

Using Gimbutas's symbolic 'language' along with the entire field of archaeomythology, especially archaeology and those methods employed by Roller, Gesell, Marinatos, and Moss, I propose to examine the artifacts from Neolithic Crete and beyond. Like Roller, I will look at representations of the deity, cult monuments, votive offerings, sacred spaces, and inscriptions (in Linear A when available). Like Marinatos and Moss, I will use comparative data from other eastern Mediterranean cultures whenever possible. Like Roller, Gesell, Marinatos, and Moss, I will be looking for the attributes and symbols of the Goddess—those they have identified, as well as others that can be discerned through Gimbutas's lens of the 'Language of the Goddess.' Renfrew's criteria will also be used to identify religious ritual, and from that identification an attempt to understand the religious beliefs underlying the ritual will be made. Like Moss, I am aware that interpretations of iconography will differ from scholar to scholar. However, using archaeomythology and feminist hermeneutics, I hope to make a plausible and highly probable case, grounded in scientific data, for my interpretation.

The character of Minoan religion and the Minoan Mother Goddess

It is apparent from the discussion above that there is some common agreement among scholars on how one may understand and identify Minoan religion and the Minoan Goddess. We know about Minoan religion from several types of evidence: pictorial representations, architectural remains, cult objects, and some written sources, most of which have not found a definitive translation. Beginning with Sir Arthur Evans in the early twentieth century and continuing through to the twenty-first century, there has been a broad consensus among archaeologists that, as stated by archaeologist Geraldine Gesell, 'there is much evidence from pictorial representations and images that the chief divinity of the Minoan pantheon is the Great Mother Goddess.'[69]

It was Evans who first began identifying the religion of the Goddess in his thirty years of excavation at Knossos, and in the publication of his multi-volume *Palace of Minos* which documented and elaborated upon his finds. The Swedish scholar Martin P. Nilsson expanded upon Evans's work, and 'brought together evidence from architectural remains and artifacts to explain the character of Minoan cult.'[70] Thus, while interpretations are revised and keep evolving, scholars have agreed that certain objects and rooms may be identified as having a religious purpose. Gesell summarizes this shared approach and understanding:

> The amount of cult material which can be substantiated gives us a picture of a highly organized religion with cult sites of many types—caves, mountain peaks, town sanctuaries, palace sanctuaries, domestic shrines, tombs—and cult objects of three main classes—goddess figurines and their cult symbols, votive offerings, and cult equipment.[71]

---

[69] Gesell 1985: 1.
[70] Gesell 1985: 1.
[71] Gesell 1985: 1.

In attempting to understand Minoan religion and the Minoan Goddess, I think one must first begin with the places of worship. Gesell notes in the above quote that Minoan religion was practiced in various places—caves, mountain peaks, town sanctuaries, and others. How have such places been identified as sites of religious worship? The lack of a decipherable written language has led Aegean archaeologists to turn to the pictorial representations found on frescoes, seals, sealings, rings, stone vases, sarcophagi, and pottery to gain an understanding of cult objects and their use. Once cult objects have been identified, when they are found in situ in rooms that are judged to be suitable for cult purposes, the rooms themselves can then be identified as sanctuaries or shrines. After archaeologists have established a pool of identifiable cult objects and sanctuaries and shrines, other rooms and other objects can be added to that pool. Gesell stresses that

> in order to establish a positive identification of the cult room, *distinctive architecture and cult objects are both necessary* [emphasis in original]. If, however, a room in one building strongly parallels, in location and architecture a sanctuary room in a second building but lacks the cult objects, it is still reasonable to conclude that it also is a cult room.[72]

We know that certain caves, mountain peaks, and sections or rooms in towns and palaces were cult sites because of the architecture of the places themselves and/or the cult objects found in them. What identifies a place architecturally as a site where religion is practiced? Archaeologists have agreed that in Minoan Crete, sanctuaries are marked by benches, lustral basins, and pillars in crypts ('pillar crypts'). A bench sanctuary is simply a built-in bench on which cult objects were placed. An architectural feature can be identified as a bench sanctuary only when corroborating evidence is found, for it is too easy for a built-in bench to have been used for other purposes. A lustral basin is identified by its sunken floor, angled stair, and often, a columned parapet.[73] Whether or not a specific lustral basin was used for ritual purposes (or perhaps for bathing purposes of some kind) depends on its relation to other architectural elements. A pillar crypt is usually a rectangular room with one central pillar. 'Not every room with a pillar could have been a cult room, so location and cult objects must be used to verify its religious function.'[74]

In addition to bench sanctuaries, lustral basins (sometimes also called *adyta*), and pillar crypts, Marinatos also identifies as architectural features of places of worship what she calls 'dining shrines' and 'balustrade shrines.' According to Marinatos, a dining shrine is a type of bench sanctuary, 'because most, although not all, of the sacred eating rooms contained benches.'[75] Such shrines also contain hearths, and can only be identified with certainty by their location (usually in the western part of one of the palaces, the part of the palace which was used almost exclusively for ritual purposes), and the equipment found in situ, which must include cult objects. Marinatos has also identified balustrade shrines: rooms in which the focal point is situated beyond a balustrade. Marinatos postulates that in such shrines a person portraying the deity would be seated, and that a ritual performance or enacted epiphany would take place.[76] Her conclusion is based again upon the location of the room in reference to other

---

[72] Gesell 1985: 2.
[73] Marinatos 1993: 77.
[74] Gesell 1985: 3.
[75] Marinatos 1993: 98.
[76] Marinatos 1993: 106.

architectural features, in the cases of Marinatos's examples, a lustral basin or pillar crypt, and cult objects found in situ.

As a general rule of thumb it can be said that in order to qualify as a shrine, a site must contain certain architectural features: focal points such as niches, platforms, and pillars; communication or barrier devices to the outside, such as large doors (or large windows if the shrine is on the upper story); benches, repositories, or treasuries, which can be used for the placing and storage of cult objects; and finally, frescoes with religious iconography.[77] 'These constitute important elements in the identification of sacred space.'[78] Marinatos reiterates that 'the identification and typology of shrines has been one of the major aims of scholars dealing with Minoan religion since the days of Sir Arthur Evans and Martin P. Nilsson.'[79]

The Minoans also celebrated their Goddess out of doors: in caves, on mountain peaks, in sacred groves, and at open-air shrines. In these cult places (the term simply means 'diverse categories of places where worship took place'[80]), while some 'sanctuary architecture' may be found, usually the remains of buildings or, perhaps more usually, rooms, it is mainly natural features such as chasms, stalagmites and stalactites, or rock formations in the shape of humans or animals, that mark the place as sacred. As archaeologist Bogdan Rutkowski wrote regarding cult places outside settlements:

> In the natural cult places everything untouched and unformed by man—the sacred area itself, the rocks, the roof of the grotto, etc.—constituted [the] basic feature. Of course the elements contributed by man—for instance the walls and the structures erected by him—could also sometimes be of great significance.[81]

In addition to those items both unformed and formed by humans, cult places outside settlements can often be identified as such by the remains of ash, indicative of burning and thus sacrifice and feasting, votive offerings, and altars.

From what has been said above it is obvious that cult objects are immensely important in identifying sacred architecture and making sense of Minoan religion. Over the years archaeologists have identified numerous cult objects and their reliable identification is a huge subject. Thus, Gesell divides cult objects into three classes: representation of the divinity, ritual equipment, and votive offerings.

Under 'representation of the divinity' Gesell places not only figures of the Goddess, but cult symbols as well. She lists as cult symbols: the double axe, horns of consecration, bull, bird, snake, agrimi, sacral knot, sun disk, and moon crescent.[82] Most of these, as we shall see, can also be considered attributes of the Goddess.

Ritual equipment is defined by Gesell as offering vessels and rhyta. Marinatos expands this list to include: horns of consecration, double axes, rhyta or libation vessels, libation tables,

---

[77] Marinatos 1993: 76.
[78] Marinatos 1993: 76.
[79] Marinatos 1993: 76.
[80] Rutkowski 1986: xix.
[81] Rutkowski 1986: xix.
[82] Gesell 1985: 3.

incurved altars, offering tables, sacrificial tables, conical cups, stone maces, composite vessels or kernoi, tubular stands or snake tubes.[83]

Gesell's third category of 'votive offerings' includes: figurines, small double axes, miniature vessels, miniature altars, and ceremonial weapons.[84] Elaborating on the subject of votive figures, Gesell writes that they are normally constructed of bronze or terracotta, and portray female, male, and animal figures. Bulls and agrimi make up the bulk of the animal figurines. The human figures are usually in a standing position. In that position, the female figurines strike a variety of poses, while the males salute or hold an offering.[85] Votive offerings, including votive figures, are found in all types of sanctuaries, but are especially prominent in caves and peak sanctuaries.

I would like here to elaborate on some of the cult symbols and the interpretive descriptions of them, for while archaeologists may agree something is a symbol, they do not always agree upon its meaning.

As for one of the most enigmatic of Minoan symbols, the double axe, Gesell thinks that it was first used as the sacrificial axe in cult rites and its status as a cult object thus derives from that use.[86] Moss notes that its origins are disputed, but that 'there may be a connection with an example of a similar, much earlier use of this motif in a religious context at Çatal Hüyük in Anatolia.'[87] Ultimately Moss identifies it as a symbol of renewal.[88] Marinatos writes that the double axe is never shown as a sacrificial device, is always held by females, and stresses that the double axe is most commonly shown 'being set up as a symbol in places where some ritual takes place.'[89] She says, 'It obviously denotes power, but more we cannot say.'[90] My hypothesis about the double axe is that it is a symbol of the Mother Goddess herself, her essence. I come to that way of thinking from observing that the double axe is very similar to the butterfly, a symbol of transformation. I believe that transformation into life, and from life to death, and back to life again are the Goddess's primary aspects.

The horns of consecration, which appear on top of altars and roofs of sanctuaries, palaces, and villas and are found painted on pottery and burial larnakes, is another of the enigmatic Minoan symbols. Gesell says we are uncertain of their meaning/use but that 'its common occurrence together with the double axe suggests that both were connected with and represent the bull sacrifice.'[91] Marinatos calls the horns of consecration one 'of the most important symbols of Minoan religion,'[92] and admits that while we do not know what they symbolized, 'the similarity with bulls' horns cannot be entirely fortuitous.'[93] Moss posits that the

---

[83] Marinatos 1993: 5-7.
[84] Gesell 1985: 2.
[85] Gesell 1985: 3.
[86] Gesell 1985: 3.
[87] Moss 2005: 17.
[88] Moss 2005: 197.
[89] Marinatos 1993: 5.
[90] Marinatos 1993: 5.
[91] Gesell 1985: 3.
[92] Marinatos 1993: 79.
[93] Marinatos 1993: 5.

origins of the symbol of the so-called 'horns of consecration' appear to lie to the east of Crete, in Anatolia or Assyria, but there seems to be sufficient evidence to argue that the use and possible meaning of the horns was influenced by their use in Egyptian religion, especially in the iconography of [the Goddess] Hathor.[94]

Moss believes that in Egyptian Hathoric iconography, the horns of consecration 'are commonly associated with protection and cyclical renewal or rebirth;'[95] Hathor was the protectress of the solar god, enabling the sun to rise at dawn. She was also the Goddess of the Dead. This suggests to Moss that the horns denote renewal and protection.[96] It is my view that the horns of consecration signified a place or thing sacred to the Mother Goddess as well as symbolizing the Goddess in her triple aspects of birth, death, and regeneration.

Nilsson convincingly argued that the horns of consecration signified a place or thing sacred to the Mother Goddess, and that shrines, as well as buildings connected with sanctuaries other than shrines, 'were adorned with sacred horns in order to stamp them as sacred.'[97] I believe the second aspect of my hypothesis, that the horns of consecration may represent the Mother Goddess in her triple aspects, may be traced back to Anatolia. We know that the people of Çatal Hüyük hunted wild cattle and eventually domesticated them. Fekri A. Hassan has made the extremely important observation, in connection with Hathor and Egyptian religion, that the association of cow imagery, in this case horns, with Goddesses in Egypt can be traced back to the time before cattle were domesticated, as early as 10,000 BC. At that time cattle were being venerated in Egypt as evidenced by the placement of horn cores of cows in burials. Hassan suggests that since women tended the homestead, it was they who began feeding and watering cows. Women eventually became associated with them, not only because they tended them, but because 'both cow and woman gave milk. Both were the source of generation and life.'[98] Hassan believes 'these mental associations were of deep psychological significance,' and that 'they laid the foundation of the fundamental notions of Egyptian religion: birth, death, and resurrection.'[99] I hypothesize that the same associations, woman and cow as sources of regeneration and nourishment, might have also had a deep psychological significance to the Anatolian settlers who came to Crete, and that the significance of woman's role as nurturer and regenerator lead to the veneration of a Mother Goddess in her triple aspects and to the use of cow horns as a symbol of places sacred to her, as well as to her powers of life, death, and regeneration.

As for the bull as a cult object, it appears as a rhyton (a ritual vessel for pouring liquid), as a votive offering, and in frescoes. Gesell says that 'it was certainly an animal of sacrifice.'[100] Susan Evasdaughter disagrees, writing that in the period from Neolithic to Classical Greece,

> The only pictorial image of a probable bull sacrifice in this long period of Cretan archaeology is from the Ayia Triada sarcophagus which dates from around 1450 BC, and, as is indicated from the building in which it was found and many aspects of the

---

[94] Moss 2005: 212.
[95] Moss 2005: 14.
[96] Moss 2005: 198.
[97] Nilsson 1949: 185.
[98] Hassan 1998: 105.
[99] Hassan 1998: 105.
[100] Gesell 1985: 3.

scenes depicted on it, [is] more representative of an alien tradition than indigenous Cretan ritual.[101]

It must be noted here that 'bull rhyta' may actually have been 'bovine rhyta.' Moss has written,

> It should be noted again, that in Egyptian art, horned bovine heads signified cows, and that the goddess Hathor was the cow-headed goddess. . . . The Minoans may have used the Egyptian iconography for the goddess Hathor in the form of the mis-named bull's head rhyta.[102]

Moss has also argued that 'Minoan bovine head rhyta may represent a goddess not unlike Hathor.'[103] Like Moss, I see the 'bulls' as possibly being cows and believe that more interpretive analysis is needed on this point.

Birds appear as votive offerings, or as symbols attached to the Goddess, or her equipment, or in the form of the Bird Goddess. There is general agreement among scholars that birds also represent the epiphany of the Goddess. Moss links birds attached to the Goddess as signifying she was a 'celestial goddess.'[104] Additionally she posits that the 'sky goddess' may have been symbolized as a bird.[105] Gesell also links birds with a Sky Goddess.[106] Marinatos proposes that the bird signifies the Goddess as Protectress of Nature.[107]

Like the bird, the snake is also connected with the Goddess. Snakes are found on her, as in the famous Snake Goddesses of the Knossos Temple Repositories, or attached to cult objects. I discuss the Snake Goddesses at length in Chapter 5. Nilsson writes that snakes are representative of the dead, based on 'a mass of evidence both of words and of images from all quarters of the world.'[108] Snakes are also, according to Nilsson, associated with chthonic deities and represent death as well as fertility. Finally, noting that 'The house snake is well known in European folk-lore,'[109] Nilsson points to the role of the snake as a protector and guardian of the house. Goodison notes that the snake has been variously understood as a symbol of the household, of death and rebirth, and that 'it usually appears with women.'[110]

The agrimi appears as an attribute on cult equipment and as a votive offering. Gesell says that 'it is one of the symbols marking the goddess as Mistress of Animals.'[111] Agrimia also appear in at least one fresco, the famous Ayia Triadha fresco, discussed at length in Chapter 5, portraying the Goddess and a votary in the landscape. There several agrimia frolic among the lush vegetation within which are situated the Goddess and her votary. Agrimia adorn vessels

---

[101] Evasdaughter 1996: 138.
[102] Moss 2005: 41.
[103] Moss 2005: 212.
[104] Moss 2005: 27.
[105] Moss 2005: 13.
[106] Gesell 1985: 65. For further discussion of birds as attributes or symbols of the Goddess see Gesell 1985: 62; Marinatos 1993: 155-156.
[107] Marinatos 1993: 149.
[108] Nilsson 1949: 324.
[109] Nilsson 1949: 325.
[110] Goodison 1990: 320.
[111] Gesell 1985: 3.

such as rhyta, pithoi, jugs, and snake tubes. Almost all of these vessels can be linked to ritual.[112] When they appear alone, agrimia 'may be interpreted as a pars pro toto representation of a holy encounter.'[113]

The sacral knot, which is a looped and knotted piece of cloth with two fringed ends hanging down, was first identified by Sir Arthur Evans who gave it the name *sacral knot*.[114] He noted the similarity of some of the double axe/sacral knot representations found on Minoan pottery to the Egyptian ankh. The most famous sacred knot of Minoan Crete is the one that appears on the nape of the neck of the 'priestess' in the fresco named by Evans as the 'La Parisienne.' There are many other examples.[115] Gesell posits that they have some connection to bull sacrifice and believes they were a part of sacral dress. She also points out that they are found joined to painted representations of the double axe.[116] Marinatos believes they were the 'accoutrements' of the priestesses, and that it was such sacred symbols that differentiated priestesses from ordinary women.[117] Moss connects the sacral knot to the worship of the Egyptian Goddesses Hathor, Isis, and Tawaret and posits that it was 'an adaptation of the Egyptian symbols [the ankh, the 'Isis Knot' (tyet), or Sa] and signified protection and life.'[118] She also sees a connection between the sacral knot of the Minoans and the sacral knot of the Goddess Inanna from Mesopotamia who, 'returning from the Underworld, was a goddess of both life and death, so the sacral knot may have an underlying symbolism of cyclical renewal.'[119] It is clear to Moss that the Minoans absorbed into their religion the iconography of foreign deities, although she admits we do not know when this happened or how much of the mythology or religious beliefs of the foreign countries were also incorporated into the Minoan belief system.

As for the sun disk and the moon crescent, Gesell believes they rarely appear as cult objects.[120] Archaeologist Lucy Goodison has stated that 'there has been a tendency to overlook or deny evidence for the importance of the sun and moon in the religion of Bronze Age Greece,'[121] and she demonstrated that solar symbolism is repeatedly shown on articles of religious function in Bronze Age Crete.[122] Goodison posits a close connection between sun symbolism and the female sex, beginning in the Early Bronze Age, when 'frying-pans' with both the sun and pubic triangle incised on them first made their appearance in the Cycladic islands and eventually also in Crete. Moreover, Goodison links sun symbolism with some of the cult symbols discussed above: snake, bird, and goat. Marinatos in her 2010 book, *Minoan Kingship and the Solar Goddess: A Near Eastern Koine*, explores the symbolism of the solar disk in Cretan iconography and neighboring countries and concludes that the chief deity of Crete was a solar Goddess. Moss points out that the Egyptians and Mesopotamians used solar and stellar symbols as religious signs, especially in connection with the Goddesses Hathor, Astarte, and Asherah. As the

---

[112] Simandiraki 2006: 100.
[113] Simandiraki 2006: 100.
[114] Evans 1964: 1:430.
[115] Nilsson lists examples in 1949: 162-164; Lenuzza also lists examples in 2012: 257-260.
[116] Gesell 1985: 3.
[117] Marinatos 1993: 143.
[118] Moss 2005: 204.
[119] Moss 2005: 204.
[120] Gesell 1985: 3.
[121] Goodison 1989: 11.
[122] Goodison 1989: 78.

Minoans were in contact with the civilizations of the Near East, they might well have been influenced by the use of such signs and incorporated them into their belief systems.[123]

We turn our attention next to ritual equipment. As noted above, there are a number of items which archaeologists have identified as serving as ritual equipment in Minoan religion. One is offering tables. Gesell lists four types of offering tables: *kernoi*, fruit stands (shallow bowls on stands), snake tubes (cylindrical stands with two rows of serpentine loop handles on which offering bowls were placed), and altar stands.[124] A kernos is a clay vessel, to which were attached a number of small cups. Its cups could be filled with various grains and liquids, and thus filled, it could be used to offer the first fruits of the harvest to the divinity. The kernos is particularly associated with the Eleusinian Mysteries of Demeter and Persephone, but there is much evidence to argue that it originated in Crete.

A related piece of ritual equipment is the incurved altar, an altar with a base formed using two concave lines. Incurved altars have been found in situ, but usually they appear as a symbol in religious iconography. The Goddess in the Crocus Gatherers Fresco, discussed in Chapter 5, sits on an incurved altar. 'One of their main functions was to form the substructure or support for a throne or platform on which the goddess sat.'[125] In other words, they often symbolized or served to make manifest the presence of the Goddess.

Also important as ritual equipment are the *rhyta*, vessels for pouring liquid, in the shape of animals or animal heads. The bull head or bovine head rhyta were discussed above. Other shapes include the head of a lioness and of a pig; one rhyton portrays three men holding on to the horns of a wild bull. Cups were also used as ritual equipment. Marinatos discusses how when conical cups are found overturned in shrines or sanctuaries, 'a ceremony of offering in which the contents were to be received by the earth can be inferred.'[126] Chalices and pottery also served as ritual equipment in cult rites.

In at least one well-known sealing from the Idaean cave, a triton shell is blown by a priestess 'to invoke the divinity.'[127] Triton shells have been found in sanctuaries as well as in funerary contexts, often in association with other ritual objects. Found throughout the Minoan period, some were used as containers for food, some as rhyta, and some, much fewer in number, functioned as trumpets. When they functioned as trumpets, archaeologists agree that they were used to summon the deity.

Archaeologists are in accord that a Goddess (or Goddesses) is at the center of Minoan religion and that one of the three main classes of cult objects is comprised of Goddess figurines. How is the Goddess herself to be identified? In addition to noting the sacredness of the find location and the context of cult objects and/or of worshippers, another important way is through the identification of her attributes. Summarized in the previous section were the various symbols which Gimbutas would consider to be attributes of the Old European/Anatolian Goddess in her Triple Aspect as Birth-Giver, Death-Wielder, and Regeneratrix. These included streams,

---

[123] Moss 2005: 201.
[124] Gesell 1985: 15, 35, 51-52, 63.
[125] Gesell 1985: 6.
[126] Marinatos 1993: 7.
[127] Marinatos 1993: 4.

chevrons, zigzags, wavy and serpentine bands, net and checkerboard patterns, waterfowl, bird women, vulva, mothers in animal form, snakes, bucranium, stiff nudes with pubic triangles, spirals, crescents, the bull, bee, and butterfly.

Gesell found the attributes of the Goddess in the vases in the shape of women with their hands under breasts with open nipples (to allow the pouring of liquids) which indicated to her the worship of a fertility and birth Goddess; in the central figure of the Old Palace period Phaistos fruit stand (a shallow bowl on a stand), holding flowers in her upraised hands and surrounded by dancers/adorants, whom Gesell identified as the Goddess of the Lilies; from that same period, the images of birds on stone libation tables that led Gesell to posit that a Sky Goddess was also worshipped; the Snake Goddesses from the Temple Repositories at Knossos, found with a large variety of marine and animal life, that led her to propose an Earth Goddess; the pillar crypts with their symbols of double axes and bulls that spoke to Gesell of a Chthonic Goddess and Goddess of Earthquakes; and the Goddesses 'with upraised hands' with their attributes of snakes and birds, that led Gesell to conclude that the Earth and Sky Goddess was venerated well into the Postpalatial period.

The previous section also listed some of the attributes that Marinatos assigns to the Goddess, namely, vessels for libations that resemble a mother holding a baby, symbolizing the Goddess's association with sustenance; bird and animal figurines and frescos indicating the Goddess's role as protectress of nature; frescoes and sealings with the motif of flowers, plants, especially the lily, and trees as further evidence of her close identification with nature; the Snake Goddesses, representing the chthonic aspect of the Goddess; and marine life, linked to the Goddess's role in regeneration.

One attribute or symbol of the Goddess that neither Gesell, Marinatos, nor Moss discuss, linked to the Goddess's role in regeneration, is the bee. The bee as the epiphany of the Goddess is a common symbol in Minoan Crete. Gimbutas discusses the bee as a symbol of regeneration in *The Living Goddesses,* writing that 'the bee is . . . [an] important regenerative symbol inherited from Neolithic and then Minoan times.'[128] Why were bees chosen as a symbol of regeneration? Gimbutas begins a lengthy discussion of the bee and butterfly as epiphanies of the Great Goddess by noting the ancient belief that bees were begotten by bulls. She quotes Antigonos of Karystos (250 BC), one of the earliest writers to observe that the bull putrefies and 'is resolved into bees.' 'The idea of a "life in death" . . . is expressed by the belief that the life of the bull passed into that of the bees.'[129]

Yet another reason bees were associated with regeneration, according to Gimbutas, is because the bee has 'antennae like bull horns and wings in the form of a lunar crescent.'[130] Finally, 'the periodic swarming and activity associated with the production of honey,'[131] must have also contributed to the use of the bee as a symbol of regeneration. Gimbutas details the many instances of the bee in Minoan iconography. Among the most well-known are: the famous gold pendant from Malia showing two bees holding a large drop of honey (seventeenth century BC); the onyx gem from Knossos portraying the Bee Goddess, flanked by winged dogs with

---

[128] Gimbutas 1999: 157.
[129] Gimbutas 1999: 181.
[130] Gimbutas 1999: 181.
[131] Gimbutas 1999: 183.

bull's horns and a double axe above the Goddess's head (1500 BC); the Early Minoan three sided bead seal of yellow steatite portraying the Goddess in the shape of a bee; and the gold ring of Isopata (found in a tomb near Knossos, dated *c.* 1500 BC) portraying a Goddess and three worshippers, 'usually assumed to be melissae, or bees.'[132] The bee in religious iconography did not end with the Minoans. When the Indo-European invaders learned the art of bee-keeping from the Minoans, 'They . . . inherited the mythical image of the Goddess as a bee, the Goddess of Regeneration, the image of her virgin priestesses or nymphs as bees and many other myths and beliefs connected with the bee and honey.'[133] Thus the symbol of the bee is found in Mycenaean and Classical Greek art as well. Gimbutas points out a Mycenaean gem of Minoan workmanship in which two genii clad in bee skins hold jugs over horns from which a new life springs in the shape of a plant.[134] She then traces the bee symbolism to Greek jewelry of the seventh to fifth centuries, to a Boeotian amphora dating from 700 BC, and to Artemis of Ephesus. The cult animal of Artemis of Ephesus was the bee, and Gimbutas postulates that 'the organization of the sanctuary in classical times rested on the symbolic analogy of a beehive.'[135]

Not only was the social organization of the temple of Artemis at Ephesus modeled on the 'symbolic analogy of a beehive,' but it is claimed that the social organization of Minoan civilization was as well. Author Susan Evasdaughter has called attention to the fact that in addition to being a symbol for regeneration, the bee was an important symbol in Minoan religion

> because its social organisation mirrored that of the Bronze Age Cretans. In both instances the success of the whole population was dependent on the cooperation of all its elements. Each individual worked for the good of the whole group.[136]

Evasdaughter also notes other ways in which the sacred associations of the bee continued from Minoan Crete into classical times: 'the omphalos at Delphi is shaped like a beehive and Pythia, the chief oracular priestess there, was called the Delphic bee.'[137]

I am persuaded by Gimbutas's arguments in favor of the bee as a representation of regeneration and the regenerative aspect of the Goddess. I also find extremely interesting archaeologist Sinclair Hood's comment that 'the ancients normally thought of the queen bee as king and described her as such.'[138] The bee as a representation of the Minoan priestess-queen is a powerful symbol. Perhaps in addition to its role as a symbol of regeneration, the bee was also a symbol of the clan mothers who guided Crete. It was perhaps with one of the clan mothers that the famous Malia pendant was buried in the Chrysolakkos burial enclosure.

Marina Moss lists many of the same attributes of the Goddess(es) as does Marinatos. The snake is an important attribute which Moss associates with 'the earth, the Underworld, regeneration and renewal, as well as being associated with the protection of the house.'[139] In Crete, the

---

[132] Gimbutas 1999: 183-185.
[133] Gimbutas 1999: 184-185.
[134] Gimbutas 1999: 184.
[135] Gimbutas 1999: 183.
[136] Evasdaughter 1996: 143.
[137] Evasdaughter 1996: 145.
[138] Hood 1976: 70.
[139] Moss 2005: 68.

snake is only associated with the female.[140] The bird (especially the dove) as a Minoan religious symbol is associated with a Bird Goddess, and with a sky deity.[141] Plants and vegetation, which figure so prominently in Marinatos's understanding of the Goddess's attributes, do so as well for Moss, who often finds a Goddess of Vegetation present. Animals of all sorts are important attributes as well, in Moss's opinion. Discussing the cat on the headdress of one of the Knossian Snake Goddesses, she writes that it may signify that the Goddess 'has power over this animal,'[142] which is another way to say that the Goddess is the Mistress of the Animals (discussed in more detail later.)

Under the subject of the Goddess's attributes, Moss includes items which can also fall under the category of cult equipment. The cult objects of the bovine rhyta, sacral knot, horns of consecration, and double axe (which as Moss notes sometimes metamorphosizes into a butterfly—a symbol of renewal), are linked by Moss not only with the Minoan Goddess, but also with the Egyptian Goddess Hathor, a fertility goddess responsible for the growth of plants, protection, and life itself.[143] The sacral knot Moss not only links to the Minoan Goddess and Hathor but additionally to the Egyptian Goddess Taweret, a birthing Goddess, and to the Sumerian Inanna. While she does not believe the Minoans adopted the Egyptian worship of Hathor wholesale, Moss does believe the worship of Hathor had some effect on Minoan religion.

> While we cannot be certain that the Minoans worshipped Hathor as such, it seems that they found her attributes, symbolism and nature appealing and relevant. There seems to be too significant an amount of directly comparable combinations of iconography here for this to be attributed to chance. . . Again, it is to be stressed that we do not know if the Minoans worshipped Hathor, or whether this evidence points to the Minoanisation of an Egyptian goddess along with her iconography and attributes in the Bronze Age on Crete.[144]

In addition to what I have called 'attributes,' there are other ways in which the Minoan Goddess may be identified in iconography. Position, size, gesture, clothing, human and animal attendants, and mythological or supernatural creatures (such as the griffin or sphinx) are all important factors in determining whether or not a Goddess is present (in contrast to a human woman). When the female figure in a fresco or sealing is seated on a platform, or a rock, or under a tree, especially if she is also more elaborately dressed, or larger in size than the other figures in the composition, or occupies the central or focal area of the work, and has female or fantastic or heraldic animal attendants, it is very likely that she is a representation of the Goddess.

Collin Renfrew in his work, *Archaeology of Cult*, set forth some guidelines for identifying deities in the iconography. There he proposed that the following criteria are important: first, scale and number:

---

[140] Moss 2005: 200.
[141] Moss 2005: 152.
[142] Moss 2005: 69.
[143] Moss 2005: 46, 204.
[144] Moss 2005: 213.

A single image of great size in a religious context, for instance larger than life size, might readily be taken as a depiction of a god. But in fact colossal size is not enough. . . . Yet if the single, very large image occupies a key, central location within a sanctuary, the case is clearly very much stronger.[145]

Renfrew's second criterion is

a highly asymmetrical role emphasized markedly by attention focusing devices. An image, focally placed, without rivals for attention and accompanied by offerings which may plausibly be interpreted as dedicated to it, may well qualify as a cult image.[146]

His third criterion is gesture, which he says is often ambiguous. Renfrew adds, however, that gestures 'displaying power must . . . be taken as an indication of the deity, since such gestures would seem inappropriate in a votive.'[147] His fourth criterion, attributes, he does not discuss in detail, however, I have reviewed these extensively above in the works of other archaeologists who specialize in the archaeology of Minoan religion. Renfrew does give one example of an attribute and how it can be used in identifying a deity. 'A cult image with the sun's rays, or with the moon's crescent might be regarded as depicting respectively the sun or moon deity, or a deity with the sun or moon as attribute.'[148] Finally, he lists mythical or fantastic beasts and notes that 'the entity who dominates them or is flanked by them, must generally have divine powers.'[149]

Renfrew's criterion of scale, number, size, focus, attributes, and mythical companion beasts are relatively straightforward. The issue of gesture is a bit trickier. A great deal of work has been done by archaeologists to classify the gestures of votive figurines and thus differentiate them from deities. Moss writes that some gestures, such as saluting, arms crossed over the chest, or arms outstretched, indicate votaries appealing to the deity or engaged in ritual.[150] She believes that 'the variety of poses may reflect the different ways in which supplicants appealed to the deity, or may depict gestures used at different times in "ritual."'[151]

Marinatos has attempted to codify the gestures of Minoan priestesses. She observes that in Minoan iconography, a priestess can be identified by, among other criteria, two characteristic gestures: in the first one, one arm is bent and the other arm hangs loose or extended to the side, and in the second gesture both hands are on the hips.[152]

Turning to the differences in gesture between priestesses and Goddesses, Marinatos emphasizes that differentiating between them in the iconography can be difficult because priestesses assume the characteristics of the divinity.[153] Nevertheless, she believes there are ways in which the priestess seems to be differentiated from the Goddess. One is that although

---

[145] Renfrew 1985: 23.
[146] Renfrew 1985: 23.
[147] Renfrew 1985: 23.
[148] Renfrew 1985: 23.
[149] Renfrew 1985: 23-24.
[150] Moss 2005: 100.
[151] Moss 2005: 100.
[152] Marinatos 1993: 185.
[153] Marinatos 1993: 184.

the 'high priestess'[154] is often larger, or in some other way different from other mortals, she is not so different as to warrant the label 'Goddess.' In Marinatos's discussion of the 'high priestess,' which is based on her analysis of eight gold rings, and some sealings, not only is the priestess identified by the two characteristic gestures listed above, but she is also either in the center of what can be described in several of the rings as a ritual action—with other figures on the periphery shaking a sacred tree or bending over a baetyl (actions meant to invoke the deity), or the priestess is portrayed either at the beginning or conclusion of the ritual—alone with the tree or baetyl. In all cases, 'She is upright; her gesture is commanding . . . she does not directly participate in the action . . . the humans are [not] . . . in awe of her. It seems that she controls and directs the ritual.'[155]

Marinatos has also proposed some formulae to help in determining when we are seeing a Goddess in Minoan iconography. One she calls the 'offering scheme'; this is 'a pictorial formula in which worshipers bring offerings to a deity.'[156] In the most common Minoan offering scenes, the Goddess 'manifests herself within a natural environment, seated under a tree or on a rock.'[157] She receives flowers or some other type of offering, and can have animals in attendance. In a sub-category of the 'offering scheme,' rather than being seated on a rock or under a tree, the Goddess is seated on a man-made construction, a type of (usually tripartite) platform. 'She always wears the flounced skirt; the breasts are bare. . . . When her adorants are not animals, they are mostly women.'[158]

Another formula Marinatos has developed to help identify the Goddess is the 'transportation of the Goddess.'[159] In this iconography she either descends from the sky and is represented as a hovering image who is descending, or she arrives by boat (in one seal the boat is in the shape of a dragon, in another a sacred tree is depicted on the boat), or chariot which is often drawn by griffins. Marinatos has found that the Goddess is also often shown in the gesture of feeding or petting an animal.[160]

In addition to the formulae proposed by Marinatos, there are other gestures archaeologists associate with the Minoan Goddess. One common gesture attributable to the Goddess is that of greeting, blessing, or benefaction. This gesture is especially apparent in the Postpalatial period LM IIIB-C, c. 1350-1070 BC, in the Goddesses with Upraised Arms figurines. Sometimes the Minoan Goddess is shown grasping animals by their tails or necks in her role as Mistress of Nature or Mistress of the Animals. Such a gesture certainly falls into Renfrew's category of 'displaying power.'

The Knossos Snake Goddesses are a prime example of the gesture of the Goddess grasping animals (or in this case snakes) and as Mistress of Nature 'displaying power.' Speaking of the Snake Goddesses from the Knossos Temple Repositories, Moss writes:

---

[154] Marinatos 1993: 184.
[155] Marinatos 1993: 187.
[156] Marinatos 1993: 160.
[157] Marinatos 1993: 160.
[158] Marinatos 1993: 162.
[159] Marinatos 1993: 162.
[160] Marinatos 1993: 154.

As snakes are among the most feared creatures in the world, these figures which show women or goddesses handling snakes without trepidation suggest that they are exhibiting some kind of super-human qualities. . . . It has been argued that the handling of wild beasts is a sign of divine power over Nature.[161]

Moss also reminds us that the snake peering over the top of the hat of one of the Knossos Snake Goddesses is reminiscent of the uraeus serpent worn on the headdresses of Egyptian pharaohs and divinities and symbolizing, for the Egyptians, 'supreme power.'[162]

The question of gestures appropriate to the Goddess is a subject of controversy among Aegean archaeologists. Archaeologist Janet L. Crowley argues in 'Images of Power in the Bronze Age Aegean,' that there are only three instances when we can identify the Minoan Goddess with any degree of certainty and without additional information 'possibly from other sources:'[163] (1) when she appears with an animal familiar, which Crowley defines as 'a living creature (either from this world or from the world of the imagination)' that is in a 'symbiotic relationship'[164] with her; (2) when a female figure exhibits 'hybridization,' that is when the artist has rendered the body of a human with the head of a bird or animal;[165] or (3) when a female figure appears in an 'Audience Scene,' that is a scene of homage or procession.[166]

Aegeanists Carol G. Thomas and Michael Wedde in their humorously titled work 'Desperately Seeking Potnia' have argued that 'the pictorial evidence offers few consistent traits associated exclusively with deities.'[167] They offer that the only certain criterion for identifying a deity is what they term 'behavior,' and the only 'behavior' they believe supplies certain identification of a deity is that of hovering in the air: 'a small hovering anthropomorphic figure is a deity.'[168] Such hovering figures are portrayed on at least half a dozen Minoan seals, sealings and rings from the New Palace Period and are discussed in Chapter 6. Thomas and Wedde conclude their work by noting that what is needed in Aegean archaeology is an explicitly formulated methodology, one that is not based on later religious developments, nor on trying to match archaeological data with Linear B texts.

Where does this leave us? In addition to cult symbols, cult equipment, cult objects, and attributes, discussed earlier, as ways in which to identify the Minoan Mother Goddess, Renfrew's criteria: scale, number, size, focus, attributes, mythical companion beasts and gestures, are extremely useful as well. The above discussion about gesture has sought to differentiate between the gestures of votaries and priestesses and Goddesses. While Thomas and Wedde recognize only one sure way of identifying a Goddess—she must be floating in the air, Crowley has supplied others: she must have fantastic animals with her, she can be shown as part-human, part animal/bird, and she is being paid homage or is the object of a procession. Crowley's categories can be used in addition to Renfrew's criteria (see earlier discussion in this chapter) and several of them certainly overlap with his. Renfrew, like Crowley, also includes

---

[161] Moss 2005: 68.
[162] Moss 2005: 68.
[163] Crowley 1995: 2:483.
[164] Crowley 1995: 2:480.
[165] Crowley 1995: 2:477.
[166] Crowley 1995: 2:487.
[167] Thomas and Wedde 2001: 6.
[168] Thomas and Wedde 2001: 6.

mythical companion beasts as a sign of divinity, and his category of 'focus' is similar to Crowley's category of 'Audience Scene.' Marinatos's discussion is also helpful in distinguishing votaries from priestesses, and priestesses from Goddesses.

I conclude by noting that dress can often help one differentiate a Goddess from a mortal. Marinatos has observed that certain ornamental motifs such as griffins and bucrania, which have a symbolic character, can pertain only to the Goddess.[169] It must also be noted that in frescos at least the dress of the Goddess is always the most elaborate of all the women present. For example, in the 'Crocus Gatherers' fresco from Thera, which is discussed in detail in Chapter 5, the face and clothing of the Goddess seated on the tripartite platform are decorated with crocus flowers. Around her neck she wears a triple necklace with beads and duck and dragonfly pendants. Marinatos identifies her as a 'mistress of nature.'[170] Paul Rehak has noted that she 'is currently the most richly dressed and bejeweled figure to survive in Aegean art.'[171]

I will be using a combination of the markers discussed in the preceding pages: scale, number, size, focus, attributes, mythical companion beasts, gesture, and dress to distinguish Goddesses or gods, priestesses or priests, other votaries or devotees, and ordinary people in ritual scenes.

The pantheon of deities: one Goddess or many? Minoan gods

Before beginning to look at the evidence for the Goddess in Crete, I want to pause here to synthesize what has been said in the previous sections of this chapter, to reiterate my methodology, explain my understanding/definition of the Mother Goddess, and summarize how Aegean archaeologists have characterized the Goddess and how my own characterization of her differs from theirs. I also want to address the worship of a Minoan god. I turn first to the synthesis.

In this chapter it has been shown that there is substantial evidence to argue that the original settlers of Bronze Age Crete came to the island from Anatolia during the Neolithic Age, bringing the worship of the Mother Goddess with them, and that her worship in Neolithic Crete was characterized by female figurines. The attributes of the Anatolian Mother Goddess, especially the bird and lion, were discussed, because by the Bronze Age, as we shall see, those attributes were attributes of the Minoan Mother Goddess as well. In this context the work of Lynn Roller, archaeologist of ancient Anatolia, who studied representations of the deity, cult monuments, votive offerings, sacred spaces, and inscriptions (which for her time period, 9th century BC to 4th century AD, are plentiful) to come to her understanding of the Phrygian Mother Goddess, is reviewed. Also discussed is Mellaart's work at Çatal Hüyük, since there is Neolithic evidence for the worship of a Mother Goddess there; and some of the earliest settlers to Knossos came during the Neolithic from the region of Çatal Hüyük.

The methodology of some of the most prominent archaeologists working in the field of Minoan religion and the Goddess was reviewed in order to determine not only how they viewed the

---

[169] Thomas and Wedde 2001: 141.
[170] Marinatos 1984: 70. In an article published in 2018, Marinatos refers to the Theran Goddess as a 'solar deity.' (Marinatos 2018: 85).
[171] Rehak 2004: 92.

Goddess—as one or many—but primarily how they propose to recognize her. Particularly considered were the work of Gimbutas, Gesell, Marinatos, and Moss.

Since the main methodological tool of this work is archaeomythology, I look in this chapter at archaeomythologist Marija Gimbutas's decipherment of the symbolic system around the worship of the Goddess of Old Europe/Anatolia, and summarize those signs and symbols that characterize the Goddess as Giver, Taker, and Renewer of Life. Many of the same attributes and symbols that Gesell, Marinatos, Moss, and others associate with the Minoan Goddess are found in Gimbutas's analysis as well. However, Gimbutas's understanding of the Goddess, one Goddess with a Triple Aspect, includes many more attributes than those found in the works of the others. Moreover, in Gimbutas's view, the attributes of the Minoan Goddess can be seen as reflected in a classification system of symbols of the Goddess of Old Europe/Anatolia comprised of four groups: Life-Giving, Renewing and Eternal Earth, Death and Regeneration, and Energy and Unfolding. Thus in addition to birds and Bird Women; goats, deer and lions; fantastic animals like the griffin or sphinx; lilies, trees, marine life, and snakes; Gimbutas includes streams, chevrons, zig-zags, wavy and serpentine bands, net and checkerboard patterns, symbols of the vulva, spirals, U-shapes, whirls, crosses, and various four-cornered designs, among others.

Gimbutas, like her colleagues, also looks at the interplay of find site, architecture, artifacts, and their relation to each other and to the landscape in order to specify sacred sites. She too takes into account accepted cult symbols, cult equipment, and cult objects.

However, Gimbutas differs from her archaeology colleagues in a number of important ways. First of all, she compares the Minoan archaeological material with a broader range of material, from over a longer time period than do Gesell, Marinatos, or Moss, for she views Minoan Crete as a part of the region comprised of Old Europe/Anatolia—two areas culturally connected during the Neolithic Age. Secondly Gimbutas differs from the others because she frames her investigation within a worldview which, as noted earlier, includes four primary components: a reinterpretation of the Neolithic, an understanding of the Goddess as tri-partite and one with nature, the deciphering of a complex symbolic system formulated around the worship of the Goddess in her various aspects, and an explanation as to how and why the civilization of the Goddess was amalgamated into the civilization that overtook it. Finally Gimbutas differs from the others in that she is using archaeomythology as her methodology: mythology, linguistics, history, and folklore as well as archaeology to interpret the material.

The work of Geraldine C. Gesell presents some wonderful summaries of attributes and symbols of the Goddess as well as architectural features which identify sacred sites (she identifies bench sanctuaries, lustral basins, pillar crypts, and open-air shrines). Like Marinatos and Moss, Gesell identifies the double axe, horns of consecration, bull, bird, snake, agrimi, sacral knot, sun disk and moon crescent as cult symbols of the Goddess(es). Especially helpful is Gesell's classification of cult objects into three groups: representation of the divinity; ritual equipment (offering vessels and rhyta); and votive offerings (figurines, small double axes, miniature vessels, miniature altars, and ceremonial weapons.)

Now to turn to the question of a male deity in Crete. Gesell, like most scholars before her, found little evidence of any male gods. She writes: 'Male figurines representing deities do not appear before the Geometric [*c.* 810-700 BC] period.'[172] On the contrary, she finds that all the evidence points to a female divinity, although Gesell is not sure whether she is one or many.[173] Based on the attributes Gesell has identified she posits one Goddess or more representing fertility and childbirth, a general protectress of women and women's affairs, Protectress of the Sky, an Earth Goddess or universal Mother, and a chthonic deity.

Nanno Marinatos combines structuralism, semiotics, anthropology of religion, and cultural anthropology along with archaeological data to learn about Minoan religion, laying great stress on comparison with contemporary Near Eastern cultures. With that methodology she determines the attributes of the Minoan Goddess as including: birds; animals—especially goats, deer, and lions; fantastic animals like the griffin; lilies, trees, marine life, and snakes; and thus she defines the Goddess's role as that of Sustainer, Protectress of Nature, Goddess of Vegetation, and Goddess of the Three Realms of Nature: earth, air and sea. Marinatos also provides a list of the cult equipment that has come to be thought of by archaeologists as the symbols of Minoan religion: horns of consecration, double axes, rhyta, libation tables, stone altars, offering tables, sacrificial tables, conical cups, stone maces, kernoi, and snake tubes. She supplies a convenient list of architectural items that indicate a sacred site: bench sanctuary, lustral basin or adyton, pillar crypt, dining shrine, and balustrade shrine.

Marinatos intimates that Evans was correct: there was only one Goddess. She asserts, 'there is an essential unity in the symbolism which connects the goddess with nature in all its manifestations.'[174] However, she goes on to say that the question of polytheism versus monotheism will probably never be solved. Disagreeing with Nilsson who noted that a male god seldom appears in Minoan iconography, Marinatos posits that the Minoans worshipped gods, 'although the representations of gods are fewer in number than those of goddesses.'[175] Marinatos believes that gods were associated with the towns and their institutions; she bases this hypothesis on the Master Impression sealing discussed at length in Chapter 7. She also sees the gods associated with nature. Here she is relying on seals, sealings, and rings which depict the male with mastery over animals. However, unlike the Goddess, the function of the god, according to Marinatos, was 'to control nature, not to nourish it.'[176] Here I would disagree for I believe, based on the iconographical evidence, that the Goddess both controlled, because she was the mother of the natural world and generated the cycles of nature, and nourished nature.

In *Minoan Religion* Marinatos writes that the Minoan gods are generally portrayed in one of three roles: Master of the Animals, hunter, or 'young god with staff.' As a Master of the Animals he has short curly hair, a broad chest, both arms are extended holding animal(s), and he wears a codpiece and belt at the waist. Another guise of the male god, according to Marinatos, is as hunter. As the hunter his attributes are a spear and shield, a bow or only a long staff.[177] In this guise he wears a kilt and often a peaked cap. Sometimes he is also depicted with one or two lions, not holding them but standing beside them. Finally he is also portrayed as a 'young god

---

[172] Gesell 1985: 61.
[173] Gesell 1985: 64.
[174] Marinatos 1993: 165.
[175] Marinatos 1993: 174.
[176] Marinatos 1993: 174.
[177] Marinatos 1993: 169.

with staff.'[178] In this role he has long hair, 'a slim but robust figure,'[179] a codpiece, and he holds a staff or spear in his outstretched arm.

Few of the cult objects, cult equipment, or cult symbols discussed at length above can be associated with Minoan gods. The rich vocabulary of iconography one finds with the Minoan Goddess is absent from portrayals of gods. In one famous sealing from Kydonia, interpreted by some scholars as a god in the guise of the Master of the Animals, the god does stand on a pair of horns of consecration. In several sealings the god is portrayed in front of a tree shrine with votaries of both sexes. However, the Goddess is also depicted with tree shrines and votaries and, as was discussed at length above, the horns of consecration are one of the symbols of the Goddess.

Marinatos substantially changes her view of Minoan gods and their attributes in her 2010 work *Minoan Kingship and the Solar Goddess*. In that book she argues that Minoan iconography made no distinction between the Minoan king and the god. Taking nearly all representations of males in the iconography to represent the king/god, Marinatos writes that the Minoan god must be seen as a 'bright star in the constellation of Minoan deities.'[180] In order to make her case for this 'bright star,' Marinatos, who believes there was a shared political and religious ideology among the regions of the ancient Near East, including Crete, compares Minoan iconography to that of the Near East, and then uses the mythology of the Near East to interpret Minoan iconography. She concludes that the Minoans had a storm god at the head of their pantheon and that he also served as a representation of the Minoan king. The book is discussed at length in Chapter 7, as is my critique of it.

Marina Moss's work, which utilizes the cognitive archaeology approach, looks at archaeological material found in religious contexts from the Middle to Late Minoan period, which she defines as *c.* 2050/2000 to *c.* 1000 BC.[181] Surveying Minoan settlement sites, palaces, hill sanctuaries, cave sanctuaries, and rural settlements, she presents for each a description of the architecture, a reference to significant features in the landscape, the context of the archaeological finds and their association with one another, a description and discussion of the finds, and, like Marinatos, a comparison of the Cretan artifacts with artifacts from contemporary eastern Mediterranean cultures. On the basis of these criteria she draws conclusions about whether a Goddess or god was worshipped at each site.

Moss provides a list of cult equipment similar to that of Marinatos, and a list of attributes and symbols of the Goddess similar to those of Marinatos as well: the snake, birds, plants and vegetation, and animals. However, Moss draws some very different conclusions about the Goddess than does Marinatos, for in contrast to one Goddess of Nature, Moss finds numerous Goddesses, including: a Bird Goddess, Goddess of the Dead, Dove Goddess, Sun Goddess, Mountain Mother, Goddess of Renewal, Snake Goddess, Stellar Goddess, and Goddess of Vegetation/ Agriculture.

---

[178] Marinatos 1993: 171.
[179] Marinatos 1993: 173.
[180] Marinatos 2010: 167.
[181] Moss 2005: 1.

Moss also finds several gods, although relatively very few of them. One she terms a 'god of initiation' and finds evidence of his worship at Mt. Jouktas, a peak sanctuary, and in the Idaean and Psychro caves. Moss bases her hypothesis that a 'god of initiation' was worshipped at Mt. Jouktas mainly on two pieces of evidence. One is the large number of votive figurines of males with long hair (which research has equated with mature young men) that were found at the site. Moss believes that they, along with the real and non-functional weapons excavated at Mt. Jouktas, are indicative of male initiation rites. The other piece of evidence is a Roman inscription to Zeus. 'The idea of male initiation rites at peak sanctuaries seems reasonable, but all the more so at Jouktas which, in later times, was associated with the young Zeus.'[182]

Also at the Idaean cave, figurines of young men and non-functional weapons, as well as the fact that the cave 'has a long tradition of the veneration of Zeus,'[183] lead Moss to posit that a 'god of initiation' was among the deities worshiped there. One wonders why the 'long tradition of the veneration of Zeus' does not lead Moss to consider a god of vegetation, consort of the Goddess, rather than a god of initiation. The figurines of young men and weapons bring to my mind the myth of the birth and seclusion of the god Zeus, accompanied by the boisterous dancing of the Kouretes. I believe Zeus in Crete should be associated with the myth of the death and rebirth of the vegetation god. If one wishes to find a god of initiation worshipped at the Idaean cave, one might postulate that the initiation was tied to the celebration of the dying and rising vegetation god.

It was R. F. Willetts, in his book *Cretan Cults and Festivals,* who explained that the god Zeus, who has come down to us through Classical Greek mythology as the supreme head of a pantheon of gods and Goddesses, was originally, as Cretan Zeus, a vegetation god. 'The name Zeus is undoubtedly Indo-European and we must suppose that it was applied to a Minoan deity whose role and function can be discerned from an enduring store of legend, myth and cult practice.'[184]

From the 'enduring store of myth and legend,' Willetts and other mythographers have deduced that originally the name Zeus belonged to the group of young male companions of the Cretan Goddess—her consort and off-spring who died and were born again. The myth of the young god Zeus's birth in Crete is the basis for the interpretation of Cretan Zeus as a vegetation god. As I said earlier, the story goes that the Goddess Rhea, to prevent her husband Kronos from devouring their infant son Zeus, hid him in a cave in Crete where he was attended by nymphs, who fed him milk and honey, and was protected by the Kouretes, mythical male dancers who clashed their shields and swords in order that the crying child would not be heard by Kronos. As Nilsson tells us, the weapons, far from indicating the dancers were war-like, were there to be used against ghosts and daemons and the dance to promote fertility; the dance of the Kouretes is a fertility charm.[185]

Mythographers like Willetts and Hawkes corroborate the interpretation of Zeus as a vegetation god and consort of the Goddess with Minoan seals dated to the sixteenth and fifteenth centuries BC (from Knossos, Archanes and Mochlos) which portray scenes with the theme of the death of

---

[182] Moss 2005: 100.
[183] Moss 2005: 125.
[184] Willetts 1962: 116.
[185] Nilsson 1949: 546.

the vegetation god, as well as with further archaeological finds and later myths and legends. Willetts explains:

> It is quite likely . . . that the death and resurrection of the god, consort of the goddess, was prominent in the myth and enacted ritual of Bronze Age Crete as elsewhere in Levant; and a number of these metal signet rings could portray scenes with this theme. On a bronze signet from Knossos a goddess stands outside a shrine or enclosure of squared masonry with a sacred tree in or behind it. A female attendant seems to have climbed the wall of the enclosure and is pulling down a bough of the tree. Behind the goddess, stooping as if in sorrow is an object shaped like a jar of the sort used for burials in many parts of Crete during the Middle Minoan period from *c.* 2000 BC onward.[186]

Similarly, reporting the myth of Zeus's birth in Crete, Vasilakis notes:

> The most interesting of the many important aspects of this myth is the role played in it by the wife-mother Rhea and the nymphs, who are of fundamental importance to life and survival in a matriarchal society like that of ancient Crete, especially in its earliest phases.[187]

Vasilakis has made a very important point about how essential myth can be for a fuller understanding of Minoan Crete, for he suggests that the roles of Rhea and the nymphs Amaltheia, Ida, and Adrasteia in the ancient Zeus myth reflect the important role of Goddesses and women in matriarchal societies.

To return to Moss and her discussion of the Minoan 'god of initiation,' at another sacred cave, the cave at Psychro, the deposition of functional weapons leads Moss to assert that male initiation rites took place there as well. However, because of the presence of bronze figurines, a bronze plaque (depicting the sun and moon, a fish, a dove, three horns of consecration with trees between the horns, a male dancing, and a tree in the center of the composition), a scarab (dating to MM IA-MM II),[188] various items made of terra cotta including storage vessels, cups, vases with reliefs of birds and agrimia, lamps, bowls, jugs, a bovine head rhyton, figurines of people and animals (mainly cattle), and, very importantly, a fragment of a female figure which if reconstructed would measure three meters in height making it 'unprecedented in Minoan archaeology,'[189] Moss believes that a Goddess of Renewal, a Dove Goddess, a Guardian of the Sun (a female Goddess), and a solar god were also worshipped at the cave of Psychro.

As for the other god Moss identifies, the solar/sky god, in addition to the cave of Psychro, Moss finds evidence for his worship at the temple-palace of Malia, and at the peak sanctuaries of Mt. Jouktas, Petsophas, and Traostalos. Her evidence consists of statuettes of young men with their fists to their chests (however, this is generally the mark of a votary); mason marks (two of them) in forms that appear to be solar symbols, but could be stellar symbols; and beetle figurines, which she associates with the male sun at dawn—an idea she adopts from Egyptian religion.

---

[186] Willetts 1977: 117.
[187] Vasilakis 2001: 34.
[188] Moss 2005: 138.
[189] Moss 2005: 136.

To summarize Moss's discussion of Minoan gods, she identifies only two: a god of initiation, and a solar/sky god, and tells us that 'there are a large number of deities [she lists five: healing, cattle, maritime, war, stellar] to whom it is not possible to assign a gender as the evidence and iconography are enigmatic.'[190] Moss finds that the gods she has identified as a god of initiation and a solar/sky god are worshipped beginning in MM IA, *c.* 2000 BC.[191] It is interesting to note that in her analysis of these gods and their places of worship, there is evidence to show that even in the places where the initiation and solar/sky god were most revered, the peak sanctuaries and caves, their popularity was rivaled by that of a Goddess whom Moss calls the Goddess of Renewal. She is worshipped in far more caves than the male gods are, and in approximately the same number of peak sanctuaries, and over a longer time period.

Before leaving the subject of Minoan gods, one more candidate for that role should be mentioned: the Palaikastro kouros, an ivory statuette that was found in fragments at the site of the Minoan settlement of Palaikastro, and dated to LM IB, *c.* 1480-1425.[192] Recovered between 1987 and 1990, and thus a relatively new discovery, the kouros is described by some as an adorant, and by others as a youthful god. The excavators have interpreted him as an early Zeus because of evidence for the worship of Zeus elsewhere on the site from the seventh century BC onward. The identity of the figurine is still debated, and the seven hundred year time gap between the dating of the kouros and evidence for the worship of Zeus, makes the figurine's identification as Zeus problematic.

To summarize the above discussion of Minoan gods, it must be noted that few of the cult objects, cult equipment, or cult symbols discussed at length above in conjunction with the Minoan Goddess can be associated with Minoan gods. The rich vocabulary of iconography one finds with the Minoan Goddess is absent from portrayals of gods. Although Moss makes much of the presence of votaries, and of solar and stellar symbols as identifiers of gods, votaries, both male and female, are associated with the Minoan Goddess, and solar and stellar symbols are part of her repertory as well. Only the beetle remains as a symbol unique to the Minoan male god—if Moss is correct in her interpretation of that symbol.

In my own analysis of the artifacts in the next chapters, I shall be taking into consideration the list of architectural features, cult symbols, cult equipment, cult objects, and attributes and symbols of the Goddess that have been identified by Gesell, Marinatos, Moss, and others. As an archaeomythologist, I will be expanding my view of the symbolism of the Goddess as Gimbutas proposed. Although I am not an Egyptologist, I will be making comparisons between Minoan and Egyptian cult symbols, equipment, objects, and attributes and symbols of the Goddess where relevant, as well as between those of Minoan Crete and other Near Eastern cultures; and between Minoan Crete and other regions of Old Europe/Anatolia. Finally, as an archaeomythologist, I will be using the disciplines of archaeology, mythology, linguistics, and history to make my interpretations of the archaeological record, iconography, and sacred sites.

---

[190] Moss 2005: 184.
[191] Moss 2005: 188.
[192] Moss 2005: 42.

The Minoan Mother Goddess defined

At this point I would like to turn my attention to a discussion of how I understand the term I am using to describe the Goddess of the Minoans: Mother Goddess. In using this term I do not mean to limit it to representations only of a literal mother and child—of which there are relatively few examples in Minoan Crete. Such representations are certainly to be included in my understanding. Also included in my understanding of the Minoan Mother Goddess is the Goddess as nurturer, birth-giver, and concerned with pregnancy and fertility, as illustrated, for example, in the Prepalatial vessels which portray a mother holding a jug like a baby. Additionally, I have a broader cultural meaning in mind. I refer back to Lynn Roller's description of the Phrygian Mother Goddess:

> We seem to see a goddess whose position of power over the natural environment, rather than any specifically maternal function, was the chief factor that gave her the status of a Mother.[193]

I believe that the Minoan Goddess's 'position of power over the natural environment', or her position of power as generatrix of the cycles of nature, a phrase I prefer, is one aspect of her role which identifies her as a Mother Goddess, and that this aspect of her role could be described, in Gimbutas's terminology, as Life-Giver.

Another aspect of the Mother Goddess's role and my understanding of her is implicit in Roller's statement about the Phrygian Mother Goddess as 'a figure of power and protection, able to touch on many aspects of life and mediate between the boundaries of the known and unknown.'[194] My understanding of the term Mother Goddess also includes that ability 'to touch on many aspects of life and mediate between the boundaries of the known and unknown,' which I read as being able to mediate between life, death, and rebirth. Thus the Mother Goddess in my definition is a mediator between life, death, and rebirth and the endless cycles of life, death, rebirth, and regeneration. In identifying her as such I am also identifying her with Gimbutas's Goddess in her Triple Aspect.

Finally, my definition of the Minoan Mother Goddess also includes a cosmological aspect. The Goddess's role as protectress, her ability to mediate between the boundaries of the known and unknown, her role as nurturer, embodiment of fertility, Life-Giver, Death-Bringer and Regeneratrix, her oneness with all of life, extends beyond the earthly plane into the cosmos. The sun, moon and stellar imagery in Minoan art illustrates this as does the bird imagery, and the Minoan Goddess's cosmological aspect is acknowledged by Gesell who calls her a 'sky goddess'[195]; Moss who hypothesizes a possible 'Stellar Goddess'[196]; Marinatos who posits a Solar Goddess[197]; and Goodison who emphasizes the importance of sun and moon imagery in Bronze Age religion, and the close association of female imagery with solar imagery in Minoan iconography.[198]

---

[193] Roller 1999: 6.
[194] Roller 1999: 113.
[195] Gesell 1985: 1, 45, 65.
[196] Moss 2005: 206.
[197] Marinatos 2010: Chapter 12.
[198] Goodison 1990: 302.

Gesell's understanding of the Minoan Goddess(es) as concerned with fertility and childbirth, as a universal Mother or Earth Goddess, Protectress of the Sky, and chthonic deity, speaks to me of a Goddess with three aspects: She who is responsible for life, death, and regeneration—which is how I understand the term Mother Goddess.

Marinatos emphasized the Minoan Goddess's role as a Goddess of Nature and a Nurturer of Nature. This role as Nature Herself and Nurturer of All is a part of what I understand the Mother Goddess's role to be, and it is encompassed in the term Life-Giver.

Moss's categories of what she sees as the Minoan Goddesses are plural: Bird Goddess, Goddess of the Dead, Dove Goddess, Goddess of Initiation, Mountain Mother, Goddess of Renewal, Snake Goddess, Stellar Goddess, and Goddess of Vegetation/Agriculture. I believe rather that these are aspects and markers of the Mother Goddess in her triple aspect, and that the Mother Goddess encompasses all the various attributes Moss would like to assign to many Goddesses.

Conclusion

Chapter 4 has attempted to illustrate that there is substantial evidence to argue that Neolithic Crete was settled by people from Anatolia who brought the worship of the Mother Goddess with them. It has discussed the methodology of the most prominent scholars working in the field of Minoan religion and the Goddess, and determined whether they identify one Goddess or many. In particular it has focused upon the criteria by which these scholars recognize the Goddess's presence in Minoan society. The criteria by which a god might be recognized have also been addressed. Finally, the definition of the term Mother Goddess has been re-stated and explained. Chapter 5 will utilize the criteria elaborated upon in this chapter to present the evidence for the worship of the Minoan Mother Goddess in Crete from the Neolithic to the Late Bronze Age.

Chapter 5

Analysis of the Iconography
of the Mother Goddess in Crete

In this chapter I present the iconographic evidence for my identification of the Mother Goddess in Crete beginning with the Neolithic and continuing through to the end of the Bronze Age, c. 6500-1000 BC. Each item—figurine, seal, sealstone, ring, or fresco—is discussed in detail, in chronological sequence, to ascertain how it fits the methodological criteria developed in the previous chapter. Those criteria for ascertaining if the figure in question is a Goddess, are found when the following questions are answered affirmatively: Was the physical location of the artifact (whether architectural context or nature) a shrine or sacred place? Was it discovered in association with 'cult equipment?' Does it have 'cult symbols' typically associated with the Goddess on it? Are the attributes of the Goddess displayed on it, or in association with it? (Cult symbols and attributes often overlap. These include horns of consecration, double axes, rhyta or libation vessels, offering tables, snake tubes, incurved altars, bulls, birds, snakes, agrimia, sacral knots, sun disks and moon crescents, among others.) Are the position, size, gestures, and clothing of the figure portrayed typically indicative of a deity (is she central, larger, giving a gesture of blessing instead of offering, and is her costume more elaborate)? Is the figure clearly female rather than male or of indeterminate sex? Are there human or animal attendants who act as devotees? Does a comparison with similar evidence from other cultures in the eastern Mediterranean or Old Europe/Anatolia indicate the presence or representation of a Goddess? And, finally, is there mythological and historical evidence that is related and can be used to support or further substantiate a claim that this is indeed a Mother Goddess?

Cretan Neolithic Mother Goddess figurines

Figurines that can be interpreted as a Mother Goddess are found in Crete beginning in the Neolithic, c. 6500-3200 BC, and are similar to figurines found around the world dating to that time period. Since the late nineteenth century, when they were discovered by archaeologists, 'The study of prehistoric human figurines has been one of the main focal points of prehistoric archaeological investigations.'[1] At the time of their discovery, and until the 1960s, scholars interpreted such figurines as representatives of the Mother Goddess, or as connected with the worship of the Mother Goddess, and recognized that they supplied concrete evidence concerning Neolithic religious beliefs. Scholars are still generally of the opinion that the figurines supply concrete evidence concerning Neolithic religious beliefs. Archaeologist L. Vance Watrous writes: 'Our knowledge of religion on Crete in this period [Final Neolithic] is dependent on the few known figurines.'[2] Watrous goes on to note that the 'larger (up to 14cm) three-dimensional clay female figurines may have been a feature of domestic cult, as in Cyprus and Anatolia.'[3]

---

[1] Ucko 1968: xv.
[2] Watrous 1994: 700.
[3] Watrous 1994: 700.

While in the last thirty years the view that the figurines are representatives of the Mother Goddess, or connected with her worship has been challenged, and alternative theories proposed, I am of the belief that at least some of the Cretan Neolithic female figurines can be considered representatives of the Mother Goddess, and that a strong argument can be made for such an interpretation. Before looking at several examples of Neolithic Cretan figurines, I want to look at the controversy surrounding the interpretation of Neolithic female figurines, and consider the corpus of Neolithic Cretan figurines as a whole.

The controversy surrounding the interpretation of Neolithic female figurines

The most oft-quoted and well-known critic of the interpretation of prehistoric figurines as representatives of the Mother Goddess is archaeologist/anthropologist Peter Ucko. His critique of the 'Mother Goddess interpretation' is presented in his 1962 article 'The Interpretation of Prehistoric Anthropomorphic Figurines' and developed further in his 1968 book *Anthropomorphic Figurines of Predynastic Egypt and Neolithic Crete with Comparative Material from the Prehistoric Near East and Mainland Greece*. I discussed Ucko's work extensively in Chapter 3. Therefore I will only summarize that discussion here. In Ucko's article and book he argues that 'the general Mother Goddess interpretation fails to cover all the known facts.'[4] Specifically he points out that the proponents of the Mother Goddess theory have not done a comprehensive examination of the figurines themselves nor considered the archaeological context in which they were found, and he asserts that absolutely no one has considered 'relevant anthropological data.'[5]

Ucko attempts to correct the situation by examining the Neolithic figurines of Crete and comparing them with those from 'pre-dynastic Egypt and other roughly contemporaneous non-literate agricultural societies.'[6] His examination of the figurines and their archaeological contexts leads him to conclude that the Mother Goddess proponents have not explained several important factors: the existence of 'sexless' figurines, the fact that most of the figurines were made of clay, rather than a precious material of some sort; they are of differing quality and artistic merit;[7] and none of them come from a "shrine." '[8]

In order to interpret the Neolithic figurines of Crete, Ucko turns to anthropological evidence. On the basis of comparisons with twentieth century non-literate tribes, Ucko determines that the Neolithic figurines could be dolls, initiation figures, or figures of sympathetic magic.[9]

As I indicated in Chapter 3, it can be argued that the criticism Ucko leveled against the Mother Goddess proponents in the 1960s fails to stand up to scrutiny, especially when it is applied to the work of Gimbutas. In Chapter 3 I stated and then deconstructed Ucko'a arguments. That material is presented here in shortened form.

As for Ucko's first criticism, that a large number of the figurines are 'sexless'—44 out of 102, I would argue that Ucko identified 44 'sexless' figurines because he looked at only several hundred; did not compare the Cretan figurines with a pool of figurines from contemporary

---

[4] Ucko 1962: 38.
[5] Ucko 1962: 38.
[6] Ucko 1962: 38.
[7] Ucko 1962: 41.
[8] Ucko 1962: 41.
[9] Ucko 1962: 47.

Old European cultures; and because he ignored the symbolism on them and of them. Gimbutas, on the other hand, looked at thousands of figurines and symbols across time and cultures, and as a result deciphered a symbolic language bespeaking a Goddess or Goddesses (she held both views open).

While Ucko believed that the male and animal figurines could not fit into the picture of a Neolithic Mother Goddess, Gimbutas's decipherment of the 'meta-language' of Old Europe/Anatolia, and her analysis of the mythology of that culture demonstrated that the Goddess often had a male consort, a vegetation god, and that animals like the hedgehog, bear, bird, snake, deer and sow, to name a few examples, were symbols for the Goddess. Gimbutas's interpretation becomes even more plausible when one considers analogously, how during the Middle Ages in Europe, 'the entire natural world was viewed as a symbol of God the Father, Son and Holy Spirit. . . . To the medieval mind, God was male, and everything in the world was symbolic of him.'[10]

Ucko's criticism that the figurines came from non-ritual contexts, and thus could not be Mother Goddesses, can be countered with the argument that in Old Europe/Anatolia there was no separation between sacred and profane. Life was not categorized in that way.

Finally, as for Ucko's criticism that the Mother Goddess theorists have not explained the use of clay in the making of the figurines rather than a more costly material, I think Ucko himself supplies an answer to that criticism when he writes that it is unintelligible 'unless some association, . . . between the Mother Earth and the use of clay is assumed.'[11] The idea that female figurines made of the earthy substance of clay could represent an Earth Mother Goddess is not a difficult association to affirm. Moreover, Ucko's assumption that only expensive or precious materials would be used to represent a deity might contain an implicit assumption that reserves the production of religious iconography to cultural elites or the wealthy rather than to ordinary people or artisans like pottery makers.

There are several more flaws in Ucko's work I must point out here. It was striking to me that he left out of his study a survey of the small find materials discovered with the figurines. As he put it: 'Of primary interest here are the figurines themselves rather than the character of the associated archaeological assemblages.'[12] However, I believe it is vital that such assemblages be included in one's interpretation. As we have seen from the discussion in the previous chapter, in attempting to identify the Minoan Goddess, Aegean archaeologists rely not only on the objects themselves, but on the architecture, landscape, and immediate context of the finds, their association with one another, and any associated symbols, or ritual equipment, in order to determine whether or not one has found a sacred site and a representation of a deity within. A consideration of the associated archaeological assemblages and find spots of the Neolithic Cretan figurines provide a different interpretation or conclusion than the one arrived at by Ucko. This is discussed further below.

Susan Evasdaughter has pointed out further flaws in Ucko's work:

---

[10] Christ 1997a: 411.
[11] Ucko 1968: 417.
[12] Ucko 1968: xvi.

> He [Ucko] uses very late ethnographic evidence as the basis for his assertion that many of them [the figurines] were dolls. In his study he never states explicitly what an identifying characteristic of a deity would be but is wary of accepting any figure in this role. Given what we know of Cretan religious practices, however, he gives an inappropriately restricted definition to the Great Goddess, assuming Her to have been associated exclusively with fertility and the earth.[13]

It must be acknowledged here that most, if not all, critics of the Mother Goddess interpretation of Neolithic figurines are also guilty of giving an 'inappropriately restricted definition to the Great Goddess.'

Archaeologist Naomi Hamilton has drawn attention to the fact that

> Ucko's own interpretations suffer from precisely the same shortcomings as those for which he berates Mother Goddess theories—application of the same idea to widely differing contexts, use of historical analogies with a massive time gap and ethnographic examples from other geographical areas.[14]

Hamilton goes on to say that in the post-modern world, work being done on the interpretation of figurines 'might question whether the sex of figurines can be assessed at all, and whether it is relevant anyway.'[15] Certainly in the 1990s archaeologists began to question many ideas that previously had been taken for granted in the interpretation of figurines such as: 'the existence of a natural division of the sexes, the relationship of sex to gender, the social construction of gender and a division of labour, the prehistory of male dominance, etc.'[16] Hamilton herself is interested in determining what can be justifiably used as sex indicators, and she has observed in her own archaeological work, and from anthropological research, that sex and gender are often fluid. Perhaps one of the most interesting points she raises is that interpretations of figurines 'are the reflection of the socio-political concerns of the time,'[17] that is to say, of the time of the interpreter, and thus that interpretations are bound to change over time.

As we saw, one of the main issues Ucko raises is the large number of 'sexless' figurines he encountered. What is to be made of them? Marija Gimbutas classified most of Ucko's 'sexless' figurines as female on the basis of her work with and understanding of the 'meta-language' of Old Europe/Anatolia. In a 2008 work, *Anthropomorphic Figurines from the Neolithic and Early Bronze Age Aegean*, Aegeanist Maria Mina attempts to account for the large number of 'sexless' Neolithic figurines. Although her approach is different from that of Gimbutas, and while she is not a proponent of the Mother Goddess theory, Dr. Mina's painstaking work, surveying 1,089 Neolithic figurines from throughout the Aegean, including Crete, has led her to propose that the 'asexual' and 'probably asexual' figurines, as she calls them, and which number 29 percent of her sample, have a stronger symbolic affiliation with the anatomically female figurines than with the male. She posits that they are 'age-related variations mainly of women.'[18] More will be said about this extremely important point below.

---

[13] Evasdaughter 1996: 46.
[14] Hamilton 1996: 283.
[15] Hamilton 1996: 285.
[16] Hamilton 1996: 285.
[17] Hamilton 1996: 285.
[18] Mina 2008a: 112.

Mina stresses, as did Ucko years before, that there are relatively very few male figurines found. In Mina's sample, while the female and female-related categories of figurines account for 67 percent of the whole, male figurines account for only 2.1 percent. Neither she nor Ucko, who identified only five male figurines from Neolithic Crete, offers an adequate explanation. I believe the best explanation is that given by Gimbutas: they are representations of the young male god who is a metaphor for rising and dying vegetation, and the consort of the Goddess. The large number of female figurines has led Mina to conclude that 'Neolithic people were particularly preoccupied with the portrayal of women's bodies and aspects related to women's life cycles.'[19] The preponderance of Neolithic female figurines has prompted archaeologist Adonis Vasilakis to write that 'The fact that female figurines are in the majority, attests to the important role played by women in Neolithic communities, which could be described in this sense as 'woman-centred.'"[20]

Finally, in attempting to interpret the Neolithic figurines, I also take into account an experience I had recently as a participant in women's mysteries and rituals. While we cannot automatically project our own spiritual experiences onto peoples of the distant past, we can use our experiences to reflect upon and perhaps develop insight into the lives of our cultural and spiritual ancestors. In September of 2010, I and twenty other women came together to celebrate the Autumnal Equinox and Eleusinian Mysteries at a three day ritual. At one point in the week-end, after spending an hour with several altars that had as their themes the subjects of death, rebirth, and compassion respectively, and which contained images of Neolithic and Bronze Age Goddesses, each of us proceeded to walk a labyrinth that had been mowed into the tall grasses. Upon entering the labyrinth we were given a piece of clay to fashion, if we so wished, along with some seeds. My experience at the altar representing death had been a profound one. Sitting in front of it, I had asked, 'Why is there so much life if it only ends in death?' A silent voice within me answered, 'It doesn't end.' As I walked the labyrinth, I began to fashion the clay, without any preconceived idea of what it would be. When I finished a few minutes later, I had in my hands a figurine similar to one found at Çatal Hüyük in Neolithic Anatolia, a Goddess with seeds in her back. I looked in astonishment at what I had created. Then I realized, of course, when one celebrates the Mysteries, when one understands death and rebirth at a heart-level (as I had when I received the answer It [life] doesn't end), one's hands may naturally fashion the Goddess. The Goddess I had fashioned carried within her body the seeds of rebirth.

A new interpretation of Ucko's 'sexless' figurines

It is with all this background information in mind that I now tackle the subject of Neolithic Cretan figurines. As I noted above, in her study of anthropomorphic figurines of the Neolithic Aegean, Maria Mina looked at a total of 1,086 published figurines. In her sample were included 110 figurines from Neolithic Crete. The majority of them were found at Knossos and are Final Neolithic in date, c. 4500-3200 BC, although figurines are also found in the earliest Neolithic levels at Knossos c. 6500-5800 BC, and at other sites in Crete including Gortyn and Phaistos. According to Mina's criteria, of the 110 Cretan figurines approximately 63 percent are female, probably female, female form or probably female form; approximately 33 percent are asexual

---

[19] Mina 2008a: 31.
[20] Vasilakis 2001: 77.

or probably asexual; with males or probably male, and ambiguous and probably ambiguous figurines making up the rest.[21]

Mina makes a number of interesting observations regarding Neolithic figurines in general, and, of course, this includes the Cretan figurines. Most importantly for this study is that she finds in her examination of all the Aegean Neolithic figurines that 'at least some' of the asexual figurines have a great deal in common with the female figurines. In her words, 'Asexual figurines show a stronger symbolic affiliation with the anatomically female than with the male grouping.'[22]

What are the symbolic affiliations that allow Mina to group some of the asexual figurines with the female figurines? First, the asexual figurines share a 'considerable number of motifs' with 'anatomically female categories.'[23] These motifs include chevrons, spirals, and zigzags—motifs that Gimbutas has interpreted as the 'language of the Goddess.' Mina has identified 24 core motifs 'that occur on both the general anatomically female grouping and asexual figurines.'[24] In addition to the chevrons, spirals, and zigzags, these core motifs include: vertical parallel lines, crosses, horizontal parallel lines, spirals, rings, diagonal lines, and variations of these motifs. Mina believes that these motifs denote body decoration (which she defines as body painting, tattooing, or scarring). The fact that they were mainly applied to female figurines indicates to Mina that 'female bodies [may have] held a central place in the practices and symbolic constructs that marked gender and cultural identity in Neolithic society.'[25] She adds the extremely important comment that 'the suggested link between women and decoration also indicates the central role played by women's bodies in the ordering of the natural and social cosmos.'[26]

The second symbolic affiliation that allows Mina to group some of the asexual figurines with female figurines is color. The use of color on Neolithic figurines is restricted to female and female-related figurines mainly of a Late Neolithic date. Mina notes that paint—white, black, or red—was applied to 'fertility-related' parts of the body: pubic, breast, and abdominal area, and that the color white seemed to be preferred. She believes that white signifies 'body fluids,' and when found on female figurines in the breast, abdominal, or pubic area, 'may have constituted a symbolic reference to pregnancy, breast-feeding, etc.'[27] Mina found 'overlap in

---

[21] Female (F) figurines are defined [by Mina] by a definite presence of primary anatomical features . . . plus occasional secondary anatomical features . . . ; Probably Female(PF) figurines are recognized by a certain presence only of secondary anatomical features . . . ; Female Form (Ff) figurines are defined by the absence of primary anatomical features but the presence of a swollen abdomen, narrow waist, wide hips, and/or protruding buttocks; Probably Female Form (PFf) figurines take the form of surviving upper and lower halves which suggest that they represented shapes conforming to the Ff category; Male (M) figurines are marked by the presence of male genitalia, beard, and/or straight torso; Probably Male (PM) figurines are recognized by the possible depiction of a penis and the absence of breasts; Asexual (A) figurines lack female or male primary and secondary anatomical features; Probably Asexual (PA) figurines take the form of upper and lower body halves which are not marked anatomically with the presence of breasts or male/female genitalia . . . ; Ambiguous (Amb) figurines are characterized by the presence of anatomical parts of both male and female bodies (Mina 2007: 268, 271).
[22] Mina 2007: 275.
[23] Mina 2007: 277.
[24] Mina 2007: 277.
[25] Mina 2008b: 126-127.
[26] Mina 2008b: 124.
[27] Mina 2008b: 126.

the use of colour between anatomically female categories and asexual figurines.'[28] Color is rarely or almost never found on male figurines of the Neolithic.

Finally, some of the asexual figurines also share with the female and female-related figurines similar postures. Mina lists ten postures including: arm stumps, arms outstretched, arms on chest, arms folded, seated, squatting, and upright. The asexual figurines shared no postures with the male figurines. Mina concludes: 'the overlap of postures between asexual and general anatomically female types is suggestive of a further identification [between the asexual and female figurines] on the level of gender representation.'[29]

If Mina's analysis of Neolithic figurines is correct, one of Ucko's main criticisms of the 'Mother Goddess proponents,' that they cannot account for the large number of 'sexless' Neolithic figurines, is shaken, if not altogether removed. For I think what Mina is indicating here is that while they may not exhibit female primary sexual characteristics, some of the 'asexual' (Mina's words) or 'sexless' (Ucko's words) figurines, because they exhibit the motifs, colors, and postures of the Neolithic female figurines, might cautiously be classified with the female figurines—thus reducing the number of sexless figurines and increasing the number of probable female figurines. And indeed, when I re-examined Ucko's illustrations of the Cretan Neolithic figurines with Mina's analysis in mind, I found that there were at least six figurines with markings on them that Ucko classified as 'sexless,' but that by using Mina's observations and analysis, might plausibly be considered probably female figurines. There were another ten 'sexless' figurines whose postures, mostly arm stumps, would qualify their cautious inclusion in the probably female figurine category.

Mina herself never discusses any need for a revision of the number of female or sexless figurines in Ucko's sample, nor does she call for a revision of his criticisms of the 'Mother Goddess proponents.' She concludes, however, in contrast to Ucko that, 'It is reasonable to argue . . . that Asexual figures . . . should be read as alternative expressions of the anatomically female gender category.'[30] Mina deduces from her analysis that asexual figurines may represent Neolithic women in childhood, adolescence, or pre- or post-pregnancy stages.[31] Her favored interpretation is that they represent 'genderless stages of life.'[32] I would posit that they might represent the Triple Goddess in her role as maiden or crone, or that they may represent one aspect of the Goddess's three aspects of Life-Giver, Death-Wielder, and Regeneratrix.

It is my hypothesis that the female Neolithic Cretan figurines, the majority of the figurines, in Mina's sample, represent the Goddess. I come to that conclusion based on several factors. One is the markings on many of the figurines. If one surveys the markings on them, and here I am consulting illustrations, drawings in books, as well as my observation of some of the figurines in the museums of Crete, one is struck by the fact that many are incised with chevrons, V's, M's, tri-lines, zigzags, lozenges, and dots. One of the Cretan Neolithic figurines even has a double lozenge on her back; one has a triangle on her right shoulder, and another, two concentric circles around her belly button. Many of these incisions are filled with white or red paint.

---

[28] Mina 2007: 274.
[29] Mina 2007: 274.
[30] Mina 2007: 278.
[31] Mina 2007: 280.
[32] Mina 2007: 280.

As discussed in Chapter 4, Gimbutas categorizes chevrons, V's, and zigzags as symbols of the aquatic world and links them with the Goddess as Life-Giver and Renewing and Eternal Earth. They are symbols 'associated with the primary aspect of this Goddess, that of life-giving moisture of the Goddess's body.'[33] Gimbutas writes that 'the zig-zag is the earliest symbolic motif recorded.'[34] She equates it with water, 'a generative force,'[35] and notes that in the Upper Paleolithic it was associated with anthropomorphic, bird, and fish images. The 'M' sign, which Gimbutas sees as a variation of the zigzag, is often found on figurines, particularly below the female breasts. Gimbutas interprets this as indicating a Goddess as 'source of milk and universal nurture,'[36] and she links the 'M' or zigzag to the Goddess in her aspect as Life-Giver. Gimbutas also links the zigzag and 'M' with female moisture and amniotic fluid.

The lozenges and dots are associated by Gimbutas to the Goddess in her Renewing and Eternal Earth form. Based on what Gimbutas has written about 'dots' and their relation to seeds,[37] I wonder if the dots on some of the Cretan Neolithic figurines might represent seeds, and if so, did the seeds represent the souls of the dead? Or did they perhaps symbolize a general resurgence of life, such as seeds scattered in a field would?

As for the tri-lines, Gimbutas believes they are also symbolic of the Goddess in her Life-Giving aspect, and can be associated with Being and Becoming. Gimbutas further links the tri-line with the power of three; the Goddess as owner of the triple source of life energy necessary for the renewal of life; and with the triple-Goddess herself.[38]

The concentric circle Gimbutas links to Becoming. And the triangle she interprets as symbolic of the Goddess's regenerative power, and as a symbol of the female pubic triangle.

The fact that many of the figurines exhibit the pubic triangle and have their hands and arms positioned so that they emphasize their chests/breasts, also points to the interpretation that they are representatives of the Goddess—especially in her Life-Giving and Regeneratrix aspects. Perhaps these early Neolithic representations of the Goddess with her hands to her chest or below the breasts were the precursors of the Early Minoan Goddesses (to be discussed later in this chapter) with their pitchers—the ones Marinatos linked to the Minoan Goddess in her role as sustainer, and Gesell named Goddess of Fertility and Birth. Here rather than a pitcher held like a baby, or breasts with holes for nipples to allow the pouring of liquid, the Goddess's nurturing aspect is simply represented with the placement of arms and hands. In such figurines I think we can see the Nurturer of All, part of what I understand the Mother Goddess's role to be, and encompassed in Gimbutas's term 'Life-Giver.'

It is also extremely important to keep in mind when considering the hypothesis that the Cretan Neolithic female figurines, and some of the asexual figurines, are Goddesses is that the majority of them were found at Knossos. Archaeologists now believe that Neolithic Knossos, and perhaps all the temple-palaces of Minoan Crete, were very ancient and important ritual centers—that is why the temple-palaces were constructed on those spots in the Early

---

[33] Gimbutas 1989: 3
[34] Gimbutas 1989: 19.
[35] Gimbutas 1989: 19.
[36] Gimbutas 1989: 22.
[37] Gimbutas 1989: 143.
[38] Gimbutas 1989: 97.

and Middle Minoan periods.[39] If one keeps in mind then, that the majority of the Neolithic Cretan figurines were found at a sacred site, or ritual center, the argument that the figurines represent the Mother Goddess, or at least two of her aspects, takes on even greater validity. It also removes yet another of Ucko's criticisms—that the figurines were found in 'non-ritual contexts.'

It is quite possible to make a plausible argument that most of the Cretan Neolithic figurines, those that are female, as identified by the presence of breasts, and/ or a pubic triangle, and some of the asexual figurines, as identified by markings, incised color, and posture, are portrayals of the Mother Goddess. I realize that for many of them their condition is too fragmentary to make a strong argument that they are the Mother Goddess as I have defined the term. Another problem in their identification as the Mother Goddess is that information regarding the material excavated with them is often difficult to access.[40] Mina has written that many of the Aegean Neolithic figurines were found in isolation. When not found alone, they tended to be associated with 'one or more other figurines of a human or animal form,' or with tools, utensils, or pottery.[41] When associated finds are known, interpretations suggesting a religious function for the figurines can in some cases be more forcefully made. For example, Italian archaeologist Luigi Pernier, who excavated at the temple-palace of Phaistos in the first half of the twentieth century, found a Neolithic female figurine (he identified her as female on the basis of breasts and a pubic triangle) accompanied by a piece of meteoritic iron, a red-painted triton shell, and dishes of a 'votive character.'[42] He determined the context was a religious one. Watrous cautiously agrees, and attributes a 'religious function' to the figurine.[43] To make a strong argument that the Neolithic Cretan figurines do represent the Mother Goddess as I have defined the term in this work, I would want to have additional detailed information about the finds associated with them to determine if symbols exist on any tools, utensils and pottery found with the figurines; what types of animal forms, if any, accompany the figurines, and the size and type of any human forms that might accompany them.

Based on a combination of Mina's analysis and Gimbutas's interpretation of symbols, there is good evidence to support the claim of my hypothesis that a majority of the Cretan Neolithic figurines represent the Goddess in her Life-Giver and Regeneratrix aspects. I predicate this assertion on the markings: zigzags, chevrons, V's, etc., and the pubic triangles and breasts that adorn the figurines, as well as their find spots: the sacred sites that eventually became the temple-palaces of Knossos and Phaistos.

As for the absence of the third aspect of the Mother Goddess, that of Death-Wielder, perhaps one can account for that absence, and the general dearth of death imagery, in the fact that as Gimbutas noted, 'there is much more emphasis on regeneration than death in the iconography [here she is speaking of Old Europe in general], [and] this reflects the belief that out of every death new life grows.'[44] Perhaps such imagery is to be found in the archaeological assemblages

---

[39] See Schoep and Tomkins 2012: 8-9; Day and Wilson 2002: 148.
[40] It is my understanding that the excavator's daybooks, as well as some other difficult–to-obtain publications, contain descriptions of finds related to the figurines excavated at Knossos, where the majority of Neolithic Cretan figurines have been found. I do not at present have access to those materials.
[41] Mina 2008a: 35.
[42] Ucko 1968: 299.
[43] Watrous 1994: 700.
[44] Gimbutas 1989: 187.

excavated in conjunction with the figurines, however, that material is not available to me at this point in time. In regard to the question of death imagery, I have noted with interest that several of the Cretan Neolithic figurines bear a similarity to the later Cretan and Cycladic 'stiff nudes,' the famous marble images found in Cycladic and Cretan graves dated to *c.* 3500-2500 BC,[45] although they are certainly much smaller and much cruder than the later Cycladic and Cretan figurines. Watrous has noted that some of the smallest Cretan stone figurines may have been worn as amulets, as was the practice in Neolithic Cyprus and Anatolia.[46] Perhaps the figurine/amulets represent some aspect of the Goddess as Death-Wielder.

The Ierapetra Snake Goddess

I would now like to turn to a discussion of two Neolithic Cretan figurines that I believe can plausibly and probably be argued to represent the Mother Goddess as I have defined her in this book. I have chosen to discuss these two examples because they are larger, more accessible, and in better condition than most of the Neolithic figurines remaining to us; and for one of them, there is a great deal of information available about the associated archaeological assemblages.

Figure 1. The Ierapetra Snake Goddess. Neolithic, c. 6000-5500 BC, 14.5cm x 9cm, clay, surface find, Ierapetra, Crete. Giamalakis Collection, Heraklion Museum, Crete. Photograph by author.

[45] Gimbutas 1989: 203.
[46] Watrous 1994: 700.

The first Cretan Neolithic figurine I would like to consider is the famous figurine from Ierapetra (now in the Heraklion Museum and part of the Giamalakis Collection). This figurine, which is 14.5cm in height and 9cm broad at the base, combines the features not only of a woman and a bird, but a snake as well. She sits cross-legged in what yogis would call the lotus pose, her left leg folded over her right, her arms resting at her sides, and her hands resting on her stomach. Her breasts are well defined and her body well-rounded, especially her buttocks. She has a long 'bird like' neck and an aquiline nose, her eyes are incised and her lips are slightly modeled, and she seems to be wearing a flat-topped hat, headdress, or crown. Her snake-like appearance comes especially from the modeling of her lower body: her legs are snake-like in their curvature and size; and from the markings on her body. She has incised lines on her shoulders, breasts, arms, and legs.

Since the Ierapetra figurine comes from an unexcavated site and was a surface find, it is impossible to speak to the issue of find spot, or to the issue of other items found with her. While Ucko makes the point that she is unlike any other Neolithic figurine found in Crete, I would argue that she is of the type widely found in the Mediterranean Neolithic, which Lynn Roller described as having 'exaggerated breasts, hips, buttocks and abdomen.'[47] Moreover, the figure meets the criterion given for recognition of a deity, the hybridization of human and animal features. In addition, the headpiece can be interpreted as a crown—indicating a special status. As Gimbutas wrote,

> A belief in the magical crown of the snake queen still survives in European folklore: whoever catches hold of the crown will know all the secrets of the world, find enchanted treasures, and understand the speech of animals.[48]

What is one to make of the figurine's bird and snake-like features? Writing about the snake in Neolithic Europe, Gimbutas said:

> The snake is life force. . . . It is not the body of the snake that was sacred, but the energy exuded . . . which transcends its boundaries and influences the surrounding world. . . . Its seasonal renewal in sloughing off its old skin and hibernating made it a symbol of the continuity of life and of the link with the underworld.[49]

Gimbutas linked chevrons, X's, and aquatic symbols to the snake, and noted that those same symbols were associated with waterfowl and the Bird Goddess. Calling the snake a transfunctional symbol, she noted that it 'permeates all of Old European symbolism,' representing not only life and creation, but fertility and regeneration as well.[50] As we saw above, Moss notes a 'possible meaning' for the snake as that of renewal, regeneration, initiation, the chthonic world, and transformation;[51] Gesell identifies the snake as a symbol of a Minoan fertility and a chthonic

---

[47] Roller 1999: 30.
[48] Gimbutas 1991: 236.
[49] Gimbutas 1989: 121.
[50] Gimbutas 1989: 121.
[51] Moss, 2005: 152.

deity;[52] while Marinatos posits that the snake in Minoan religion has the 'positive connotations of renewal,'[53] noting that 'in folklore, the snake has the ability to restore life to the dead.'[54]

As for the bird aspect of the Ierapetra Goddess, Marinatos has called the bird one of the animals sacred to the Goddess, her 'celestial messenger.'[55] As Goddess of Nature, the Minoan Goddess, according to Marinatos, has a 'special relationship with the animal world.'[56] Her birdlike features can perhaps be said to reinforce the life-giving qualities associated with the snake for, as noted above, Gimbutas believes the Bird Goddess is also a symbol of life and life giving, and that the association between the Snake and the Bird Goddess in Old European imagery is intimate and continuous throughout prehistory. They are both guardians of the springs of life.[57]

All the archaeologists discussed above identify the snake and bird as attributes of the Minoan Goddess, and as her cult symbols, because of their frequent association. I would suggest that one can imply that those symbols that denote the Goddess in the Bronze Age may well have also denoted the Goddess in the Neolithic.

Is the Ierapetra Goddess a representation of the Mother Goddess? I said above that one aspect of my definition of a Mother Goddess is that she has power over the natural environment. As bird and snake and woman, the Ierapetra Goddess could symbolize the Mother Goddess's 'special relationship with the animal world,' and her oneness with Nature, which is another way to say, her power over the natural environment. Moreover, because the snake sheds its skin, hibernates, or 'dies,' and comes back to life or is 'reborn,' it seems to mediate the boundaries between life and death, a crucial aspect of my definition of the Mother Goddess. Because the Ierapetra Goddess is snake-like in many of her attributes, she could be said to symbolically embody that ability to mediate between life and death and rebirth. Moreover, the combination of female, bird, and snake indicates a mythical rather than a human being.[58] The Ierapetra Goddess of Neolithic Crete embodies all the qualities essential to a Mother Goddess as I have defined her, and thus I believe she can plausibly and very probably be interpreted as one.

The Goddess at the Eileithyia cave at Amnisos

The second icon of the Goddess which dates to the Neolithic which I wish to discuss is found in the cave of Eileithyia at Amnisos, the ancient port town located about nine kilometers east of Heraklion on the northeast coast of Crete. The cave is so-called because there is archaeological evidence to show that from the Bronze Age to the Roman era, the Goddess of childbirth,

---

[52] Gesell 1985: 65.
[53] Marinatos 1993: 158.
[54] Marinatos 1993: 159.
[55] Marinatos 1993: 156.
[56] Marinatos 1993: 152.
[57] Marinatos 1993: 121.
[58] Dexter notes:

> Two prevalent [Goddess] hybrids in the European and Near Eastern Neolithic were those of the *bird-woman and snake woman*. Figurines of such goddesses have been found in Greece, Italy, Yugoslavia, Bulgaria, Romania, and Central Europe, and nearly forty percent of the figurines excavated in these areas are combinations of female figures with these avian or serpentine attributes (Dexter 1990: 5-6).

> Dexter dates these figurines to between 7000-3500 BC, and remarks that they are quite numerous, remarkably similar to each other and have Paleolithic precursors as well as Indo-European antecedents (Dexter 1990: 5-6).

Eileithyia, had been venerated in that cave. It was Homer's *Odyssey* which first alerted scholars to the fact that a cave dedicated to Eileithyia was located near Amnisos.[59] The *Homeric Hymn III to Delian Apollo* further names Eileithyia as the Goddess of childbirth.[60] Moreover, Linear B tablets recording offerings of honey to 'e-re-u-ti-ja' identify Eileithyia as a pre-Greek Goddess. Excavations in the cave have uncovered sherds dating from the Neolithic to the Roman period.

This cave is extremely important for my discussion as it contains a number of concretions, 'many of which resemble women,'[61] and which may be thought of as cult images of the Goddesses. How or why might they be regarded as such? Rutkowski explains:

> In ancient times the stalactites and stalagmites which nature herself had formed into the shape of humans and animals were looked upon as miraculous, and were worshipped like idols. This supposition is corroborated by the fact that rocks shaped like human beings have also been found in the domestic sanctuary in the Little Palace at Knossos . . . and in the tholos tomb at Apesokari, where they must have been used as cult idols. . . . There were other examples, too, of fragments of stalagmites having been brought into the Minoan houses. So properties must have been attributed to them.[62]

Extremely interesting for our discussion is the fact that Rutkowski also notes that in other Mediterranean cultures, stalagmites and stalactites were often brought into homes.

> At Çatal-Hüyük one of the statuettes, representing an old goddess, was made of a piece of stalagmite which someone had roughly fashioned to give it human form. Bits of stalactites were also found in one of the sanctuaries.[63]

Also of note is the fact that at least several of the concretions have been shaped and polished by human hands to resemble people, in particular, women. Moss cautions that there is no way of knowing when these concretions were so shaped and polished.[64]

The cave of Eileithyia itself is long and gently sloping down into the hillside above the harbor of Amnisos. It is approximately 60 meters long, 24 meters wide and up to 4 meters high in some spots. Upon entering the cave of Eileithyia one first encounters a large round stone with an indentation in the center that has been described as resembling an *omphalos*. Moss remarks that even this round stone has a connection with women in that 'it may serve as a reminder to pilgrims of their own birth, or it may suggest that as they walk inside, they are about to enter the womb of the earth.'[65]

Six meters to the west of the *omphalos* and nine meters from the entrance,

> There is a rock 1.10m high resembling a female figure; the head has been cut off with the blow of an axe. This rock is surrounded by an ancient wall. . . . In the middle of

---

[59] Homer, *Odyssey* XIX, 188.
[60] *The Homeric Hymns,* lines 95-96.
[61] Moss 2005: 122.
[62] Rutkowski 1986: 51.
[63] Rutkowski 1986: 51.
[64] Moss 2005: 122.
[65] Moss 2005: 122.

the cave, 18m from the 'woman figure', there is a stalagmite 1.40m high and 1.17m in circumference. This is encircled by a stone wall. . . . The upper part of this stalagmite has been deliberately cut off, but the discerning eye can still make out the legs and abdomen of a woman.[66]

Rutkowski notes that this stalagmite has been rubbed smooth by human hands, indicating that the pilgrims who visited the cave thought that it had miraculous powers. Nearby is another stalagmite of the same height. These are not the only 'cult stalagmites' in the cave. Forty-eight meters from the entrance 'there was another large stalagmite 4.8m high, also shaped like a female figure and also with the upper part cut off.'[67] In the rear part of the cave, water collected in numerous hollows in the rocks. Judging from the votive offerings found nearby, Rutkowski remarks that 'It is certain that miraculous powers were attributed to the water here.'[68]

The most interesting of the female concretions in the cave, and the one I wish to focus on, is the one located in the middle of the cave. This is the concretion that Rutkowski has described as a figure of a woman with the upper part cut off, having been rubbed smooth by pilgrims, and with another stalagmite of the same size close by. This pair has been described as: a seated figure accompanied by a standing figure; as representing a mother holding a child (with the nearby stalagmite representing a phallus); as a mother and daughter;[69] and as a Goddess with a young god.[70] To me it looks like a mother holding a child. Of great importance is the fact that these two stalagmites are surrounded by a low four-sided, meander-shaped wall 'probably built to separate the most holy spot around stalagmites.'[71] There is a raised area between the two stalagmites 'which probably served as a natural altar,' and 'an unhewn rock in front of them was probably an altar base.'[72] Archaeologist Loeta Tyree has written that within this area of the low wall enclosing the two stalagmites, pot sherds from all Minoan and Post-Minoan periods were found by early investigators of the cave. '[Spiros] Marinatos later reported additional sherds belonging to all periods from Neolithic to Classical ages.'[73]

Finds inside the cave have consisted almost entirely of pottery fragments (from shallow vessels, large jugs, and bowls) dating from the Neolithic period onward. Almost all of the finds are of clay—except for one lead bovine figure, and a stone axe dating to the Neolithic.[74] It is interesting to me that almost all the finds recovered at the cave have been clay sherds. I am reminded of Ucko's comment that 'the predominant use of clay for the manufacture of figurines . . . is strange if they represent the Mother Goddess . . . , for the representation of the major deity of the time could be expected to deserve the use of a more costly material.'[75] Certainly the least costly materials to represent the divinity include stalagmites, stalactites, and clay, and yet here in the cave of Eileithyia, they clearly have been attributed a sacred nature.

---

[66] Rutkowski 1986: 51.
[67] Rutkowski 1986: 51.
[68] Rutkowski 1986: 53.
[69] Christ 1995: 36.
[70] Tyree 1974: 26.
[71] Rutkowski and Nowicki 1996: 81.
[72] Tyree 1974: 26.
[73] Tyree 1974: 26.
[74] Rutkowski 1986: 65.
[75] Ucko 1968: 417.

Archaeologists have debated as to whether or not the cave of Eileithyia at Amnisos or any of the other Cretan caves were used as places of worship in the Neolithic. Rutkowski and fellow Polish archaeologist Krzysztof Nowicki are convinced the cave of Eileithyia was, and they include it in their list of caves 'certainly used for cult purposes.'[76] Indeed, they argue persuasively that since Neolithic pottery and a stone axe were discovered in the depths of cave of Amnisos, and not at its entrance, where it is drier and thus more suitable for habitation, then clearly these objects were meant as offerings and not as utensils of daily living. Rutkowski reminds his reader that stone axes were used in the Neolithic for offerings, just as bronze and gold ones were in Minoan times. And, as if speaking in answer to Ucko, he declares that in the Neolithic era, 'pottery—even ordinary vessels such as kitchenware—could have been used as offerings to the gods, for the sacrifices to the gods were held in these containers.'[77]

Who then was worshipped in the Eileithyia cave at Amnisos? Gimbutas hypothesizes that a cave like Amnisos is, '[a] natural manifestation of the primordial womb of the Mother,'[78] and the stalagmites and stalactites 'probably symbolized the embryonic, concentrated life force materializing in the womb of the Goddess.'[79]

Rutkowski, referring to caves and rituals around the Aegean, believes that in pre-Greek times, 'rites connected with the great mysteries of birth and death in the whole realm of man, animals and plants were performed in the caves.'[80] He is of the opinion that whichever Goddess was worshipped there, her cult was chthonic and she had a variety of roles and duties.

> Thus in earlier times (in the Neolithic, for example), the goddess who appeared to humans in the grottoes possibly had a very wide range of functions. As time went on, and depending on the cult place, some aspects of the goddess . . . predominated over and obscured her other characteristics. Consequently, it sometimes happened that local deities came into existence whose principal characteristic was different from the previous multi-functions of the Great Goddess.[81]

It seems to me that there is stronger evidence than Rutkowski allows for indicating that Eileithyia was a pre-Greek Goddess. As noted above, her name appears in a Linear B tablet. Nilsson states that 'philology agrees with our other evidence in postulating a pre-Greek origin of Eileithyia. She was especially venerated in Crete, on the neighboring islands and in Laconia, and this adds to the probability of her Minoan origins.'[82] Willetts writes that 'The name Eileithyia is not Indo-European, which strengthens the possibility of a direct descent from a Minoan goddess of childbirth.'[83]

Moss believes that the cave may have been the site of some sort of water cult. Rutkowski hints at this as well. Moss thinks, 'There may have been an element of renewal or rebirth for the

---

[76] Rutkowski and Nowicki 1996: 21.
[77] Rutkowski 1986: 66.
[78] Gimbutas 1989: 151.
[79] Gimbutas 1989: 223.
[80] Gimbutas 1989: 223.
[81] Gimbutas 1989: 64.
[82] Nilsson 1949: 522.
[83] Willetts 1962: 168.

supplicants (rather than a connection with childbirth) at the Cave of Eileithyia at Amnisos.'[84] Both Rutkowski and Moss point out that even though Homer's *Odyssey* links Amnisos with a nearby cave dedicated to Eileithyia, and the *Hymn to Delian Apollo* names Eileithyia as the Goddess of childbirth, 'it is not certain whether the cave was used to venerate this deity in Minoan times.'[85]

I believe it can plausibly be argued that the concretions in the center of the cave, those surrounded by the wall marking off the holy space and found with sherds dating from the Neolithic, represent the Mother Goddess. She is not only an early representation of the Goddess of Childbirth, who should be called Life-Giver, I think, but more. She is the Goddess of Death as well, for in the Early Minoan period, the cave of Eileithyia at Amnisos was used as a burial ground,[86] most likely because, as Gimbutas wrote, caves were the 'the primordial womb of the Mother,'[87] and because ancient peoples envisioned the stalagmites and stalactites as symbolizing 'the embryonic, concentrated life force materializing in the womb of the Goddess.'[88] I believe, like Rutkowski, that she who was worshipped at Amnisos was connected with 'the great mysteries of birth and death in the whole realm of man, animals and plants,' and had a 'wide range of functions.'[89] At the cave of Eileithyia at Amnisos, she who was worshipped was the great mediator, the mediator between the known and unknown, between life, death and rebirth, the Mother Goddess.

The Early Minoan Period

The Neolithic in Crete was followed by a period of rapid development that eventually culminated in the 'palatial' civilization of Minoan Crete. The period between the Neolithic and the establishment of 'palatial' civilization is known as the Prepalatial, or more usually, as the Early Minoan Period. It begins in *c.* 3200 BC and is divided into three periods: EM I, *c.* 3200/3000-2600 BC, EM II, *c.* 2600-2300 BC, and EM III, *c.* 2300-2100 BC.[90]

The Early Minoan Period, also known as the Early Bronze Age, is a time of probable immigration from Anatolia, increased contact with the Cyclades, Egypt, and the Near East, the introduction of metallurgy, rapid economic development, and the building of sizable houses and tombs. It marks the appearance of elegant stone vases, skillfully crafted seals, and 'a high degree of perfection'[91] in the art of jewelry making, as well as new pottery shapes and decoration. Although there were as yet no 'palaces,' there were settlements, most notably in the eastern and southern part of the island, and what Marinatos has called 'monumental'[92] funerary architecture. It is also important to note that this time period is generally understood to be one in which a relatively equalitarian society existed as evidenced in the communal tombs of the period and the settlement of Myrtos, which indicates a communal social organization.[93]

---

[84] Moss 2005: 122.
[85] Moss 2005: 122.
[86] Moss 2005: 122.
[87] Gimbutas 1989: 151.
[88] Gimbutas 1989: 223.
[89] Rutkowski 1986: 65.
[90] Dimopoulou-Rethemiotakis 2005: 23.
[91] Davaras 1976: 80.
[92] Marinatos 1993: 13.
[93] For a discussion of Myrtos's social organization see Warren 1972: 266-267.

From the Early Minoan Period in Crete, I shall look at figurines that come from one settlement (few of these have been discovered for the Early Minoan Period) and from several tombs, to determine if a case can be made for interpreting any of them as a Mother Goddess. I shall be focusing on three particular figurines, but I should point out that they are a part of a larger group of at least nine Early Minoan figurines which exhibit a great deal of similarity and are often discussed in conjunction. These figurines were found at Myrtos, Koumasa, Malia, Mochlos, Trapeza Cave, Pyrgos Cave, and Aghios Myron.[94] Only one comes from a settlement, the rest come from burial sites.

The Goddess of Myrtos

The 'Goddess of Myrtos' was named after the settlement of Myrtos in southeastern Crete, where she was found, and dated to EM II, *c.* 2650-2300 BC. British archaeologist Peter Warren, the excavator who discovered her, prefers the title 'Household Goddess.'[95] This will be discussed further below.

Found in a shrine within the settlement of Myrtos, also called Fournou Koriphi, the name of the hill on which it was built, the settlement itself contains about ninety rooms, but 'has the appearance of one large building complex which cannot be divided into individual houses.'[96] The shrine room where the Goddess of Myrtos was found was equipped with offering vessels, eighteen in all, and an altar, or stone bench, from which the figurine fell, with an adjacent store room filled with fine pottery, and another room with 'grinding and draining equipment for preparing liquid offerings.'[97] These rooms had an entrance that was independent of the rest of the settlement. Gesell notes that 'the arrangement of the [shrine] room complex, which resembles the later LM III [*c.* 1400-1070 BC] sanctuaries, supports the cult identification.'[98] She also argues that the separate entrance indicates that the Goddess of Myrtos was not a household Goddess, but that her shrine was 'the cult center of the whole settlement.'[99]

The Goddess of Myrtos is 21 centimeters high and holds a miniature jug in the crook of her left arm; the only entrance to the interior of the Goddess is through this little jug. Her right arm comes across her body and holds the jug by the handle (the end of this arm is missing). Her exposed breasts are composed of carefully modeled lumps of clay. Her bell-shaped body contains a series of panels with a net pattern, with a triangular panel emphasizing her pubic area. Warren thinks the painted panels represent clothing.[100] She has a long bird-like neck which the excavator believes signifies that she does not represent a human being.[101] Her nose and chin are made from pieces of clay added to the head, the nose is pinched out from the head, and her eyes are incised circles painted red inside. In addition to the eyes being painted red, her nose, chin, eyebrows, and breasts are also red, as are the panels of net patterning. The

---

[94] A full description of these can be found in Warren 1973: 138-139.
[95] Warren 1972: 266.
[96] Gesell 1985: 7.
[97] Gesell 1985: 7.
[98] Gesell 1985: 7.
[99] Gesell 1985: 7.
[100] Warren 1972: 209.
[101] Warren 1972: 210.

Goddess of Myrtos has two thin bands of red around her neck; Warren suggests they represent collars or necklaces; and a band of red paint along the length of her arms up to her shoulders.[102]

As stated above, Warren (in contrast to Gesell noted earlier) has called the Goddess of Myrtos a 'Household Goddess.' He writes:

> With the evidence of Minoan cult figures on or beside low benches, with adjacent vessels for offerings, in the later shrines of Knossos (Double Axes), Gournia, Gortyn, Kannia, Gazi and Karphi there can be little doubt that the Myrtos figure represents a domestic goddess in a household shrine. . . . With her particular attribute, the jug, she was perhaps protectress of the water supply, a fundamental necessity for life in a village settlement on a hilltop without water.[103]

Gesell and Marinatos argue for a larger role for the Goddess of Myrtos than that of a domestic protectress of the water supply. Gesell points out that the pubic triangle and the bell-shaped body (which Gesell believes symbolized pregnancy) indicate that she is a 'fertility goddess.'[104] Marinatos argues that she is a Goddess of Nature and that one of her most important functions must have been to personify fertility, for her hollow body and little jug suggest it is she who supplies life-giving liquid.[105]

Not only do the bell-shaped body, exaggerated pubic triangle, and association with life-giving liquid emphasize fertility or life-giving properties. But her life-giving aspect is further enhanced by her prominent breasts, once again drawing attention to the life-giving liquid; the net pattern on her body, which Gimbutas has counted among the Life-Giver symbols of the Goddess; and the Goddess of Myrtos's long bird-like neck, which links her with another symbol of life-giving and of regeneration, the bird. Do these attributes make her a Mother Goddess?

Before considering that question, several other figurines of the Early Minoan period which have a close relationship to the Goddess of Myrtos must be discussed. These are the Koumasa I Goddess, and the Mochlos Goddess.

The Koumasa I Goddess

The Koumasa I Goddess, dated to EM II, *c.* 2650-2300 BC, is one of four similar figurines found at the Koumasa cemetery. Fifteen centimeters high, she has an almost bird-like face with a very beak-like nose. Her face is much less human looking than that of the Goddess of Myrtos, but like her, the Koumasa I Goddess is also bell-shaped. Like the Goddess of Myrtos, she too cradles a small jug in the crook of her arm. The front of her body is decorated with X's down the center, and to each side of the X's, two lines of plants, or what I prefer to call representations of the tree of life. What is also highly significant about her appearance is that a snake runs from the hand to shoulder on each side of her body, appearing to wrap itself around her neck as well. Markings on the snake are in red, as are the markings on her body. There is a handle on her back for holding her as one pours liquids from this vessel.

---

[102] Warren 1972: 209.
[103] Warren 1973: 142.
[104] Gesell 1985: 7.
[105] Marinatos 1993: 30.

As regards the find spot of the Koumasa I Goddess, she was uncovered in the archaeological area named Delta, the paved area between tholos tomb A and rectangular ossuary C in the Koumasa cemetery, which is located in the Mesara Plain of south-central Crete, by Greek archaeologist Stephanos Xanthoudides in the early twentieth century. The Mesara Plain was the most important and prosperous area of Crete in antiquity, with the exception of Knossos, and it includes within its boundaries most of the tholos tombs of the Early Minoan Period, and 'a great number of other Minoan settlements, sanctuaries and cemeteries.'[106] It should be explained here that 'cemeteries were the ritual foci of the communities of Prepalatial times,'[107] playing a prominent part in the lives of the people of the Early Minoan Period. Archaeologist Keith Branigan has argued that dancing often took place in the paved areas of the Mesara cemeteries and that these areas were the location 'of rituals and ceremonies which were concerned with the vegetational cycle and fertility.'[108]

Found with the Koumasa Goddess in area Delta were several other Goddesses, as well as 'several bulls, one with men hanging from the horns; several birds; three jugs with humans clinging to their necks; and, in addition, a vessel in the shape of an egg.'[109] The other Goddesses found with the Koumasa Goddess resembled her in many aspects. The Koumasa Goddess II is similar in shape and also holds a jug, however she does not have the snake on her arms and shoulders and there are traces of white and black decoration on her body. The Koumasa Goddess III is missing her head and appears to have no spout. She is decorated with red diagonal bands on her body and has a handle at the back. The Koumasa Goddess IV is also missing her head, but is similar to Koumasa Goddess I as regards her spout and snake markings.[110]

It is generally accepted by archaeologists that the Koumasa I figurine is a Goddess (indeed all four of the Koumasa Goddesses are labeled Goddesses by experts). Branigan has argued that she is 'an early appearance of the snake Goddess.'[111] In this he echoes an observation originally made by Evans.[112]

The Koumasa I Goddess certainly has two of the attributes of the Minoan Goddess: the snake and the bird. Like the Goddess of Myrtos, she carries a jug to provide life-giving water and is herself the provider of life-giving liquid, most likely both water and milk. The markings of X's and the tree of life reinforce her life-giving aspects. Branigan has noted that the X's or lattice work on the front of her dress is also found on the apron of the Snake Goddess from Knossos.[113] The fact that she was found with bulls, birds, and an egg-shaped vessel might argue further for her connection with life-giving. As we have seen, birds and bulls are often considered attributes of the Minoan Goddess. Moreover, Marinatos has argued that when bull figurines are found in funerary contexts, they may represent the continuation of life.[114] The egg symbol is particularly important in regard to the continuation of life. Gimbutas has

---

[106] Davaras 1976: 195.
[107] Marinatos 1993: 13.
[108] Branigan 1993: 135.
[109] Marinatos 1993: 16.
[110] Warren 1973: 138.
[111] Branigan 1993: 136.
[112] Evans 1964: 4:163.
[113] Branigan 1993: 136.
[114] Marinatos 1993: 3. Marinatos suggests that 'death rituals are associated with activities that negate death by affirming the vitality of life' (Marinatos 1993: 28). One such activity she cites is Minoan bull wrestling, which is suggested by bull vessels and figurines found at various burial sites.

said of the egg, it 'bears not so much upon birth as upon a rebirth modeled on the repeated creation of the world.'[115] She has pointed out that from the Neolithic onward, burial pithoi are egg shaped, 'symbolizing the womb of the Goddess from which life would re-emerge.'[116] Also from the Neolithic onward, eggs were placed as offerings in graves to ensure regeneration.[117] Interestingly, Gimbutas has also noted that the combination of the symbols of eggs, birds, water, and bulls, symbols of becoming and regeneration, are found throughout prehistory.[118] Marinatos has written about the significance of finding the Koumasa I Goddess with an animal vessel; referring here to the bull with the humans hanging off the horns, one of the cult objects found with the Koumasa I Goddess. She posits that the existence of such an artifact along with the representation of the Goddess shows a concern for 'fertility and regeneration.'[119] Benaki Museum curator Irini Papageorgiou has argued that since EM II, c. 2600-2300 BC hunting was associated, in Aegean iconography, with the concept of transition. In the case of the artifact of the bull and humans what is symbolized is the transition to the afterlife, and by implication, I think, a transition involving fertility and regeneration.[120]

I said above that Branigan considered that dancing often took place in the paved areas of the Mesara cemeteries and that these areas were the location 'of rituals and ceremonies which were concerned with the vegetational cycle and fertility.'[121] Branigan bases these conclusions on a number of factors, one of which I wish to discuss here: mythology, and specifically, the myth of Ariadne.

Because Homer described the dancing ground which Daedalus made for Ariadne at Knossos, as well as the dances performed there, dancing in ancient Crete has long been associated with the Goddess Ariadne. Ariadne is a Goddess who had two festivals celebrated in her honor: one of sorrow, that depicted her dying after having been abandoned by Theseus of Athens on the island of Naxos; and one of rejoicing, that depicting her resurrection. Nilsson has argued that the death and resurrection of a vegetation Goddess (rather than a god) is unique, known only in Crete. Vasilakis believes that Ariadne the Goddess is to be identified with Europa, Pasiphae, or Britomartis, all forms of the great Minoan Goddess. The name Ariadne means 'pure;' like Britomaritis 'sweet-maiden.'

> When she was demoted to the status of demigod, legend adapted her to the type of the princess who helps the young warrior to achieve his aim, like Medea in the legend of Jason. . . . Theseus's feat may be regarded as a reflection of conflicts between the cities of mainland Greece . . . and Minoan Crete, which seem to have taken place at this period.[122]

Nilsson, writing of the myth of Ariadne, adds further to our understanding:

> Ariadne is more than a heroine of mythology, the common opinion now is that she was an old goddess of Nature venerated on the islands of the Aegean. It deserves to

---

[115] Gimbutas 1989: 213.
[116] Gimbutas 1989: 213.
[117] Gimbutas 1989: 213.
[118] Gimbutas 1989: 213.
[119] Marinatos 1993: 17.
[120] Papageorgiou 2018: 323.
[121] Branigan 1993: 135.
[122] Branigan 1993: 51.

be noticed that the memory of her cult is not recorded by inscriptions, only by the mythographers, but those accounts show that she had very remarkable festivals. The character of her cult, her association with Crete and king Minos and the appearance of her cult on the islands make it probable that she is of Minoan origin.[123]

Ariadne as the Death-Wielding and Regenerative aspects of the Goddess is a far cry from Ariadne as the love-struck victim of Theseus that the later myths portray.[124]

Branigan posits that cemetery areas were proper locations for rituals in Ariadne's honor, especially in the Early Minoan Period when the temple-palaces with their central courts and other areas that could accommodate dancing had not yet been built; that perhaps two festivals each year were celebrated at the tombs, one in the spring and one in the fall.[125] It is an interesting hypothesis and one that underscores the life-giving and regenerative aspects of the Goddess celebrated in the tomb areas.

Before drawing any further conclusions about the Koumasa I Goddess, I would like to turn to my final example for the Early Minoan Period, the Mochlos Goddess.

The Mochlos Goddess

Like the Koumasa I Goddess, the Mochlos Goddess was also found in a cemetery with collective burials. This one was a rock cut tomb cemetery rather than a tholos or rectangular tomb cemetery. Like the cemetery in which the Koumasa I-IV Goddesses were found, the area outside the tombs at Mochlos is 'capable of serving communal gatherings.'[126]

Mochlos, an important trading center throughout the Minoan era with an excellent harbor, is located off the northeast coast of Crete. Now a tiny island, Mochlos was, from the Bronze Age to the Roman era, when the sea level was lower, a peninsula.[127] The tombs, which stand above the ground like houses, are 'on a wide ledge on a high cliff over the sea on the west side of the island.'[128]

The Mochlos Goddess is 18 centimeters high and bell-shaped like the other figurines under consideration. She has 'hollow tubular breasts held or pressed by the carefully rendered hands.'[129] There is a white painted pattern on her red-brown body [130] which includes spirals and zigzags, and, as Warren has pointed out, what looks like a snake coiled like a headband on

---

[123] Nilsson 1949: 524.

[124] In the most well-known version of the myth of Ariadne and Theseus, the pair sailed to Naxos after Theseus killed the Minotaur (with the aid of Ariadne). There 'she was deserted by Theseus for love of another woman: For strong love for Aegle the daughter of Panopeus overpowered him' (Hesiod 1977: 207). Some versions of the myth say Ariadne then hanged herself. In other versions she attempts suicide by drowning and is rescued by the god Dionysos, who then makes Ariadne his bride.

[125] Branigan 1993:133.

[126] Marinatos 1993: 14.

[127] Rackham and Moody 1996: 202.

[128] Davaras 1976: 200.

[129] Warren 1973: 138.

[130] Warren believes that the white pattern suggests a robe, noting that robes and girdles were found with the Snake Goddesses of Knossos, and in Greek religion the 'presentation of a special robe played an important part in the cult of Athena' (Warren 1973: 143).

Figure 2. The Mochlos Goddess (on the right). The Malia Goddess (on the left). Mochlos Goddess: Early Minoan III, c. 2300-2150 BC, 18cm in height, clay, found in Tomb XIII, Mochlos, Crete. Malia Goddess: Early Minoan III, c. 2300-2150 BC, 16.4cm in height, clay, found in cemetery, Malia, Crete. Heraklion Museum, Crete. Photograph by author.

her head.[131] Her head is tilted back slightly, as is that of the Koumasa I Goddess. Warren believes that this is a pose of acknowledging worshippers or adorants.[132] On her back is also a handle for pouring.

The Mochlos Goddess was found in Tomb XIII, which is dated to EM III, c. 1580-1450 BC. Within the same tomb, excavator American archaeologist Richard Seager also found a number of marble, clay, and steatite cups, jugs, and bowls of 'exquisite quality and craftsmanship,'[133] which indicate ritual toasting of the dead. In nearby tombs were placed stone palettes used for coloring the dead, and delicate gold jewelry, especially made for funerary purposes.

It is apparent from the above description that the Goddess of Mochlos has at least one of the attributes deemed indicative of the Minoan Goddess by Aegean archaeologists: the snake on her head. The snake is found as an attribute of the Goddess throughout the Minoan period, and it also appears attached to cult objects. I said above that the Minoan Goddess can also be identified by gesture—in this case the head of the Mochlos Goddess is tilted back as if acknowledging her worshippers. The place she was found—a tomb—is also indicative of her role, for the tomb is a sacred place, a ritual context. Most important, however, are her breasts. Gimbutas has said that the breasts of the Goddess are associated with her primary aspect, that of life-giver, for they symbolize moisture of the Goddess's body.[134] Archaeologists concur that the Mochlos Goddess is indeed a Goddess (as well as the Koumasa I and Myrtos Goddesses), and one of the main reasons for this identification is her breasts and the associated emphasis on nurturance that the prominent breasts denote. Marinatos notes that the Goddesses of Mochlos, Koumasa, Archanes, and Malia should be considered nurturing figures because of the life-giving liquid they supply.[135] Warren, who considers the breasts of the Goddess of Mochlos the key factor indicating her status as a Goddess, calls her a 'fertility goddess.'[136] Elizabeth

---

[131] Warren 1973: 139.
[132] Warren 1973: 142.
[133] Marinatos 1993: 15.
[134] Gimbutas 1989: 3.
[135] Marinatos 1993: 29.
[136] Warren 1973: 143.

Fowden, writing of the Goddess of Myrtos, the Koumasa I Goddess, and the Mochlos Goddess, as well as the similar figurines from Malia and the Trapeza Cave, also burial sites, writes:

> In the vessels is captured the act of provision and the flow of nourishing liquid – the goddess is seen as provider of this necessary source of life, and in burial contexts she symbolically provides regeneration for the dead when these vessels are used in funerary ritual. She remains in the tomb for symbolic, spiritual provision just as the bowls and other objects are left for material provision.[137]

Fowden has struck upon another very important point: the Goddess represented at Mochlos, Koumasa, Myrtos, Trapeza Cave, and Malia is not only Life-Giver, but Regeneratrix as well. The fact that very similar looking Goddesses are found in both burial and shrine contexts indicates to Fowden that the Minoans called upon their Goddess not only in the face of death, but in daily life. For Fowden, the Goddess of Mochlos and her 'sister' Goddesses I and II from Koumasa, the Goddess of Myrtos, the Goddess of Malia, and the Goddess of the Trapeza cave, are protectresses, not only of the water supply, as Warren believed of the Myrtos Goddess, but of the earth and sky, and ultimately, Fowden believes, they are the Nature Goddess herself.[138]

Conclusion: Early Minoan Mother Goddesses

I return now to the question of whether or not these three Goddesses are Mother Goddesses. I believe I have established that the find spots, architecture, attributes, cult equipment, and symbols found with the figurines all point to an interpretation of these figurines as Goddesses. Moreover, they can be interpreted as Goddesses of Life-Giving, Death and Regeneration. The Goddess of Myrtos was found in a shrine that appears to have served the entire settlement. The shrine complex contained not only the shrine room with the Goddess herself, an altar, and numerous vessels, but an adjacent storage room which also contained numerous vessels, as well as a room for the preparation of liquid offerings, probably wine, milk, or water. Similar shrine complexes, also containing Goddesses, are found in the Late Minoan period, thus further validating that this was a shrine complex. The Goddess herself has the attribute of a bird, her long neck, signifying not only that she is a Goddess but that she is a 'bird woman' and Life-Giver. She has other attributes of life-giving as well: her breasts, bell-shaped body, net patterning,[139] pubic triangle, and the little jug held in the crook of her arm as one would hold a child.

The Koumasa I Goddess was found in the paved area of a cemetery between a tholos tomb and an ossuary. Thus she was found in a sacred site, a cemetery, where communal ritual was performed throughout the Early Minoan era. She was found with three other similar-looking Goddesses, as well as bull figurines, bird figurines, and an egg-shaped vessel. As argued above, the bull, the bird, and the egg shape are all symbolic of the continuation of life or of regeneration. The bull and bird are generally recognized as cult symbols as well. The Goddess herself also exhibits the symbols of life-giving and regeneration: she is bell-shaped; is decorated with X's,[140] symbolic of

---

[137] Fowden 1990: 17.
[138] Fowden 1990: 18.
[139] Gimbutas has discussed the meaning of the net motif in her book *The Language of The Goddess*. According to her, pottery painting and the net motif emerged in the early Neolithic. Gimbutas interprets the net pattern as part of the aquatic symbol family indicative of the waters of life and the life-giving power of the Goddess (Gimbutas 1989: 81).
[140] The X or 'cross-band' as Gimbutas also calls it, she identifies as being associated with the Bird Goddess as well as

life-giving; and with trees of life, also symbolic of life-giving; carries a small jug as one would a child; and has a snake, one of the attributes of the Goddess and a symbol of regeneration, draped along her shoulders and arms. Finally, through the use of mythology, we can link her to Ariadne, a very ancient Minoan Goddess of Death and Rebirth.

The Mochlos Goddess was also found in a sacred/ritual site: a tomb. The snake on her head marks her as a Goddess and Regeneratrix, and the snake is a cult symbol as well. Her prominent breasts, which mark her as provider of the necessary source of life, point to her role as Regeneratrix and Life-Giver.

As for the question of whether or not they are Mother Goddesses, I believe the answer is affirmative. All three personify the role of Life-Giver, in their attributes, the symbolism on them and around them, in the very shape of their bodies; and the objects they hold—jugs and breasts—provide the necessary source of life. The Koumasa and Mochlos Goddesses, present as they are in tomb contexts, are obviously Goddesses of Death and Regeneratrixes as well—for they were believed to provide the necessary source of life for the dead. Even the Myrtos Goddess can be seen as a Regeneratrix. Her long neck, which can give her the appearance of a Bird Goddess, and the symbols of the net and the triangle over the pubic area, point to a 'transfunctional Goddess' (as Gimbutas said). For when such symbols are found with the Bird Goddess, 'they are associated with life creation and regeneration.'[141]

The Old Palace Period, c. 2100-1700 BC

A period of unusually rapid development from *c.* 2100-1900 BC culminated in a brilliant new era for Minoan civilization that has been referred to variously as the First Palace Period, Old Palace Period, Protopalatial Period, or Middle Minoan Period, MM I, *c.* 2100-1900 BC, and MM II, *c.* 1900-1700 BC. This is the time of the creation of the 'palaces' at Knossos, Phaistos, and Malia in central and eastern Crete. It is also characterized by the growth of urban centers at Zakros, Kydonia, Kommos, Palaikastro, and Archanes; the invention of the potters' wheel and the production of the exquisite pottery known as Kamares ware; advances in technology, especially for crafting jewelry and engraved sealstones; the establishment of overseas links with every area of the eastern Mediterranean (Egypt, the coast of Syria and Palestine, mainland Greece, the Aegean islands, and Asia Minor); and the introduction of writing, first of Cretan hieroglyphic and then Linear A.

Before continuing, I should say here that I prefer, and will from now forward refer to the Minoan 'palaces' as 'temple-palace' complexes: meaning that they were primarily religious centers that had important administrative and economic functions. There are a number of reasons for calling them temple-palace complexes and the argument is well-stated by Marinatos in *Minoan Religion*. To explain briefly, throne rooms and residential areas, although thought to be typical of 'palaces,' are not well documented in the 'palaces' of Minoan Crete. The one throne room that has been found, at Knossos, has convincingly been shown to be the throne of a priestess-queen, not a king, and thus the seat of a theacracy, not a kingdom. Moreover, the architecture of all the palaces, their uniform orientation, and the uniform dimensions of their central courts

---

with streams, net patterns, snakes, and breasts. It is one of the hieroglyphic symbols of the iconography of the Goddess and is closely linked to the life-giving aspect of the Goddess (Gimbutas 1989: xxiii, 12-13).

[141] Gimbutas 1989: 1.

illustrate an adherence to sacred architectural principles. The west wings of the 'palaces' have an especially sacred character to them with courts surrounded by shrines, storage rooms, and cult equipment (found in situ), raised pathways, stone platforms, and granaries. Even the east wings had ceremonial areas. As for their economic function, the 'palaces' provided sizable areas for the storage of agricultural products, and interestingly, these storage areas were often marked with religious symbols. 'The palaces were also "factories" where materials . . . were worked and agriculture produce processed.'[142] Finally, the strongest argument in favor of the 'palaces' being religious centers is 'the religious content of the wall paintings.'[143] These will be discussed in detail below.

When one looks for the iconography of the Goddess in the 'Old Palace Period,' one is disappointed to find a scarcity of material. This is so for several reasons. First of all, seals and sealings, usually a rich source of iconographic information, are not helpful for this time period as they tend to portray abstract symbols rather than ritual or religious scenes. Secondly, clay figures of what can be identified as deities, such as we have seen for the Neolithic and Early Minoan Period, are missing from the archaeological record for the Protopalatial period. For the Protopalatial period one must turn to pottery to find iconography of the Goddess.

The Bowl of the Snake Goddess and the Fruitstand of the Goddess of the Lilies

There are several pieces of pottery that give one a glimpse of the Goddess and I wish to discuss those here. Both are from the temple-palace of Phaistos which is located in the central, southern part of the island. The pottery under discussion comes from the Lower West Court Sanctuary Complex of Phaistos, an area containing eleven rooms, all of which were either storage rooms for cult equipment or preparation rooms. Gesell believes that the cult rites which these rooms served may have been carried out in the West Court, or in a room further to the east, or even in a room upstairs.[144] She notes that the complex opened out from the temple-palace and thus was available to people both inside and outside the temple-palace, in other words, it was a public sanctuary.

In addition to the several pieces of pottery with iconography of the Goddess that I will focus on, a great deal of cult equipment was found in this complex. In one storeroom, Room IL, the northern most room of the complex, besides three stone benches, and three circular offering tables, archaeologists discovered two pots with horns or breasts, three bull rhyta, an agrimi horn, a piece of a fruitstand with a double axe incised on it, a bridge-spouted pot with a double-axe painted on it, and a quantity of pottery.[145] In the southern area of the Lower West Court Sanctuary complex, were large facilities which contained a hearth room, preparation rooms with cult equipment and tools, an anteroom with a storage closet filled with cups, a probable cult dining room, and several storage rooms with pithoi and cult equipment suitable for holding food and liquid offerings as well as presenting them.[146]

---

[142] Marinatos 1993: 48.
[143] Marinatos 1993: 50.
[144] Gesell 1985: 11.
[145] Moss 2005: 84.
[146] Gesell 1985: 65.

In a cupboard under the stair of Room LV was found what is now referred to by archaeologists as the 'Bowl of the Snake Goddess.' The bowl, which measures 0.049m in height and 0.184m in diameter, has a small handle on one side. In the center of the bowl, painted on the inside, is a female figure with a triangle shaped body. The triangle has been painted red. Neither her arms nor legs are visible. The two long sides of her triangle/body have white loops along them, reminiscent of snakes. Her round head is turned sideways, and the viewer sees a large eye, a beak-shaped nose and four large curls on the top of her head representing hair. She is accompanied by two women, who occupy the space to either side of her. The lower bodies of these women are tear-drop shaped, their torsos, arms, one held up and one held down, and feet are visible. Their heads, eyes, noses, and hair are very similar to those of the central figure. There is a flower to the right below the central figure which has been identified as a lily. The hands of the two figures flanking the central figure have a shape similar to the lily below the central figure.

Room LIV of the Lower West Court Sanctuary Complex, described by Moss as a 'Preparation Room,' contained the fragments of the other important piece now referred to as the 'Fruitstand of the Goddess of the Lilies.' In this piece, the plate of the fruitstand also shows three women, two of whom appear to be votaries and resemble the two women on the 'Bowl of the Snake Goddess.' Gesell notes that 'the votaries of both vases are dressed alike in animal hide skirts and have their hair in loose ringlets.'[147] The votaries are placed on each side of the central figure and seem to be dancing. The female figure in the center faces right and holds what archaeologists have determined to be lilies, one in each hand. On the outside edges of this rather thick plate are female worshippers, resembling the votaries on the upper portion of the plate, who appear to be bowing forward, their hair flopping over their foreheads. Moss suggests they may be bowing forward to pick flowers, 'although there are no flowers in the scene.'[148] The column holding the plate with the three figures was never found so it is not known what it looked like or how tall it was. The circular base of the fruitstand is decorated with women dancing, hands on hips, reminiscent of the two dancing figures on the upper plate. Moss remarks that they 'may be dancing in honor of the goddess.'[149] Found in the same room with the 'Fruitstand of the Goddess of the Lilies' were a rectangular 12-holed kernos, a stone lamp with a double axe symbol on it, and other lamps.[150]

The Bowl of the Snake Goddess and the Fruitstand of the Goddess of the Lilies, two important pieces of Middle Minoan I and II evidence for the Minoan Goddess, have been interpreted in a number of ways. There is general agreement among Aegeanists that the central figures in each of the pieces are Goddesses. Gesell writes that they are 'almost certainly goddesses.'[151] But what sort of Goddesses are they? Whom do they represent?

Gesell does not identify the Goddesses in either piece specifically. She notes only that the central figure on the bowl is 'identified as a snake goddess because the loops down her robe suggest snakes.'[152] She observes that the female figure on the fruitstand, the Goddess of the Lilies, is the predecessor of a similar figure depicted on a LM I mold found near Palaikastro

---

[147] Gesell 1985: 17.
[148] Moss 2005: 86
[149] Moss 2005: 86.
[150] Moss 2005: 84.
[151] Gesell 1985: 17.
[152] Gesell 1985: 17.

(eastern Crete.)[153] Gesell makes the important point that 'Both scenes appear to be forerunners of the ecstatic cult scenes on certain LM gold rings.'[154] She is not certain whether one Goddess in several aspects, or several different Goddesses are depicted in the bowl and fruitstand. She does say that 'The two scenes may give us our only view of cult rites during the Protopalatial period.'[155]

Marinatos offers an interpretation of the bowl and fruitstand in *Minoan Religion*. She finds the lilies the most significant feature, in addition of course to the central figures, the Goddesses, in both pieces. She believes the lilies connect the Goddess 'with vegetation and a seasonal cycle.'[156] Thus Marinatos sees a Vegetation or Nature Goddess being represented in these Middle Minoan artifacts.

Moss has a detailed discussion of the two pieces in her work. She offers several ideas in regards to the Bowl of the Snake Goddess. First of all, she draws attention to the fact that the loops down the side of the Goddess's body are like the loops found along the sides of the 'snake tubes,' offering vessels decorated with snakes found from the MM III, *c.* 1700 BC through LM III C, *c.* 1070 BC period. If the Minoans thought of the snake as symbolic of regeneration, then such symbolism on the Goddess's body is important. Moss believes the central figure on the Bowl of the Snake Goddess is both smaller and younger than her two companions and that she appears to be rising up. Moss posits that what is being depicted is a 'rite of passage into puberty or the celebration of the coming of fertility (spring or summer).'[157]

Interpreting the loops on the Goddess's side as the sloughed off skin of the snake, rather than the snake itself, Moss also takes the view that the central figure is emerging from a period of transition 'just as a snake emerges from its old skin, renewed, larger and more mature than before.'[158] Thus she calls the central figure on the Bowl of the Snake Goddess a 'regenerative goddess.'[159] In a footnote she also points out that perhaps this scene represents the return of the 'Spring Maiden' Persephone, or even her descent.[160]

It is not only Moss who hypothesizes that the central figure on the Bowl of the Snake Goddess may be Persephone. Historian of myth, Karl Kerenyi, calling the bowl 'the earliest extant representation of Persephone,' and terming it 'Persephone with two companions,' writes: 'we recognize the same scene preceding the abduction of the goddess in the hymn [*Homeric Hymn to Demeter*] and in the Phaistos cup: Persephone admiring the flower.'[161]

Scholars Anne Baring and Jules Cashford in their work *The Myth of the Goddess: Evolution of an Image* also discuss the bowl and fruitstand from Phaistos. They come to the same conclusion as Kerenyi: 'two female figures appear, from the drooping gesture of their arms, to be mourning

---

[153] Gesell 1985: 17.
[154] Gesell 1985: 12.
[155] Gesell 1985: 17.
[156] Marinatos 1993: 149.
[157] Moss 2005: 85.
[158] Moss 2005: 85.
[159] Moss 2005: 85.
[160] Moss 2005: 247.
[161] Kerenyi 1967: xix-xx.

a third figure between them apparently about to pick a narcissus . . . , and the direction of the picture is downwards into the earth.'[162]

Turning their attention to the Fruitstand of the Goddess of the Lilies, they write:

> the same three figures are gesturing upwards together as in a celebration, the central one holding up a flower in each hand, and the scene has the feeling of rising movement, such as a return from below the earth.'[163]

Baring and Cashford call the first cup 'Descent of the Goddess,' the second, 'Return of the Goddess.'

Returning to Moss and her interpretation of the Fruitstand of the 'Goddess of the Lilies,' she likens it, with its circle of dancers on its base, to a well-known artifact from the Kamilari tomb, MM III, c. 1700-1580 BC, near Phaistos in the Mesara. This terracotta piece consists of a group of naked figures dancing in a circle within an enclosure topped by the cult symbol of the horns of consecration. If Marinatos is correct about the lily being a seasonal symbol of spring, says Moss, then 'this may be a depiction of a seasonal rite of a goddess which includes dancing in a circle.'[164] Noting that bovine rhyta as well as painted and incised double axes were found in Room IL, in the same complex as both the Bowl of the Snake Goddess and the Fruitstand of the Goddess of the Lilies, Moss argues that since bovine rhyta can be connected with the Egyptian Goddess Hathor in her aspect as a Goddess of Renewal, and double axes can be said to symbolize renewal as well, the idea that the cult assemblage found in the complex has to do with rites of renewal is reinforced.[165] She concludes that it is impossible to determine whether only a Goddess of Renewal was worshipped at Phaistos, or a Goddess of Vegetation and Agriculture as well.[166]

In the previous section on the EM II, c. 2600-2300 BC, figurines from Koumasa, it was noted that Branigan has argued that dancing often took place in the paved areas of the Mesara cemeteries and that these areas were the location 'of rituals and ceremonies which were concerned with the vegetational cycle and fertility.'[167] Branigan based these conclusions on a number of factors: architecture, the Koumasa I Goddess, as well as other Goddesses, cult equipment, cult symbols, votive offerings, and mythology: the myth of the dancing floor of Ariadne at Knossos and the celebration of her life and death as the Vegetation Goddess who dies and is reborn. Looking at the bowl and fruitstand found at Phaistos (which it must be remembered is located on the plain of the Mesara, near to some of the tholos tombs of the Mesara), Branigan hypothesizes that 'dances to Ariadne may not have been the only choreography seen on the cemetery pavements.'[168] He conjectures that the dancers on the Phaistos bowl and fruitstand

> are performing in honour of the Snake Goddess, and that these two plates from Phaistos therefore preserve remarkable near-contemporary 'snap-shots' of the sort of dances

---

[162] Baring and Cashford 1991: 116.
[163] Baring and Cashford 1991: 116-117.
[164] Moss 2005: 86.
[165] Moss 2005: 85.
[166] Moss 2005: 86.
[167] Branigan 1993: 135.
[168] Branigan 1993: 136.

which the people of Koumasa may have performed on the pavement outside their tholos tombs in the centuries around 2000 BC.[169]

All the archaeologists who have discussed and interpreted the bowl and fruitstand are in agreement that a representation of the Goddess is found on each and that this Goddess most probably represents Renewal or Regeneration and Vegetation or Nature. Is she a Mother Goddess? I would argue that she is. These two representations of the Goddess are found in the West Lower Court Sanctuary of the temple-palace of Phaistos. The larger find spot, which is identified as a preparation room for rituals to be carried out in nearby rooms, is located in the part of the temple-palace (the western) that is most associated with rebirth and regeneration, the storage of agricultural products, and the celebration of harvest festivals. Moreover, these Goddesses are surrounded by virtually every type of cult equipment and cult symbol that archaeologists have identified as pointing to the worship of the Minoan Goddess: one finds in this complex the cult symbols of the double axe, horns of consecration, bull, snake, and agrimi. These same symbols are also attributes of the Goddess. As for cult equipment, one finds offering vessels of various types, including rhyta, and offering tables. Not only does the sanctuary contain a bench but a cult dining area as well.

The Goddess at the center of the Bowl of the Snake Goddess is associated with the lily, which appears at the bottom edge of the plate, and with the snake, which loops down on either side of her triangular body. The Goddess on the Fruitstand of the Goddess of the Lilies is also associated with the lily. Marinatos has shown that beginning in this period, c. 2100 BC, and continuing into the MM III, c. 1700-1580 BC, the Goddess of Minoan Crete is often shown receiving, smelling, and surrounded by lilies, and has argued that the lily is an important symbol of her association with Nature, identifies her as the Goddess of Nature, and associates the Goddess with renewal since the lily appears in Crete in the spring, a time of seasonal renewal.[170] The snake identifies the Goddess with renewal as well, as in the snake shedding its skin, or emerging from hibernation or from 'death' into life. I think the snake also connects the Goddess to death, but in the sense of death as the precursor to new life, to rebirth.

Gimbutas has also connected one of the figures on the Bowl of the Snake Goddess to death and rebirth. For the figure to the left of the central figure on the Bowl of the Snake Goddess, Gimbutas offers the interpretation that she is an example of the 'Goddess of Death: Announcer of Death as Bird of Prey and Poisonous Snake.' She calls the figure a 'Bird Goddess design with snake crest on painted pottery from Phaistos, Crete, early 2nd mill. BC.' Gimbutas interprets the figure as a representation of the Bird Goddess because, I believe, of her bird-like face, especially her beak-like nose. The ringlets on her head Gimbutas interprets as snakes. Her arm position, one arm up and one down, Gimbutas calls 'a gesture of power or verdict.'[171] Gimbutas places her in a lineage, beginning with Çatal Hüyük, of the Vulture Goddess, a manifestation, since Neolithic times, of the Death Goddess. This is of course a different interpretation than that offered by other archaeologists. Most call her a votary. For those who would interpret the Bowl of the Snake Goddess as an illustration of Persephone's descent into the underworld, as Moss, Kerenyi, Baring, and Cashford would, the figure of a Goddess of Death fits in well with the interpretation.

---

[169] Branigan 1993: 136.
[170] Marinatos 1993: 149, 152, 195.
[171] Gimbutas 1991: 240.

In her close association with Nature through the symbol of the lily, I believe the Goddess on the bowl and fruitstand can be thought of as a Mother Goddess, for it is her 'position over the natural environment, rather than any specifically maternal function'[172] which I said was one aspect of my definition of a Mother Goddess. It seems to me that the discussion above also makes clear that these two manifestations of the Goddess encompass a Goddess who mediates over life, death, and rebirth. All the attributes, cult symbols, equipment, architecture, and find spots point to a Goddess who can be identified with life, death, rebirth, and regeneration. She who is responsible for life, death, and regeneration is, in my definition of the term, she who is the Mother Goddess.

The New Palace Period, c. 1700-1450 BC

In about 1700 BC an earthquake or series of earthquakes caused widespread destruction to the civilization of Minoan Crete and brought the Old Palace Period to an end. There followed a period of massive rebuilding ushering in a time which is considered the apogee of Minoan Civilization: the Neopalatial, New Palace Period, or Middle Minoan to Late Minoan Period, MM IIIA to LM I A/B, c. 1700- 1450 BC.

The Middle to Late Minoan IA/B is characterized by flourishing temple-palaces. In addition to the rebuilding of Knossos, Phaistos, and Malia, temple-palaces were built at Zakros and Petras in eastern Crete, and Galatas in the center of the island. Temple-palaces are also attested at Khania in western Crete and Archanes in north-central Crete. There was 'urbanization on a scale not seen elsewhere in the Aegean.'[173] Great works of art and craftspersonship also characterize the period: wall painting, fine pottery in the Floral and Marine Styles, jewelry, faience, ivory, bronzes, stone vases with reliefs and without, and seal engravings. 'The subtlety and complexity of the scenes on the Minoan seals is unsurpassed even in the Near East.'[174] There was economic prosperity, and continued and expanded trade with Egypt, the Near East, Anatolia, and mainland Greece. 'Indisputable Minoan influence' on some of the islands of the Aegean is discernable during this period.[175] 'The islands of the Aegean became very "Minoanized" at this time. Excavations on Melos, Kea and Thera, in particular, have revealed extensive towns that owe much to Crete in their lifestyle and material culture.'[176]

The Snake Goddesses from the Temple Repositories at Knossos

I shall begin my discussion of the iconography of the Mother Goddess in the New Palace Period with the two most well-known artifacts of that period, indeed of any period of Minoan history: the Snake Goddesses from the temple-palace of Knossos. According to Gesell, these are the only figurines of the New Palace Period 'with attributes which allow them to be identified as goddesses.'[177] There are three of them. Two have been reconstructed: the larger is 34 centimeters high, the smaller, 20. The lower half of a third figurine was also found. Moss points out that this fragment, which measures 17 centimeters from the waist to the lower hem of the skirt, would have been the largest of the three if she had been complete. Interestingly, three arms

---

[172] Roller 1999: 6.
[173] Fitton 2002: 131.
[174] Marinatos 1993: 4.
[175] Marinatos 1993: 4.
[176] Fitton 2002: 164.
[177] Gesell 1985: 34.

Figure 3. Small Snake Goddess, Temple-Palace of Knossos. LM I, c. 1580-1450 BC, 20cm. in height, faience, found in Knossos Temple Repositories. Heraklion Museum, Crete. Photograph by author.

Figure 4. Large Snake Goddess, Temple-Palace of Knossos. LM I, c. 1580-1450 BC, 34cm. in height, faience, found in Knossos Temple Repositories. Heraklion Museum, Crete. Photograph by author.

and several hands were also found in the same location as the Snake Goddesses, indicating to archaeologist Marina Panagiotaki, who re-excavated the Central Palace Sanctuary at Knossos in 1993, that the Sanctuary originally contained five or six figurines.[178]

Before discussing the Goddesses themselves, I would like to examine their find spots and the items found with them. The two more intact Snake Goddesses under review were found in two cists in a room to the west of the Central Court of the temple-palace of Knossos—a room which Evans termed the Temple Repositories—part of a larger area known to archaeologists as the Central Palace Sanctuary. The larger Snake Goddess, the bottom half of the smaller Snake Goddess, and the fragment of a third Goddess were found in the Eastern Repository cist. The top part of the smaller Snake Goddess was found in the Western Repository cist.

Evans and his assistant, Duncan Mackenzie, noted in their excavation diaries and annual reports that in addition to the Snake Goddesses, in the Eastern Temple Repositories, the following items were also found: objects of faience—beads, vessels, small bowls, ewers, chalices and flying fish; ivory, bone, a clay tablet, roundels and sealings, an equal-armed marble cross,

---

[178] Panagiotaki 1999: 98.

Figure 5. Shells, flying fish and argonauts. LM I, c. 1580-1450 BC, fish and argonauts of faience, shells are natural but painted, found with the Knossos Snake Goddesses in the Temple Repositories. Heraklion Museum, Crete. Photograph by Dr. Mara Lynn Keller. Reprinted with permission.

Figure 6. Goat with kid (on the left), and cow with calf (on the right). LM I, c. 1580-1450 BC, faience plaques, found with the Knossos Snake Goddesses in Temple Repositories. Heraklion Museum, Crete. Photograph by Dr. Mara Lynn Keller. Reprinted with permission.

stone libation tables, antlers, carbonized corn, painted seashells, and two beautiful plaques, one of a goat suckling her kid, another of a cow and a calf.[179]

In the Western Temple Repositories, the excavators' diaries and reports note the lower half of a Snake Goddess, gold foil, crystal plaques, a disc, objects of bronze, and a mallet of limestone.[180]

These objects were found in layers in the cists. The upper layer was clay, then a soil mixture of rubble and charred wood, pottery was found next and gold foil, below these, in the earth, the rest of the objects listed above.[181] Panagiotaki has remarked that

the finds were not simply thrown in the T[emple] R[epositories], as was the case with all other cists in the Palace; on the contrary, the objects were placed in the T[emple]

[179] Panagiotaki 1999: 73.
[180] Panagiotaki 1999: 73.
[181] Panagiotaki 1999: 73.

R[epositories] according to their material with the vases always on top. There was, therefore, a kind of stratigraphy which makes it clear that the objects placed in the T[emple] R[epositories] were honoured and treasured, not so much because gold was involved but because of the figurines representing goddesses or priestesses; the idea that the figurines had been 'ritually buried with their cult equipment' has already been rightly expressed by Gesell.[182]

Panagiotaki has hypothesized that the faience items (fifty pieces in all and composing the bulk of the preserved items, aside from the shells and the sealings), were meant as inlays for display, as embellishments to the shrine furniture, or votive offerings.[183] Among the faience pieces were plants and flowers: lilies, and papyrus, both connected with cult symbol; and a lotus flower, which Panagiotaki associates with Egypt, Hathor, and renewal.[184] Marine objects such as flying fish and argonauts also make up the faience assemblage, and Panagiotaki thinks they may represent fertility: 'The fact that the argonaut shell is created to house the eggs of the female may suggest that argonauts symbolize not only the sea . . . but also fertility.'[185] Panagiotaki wonders if the wide variety of sea creatures portrayed in faience in the Temple Repositories might not suggest the 'veneration of the sea, perhaps in the form of a sea goddess.'[186]

Referring to the 'land animal plaques' including the ones of the goat and kid and cow and calf, Panagiotaki notes that all the plaque and plaque fragments found in the Temple Repositories bring out the tender side of the animal.'[187] She hypothesizes that 'the shared peaceful atmosphere of the T[emple] R[epositories] animals' point to a deity who 'was a mother figure, *kourotrophos,* concerned with the softer and maternal aspects of life.'[188] She also proposes that the animal plaques symbolize life and the renewal of life.[189]

Also of significance are the three miniature dresses and three girdles or belts, made of faience. Decorated with crocuses and lilies, Panagiotaki posits that these 'point to a religious aspect in the material recovered from the T[emple] R[epositories], and by association the general area.'[190] She surmises that they were offered to the Goddess

> in a manner akin to the dedication of items of dress . . . depicted on Minoan seals, or in contemporary Theran frescoes, or in Classical Greece, such as the peplos offered annually to Athena in the Parthenon at Athens.[191]

Finally, approximately two thousand faience beads were also found in the Temple Repositories. These Panagiotaki believes were offerings to the shrine.

In addition to the faience objects, more than five hundred sea shells, some of them painted, were unearthed in the Eastern Temple Repositories. Panagiotaki notes that seashells 'have

---

[182] Panagiotaki 1999: 74.
[183] Panagiotaki 1999: 148, 105.
[184] Panagiotaki 1999: 78.
[185] Panagiotaki 1999: 80.
[186] Panagiotaki 1999: 81.
[187] Panagiotaki 1999: 87.
[188] Panagiotaki 1999: 87.
[189] Panagiotaki 1999: 90.
[190] Panagiotaki 1999: 103.
[191] Panagiotaki 1999: 103.

Figure 7. Faience dresses. LM I, c. 1580-1450 BC, faience, found with the Knossos Snake Goddesses in Temple Repositories. Heraklion Museum, Crete. Photograph by author.

been found in contexts, or directly connected with objects that carry religious overtones' in MM II-LM I, c. 1900-1450 BC, at Phaistos, Juktas and Pyrgos, Crete, and LH III, c. 1375-1100 BC, at Phylakopi (Melos) and in many sites of all periods in Cyprus and the Near East.[192]

Also found in large numbers in the Temple Repositories were vases. Evans discovered almost fifty vases including: five bird-shaped vases, amphorae and jars decorated with spirals and floral patterns as well as at least one with an inscription in Linear A. It is important to take note of the birds and the spirals. The bird is a cult symbol and attribute of the Goddess, the spiral a symbol of the life force.[193]

As for the Snake Goddesses themselves, the larger of the two Snake Goddesses wears what has come to be seen as a priestess costume: an open bodice to reveal her breasts, a necklace, a laced corset, and a skirt decorated with horizontal stripes and a net pattern at the hem area, with a kind of double apron over it. What is very special about her appearance are the snakes on her body. She has three snakes coiled around her. The head of one is in her right hand. From her hand the snake moves up her right arm, continues around her upper back and shoulders, and then moves down her left arm. The Goddess holds its tail in her left palm. The two other snakes are at her waist where they form an elaborate knot with their bodies. One snake continues from the Goddess's waist around to the front of her apron and then around and all the way up her back to her right ear, where it coils its tail. The third snake continues from the Goddess's waist, where it formed part of the knot, to decorate the front of her apron. It then moves along her back until it reaches all the way to the top of her headdress. Its head projects from the top of the Goddess's headdress.

---

[192] Panagiotaki 1999: 130.
[193] Gimbutas 1989: 282.

The second, restored Snake Goddess is similarly dressed except that her skirt is flounced. Her arms are slightly bent at the elbows, almost in the shape of horns of consecration, and in each hand is a snake held with the tail pointing upwards. On her head is a tiara with a cat sitting on top of it. Panagiotaki identifies it as a leopard because of its black spots.[194]

The Snake Goddesses are dated to LM I, c. 1580-1450 BC, possibly LM IA, c. 1600/1580-1480 BC. However, as Moss has so importantly pointed out, they were sealed into the Temple Repositories at that time and most probably were in use before then. She bases this conclusion on the work of Panagiotaki whose research has led her to hypothesize that the items placed in the Repositories had been damaged (by some sort of disaster) and it was not the intention of those who placed them in the cists that they be retrieved at a later date. Gesell has dated them to MM IIIB. This puts them at the beginning of the New Palace Period.

How are the Snake Goddesses to be understood and interpreted? Evans believed that only the larger one of the two was a Goddess and that the smaller was her votary. However, he made this judgment before the tiara and cat/leopard had been determined to fit the head of the smaller Goddess.[195] Marinatos identifies both figurines as Goddesses and believes they belong to the category of the Goddess as Mistress of the Animals. She also stresses that the snake is a 'potent religious symbol.'[196] Not only do snakes cause terror and come from the underworld, 'but at the same time they have positive connotations of renewal.'[197] Marinatos views snakes as creators, death-bringers, and renewers of life.

Moss's interpretation of the Snake Goddesses is similar to that of Marinatos: they are images of the Mistress of the Animals and they represent regeneration and renewal. She further believes that their iconography 'may have been influenced by Egyptian religious symbolism.'[198] In support of this argument Moss cites the snake that is peering from the top of the tall hat of the larger Goddess. She likens it to the uraeus worn on the headdresses of Egyptian divinities and pharaohs (Hathor was sometimes depicted with a uraeus on her headdress of horns and solar disc). Moss notes that it represents life as well as the protection of the sovereign. Moss also points out that the loop at the top of the lacing of the Goddesses' bodices resembles the Egyptian Isis Knot symbol of life and divine power. Moss sees the cat on the tiara of the smaller Snake Goddess as reinforcing the association with Hathor, who was associated not only with snakes, but with cats as well.

Panagiotaki suggests that the larger of the existing Snake Goddesses may represent 'a maternal *kourotrophos* [childbearer], and the smaller "a younger daughter figure."'[199] She argues that the nurturing aspect of the Goddess 'is picked up emphatically by the plaques of the goat and cow with young, but also by the stressed breasts of the goddesses themselves.'[200] Panagiotaki hypothesizes that all of the cosmos, all of nature, is represented by the Snake Goddesses, but that their nurturing aspect, their life-giving and regenerative aspects, are being emphasized.

---

[194] Panagiotaki 1999: 98.
[195] Nilsson 1949: 86.
[196] Marinatos 1993: 157.
[197] Marinatos 1993: 158.
[198] Moss 2005: 69.
[199] Panagiotaki 1999: 104.
[200] Panagiotaki 1999: 104.

Why does Panagiotaki believe the Snake Goddesses represent all of nature? Because of the material found with the Goddesses as well as the Goddesses themselves.

> Animals of land and sea are well represented, flowers and fruits too. The snakes might have a chthonic and regeneration value, and the cross and 'sun' symbol (made of rock crystal and precious metal foil) an astral one.[201]

How were the Snake Goddesses used? In re-excavating the Central Palace Sanctuary at Knossos and looking once again at all the items found with the Snake Goddesses, Panagiotaki has concluded that the objects from the Temple Repositories must have been used for a nearby shrine. Evans himself identified such a shrine, what he termed the Tripartite Shrine. Panagiotaki believes it more likely that the shrine was on the floor above Evans's proposed shrine. Wherever the shrine was actually located, the presence of the Goddesses proves to Panagiotaki that we are looking at material (all of the artifacts from the cists) that had a religious significance. Why? One reason is the Snake Goddesses and the fact that the figurines 'exhibit a concern with matters outside the realm of ordinary day-to-day life. Snakes never have been an accoutrement of normal daily attire.'[202] The other piece of evidence that makes the use of the artifacts in a shrine a certainty is the stone offering tables that were among the findings.

Based on the Goddesses' attributes: the snakes, sacral knots, cat/leopard, the patterns on their dresses; their find spots: cists within the Knossos Central Palace Sanctuary's Temple Repositories area; and the archaeological assemblage they were found with (which was described in detail above); one can make a very strong argument that these figurines are Goddesses. Are they Mother Goddesses as well?

Certainly their role as Mistress of Nature, because of their association with snakes, the cat/leopard, sea creatures, and land creatures, ensures their interpretation as Mother Goddesses in the definition I gave earlier. Moreover, they are associated above all with snakes, and also with spirals, nets, and knots, which implies their association with not only death, but rebirth and renewal as well. They are divine mediators of life, death, and rebirth, 'otherworldly matters,' and are able to mediate the boundaries between this world and the next.

The Minoan frescoes

Almost as well-known as the Snake Goddesses of the Knossos Temple Repositories are the Minoan frescoes of the New Palace and Third Palace periods, MM II/MM IIIA-LM IIIA, c. 1900-1400 BC. Frescos of the figural type have been found only at Knossos, Ayia Triadha, Pseria, and Akrotiri/Thera, but mural decoration was also present in the villas of Amnisos, Tylisos, and Nirou Hani in Crete and the island of Thera. The extensive fresco decoration at Knossos led archaeologist and fresco restorer M. A. S. Cameron to theorize that the wall paintings at Knossos all revolved around one theme: 'a festival of birth/regeneration with the "great goddess" in the centre.'[203] It is possible that such a wall program also existed at other temple-palaces and villas.

---

[201] Panagiotaki 1999: 149.
[202] Panagiotaki 1999: 148.
[203] Cameron 1987: 323.

I will focus on several frescoes here: one from Ayia Triadha, Crete, and one from a building known as 'Xeste 3' at Thera. I have chosen these because they give us two clear examples of the Minoan Goddess.

The fresco in room 14 of Ayia Triadha

First I must briefly discuss the site of Ayia Triadha itself. Located approximately two miles from the temple-palace of Phaistos, the relationship between Phaistos and Ayia Triadha has never been clear. Ayia Triadha is often referred to by archaeologists as a royal villa or a 'building with palatial functions.'[204] Archaeologist L. Vance Watrous has shown that Ayia Triadha was essentially two villas (which he termed A and B), and that 'villa A functioned as an administrative center related to the wider palatial system on Crete.'[205] Originally inhabited in the Early Minoan and Old Palace periods, Ayia Triadha had, by the beginning of the Late Minoan period, become an important center as witnessed by the many religious, artistic and prestige items found within: frescoes, fine pottery, stone vases, figurines, votive double-axes, tools, copper ingots, one hundred and forty-seven Linear A tablets, and one thousand clay sealings. Like many other sites in Minoan Crete, Ayia Triadha was destroyed by fire in LM IB, c. 1480-1425 BC. During the Third Palace or Final Palatial period, c. 1450-1300 BC, it was occupied by the Mycenaeans who conducted an extensive building project there.

The fresco in question, which was probably painted in LM IA, c. 1580-1450 BC, comes from Villa A, room 14, which is located in the northwest section of the villa, and is part of a 'shrine complex' which also included rooms 13 and 52. Frescoes originally covered the walls of rooms 13 and 14, but only scanty traces of paint now remain in room 13. According to archaeologist Paul Rehak, 'vegetation, non-figural decoration, and a fragment of relief fresco, perhaps part of a seascape or river landscape,' decorated room 13.[206]

Room 14 measures 1.55 x 2.35 meters; its entrance is at the west end of the room; and there is a low platform at the east end of the room facing the entrance. Archaeologists have theorized that this whole suite of rooms (rooms 13, 14, and 52) was a ritual area, because of the polythyron or pier-and-door partition in Room 13, the platform in Room 14, and of course, because of the fresco or traces of fresco in both rooms 13 and 14. Since the fresco under review is now fragmentary and severely damaged, Ayia Triadha having suffered like the rest of Crete from the disaster that struck at the end of LM IB, c. 1450 BC, interpretations of the fresco must be based on an extensive reconstruction by M. A. S. Cameron.

Rehak provides the following description of the fresco as reconstructed by Cameron:

> The painting formed a continuous megalographic frieze around the three walls of room 14: at its east end, above the low dais, was a female figure in flounced skirt, close to an architectural platform or façade in a meadow of myrtle or dittany; she raises her hands in a gesture interpreted as hieratic or epiphanic. Both long side walls show a rocky landscape dotted by clumps of lilies, crocus, ivy and violets, one kneeling female figure

204 Fitton 2002: 133.
205 Watrous 1984: 123.
206 Rehak 1997: 165.

130

(a 'votary' or 'flower-picker'), and some representations of fauna, including stalking cats, birds and agrimia.

The two landscape compositions on the north and south side walls are differently structured. The south wall to the right of the entrance shows a rough landscape with variegated rocks. Rocky masses . . . create the impression of a mountainous hillside.

The background of the north side wall to the left of the entrance, by contrast, is painted with undulating red bands which encircle irregular white reserved areas.[207]

Found in room 14 along with the fresco were pottery fragments decorated with plant and marine motifs. However, Rehak makes the point that these fragments most likely fell from the floor above and were not originally in Room 14.

It is the female figure in the flounced skirt, close to the platform, with her arms raised at the elbows who is the representation of the Goddess in this fresco. She can be identified as a Goddess for a number of reasons. First of all she is placed opposite the door on the main axis of Room 14, thus occupying the focal point of the room—the most important position, according to Renfrew's list of criteria for recognizing a deity.[208] Additionally, she is placed above the dais or platform in room 14, again a position that focuses attention upon her.

Yet another aspect that identifies the central female image as a Goddess is the fact that in the fresco she is standing next to an architectural façade that looks like a platform or a seat. I said in the previous chapter that Marinatos has determined that one of the ways the Goddess is portrayed in Minoan iconography is seated on a platform where she accepts offerings from either female adorants or animals. Rehak also notes that 'in pictorial art an architectural platform is one of two seats commonly used by Minoan goddesses.'[209]

The natural landscape surrounding the Goddess and her votary also identifies her as a divinity. In the Ayia Triadha landscape we find crocuses, which we shall see again with the Goddess in the Xeste 3 landscape (discussed below), and which also appeared as decoration on the Temple Repositories' belts and the offering dresses of faience described above. Crocuses are one of the most often represented of the flowers in Minoan frescoes of a religious character. Present also in this fresco are lilies, and one is immediately reminded of the use of lilies with the Goddess on the fruitstand from the Old Palace Period at Phaistos. Faience lilies were found with the Snake Goddesses of Knossos (discussed above). Agrimia, one of the animals sacred to the Goddess, appear in the landscape, as do cats. The appearance of the cats reminds us of the feline on the head of the smaller of the two New Palace period Snake Goddesses, and also of the lions that appear with the Mother Goddess of Çatal Hüyük, with the Hittite and Phrygian Goddesses, and with the Minoan Goddess herself on the Mountain Mother sealing (to be discussed below). Finally, in regard to the landscape, art historian Anne P. Chapin makes the interesting point that the fresco cycle of Room 14 at Ayia Triadha contains 'floral hybridizations, innovative

---

[207] Rehak 1997: 167.
[208] Renfrew 1985: 23. Renfrew writes that 'an image, focally placed, without rivals for attention . . . may well qualify as a cult image' (Renfrew 1985: 23).
[209] Rehak 1997: 170.

depictions of native plants, and simultaneous blossoming.'[210] The 'floral hybridizations' she is referring to are the lilies in the fresco which were created by combining the features of two different types of existing lilies. The simultaneous flowerings were accomplished through the depiction of lilies, violets, and crocuses in the fresco. In nature these different species flower months apart. Chapin believes the hybridizations and simultaneous blossoming are not merely 'meaningless artistic devices' but, rather, they 'reinforce a sense of divine abundance,' and 'signal the presence of divinity.'[211]

Rehak points out that the Goddess in the Ayia Triadha fresco is 'similar to other representations of females identified as Goddesses in frescoes and reliefs from Knossos, Palaikastro, Pseria, and Phylakopi in Melos.'[212] W. S. Smith has indicated that the fresco, along with other frescoes in the room, may have been arranged to represent a mountaintop sanctuary similar to the one portrayed on the stone rhyton from the temple-palace at Zakros.[213]

Marinatos, who also discusses the fresco, using it as her first example of the New Palace period's preoccupation with portraying the Minoan Goddess as a Goddess of Nature, writes: 'the goddess is thus shown in a setting bursting with life, full of animals and vegetation.'[214] Archaeologist Litsa Kontorli-Papadopoulou calls the Ayia Triadha Goddess a Goddess of Vegetation, as do archaeologists Cameron and Sara Immerwahr.[215]

Moss sees a Goddess of Nature portrayed in the Ayia Triadha fresco. However, she is not sure if there is only one Goddess of Nature portrayed or two, for unlike Rehak, she admits the possibility that the kneeling female figure may also be a Goddess, not a votary. She makes this argument based on her observation that the figure of the votary appears to be larger than the figure of the Goddess, and that if the kneeling votary stood up, she would be larger than the Goddess, indeed larger than life size.[216] I am more convinced by the argument of archaeologist Bernice Jones, who has reconstructed the kneeling figure and the whole north wall on which she appeared, based on several newly found fragments of the fresco, her observation of the original fragment in the Heraklion Museum, her reconstruction (in linen) of the garment of the kneeling figure, and comparisons with Aegean seals and frescoes. Jones concludes that the kneeling figure is a votary hugging a baetyl.[217]

Certainly a strong case can be made for the central female figure in the Ayia Triadha fresco to be called a Goddess. The find spot, a shrine complex, her position within the shrine complex, and her attributes all point to that interpretation. Is she a Mother Goddess as well? The lack of other archaeological artifacts in room 14 makes interpretation more difficult than in some other cases. Nevertheless, I think one can refer to the Goddess in the fresco as a Mother Goddess because of her association in this fresco with so many aspects of Nature, and especially those aspects which are known attributes or symbols of the Minoan Goddess: crocus, lilies, cats, and agrimia. Also, it must be remembered that Ayia Triadha is an important site in Minoan

---

[210] Chapin 2004: 58.
[211] Chapin 2004: 56-57.
[212] Rehak 1997: 168.
[213] Smith 1965: 78.
[214] Marinatos 1993: 49.
[215] Kontorli-Papadoupoulou 1996: 99.
[216] Moss 2005: 9.
[217] Jones 2007: 151-157.

Crete, one with 'palatial functions,' and that fresco expert Sara Immerwahr has written that this fresco 'may have been the finest of all Minoan nature frescoes.'[218] To me, the Ayia Triadha fresco portrays a Goddess who exhibits a 'position of power over the natural environment,'[219] who appears as generatrix of the cycles of nature, and it is this that gives her the status of a Mother.

Better known than the Ayia Triadha fresco are the frescoes from the island of Thera, and the Theran settlement of Akrotiri, which was perfectly preserved beneath a layer of volcanic ash when an eruption occurred.[220] We turn next to a fresco on Thera at Akrotiri.

The frescoes at Xeste 3 at Thera, Akrotiri

Perhaps first a word must be said about why I am using as an example of the Minoan Goddess an illustration that comes from the Theran town of Akrotiri. Experts in Aegean Bronze Age history have long recognized that there was a very close association between Minoan Crete and the island of Thera, indeed, many have considered Akrotiri a Minoan settlement. Marinatos has written that Akrotiri was strongly 'Minoanized,'[221] and that 'Theran religion had strong Minoan components.'[222] The Theran frescoes are important because they are preserved in larger fragments than contemporary murals from Crete and because archaeologists can observe their actual position on walls, since the frescos and the walls on which they were painted remain in situ. As Jeremy Rutter has noted in speaking of the Theran frescos, 'the decoration of entire rooms can be reconstructed with a considerable degree of confidence.'[223]

The fresco I wish to discuss comes from a building known as Xeste 3 in Akrotiri and is dated to LM IA, *c.* 1675-1580 BC.[224] Xeste 3 is one of several buildings excavated thus far on Thera that exhibit a primarily religious function. Indeed, experts are now of the opinion that Xeste 3 'was a centre of ritual activity for the community.'[225] Divided into an eastern and western section, the western half of Xeste 3 was at least three stories high and was composed of rooms for storage, food preparation, and perhaps, on the second floor, sleeping quarters.

In the eastern section all the rooms contained frescoes. Rooms 2, 3, 4, and 7 of the ground floor and 2, 3, and 4 of the second floor are connected by a series of pier-and-door partitions which could be opened to create a large space for public gatherings. In room 3 of this eastern section, at its northern end, a lustral basin is located. It will be remembered that lustral basins or adyta are one of the architectural markers of sacred space in Aegean archaeology. Rehak summarizes the frescoes in the eastern section of Xeste 3 as follows:

> The vestibule, Room 5, includes an unpublished mountainous landscape with a male figure. A frieze around the upper wall of Room 4 depicts more rockwork, with crocus

---

[218] Immerwahr 1990: 49.

[219] Roller 1999: 6.

[220] As I noted in my methodology chapter, scholars are divided over the date of the eruption with some favoring a date of *c.* 1628 BC, while others favor a date of *c.* 1530/1520 BC.

[221] Marinatos 1984: 28.

[222] Marinatos 1993: 289.

[223] Rutter and Dartmouth College n.d.

[224] Kontorli-Papadoupoulou 1996: 55.

[225] Vlachopoulos 2008: 454.

plants and animals that include swallows and a nest, red dragonflies, and blue monkeys holding gold lyres, a sword and a scabbard. Room 2 features a decorative frieze of spirals. Room 3, subdivided into compartments by pier and door partitions, has a closet displaying male figures holding a metal vessel and a cloth, as well as a sunken Lustral Basin, on two walls of which were painted women and a shrine façade and tree. On the upper floor, Room 3 has two walls depicting girls gathering crocus blossoms in a mountainous setting and offering them to a goddess, the latter is enthroned on a platform and attended by a blue monkey and a griffin. An adjacent wall illustrates a marshy scene. Another composition from the upper floor represents at least three women in procession. Finally, Room 9 on the upper level housed an abstract relief fresco.[226]

The fresco I wish to focus on is in room 3, on the upper level, above the lustral basin. In this fresco three young women collect crocus blossoms while the fourth empties them into a basket. Taking saffron from the basket, a monkey then offers it to a female figure sitting on a tripartite platform (whom Rehak has identified as a Goddess in the quote above) while a griffin flanks the Goddess's other side. The clothing of the Goddess is elaborately decorated with crocus flowers, and she wears two necklaces, one with duck pendants and one with dragonfly pendants. On her cheek is painted or tattooed a crocus blossom. In her hair and on her head a snake slithers up and flicks out its forked tongue.[227] On the wall immediately above the lustral basin (and one floor below the fresco I have just described), is the depiction of three young women picking crocus blossoms, one of whom has wounded her foot. Blood drips from the bottom of it.

Marinatos has interpreted these scenes in room 3 of Xeste 3 as symbolic of the renewal of nature in the spring, and specifically the frescoes above the adyton as initiation rites of young girls related to the general theme of nature and womanhood.[228] She proposes that the frescoes represent a coming-of-age ritual for the maiden. Rehak has written that the frescoes in the lustral basin area celebrate the first menses of young women, and adds that

> If this interpretation is correct, we would also have an important clue to the function of lustral basins during the Neopalatial period, as well as further confirmation of the importance of women in Aegean society.[229]

Archaeologist Andreas Vlachopoulos remarks,

> Scholarship in the last several years [the book was published in 2008] seems to support the idea that this monumental composition represents an important festival in honour

---

[226] Rehak 2004: 85.
[227] According to Doumas:
> The outline of her flowing luxuriant locks is followed by a serpentine band with a row of dots along its outer side. This band, which describes a loop, high up and behind, levels and narrows over the crown and terminates in two spiral tongues. The fact that the band is quite separate from the hair, and the way in which it narrows as it leaves the shoulder, strongly suggest that the artist was attempting to depict a snake. . . . The snake slithering up the figure's neck has begun moving horizontally on her head, flicking out its forked tongue. (Doumas 1992: 131).
[228] Marinatos 1984: 71.
[229] Rehak 2004: 94.

of the *Potnia*, in which young girls participated as part of their ritual education, during which they were initiated into womanhood, including motherhood.[230]

While the ultimate meaning of the fresco program in the Xeste 3 lustral basin area is difficult to know with any certainty, what does seem certain here is that there is a depiction of the Goddess of Minoan Crete within the fresco. Why is the Xeste 3 Goddess a Goddess, and why can she be identified as a Mother Goddess? There are a number of reasons. First of all there is the architectural evidence: All of Xeste 3 is architecturally suited for 'cult activities of a mystical character.'[231] As noted above, Xeste 3 was three stories high in some places; the layout of the ground floor with its fourteen rooms, was repeated on the second floor, some rooms on the first floor were connected by pier-and-door partitions which involved the construction of nearly hollow walls, a 'difficult engineering feat,'[232] and the building had two staircases. Its 'monumental aspect' was 'enhanced by the revetment of ashlar blocks on its entire east façade and the eastern section of the north side.'[233] The area where the fresco is located is particularly suited for cult purposes because of the lustral basin or adyton, which as I have explained in Chapter 4, archaeologists have recognized as an indicator of sacred space. Moreover, room 3's pier-and-door partitions 'allow control of visual access and admittance into the vicinity of the adyton.'[234]

Yet, the architectural element is not enough to prove that the woman on the tripartite platform is a Goddess. In Chapter 4, I stated that in addition to the presence of architecture indicative of sacred space, cult objects must be found in situ. Akrotiri has yielded a huge amount of pottery. Xeste 3 contains some of the best stone vessels from the site, as well as several of the most unique pots found on the site. One, which particularly intrigues me, is a beehive-shaped vessel known as a *simbloi*. It was found in room 3. Xeste 3 also has a large number, 33, of nippled jugs (pitchers with breasts or nipples as formal or decorative features.) A. Papagiannopoulou, who did a study of the pottery of Xeste 3, found that pouring vessels, indicative of ritual, were the most often found.[235] The vessels found in Xeste 3 exhibited a wide variety of decorations. One particularly beautiful ritual vase depicted swallows, lilies, and crocuses. On others, spirals abound. Birds, lilies, and crocuses are attributes of the Goddess, and spirals are symbolic of her role of life-giving.

Cult symbols are also found in abundance in Xeste 3. In the room containing the image of the Goddess, there is a fresco of an altar in the form of horns of consecration with three women in 'rich Minoan garments, elaborate coiffures, and ornate jewellery of precious metal'[236] processing towards it. The other restored frescoes in Xeste 3 contain three very interesting symbols: spirals, rosettes, and lozenges. Gimbutas has identified spirals with the life force or life-giving aspect of the Goddess; lozenges, as the symbol of the vagina,[237] with renewing and eternal earth; and rosettes with regeneration.

---

[230] Vlachopoulos 2008: 453.
[231] Marinatos 1984: 74.
[232] Marinatos 1984: 73.
[233] Doumas 1992: 218.
[234] Marinatos 1984: 73.
[235] Papagiannopoulou 1995: 213.
[236] Doumas 1992: 129.
[237] Gimbutas 1989: 223

The attributes of the Goddess are also present in the fresco: we find plants, vegetation, birds, and animal guardians. Earlier I noted that both Moss and Marinatos listed lilies and crocuses as attributes of the Goddess. Crocuses abound in this fresco, they are growing, being picked, and being offered to the Goddess. Animals abound as well: a monkey and a griffin flank the Goddess. Fantastic animals in the iconography indicate the presence of the Goddess, as do monkeys who often act as her servant.[238] There is a snake on the Goddess's head, making her a descendant of the Early Minoan Snake Goddesses of the Messara. Finally, birds, in the form of duck pendants, another attribute of the Goddess, adorn her necklace.

In addition to her attributes, Chapter 4 identified other ways in which archaeologists identify the Minoan Goddess in the iconography. There I referred to Renfrew's criteria for identifying the deity: position, size, gesture, and clothing. In the Crocus Gatherers fresco, the Goddess is seated on a platform. Not only is it tripartite, but it is held up by incurved altars—one of the pieces of Minoan cult equipment.[239] She is the focal point of this fresco, larger than the women bringing her offerings of crocus, and very elaborately dressed. In fact, 'the goddess is currently the most richly dressed and bejeweled figure to survive in Aegean art.'[240] She is extending a hand to receive an offering of crocus stamens from the blue monkey, thus she is in the gesture of receiving, and she is flanked by a fantastic animal—the colorful griffin which is wearing a collar and a leash as if to further emphasize her mastery over him. Her clothing is elaborately decorated with crocus blossoms.[241]

I believe that the evidence cited above confirms that the female figure on the tripartite platform in the Crocus Gatherers fresco is a Goddess. Most archaeologists seem to agree that she is indeed a Goddess, and that she appears here in her guise as Mistress of Nature. I noted above that Marinatos has stated that during the New Palace period the Goddess is most often evident as Mistress of Nature. Referring to the Thera fresco she notes that the Goddess portrayed there incorporates not only water animals, but animals of the earth, as well as insects and flowers.[242] To Marinatos, the Goddess of the Crocus Gatherers is the most important testimony to the Minoan Goddess as Goddess of Nature. [243]

Christos Doumas, the excavator of Akrotiri since 1976, says that 'perhaps in the representation of crocus gathering we have the largest representation of the Nature Goddess in the Aegean world.'[244] Spiro Marinatos, Doumas's predecessor at Thera, called the Goddess of the Crocus Gatherers the Mistress of Animals (*Potnia Theron*),[245] as does Rehak.[246]

---

[238] Marinatos 1993: 63.
[239] Marinatos has made the observation that four such incurved altars were found by E. and J. Sakellarakis in their excavations at Archanes and that it is likely that they supported a platform much like that portrayed in the Crocus Gatherers fresco (Marinatos 1993: 161).
[240] Rehak 2004: 90.
[241] Both Marinatos and Rehak remind their readers that crocus blossoms are also found on the faience votive dresses and girdles that were deposited with the Snake Goddesses in the Knossos Temple Repositories (Rehak 2004: 94; Marinatos 1993: 141).
[242] Marinatos 1993: 151.
[243] Marinatos 1984: 61-62.
[244] Doumas 1992: 131.
[245] Doumas 1992: 131.
[246] Rehak 2004: 90.

Based on the evidence cited above, a very strong case can be made for arguing that the female on the platform of the Xeste 3 fresco of Crocus Gatherers is a Goddess. Indeed, Nanno Marinatos writes, 'that this figure is a goddess is certain.'[247] Is the Goddess of the Crocus Gatherers fresco a Mother Goddess? I believe she is. In my definition of Mother Goddess I said she had power over the natural environment. Everything about this fresco points to a Goddess with power within all of nature; nature is part of her realm. The fresco also portrays her as a mediator *par excellance* between this world, as symbolized by the girls picking crocuses to her left, and the next, as symbolized by the griffin to her right. The spirals, rosettes, and horns of consecration on the walls serve to further emphasize the role of the Goddess as mediator between worlds.

The eruption at Thera and the arrival of the Mycenaeans

Mention was made earlier to the fact that it was because of the volcanic eruption at Thera that the wall-paintings of Akrotiri are preserved for us today. Recently scholars have demonstrated that the Theran volcano probably erupted sometime between 1650-1625 BC. It is not yet fully understood what the exact impact was upon Crete. Opinions range from the view that Crete, especially eastern Crete which, due to prevailing winds, would have been most affected by the ash fall, experienced widespread famine; to the opposite opinion, that Thera's destruction had very little effect on Crete at all. It is an issue that is still greatly debated by Aegean archaeologists.

Two other hotly debated and related issues are (1) the timing of the arrival of the Mycenaeans in Crete, and (2) whether or not it was the invasion of the Mycenaeans that caused the massive destructions of the temple-palaces and 'mansions' that occurred in Crete *c.* 1450 BC. Although Moss believes the Mycenaeans may have arrived in Crete at the time of the Thera eruption,[248] the majority of scholars place the arrival of the Mycenaeans in Crete at a much later date: *c.* 1450 BC. The period from *c.* 1400 until 1070 BC, LM II to LM IIIC has become known as the Postpalatial period.[249]

But even the date of *c.* 1450 BC for the massive destructions that ended the New Palace Period is not certain. Nanno Marinatos has written that the only thing that is certain is that during the period, LM IB-LM IIIA/B, *c.* 1500/1490 to *c.* 1360/1325 BC, the Mycenaeans from mainland Greece arrived in Crete, and seized the palace of Knossos, where, as is attested by the Linear B tablets found there, they also introduced their own language.[250]

Nevertheless, scholars generally use the date *c.* 1450 BC to mark the 'untoward event'[251] which led to the destruction of all the temple-palaces and 'mansions' of Crete with the exception of Knossos, which continued, under Mycenaean occupation until approximately 1350/1300 BC. It has been believed that it was the Mycenaeans that were the cause of that 'untoward event.'

---

[247] Marinatos 1984: 61.
[248] Moss 2005: 3.
[249] Postpalatial is not quite an accurate term for the period because Knossos continued in existence as a temple-palace until *c.* 1375. Archaeologist Andonis Vasilakis has suggested that the term 'Third Palace Period' would be a better reference to this period in the history of Minoan Crete (Vasilakis n.d.: 33). Dimopoulou-Rethemiotakis, also acknowledging the continued existence of the temple-palace of Knossos, calls the period 1450-1350/1300 BC the Final Palatial Period (Dimopoulou-Rethemiotakis 2005). Some scholars refer to it as the Monopalatial Period.
[250] Marinatos 1993: 221.
[251] Marinatos 1993: 221.

Vasilakis offers a typical explanation when he writes: 'About 1450/30 the brilliant civilization of the second palaces was delivered a severe blow by a natural disaster, a fire that was possibly the result of an enemy invasion from mainland Greece.'[252] Nanno Marinatos offers what she calls a more 'complex' view of what happened: 'a combination of various factors, such as economic impoverishment (which could have been caused by a natural disaster), a famine or a plague, social unrest, and social rebellion' led to the 1450 BC destructions.[253] She believes that if one can accept a 'combination of causes,'[254] one can better understand the eventual collapse of the Minoan civilization. I will continue to explore these questions below.

The Third Palatial and Postpalatial Periods, c. 1450-1070 BC

It is with these dates and controversies in mind that I begin my discussion of several images of the Minoan Mother Goddess that are dated to these Third Palatial and Postpalatial periods after *c.* 1450 BC, lasting until *c.* 1070 BC, when another invasion, possibly of the Dorians from mainland Greece occurred, and Cretan society underwent major changes yet again.

The scholarly literature seems to agree that for a long time, perhaps as late as 1000 BC, the old religion of Crete remained with the Goddess at its center. For hundreds of years after the fall of the temple-palaces, one can still speak of a continuing Minoan religion and perhaps at some point, exactly when scholars cannot say, a Mycenaean-influenced Minoan religion. However, scholars point out that Minoan-influenced Mycenaean religion can be found on the Greek mainland as well. One of Gimbutas's contributions to the scholarship of the history of religion is her discernment that the religion of the Mycenaeans retained strong Old European-Minoan beliefs. 'The Mycenaean civilization demonstrates that significant worship of the goddess persisted in Bronze Age Europe, even within heavily Indo-Europeanized cultures.'[255] What is found on Crete in the waning years of the Aegean Bronze Age is a religion different from that of the mainland, which to an important extent retains its traditional beliefs.[256]

Moss treats Minoan religion in the period after 1450 and indeed the whole period down to 1000 BC, as a continuation of the earlier periods. She does not remark upon any other than minor changes to the religion, and her title *The Minoan Pantheon* is used to cover the entire period from 1900-1000 BC. Marinatos titles the chapter in her book *Minoan Religion,* which deals with the period 1450 BC to 1200 BC, 'Minoan religion after the fall of the palaces.' She writes: 'The continuity of the symbols and attributes of the goddesses show that there is essential unity in the beliefs. What changes is the external manifestation of the cult.'[257] Elsewhere she says: 'the essential beliefs were maintained.'[258] What are the external changes Marinatos refers to above? Lustral basins and pillar crypts are no longer used, polythyron—rooms with pier and door partitions—are no longer constructed, the production of high-quality frescoes and seal

---

[252] Vasilakis n.d.: 31.
[253] Marinatos 1993: 221.
[254] Marinatos 1993: 221.
[255] Gimbutas 1999: 152.
[256] See articles in Driessen and Farnoux 1997.
[257] Marinatos 1993: 222.
[258] Marinatos 1993: 244.

rings slows down or ceases entirely, and 'style becomes more crude and expressionistic.'[259] Moreover, bulls head rhyta, sacral knots, and miniature libation tables also drop out of use.[260]

However, it is important to realize that all the major Minoan cult symbols continued to appear in the Postpalatial period: birds, bulls, snakes, agrimia, double axes, and horns of consecration, but as Gesell points out, 'these are not independent objects, but attached to other cult objects (goddesses, snake tubes, stands) or used as pottery decoration.'[261]

For Marinatos, the fact that cult objects associated with the Goddess in Palatial religion continue to appear in the Postpalatial period indicates 'that there is continuity of belief with the preceding era and that the figures [here she is referring in particular to the Goddesses with Upraised Arms] do, in fact, represent goddesses.'[262] For Gesell as well, there is continuity. As she says, speaking of the Postpalatial period, 'The goddess comes forth in this period as the dominating figure in cult. The male figure appears only in the role of votary.'[263] However, Gesell also observes that the horns of consecration, as well as the double axe, snakes, birds, and other symbols connected with the Goddess, have now been relegated to 'relief or painted decoration' or appear 'in miniature on her tiara or on snake tubes.'[264] She sees this as a hint of the change to come—a hint that is repeated and magnified in the LM IIIC Spring Chamber, where the Goddess appears enclosed in a hut urn.[265]

What is new and most obviously apparent in the Postpalatial period is the changed shape/ size/look of the Minoan Goddess. She is larger than before, with upraised arms, and is now usually found in groups. Also, her body has become more uniform, more abstract. No longer are bare-breasts depicted, nor naturalistic shape, nor elaborate costumes.

The Ayia Triadha Sarcophagus

The still paramount importance of the Goddess in Minoan religion is apparent in an artifact dating from this transitional, Third temple-palace period: the Ayia Triadha Sarcophagus dated to *c.* 1450-1350/1300 BC.

The Ayia Triadha sarcophagus, a limestone coffin painted with scenes of human figures reminiscent of the wall paintings of Knossos or Thera, 'was found . . . inside a destroyed building assumed to have been a tomb.'[266] Very few other artifacts were found inside the tomb: a serpentine bowl, two bronze razors, and a carnelian lentoid seal engraved with a pouncing sphinx.[267] The sarcophagus itself contained the remains of parts of two male adult crania, indicating that it was used for at least two burials. The Ayia Triadha sarcophagus is considered to be of major importance by scholars of Minoan religion because it preserves the essence of Minoan ritual as it had been practiced since the Prepalatial period.[268]

---

[259] Marinatos 1993: 222.
[260] Gesell 1985: 41.
[261] Gesell 1985: 41.
[262] Marinatos 1993: 227.
[263] Gesell 1985: 54.
[264] Gesell 1985: 54.
[265] Gesell 1985: 54.
[266] Gesell 1985: 31.
[267] Long 1974: 13.
[268] Marinatos 1993: 31.

Figure 8. Front of Ayia Triadha sarcophagus. Third Temple Palace/ Postpalatial period, LM IB-LM IIIB, c. 1450-1350/1300 BC, sarcophagus is 0.895m in height, 1.373-1.385m in length, and 0.45m in width, limestone, found inside a tomb, Ayia Triadha, Crete. Heraklion Museum, Crete. Photograph by author.

Representations of the Minoan Goddess appear on the two end sides of the Ayia Triadha sarcophagus. Before describing those, I shall briefly describe the two longer sides so that the full picture can be grasped. One long side, identified as the front because of its 'superior finishing' and its position in the tomb,[269] facing the east entrance to the tomb,[269] depicts a priestess pouring the blood of a sacrificial victim from a container into a krater set between two double axes on which birds have alighted. To her right, another priestess carries two buckets supported on a pole. She is followed by a musician playing a seven-stringed lyre. On the right half of the composition, three men wearing sheep-skins offer animals and a model of a ship to a male figure, on the far right, who is presumed by most experts to represent the deceased man. This man stands between a building and a tree with a stepped altar in front of it.

On the long back panel of the sarcophagus, in the center, a bull is sacrificed to the accompaniment of a flute. The blood of the sacrificial animal is collected in a bucket. To the left, a priestess places her hands on the sacrificial victim. There is a procession of women behind her. To the right of the sacrificed bull, another priestess[270] offers a bloodless sacrifice on an altar in front of a sanctuary with horns of consecration and a sacred tree. Hovering above the altar in midair are a libation jug and bowl of fruit, while behind the altar is a long pole with a double axe and a bird atop it. Clearly the sarcophagus iconography on the long sides is replete with images of ritual activity and symbols of the Minoan Goddess.

It is the short sides of the sarcophagus which feature the figures of the Minoan Goddess. On the west short side, in the lower register, two women are being drawn in a chariot by wild goats or agrimia. On the register above them, which is very poorly preserved, is a procession of men. On

---

[269] Long 1974: 73.

[270] Long has made an interesting point in regard to this priestess's skirt. Remarking on the 'forked pattern' on her skirt, she says that the German scholar Johannes Sundwall 'may be close to the truth in identifying it as the reed sign and linking it with the cult of the mother goddess in Anatolia' (Long 1974: 65). Long also links the double pipes being played by the man behind the sacrificed bull with the 'Phrygian pipes which were played in the first millennium B.C. in the Anatolian cult of Cybele' (Long 1974: 65). Of course the Ayia Triadha sarcophagus predates the first millennium BC; however, given the parallels I have drawn between the iconography of the Great Mother of Neolithic Anatolia and Minoan Crete, I find these later parallels of great interest.

Figure 9. Back of Ayia Triadha sarcophagus. Third Temple Palace/ Postpalatial period, LM IB-LM IIIB, c. 1450-1350/1300 BC, sarcophagus is 0.895m in height, 1.373-1.385m in length, and 0.45m in width, limestone, found inside a tomb, Ayia Triadha, Crete. Heraklion Museum, Crete. Photograph by author.

the other short side, the east side, there is only one scene taking up both registers: two women drawn in a chariot by griffins. A bird (or baby griffin?) has landed on the back of one of the griffins and faces the women.

The Ayia Triadha sarcophagus has been interpreted as portraying both the worship of the deity and the cult of the dead. Marinatos writes that it 'condenses the major cycles of death/ fertility/regeneration into a few coherent scenes.'[271] Charlotte R. Long, in her classic work on the Ayia Triadha sarcophagus, concludes that:

> The scenes on the front and back panels of the sarcophagus may be interpreted as rites performed during the funeral of the person for whom the sarcophagus was intended, rites designed to dispatch the spirit of the deceased with all due solemnity and make certain his reaching and being admitted to the afterworld. [272]

As for the short sides with the Goddesses in the chariots, Long writes: 'They were expected to escort the spirit of the dead . . . on his journey to the afterworld to ensure his safe arrival.'[273] Archaeologist Costis Davaras in his *Guide to Cretan Antiquities* posits: 'The scenes of the coffin . . . relate to the worship of the dead, the admission of the spirit to the afterworld in a happy after-life, and perhaps indirectly to the vegetation cult.'[274]

All experts are agreed that the two short sides of the sarcophagus depict Goddesses. Long hypothesizes:

---

[271] Marinatos 1993: 36.
[272] Long 1974: 74.
[273] Long 1974: 74.
[274] Davaras 1976: 276.

Figure 10. Side panel of Ayia Triadha sarcophagus with two Goddesses being pulled by griffins. Third Temple Palace/Postpalatial period, LM IB-LM IIIB, c. 1450-1350/1300 BC, sarcophagus is 0.895m in height, 1.373-1.385m in length, and 0.45m in width, limestone, found inside a tomb, Ayia Triadha, Crete. Heraklion Museum, Crete. Photograph by Dr. Mara Lynn Keller. Reprinted with permission.

They [the Goddesses] were expected to escort the spirit of the dead . . . on his journey to the afterworld to ensure his safe arrival. . . . In Egypt, figures of Isis and Nephthys, goddesses who were regarded as protectors of the dead, were painted on the ends of coffins and possibly these Minoan/Mycenaean deities had some similar function.[275]

Marinatos notes that it is unlikely that the women are mortals because the short sides of the sarcophagus depict the supernatural sphere, (in contrast to the long sides which illustrate cult practices). It seems certain that the women coming to the shrine are Goddesses, for mortal women would not arrive in a griffin-drawn chariot.[276]

Marinatos postulates that the priestess offering the bloodless sacrifice at the sanctuary (depicted on the back side of the sarcophagus) may have called the Goddesses with her sacrifice, and the short sides shows their imminent arrival.[277] She posits that the Goddesses in the agrimia-drawn chariot is present because the cult of the dead is being celebrated, and that they represent chthonic divinities. Long has pointed out that agrimia are found with the Goddess on a gold diadem from Zakros, that they appear with the Goddess on at least one sealing, and that they are depicted in the vicinity of shrines, for example, on the Zakros Sanctuary rhyton.[278] I have stressed again and again that agrimia are one of the attributes of the Goddess. Long has noted that there is evidence for the 'cult' of a 'Goddess of Wild Goats'

[275] Long 1974: 74, 32.
[276] Marinatos 1993: 35.
[277] Marinatos 1993: 35.
[278] Long 1974: 55.

at Zakros for the Neopalatial period, and 'it [the cult] might be much older.'[279] John Younger has hypothesized, based on his on-going identification and analysis of myth and narrative illustrated in Bronze Age art, that the Goddesses arriving in the chariot drawn by agrimia represent the Goddess Eileithyia arriving to assist in a birth, as she did with Leto in Delos, and that 'the coffin may have held an infant.'[280]

Griffins have religious associations as well. In Chapter 4 I listed griffins as one of the attributes of the Goddess. Griffins flank the throne of the priestess-queen at the temple-palace of Knossos in the Throne Room, the Goddess on the Akrotiri, Thera Crocus Gatherers fresco (discussed above), and on sealings. They, along with lions and daemons, are one of the three fabulous 'animals' that are the Goddess's protectors. The bird on the back of the griffins adds yet another attribute of the Minoan Goddess to the scene on the sarcophagus and lends further weight to the idea that the females in the chariot drawn by griffins are Goddesses.

Finally it may be noted again that other attributes of the Minoan Goddess as well as identifiable pieces of cult equipment appear on both long sides of the sarcophagus. In addition to the agrimia, griffins, and bird already cited, there are: the double axe, horns of consecration, sacred tree, altar, sacrificial table, and axe stand.

Are the Goddesses on the short sides of the Ayia Triadha sarcophagus Mother Goddesses? I said earlier that my definition of Mother Goddess was not limited to fertility and nurturing. While she would have those qualities, she would also be, as Roller put it: 'a figure of power and protection, able to touch on many aspects of life and mediate between the boundaries of the known and unknown.'[281] Those last words, 'mediate between the boundaries of the known and unknown,' could refer, I think, to death and rebirth, and I believe that the Minoan Mother Goddess was a powerful protector and mediator as well. If the Goddesses in the agrimia- and griffin-drawn chariots are, as Marinatos believes, chthonic deities, or as Long suggests, escorting the deceased to the afterworld,[282] or as Younger suggests, assisting in a birth (or perhaps a rebirth), then they are indeed mediating the boundaries of known and unknown and providing protection. They are Mother Goddesses.

The short sides of the sarcophagus also present us with a picture of the Goddess as Mother Goddess in her role of Mistress of Nature. The griffins and agrimia drawing her chariots give the Minoan Goddess an image of strength and mastery over the natural environment. Such strength and mastery identify her as the Mother Goddess of the natural world.

The Mountain Mother seal impression

The artifact I wish to discuss next also bridges the transition from the New Palace period to its succeeding phase known as the Postpalatial. Contemporary with the Ayia Triadha sarcophagus, and unanimously regarded as a representation of the Minoan Goddess, is the female figure found on what is termed the Mountain Mother seal impression. Fragments of this seal impression (the seal itself has never been found) were discovered by Evans at Knossos

---

[279] Long 1974: 57.
[280] Younger 2020: 76.
[281] Roller 1999: 6.
[282] Long 1974: 32.

in 1901 in two different locations on the western side of the Central Court of Knossos: in the Central Shrine itself, and in an area to the north of the Central shrine. Evans dated the seal impression to LM II, *c.* 1450-1400 BC, and many scholars accept that date. Others prefer a date of LM IIIA1, *c.* 1400-1370 BC, near the time of the final destruction of Knossos. Krattenmaker points out, however, that 'an earlier date cannot be ruled out.'[283] Moss notes that 'This [the LM IIIA1 date] does not tell us when the ring or seal, with which these impressions were made, was created.'[284]

The seal may be described as follows: In the center is a depiction of a mountain with a female figure standing on its summit. This female figure exudes power and authority. She is attired in the traditional Minoan flounced skirt and bare to the waist. In her outstretched left hand she holds out a staff, her right arm is bent and her right hand is at her waist. Flanking her in the 'heraldic' position are two lions who rest their paws on the sides of the centrally situated mountain. To her left is part of a tripartite building with three pairs of horns of consecration visible. To her right, is a man dressed in a belt and codpiece, in the pose of adoration, one hand raised to his forehead, lower body straight and stiff, upper body leaning back. He is standing at the foot of the mountain looking up at the Mountain Mother. 'She is the focus of attention—ours, that of the lions and the man.'[285]

Before determining whether or not the Mountain Mother is a Goddess and a Mother Goddess, the find spots of the seal impressions and the artifacts found with them must be addressed. As stated above, the fragments of the sealings were found on the western side of the Central Court of the temple-palace of Knossos in areas that are part of the Central Palace Shrine. Three fragments of impressions from the Mountain Mother seal were found in the sacred area known as the Tripartite Shrine, near the Temple Repository cists where the Snake Goddesses were found. Fragments of five other sealings, which are probably impressions of the Mountain Mother seal, but are too small to be identified for certain, were also found in the Tripartite Shrine.[286] Another impression was found in the Great Pithos Room, which is also a part of the Central Palace Sanctuary.[287]

As for other finds in the Great Pithos Room and the Tripartite Shrine, Panagiotaki, who re-excavated sections of the Central Palace Sanctuary in 1993, and reviewed all the material known to have been found in that area of the temple-palace in previous excavations, records eight large decorated and undecorated pithoi, a stirrup jar, a lamp foot, and a clay inscribed tablet.[288] As for the finds in the Tripartite Shrine: in addition to the eight fragments of sealings,

---

[283] Krattenmaker 1995: 49-50 n2.

[284] Moss 2000: 13 n21.

[285] Moss 2005: 63.

[286] The Tripartite Shrine is the name given by Evans to the main shrine at Knossos (Evans 1964: 1:425). The central section, which had a single column, was higher than the two wings at the side, which had two columns each. Panagiotaki describes the position/location of the Tripartite Shrine at Knossos as follows:

> The north wing is a niche formed by the Stylobate to the east, the east wall of the Temple Repositories and the Great Pithos Room to the west, the south load bearing wall of the E-W staircase to the north and by the gypsum block of the recess in the Lobby of Stone Seat to the south. . . . The south wing is the space north of the staircase in the Lobby of the Stone Seat, . . . while the central part cannot be described in the same way, since it is conjectural (Panagiotaki 1999: 235).

[287] The Central Palace Sanctuary consists of the rooms known as the Lobby of the Stone Seat, the Great Pithos Room, the Temple Repositories Room (which was discussed above in relation to the Snake Goddesses), the East Pillar Crypt, the West Pillar Crypt, the Vat Room and the Tripartite Shrine (Panagiotaki 1999: 235).

[288] Panagiotaki 1999: 215.

three of which can be identified as the Mountain Mother sealing, the other five appear to be, but cannot certainly be identified as coming from the Mountain Mother sealing; a piece of fresco was discovered 'showing part of the entablature in the miniature fresco style.'[289]

The fragments of the Mountain Mother sealing led Evans to believe that the place in which they were found was a shrine, thus he termed the area the Tripartite Shrine. Panagiotaki differs with Evans in that she believes the distribution of the fragments argues for placing the original location of the sealings on the floor above, and thus she locates the main temple-palace shrine there. She notes that all extant representations of Tripartite Shrines show them to be elevated.[290] Although the exact location of the Tripartite Shrine of the temple-palace of Knossos may never be known, the fact remains that the presence of the Mountain Mother sealing fragments, in addition to the finds of the Temple Repositories (discussed above in connection with the Snake Goddesses), as well as architectural details, all point to the Central Palace Sanctuary as indeed being the central shrine of the temple-palace of Knossos 'from the very beginning'[291] and continuing into the Post-Minoan period. Although there is no evidence that the sealings themselves were used in cult, Panagiotaki thinks the actual ring could have been.[292]

Archaeologists thus have established that the Mountain Mother seal impressions come from an area of religious worship. What were they actually used for? While the use of these particular sealings has not yet been definitively determined, Panagiotaki seems to suggest that 'they could be seen as related to the workings of the shrine's business as a religious institution.'[293]

Archaeologists are in agreement that the woman in the center of the seal impression is indeed a Goddess. Evans called her 'the Minoan Mother Goddess.'[294] Nilsson also called the Mountain Mother a Goddess, as well as Mistress of the Animals, and associated her with the Great Mother of Asia Minor.[295] Marinatos labels her a Goddess, and notes that the male in the picture is probably a votary.[296] Moss identifies the Mountain Mother as a Goddess and links her back to Kybele and ultimately the enthroned Goddess of Çatal Hüyük.[297] Moss also posits that she could be 'a depiction of a goddess like Rhea who was associated with mountains and wild animals.'[298]

My own view is very much in accord with that of Moss. As I wrote in the beginning of Chapter 4 in my introduction to interpreting the archaeological record, it is possible to argue that aspects of Minoan Goddess iconography evolved from the Neolithic symbols of the Goddess that early

---

[289] Panagiotaki 1999: 238. Evans believed this fragment may have been part of a fresco of a tripartite shrine similar to the one portrayed in the Grandstand Fresco. An entablature is a superstructure of moldings and bands placed horizontally above columns.

[290] Panagiotaki 1999: 238.

[291] Panagiotaki 1999: 275.

[292] Panagiotaki 1999: 275.

[293] Panagiotaki 1999: 117.

[294] Moss 2005: 63.

[295] Nilsson 1949: 389.

[296] In a footnote Marinatos notes that Rutkowski in *Cult Places of the Aegean* calls the male a king 'receiving his staff of authority from the goddess' (Marinatos 1993: 278n34; Rutkowski 1986: 88). Marinatos disagrees, 'Yet he is not receiving, nor is the goddess handing it out. Her gesture and the staff typify gods who do not necessarily interact with their worshipers' (Marinatos 1993: 278n34). Moss on the other hand seems to favor Rutkowski's interpretation (Moss 2005: 65).

[297] Moss 2005: 63.

[298] Moss 2005: 64.

settlers to Crete brought from Anatolia: especially the Çatal Hüyük enthroned Goddess with lions, and the Hittite images of the sacred mountain in association with the divinity. This is not to say that the Mountain Mother seal impression derives exclusively from foreign influences. The Goddess's dress, the votary's stance and costume, which is just like those of votaries found at Minoan peak sanctuaries, and the horns of consecration on the shrine, are all purely Minoan elements. Yet the association of the Goddess with lions and mountainous terrain could owe a great deal to Anatolian influences.

The Mountain Mother sealings were found in the central sanctuary area of the temple-palace of Knossos, an area used for religious worship from the time of the Old Palace Period to the Post-Minoan era. It was an area filled with Minoan cult equipment, and cult symbols, and characterized by sacred architecture. Thus the identification of the woman at the center of the seal as a Goddess is upheld by these important criteria.

The identification of the Mountain Mother image as a Goddess is also validated by Renfrew's criteria for identifying deities in the iconography: her large size; position in the center where she is the focus of attention of the votary, the lions, and the viewer; her gesture of authority; the shrine with its cult symbol of the horns of consecration and the lions in heraldic position. All of this verifies that what we see before us is a Goddess.

Is the Mountain Mother a Mother Goddess as well? Like her Anatolian predecessor, the Mother Goddess of Çatal Hüyük, she exhibits mastery over the natural environment, from the lions at her side to her position on the peak of the mountain. No mortal could stand atop the peak of a mountain with lions on either side. The natural environment is part of the Mountain Mother's realm; she holds power within all nature; she generates the cycles of nature, and it is this that gives her the status not only of a Goddess, but of a Mother Goddess as well.

The Goddesses with Upraised Arms

The Ayia Triadha sarcophagus and the Mountain Mother sealings date to the period soon after the 'untoward event' of 1450 BC that caused the destruction of the temple-palaces and 'mansions' of Minoan Crete with the single exception of Knossos. The artifacts I wish to discuss now date to the period between the final destruction of the temple-palace of Knossos, c. 1350/1300 BC, and the end of the Bronze Age in Crete, c. 1000 BC. There are certainly Mycenaeans in Crete at this time, but as archaeologist Eleni Andrikou points out, 'the presence of a Mycenaean ruling class or the exercise of political control on the island on behalf of the Mycenaeans does not necessarily lead to profound changes in the population.'[299] I understand her to include the religion of the population here. Archaeologist Robin Hägg seconds her opinion when he writes:

> The archaeological evidence does not support the hypothesis of a Mycenaean-Minoan religious syncretism in post-palatial Crete in general. . . . The real Mycenaeanization or rather Hellenization of Crete started only with the massive population movements from the Mainland close to the end of the Bronze Age, and even then it took a long time:

---

[299] Andrikou 1997: 22.

Figure 11. Goddesses with Upraised Arms. The Goddesses depicted here are from the sites of Karphi, Kannia, and Gazi. Postpalatial period, c. 1350/1300-1000 BC, clay. Heraklion Museum, Crete. Photograph by Dr. Mara Lynn Keller. Reprinted with permission.

even in Classical times the Cretan cults retained more peculiar traits, inherited from the Minoan past.[300]

As I noted above, the attributes of the Minoan Goddess are to a large extent conserved. Now, however, they appear as part of the Goddess's attire rather than separate objects surrounding her. While certain cult symbols or equipment items fall out of use, like the bull's head rhyta, sacral knots, and miniature libation tables, others remain, for example, birds, bulls, snakes, agrimia, double axes, and horns of consecration. So what does the iconography of the Goddess look like at this point in time--post 1350 until the Dorian invasion of c. 1100 BC?

My first example comes from Gournia, a settlement and a temple-palace, located on the north coast of eastern Crete. Excavated by Evans in the late nineteenth century and then by Harriet Boyd Hawes from 1900-1904, it has been studied numerous times since then and is currently being excavated yet again. Gournia was originally built in MM I, c. 2100-1900 BC, destroyed in LM BI, c. 1450 BC, and then reoccupied during the Third Palatial and Postpalatial periods, c. 1400-1070 BC.

Three terra-cotta Goddesses with Upraised Arms, one in very good condition, were found at Gournia in what Gesell calls an 'Independent Bench Sanctuary.'[301] The shrine or sanctuary, which was probably not used as such until LM IIIB1, c. 1360-1325 BC, measures 3x4 meters and has three steps leading into it. 'There may have been a bench at the southern side as there was a recess in that wall, although the remains are confusing.'[302]

---

[300] Hägg 1997: 68.
[301] Gesell 1985: 72.
[302] Moss 2005: 16.

The Goddess with Upraised Arms (the one that remains in good condition) is 37 centimeters in height and appears to have a snake encircling one shoulder and arm, with the remains of a second snake on her back. She is naked to the waist and wears a tapered skirt and a plain headdress. Her long hair flows down her back. Found with her were fragments of two other Goddesses, one of which had a part of a snake on her shoulder; an offering table; three complete snake tubes decorated with horns of consecration, one of which has a disc between the horns; the remains of two other snake tubes; four terracotta doves; a fragment of pottery with a double axe in relief with a disc above the upper edge of the axe; and a terracotta snake head. The birds and extra snake head may have been attached to the Goddesses or the snake tubes.[303] Gesell has noted that the Gournia sanctuary included almost all the sacred symbols used in Neopalatial cult. However, she has also stressed that now the symbols are attributes of the Goddess and her cult equipment, they do not stand alone.[304] Marinatos hypothesizes that the figures of the Goddess with Upraised Arms at Gournia stood on the bench and that the offering table and snake tubes were placed around them or on the floor.[305]

Moss has commented on the amount of snake imagery in the Gournia shrine, especially on the figurines of the Goddess.[306] Gesell has written that although they are made of much cruder material, the Goddess figures of Gournia with their snake attributes, are related to the MM II Snake Goddesses from Knossos.[307] Marinatos has remarked on the prominence of snakes in Postpalatial cult, noting, 'there are now several "snake goddesses."'[308]

Goddesses similar to those of Gournia, also with a preponderance of snake iconography, were found at a villa in Kannia, near Phaistos. The shrine complex at Kannia has five rooms, as opposed to the one room at Gournia, and is also dated LM IIIB1, c. 1360-1325 BC. In room I, four Goddesses were arranged on the bench with snake tubes on the floor in front of them. Found with them were small votive figures of worshippers, and a plaque. Excavators were able to reconstruct two of the Goddesses from room I. The taller of the two, 52cm tall, stands with her lower arms raised at right angles to her body. Her breasts are full and she wears a headdress over the top of which snakes peep out. The second figurine is smaller, 34cm in height, and wears a row of snakes on her headdress, the largest of which peers over the top of the headdress. Her hands are outstretched from her body at shoulder level and a snake is entwined around each arm. The fragment of the plaque bears the torso and arms of a Goddess with Upraised Arms, in relief; 'the bodice of her blouse is decorated with concentric circles which cover and emphasize her breasts.'[309]

Room IV, located to the south of room I, contained miniature objects and bowls and 'served as anteroom and repository of offerings.'[310] Room V, a storeroom with side benches and hearth, held more figurines of the Goddess with Upraised Arms; more snake tubes; various other human, animal, and bird figurines; a triton shell; and a plaque decorated with relief. The Goddess figure in room V is small, 0.22cm high, and wears a headdress similar to those worn

---

[303] Gesell 1985: 43.
[304] Gesell 1985: 43.
[305] Marinatos 1993: 222.
[306] Moss 2005: 16.
[307] Gesell 1985: 43.
[308] Marinatos 1993: 223.
[309] Moss 2005: 20.
[310] Gesell 1985: 43.

Figure 12. Goddesses with Upraised Arms from Kannia, Crete. Postpalatial period, LM IIIB, c. 1360-1325 BC. The figure on the left is 52cm. in height, the one on the right is 32cm. in height, clay, found in Kannia Sanctuary Complex. Heraklion Museum, Crete. Photograph by author.

by the figures from room I, but without snakes peering over her headdress. (As the top of her head is missing, snakes could have been part of her attire.) Moss describes the plaque in room V as 'unusual:'[311] in relief are antithetical winged sphinxes; an incurved altar appears between them and bears a tree. Room XV, another storeroom, yielded a Goddess with Upraised Arms with snakes on her tiara, a snake tube, various pottery items and a stone libation table bearing incised horns of consecration on one side.

Moss notes the snake imagery everywhere at Kannia. In addition to the snakes, many of the attributes of the Minoan Goddess are found at Kannia. Birds 'of attribute size'[312] were found belonging, most probably, to a columnar libation table; the hands of a male votary; horns of consecration are incised on a stone libation table; bull figurines were found as well as bulls' heads attached to snake tubes; agrimia also appear as images on a snake tube; and an incurved altar appears on a plaque. In short, there is 'a variety of cult material of all classes scattered throughout this sanctuary.'[313]

The last set of Goddess figurines I will consider for the Postpalatial period come from Vronda in northeastern Crete, they date to LM IIIC, c. 1190-1070 BC, the very end of the Minoan period. Vronda is located on a hilltop six miles east of Gournia, and like Gournia, it was first excavated in the early part of the twentieth century by Hawes and then re-excavated in the 1980s by a team of archaeologists from the American School of Classical Studies.

Originally settled in MMI, Vronda was abandoned after LM IIIC, c. 1190 to 1070 BC. However, it continued to be used for tholos burials until the Byzantine Age. The settlement of Vronda consists of a number of houses and Building G, which excavators have identified as a shrine.

---

[311] Moss 2005: 20.
[312] Gesell 1985: 43.
[313] Gesell 1985: 43.

Made up of two rooms and containing a bench, Building G, and the slope next to it, yielded more than twenty-six Goddesses with Upraised Arms figurines, parts of thirty-three snake tubes, and thirty-seven terra cotta plaques, at least one of which was decorated with horns of consecration on the upper edge.

One of the excavators of Vronda, Nancy L. Klein, has pointed out the uniqueness of Building G. She writes:

> At Vronda, Building G was constructed . . . to serve a single function, as a shrine of the Goddess. . . . It is the only free-standing structure on the site . . . the western wall was made of particularly large boulders along its entire length . . . this indicates a much greater effort expended in its construction than in other buildings of the settlement. . . . Building G has an impressive bench along the western façade. . . . The presence of the bench and the great care taken in the building of the wall suggest to me that the western façade of the building merited special attention and may have been a place of assembly or display. . . . It faces a large open area suitable for congregation.[314]

So many artifacts were found on the slope next to Building G rather than in the building itself because room 1 was used for a burial in the Late Geometric period, at which time the ritual equipment in room 1 was discarded and thrown onto the slope. Gesell thinks that prior to this late burial, many of the Goddess figurines and their ritual equipment were grouped on and in front of the bench in room 1. 'A second group of ritual equipment was discovered in room 2 intact or nearly so, though none was in situ on the floor.' [315]

As for the artifacts from Building G and the adjoining slope, the snake tubes are of the type familiar from this period. It will be remembered that snake tubes are ritual stands for holding bowls filled with offering material. They are made on a pottery wheel with a ringed top, beveled bottom and serpent-like loops down both sides. One was unique, however. Found in room 2 of Building G, 'this unusual snake tube had a kalathos-shaped top and small horns of consecration on the upper rim, in line with the loops down the side.'[316] Moss has also written that while most of the cups or kalathoi from Vronda were plain, 'one had relief terracotta snakes inside it.'[317] She has also noted that one of the plaques found was decorated with horns of consecration on both edges.[318] Archaeologist Peter M. Day and his co-authors remark that it is likely that originally all plaques were decorated with ritual scenes.[319]

As for the Goddesses, Day and his colleagues have suggested that each Goddess with Upraised Arms is usually associated with a particular snake tube and plaque, and the three thus comprise a set. These sets can be identified as such because they are made from the same fabric.

> The goddess figures from Kavousi [Vronda] fit into the general pattern, that each was part of a ritual assemblage, together with a snake tube and plaque belonging to a shrine.

---

[314] Klein 2004: 100.
[315] Day et al. 2006: 140.
[316] Moss 2005: 27.
[317] Moss 2005: 27.
[318] Moss 2005: 27.
[319] Day et al. 2006: 143.

It is clear that this assemblage . . . was a matching set, not only in the way it was used, but in the way it was produced.[320]

At this point it is appropriate to summarize the features common to the shrines and the Goddess figurines of Gournia, Kannia, and Vronda (as well as other shrines like Gazi, Karphi, Shrine of the Double Axes at Knossos, Prinias, Kephala Vasilikis, and Chalasmenos Monastriakiou, which are not discussed here but which date to the period under review). In all of them Goddesses, benches, and snake tubes are found. Sometimes votaries, cups and plaques are found as well. Marinatos reports that 'The goddess figures are the most conspicuous feature of Postpalatial cult.'[321] Despite their variation in height, it is obvious from the discussion above that the Goddesses have some common features. They are simply shaped, their clothing is not articulated, and their breasts are small, but unmistakable. All of the Goddesses have their arms upraised, although the position of their hands varies. Their heads are their most conspicuous feature: they are large, the expression on their faces is otherwordly and awe-inspiring, and they are crowned with headdresses exhibiting a variety of attributes and/or cult objects: horns of consecration, birds, and snakes to name a few. As Marinatos has noted, these same attributes and cult objects were associated with the Goddess during the Palatial period.[322] Day and his co-authors, comparing Goddesses with Upraised Arms from the different sites, note that all the Goddess figures are similar in dress and pose but they differ in details of arm positions, decoration, and ritual symbols on their tiaras.

The Minoan Goddesses with Upraised Arms from the Post-Palatial Period from Gournia, Kannia, and Vronda are all found in bench shrines. Thus their find spot indicates an association with the sacred. That argument is reinforced if Marinatos is right about the exact positioning of the Goddess with Upraised Arms in the shrines: on the benches surrounded by snake tubes with their offerings to the Goddess on the floor in front of them.[323] Their attributes: snakes, birds, horns of consecration, poppies;[324] the cult symbols found with them: horns of consecration, sphinxes, double axes, triton shells, bulls, birds, and agrimia; and the cult equipment found with them: snake tubes with attributes like snakes, a bull's head, birds, an agrimi, and horns of consecration adorning them; offering tables and cups, all lend further weight to the argument that the Goddesses With Upraised Arms are just that—Goddesses. Are they Mother Goddesses as well?

Marinatos argues that a Goddess of Nature furnished the iconographical prototype for the Goddess with Upraised Arms.[325] Gimbutas, looking at examples of the Goddess with Upraised Arms from Gazi and Kannia, both of which have pronounced cone-shaped headdresses, terms them the 'rising Earth Mother and the omphalos,'[326] and remarks: 'Fruits, birds and upraised arms suggest that the image portrays a blessed emergence of the Earth in all her splendor.'[327] I also think that the tree-like appearance of the lower half of her body links the Goddess with

---

[320] Day et al. 2006: 143.
[321] Marinatos 1993: 225.
[322] Marinatos 1993: 227.
[323] Marinatos 1993: 222.
[324] Day and his co-authors believe the poppies might signify the use of opium in ritual (Day et al. 2006: 142).
[325] Marinatos 1993: 227.
[326] Gimbutas 1989: 150.
[327] Gimbutas 1989: 150.

Upraised Arms to nature and specifically to the image of the tree and the tree of life.[328] One is reminded of the importance of sacred trees in Minoan religious iconography, especially on rings and sealings.

Is the Goddess with Upraised Arms a Mother Goddess? As the bountiful mother, as Gimbutas calls her, and Goddess of Nature, as Marinatos terms her, certainly the Goddess with Upraised Arms includes nature as part of her realm. Mastery within all of nature would qualify the Goddess with Upraised Arms as a Mother Goddess in my definition of the term Mother Goddess. I also believe that what Gimbutas called the 'mask-like face'[329] of the Goddess with Upraised Arms, gives her an otherworldly appearance and a clue into another of her aspects: she who is a mediator between life and death, she who moves between the boundaries of life and death. Archaeologist Stephanie Budin supports this assessment when she comments that the Goddess with Upraised Arms is associated with 'worship, death, and possibly the afterlife.'[330] A Goddess who mediates life and death, who is responsible for death and rebirth is, in my definition, a Mother Goddess.

The last Goddess with Upraised Arms (thus far discovered) is the one found at the Minoan refugee settlement at Karphi LM IIIC. By this time, c. 1070 BC, another disaster had befallen Crete, the invasion of the Dorians. Now the Goddess with Upraised Arms metamorphoses into the Goddess with Upraised Arms enclosed in the hut urn. I could not agree with Gesell more when she notes this artifact as signaling the end of the preeminence of the Goddess, and her replacement by male gods.[331] However, as Gimbutas so brilliantly made clear, the Goddess never really disappeared, but merely went underground, to be found in folktale, legend, mythology, submerged in patriarchal religions as Mary, or one of the female saints. The Goddess in the Hut Urn seems to me a fitting image to symbolize the end of a period in which the divine in Crete was visualized as female, and the beginning of the ascendancy of a male deity or deities that continues to the present day.

Conclusion

This chapter has argued that from the Neolithic to the Postpalatial period, c. 6500-1070 BC, a timeframe spanning more than five thousand years, a Mother Goddess was worshipped in Minoan Crete as the central deity. Chapter 4 established the definition of Mother Goddess utilized here: She was Life-Giver, Death-Wielder, and Regeneratrix; a 'figure of power and protection, able to touch on many aspects of life and mediate between the boundaries of the known and unknown;'[332] and she was a Goddess who generated the cycles of nature, and had power within all nature. Chapter 5 has looked at the iconographic evidence for the Minoan Mother Goddess during the period under review, and analyzed why each figurine or image under consideration, whether it appeared on a piece of pottery, a seal, sealstone, ring, or a fresco, could be considered a representation of the Mother Goddess. Each item was analyzed according to the criteria developed in Chapter 4: Was the physical location of the artifact (whether architectural context or nature) a shrine or sacred place? Was it discovered in

---

[328] It was an article by archaeologist Stephanie Budin that pointed out the similarity of the lower half of the body of the Goddess with Upraised Arms to a tree (Budin 2005: 194).
[329] Gimbutas 1989: 150.
[330] Budin 2003: 55.
[331] Gesell 1985: 54.
[332] Roller 1999: 33.

association with cult equipment? Does the artifact have cult symbols typically associated with the Goddess on it? Are the attributes of the Goddess displayed on it, or in association with it? Are the position, size, gestures, and clothing of the figure portrayed typically indicative of a deity? Is it clearly female rather than male or of indeterminate sex? Are there human or animal attendants who act as devotees? Does a comparison with similar evidence from other cultures in the eastern Mediterranean or Old Europe/Anatolia indicate the presence or representation of a Goddess? And, finally, is there mythological and historical evidence that is related and can be used to support or further substantiate a claim that this is indeed a Mother Goddess? Additionally, a wide range of archaeological and archaeomythological studies and interpretations were consulted.

Having established in the affirmative that a Mother Goddess was worshipped in Minoan Crete, and that she was the central deity, one of the major questions of this study has been addressed and answered. In the next chapter I look at the role of women in Minoan society. Is the Mother Goddess's preeminence reflected in the economic, social, religious, cultural, and political position of the women of Minoan Crete? What was the role of women in Minoan society? It is only by answering that question that one is able to provide an answer to the overarching question of this study: Can a plausible case be made to argue that Bronze Age Crete was a matriarchal society?

Chapter 6

The Role of Women in Bronze Age Crete: Bull-Leapers, Priestesses, Queens, and Property Holders

In the previous two chapters I have attempted to show that a plausible and highly probable argument can be made for the assertion that a Mother Goddess was at the center of Cretan Bronze Age religion, and that she held that central position from the Neolithic to the Iron Age. My argument was based on an examination of the relevant archaeological studies, archaeomythological studies, and my own examination of the shrines, architecture, artifacts, and religious iconography of ancient Crete.

In this chapter I will go on to demonstrate that a strong case can also be made for the argument that Minoan Crete was a woman-centered society. I will examine the archaeological evidence regarding women and their economic, social, political, and religious roles in Minoan society. I will be using archaeological artifacts and interpreting them through the lens of archaeomythology as well as Women's Spirituality, and the history of religion. Since there are not yet any deciphered written records, the artifacts will include mainly frescoes, seals, sealings, and signet rings because these are the most numerous, and because they reveal the most about the role of women in Bronze Age Crete.

Bull-leaping

I begin with the subject of bull-leaping, for I believe that women's participation in this ritual activity can be seen as one indication of their equality with men in Minoan society. Bull-leaping was an extremely dangerous, demanding ritual activity, the sort of activity that women most probably would not participate in, in a patriarchal society, where gender roles generally assign dangerous work to men and childrearing and domestic chores to women. Bull-leaping shows women in an unusual light by patriarchal standards: participating with men, and physically equal to men in a contest of great courage and skill. Women bull-leapers are very prominent on a very famous fresco (which Evans named the 'Taureador Fresco'), and on fragments of at least two other fresco panels.[1] Combined with other representations of women, the artistic representations of women bull-leaping convey the message that in Minoan society women were at least equal to the men in realms of physical strength, agility, and courage not only in the area of bull-leaping, but in Minoan life in general.

The literature on bull-leaping, and the related customs of bull-hunting and bull-wrestling, is extensive. Bull-leaping, which appears in Minoan artistic representations (frescos, sealstones, and sealings) beginning in LM I, *c.* 1580 BC, and continuing until the close of LM IIIA, *c.* 1390/70 BC, is an acrobatic feat which seems to have had at least three different variations.[2] In the most often portrayed version, one of the leapers

---

[1] Immerwahr 1990: 91.
[2] Younger 1995: 2:510.

Figure 13. Bull-leaper or 'Taureador' Fresco. LM IA, c. 1600/1580-1480, or LM IB, c. 1480-1425 BC, 78.2cm x 104.5cm, fresco, found in east wing of Temple-Palace of Knossos. Heraklion Museum, Crete. Photograph by author.

approached the bull from an elevated position and dived down the bull's neck so that they landed first on the bull's shoulders, then somersaulted over to land feet-first on the ground behind the bull.[3]

In the second version, the leaper

must have grabbed hold of the bull's horns, anticipating that the bull would toss its head obligingly back so the leaper could be flipped over the bull's head … landing feet-first on the bull's back and finally jumping neatly off.[4]

In the third version, called the 'floating leaper schema,' 'the leaper hangs poised above the bull, one hand holding onto the bull's neck, the other usually supported on the bull's horn, the legs out horizontally.'[5]

It was Sir Arthur Evans who first identified women bull-leapers. Discussing the Toreador Fresco in his work *The Palace of Minos*, Evans noted their white skin color, their festive clothing, including necklaces and headbands, and the curls falling over their foreheads.[6]

It was Evans who was also the first to interpret the 'bull-games,' as they are often called, and his dual interpretation has continued down to the present day. On the one hand, Evans believed

---

[3] Younger 1995: 2:510.
[4] Younger 1995: 2:511.
[5] Younger 1995: 2:511.
[6] Evans 1964: 3:212.

they had been performed in a religious context, but he also thought that 'they could best be described as the glorification of athletic excellence.'[7]

Many archaeologists treat bull-leaping as though it were only 'a glorification of athletic excellence,' and mainly concern themselves with questions like: what are the different schema of bull-leaping that can be identified? What did the bull-leapers wear? Representative of this group is Anne Ward, who in her article 'The Cretan Bull Sports' writes: 'There remain many unclarified questions about its [bull-leaping's] motivation and purpose, the identity of its performers, its frequency, and above all its location.'[8] Her work then goes on to analyze whether the games took place in the palaces' central courts or outside the palaces. She concludes that 'impractical as it may seem, the bull sports did actually take place in the Central Courts which lay at the heart of all the Cretan palaces.'[9]

Following Evans's first line of inquiry, many scholars do look for some religious significance behind the practice. Archaeologist S. Alexiou suggests that bull-leaping took place in the context of a festival, probably religious, in which contests were performed.[10] W. Geoffrey Arnott and R. F. Willetts hypothesize that bull-leaping was a form of initiation:

> Since the participants in the performance seem all to have been young, it is not surprising that the alleged religious ceremony has sometimes been interpreted as an initiatory ordeal, a *rite de passage* from childhood to adult status.[11]

Arnott compares bull-leaping to a similar *rite de passage* he has observed among the Ormo culture in Ethiopia.

Nanno Marinatos in her article 'The Bull as an Adversary: Some Observations on Bull-Hunting and Bull-Leaping' also sees bull-leaping as a rite of passage. As the title of her work suggests, she believes bull-leaping grew out of bull-hunting:

> The hunting urge goes back to the beginnings of mankind. While it was originally necessary for sustenance, as human societies and cultures became increasingly complex, it became a symbolic, behavioural pattern, one aspect of which is dominance over nature. In Crete, the most ferocious animal indigenous to the island was the bull. . . . If the above thesis, that the hunt represents a contest between man and wild animal is correct, then bull-leaping can be seen as a feat of similar character. . . . Bull-leaping then represents a metamorphosis of the more primeval hunting into an acculturized form; a transference from the wilderness into the urban centre under the control of the palace of Knossos.[12]

Echoing the sentiments of Alexiou, Willetts, Arnott, and Marinatos, John Younger also says the bull-games 'contributed to a palatial ceremony of "coming of age."'[13] Elaborating upon

---

[7] Marinatos 1989: 24.
[8] Ward 1968: 117.
[9] Ward 1968: 117.
[10] Marinatos 1989: 23.
[11] Arnott 1993: 115.
[12] Marinatos 1989: 25.
[13] Younger 1995: 2:521.

the theme in a later work he adds that the ceremony had the greater objective of 'maintaining social stability and predicting and predicating the preservation of the state.'[14] Younger thinks that at the end of the 'games,' the bull was probably sacrificed.

> What happened after the process of bull-leaping is unknown. I imagine that sacrificing the bull would have formed a fitting close to the bull-games. The sacrifice of bulls is well illustrated and has received much attention; it undoubtedly occurred often during several kinds of rituals, including funeral rites and perhaps hero/ancestor worship.[15]

Gimbutas also discusses the religious and symbolic meaning of bull-leaping at length and offers a very different interpretation of its meaning and purpose. Rather than viewing it as a symbol of 'man's' triumph over nature, or even as a rite of passage, she sees it as a reflection of the Minoan's understanding of regeneration.

In *The Language of the Goddess*, Gimbutas discussed the bull as a symbol of regeneration and becoming, and the similarity between its head and the female reproductive organs. It was this similarity which caused the bucrania to be associated, since the Paleolithic, with symbols of regeneration and becoming such as water, the moon, eggs, and plants.[16]

For Gimbutas, the women bull-leapers in the Toreador Fresco are an example of the place of honor women held in Minoan society. Yet there is controversy in the archaeological literature as to whether or not two of the leapers portrayed in the Toreador Fresco are women. It was Evans who first identified the two white skinned leapers as girls/women. The third, a red hue, he identified as a man. It is commonly understood in Aegean archaeology that the color white is used exclusively in works of art to designate women.

However, Marinatos argues that in the case of the Toreador Fresco 'color was manipulated to express more than just the male-female distinction.'[17] She goes on to say that it is likely 'that a type of hierarchy is expressed' by the color white. White in this case, according to Marinatos, indicates not that the leapers are female, but that they are younger and less skilled, and thus more 'female.'[18] She believes that such a hypothesis fits perfectly with her theory that the bull games were a rite of initiation. According to Marinatos there are other reasons for calling the white-skinned leapers male: they are wearing male costumes, including a phallus sheath, and they have no breasts but 'pronounced abdominal and stomach muscles' instead.[19]

Marinatos is supported in some of her conclusions by Silvia Damiani-Indelicato who, in an article entitled 'Were Cretan Girls Playing at Bull-Leaping?' also argues that the white skinned acrobats in the Toreador Fresco could not be women. Like Marinatos, Damiani-Indelicato is disturbed by the masculine appearance of the female leapers.

> Why should the Minoan artist represent bare-chested girls with male anatomical features? We know only too well that he [*sic*] used to depict female figures with

---

[14] Younger 2020: 72.
[15] Younger 1995: 2:518.
[16] Gimbutas 1989: 266.
[17] Marinatos 1989: 32.
[18] Marinatos 1993: 220.
[19] Marinatos 1989: 29.

appropriate attributes: suffice it to look at the chattering ladies of the Grand stand fresco . . . and at their well-marked breasts. Even in seals or signet-rings the female silhouette appears definitely full-bosomed.[20]

Echoing Marinatos, Damiani-Indelicato asks why not suppose that the white color, in particular contexts, could convey a different message than the traditional one. In this case she believes the color white is conveying 'a mental picture.' Her thesis is that each figure is reproducing a different moment of the same leap or three phases of the same jump.

John Younger's work 'Bronze Age Representations of Aegean Bull-Games III' responds to both Damiani-Indelicato's and Marinatos's claims that white may not signify women. He believes the white leapers are women even though he too believes the bull-games were a rite of passage.

> I follow P. Rehak who questions (AegeaNet, 12 October 1994) the idea that color conventions so rigidly adhered to elsewhere, should suddenly mean something different only in bull-leaping; instead white-painted people should always be female in the Aegean.[21]

While he does not argue for or against women bull-leapers, archaeologist and archaeological artist M. A. S. Cameron offers a unique interpretation of the Toreador Fresco. He sees it as part of a large fertility festival. His interpretation of the Toreador Fresco and the other Knossian frescoes sheds light on the role of women in Minoan Crete that leads further into the subject of the portrayal of women (and of the Goddess) in Minoan frescoes.

Women in Minoan frescoes

I noted in the previous chapter that Cameron hypothesized that the theme of the 'wall programme' of the Knossos frescoes was the worship of a Great Goddess and her festivals celebrated throughout the year. He believed the Goddess's festivals were acted out by human beings as well as painted on the palace walls. Within this context Cameron explained the Procession Fresco, which features a procession of male offering bearers and some female figures, as the escorts of the Goddess accompanying her to the temple-palace. The Jewel Fresco, which he restored as a male removing a necklace from a woman's neck, he interpreted as 'a derobing scene, a prelude to the sacred marriage.'[22] The Campstool Fresco, a scene of males sitting on camp-stools in pairs, knee to knee, toasting and drinking, in the presence of two larger female figures wearing long white cloaks (the two larger female figures Cameron interpreted as Goddesses), he saw as a feast prior to the sacred marriage. The Toreador Fresco was the shedding of blood in connection with the fertility festival. The Sacred Grove and Dance Fresco, Cameron interpreted as 'a crowd assembled to witness the epiphany of the Great Goddess.'[23] And in the Temple/Grandstand Fresco, according to Cameron, the Goddess has been escorted to her shrine, surrounded by the seated ladies, her attendants. Finally, in the Throne Room Fresco, the Goddess sat on her throne which had the shape of her sacred

---

[20] Damiani Indelicato 1988: 40.
[21] Younger 1995: 2:515.
[22] Cameron 1987: 324.
[23] Cameron 1987: 325.

mountain. There, flanked by griffins and palms, 'the actual or symbolic birth of the child would take place.'[24]

The frescoes cited above are important for illustrating not only the major significance of the Goddess in Minoan religion, but also the role of women in Minoan society, because these frescoes and others like them 'provide the fullest picture of Minoan life'[25] that we have. They point not only to the importance of women as representatives of the Goddess and her attendants, and thus women's supreme role in the religious sphere, but to women's major role in all aspects of Minoan society.

Before looking at the frescoes in more detail, a few words must be said about fresco painting in Crete, and the dating of the frescoes under consideration. The Minoans began decorating their walls with plaster and paint as early as the Neolithic. By the time of the Old Palace Period, c. 2100-1900 BC, geometric and floral designs had been added to the repertoire. It was not until the New Palace Period, c. 1700-1450 BC, however, that human figures began to appear in the frescoes.

The largest groups of figural paintings come from Knossos in Crete; and also from Akrotiri, on Thera. While it is fairly certain that the frescoes from Akrotiri are sixteenth century in date, the frescoes from Knossos are more difficult to date with any certainty. The preserved paintings of Knossos do not all belong to the same period of the 'new palaces,' which spans a time frame of c. 1700-1450 BC. The frescoes under discussion below date from c. 1700 to 1370 BC.

Cameron has written that a 'comprehensive, unifying, thematic formula in Knossian palatial mural decoration [described above] could have been devised in early MM IIIA [c. 1700 BC].'[26] He believed that when 'extensive redecoration' took place, the thematic formula was repeated. Thus even though the frescoes vary in date, in Cameron's opinion, the newer frescoes still reflect the themes prevalent three hundred years earlier. Cameron also believed 'that the later phases of the palace (LM II onwards) [c. 1450 BC on] represented a Mycenaean occupation and that the theme of the goddess's great festival survived through the ages so that it is represented even in the pictorial scheme of the Mycenaean levels.'[27]

Evans was the first to note the importance of women in Minoan society and the first to term Minoan Crete a matriarchal society. He based these observations on the frescoes as well as seals, rings, and sealings. Moreover, he noted women's importance in two spheres: the religious and the secular. Commenting on the role of women in Minoan religion Evans wrote, 'the female ministers of the Goddess took the foremost place in her service.'[28] He said over and over again that women were primary in the religion of the Goddess. 'It is observable, moreover, that the most intimate associations of the divinity are reserved for members of her own sex.'[29]

---

[24] Cameron 1987: 325.
[25] Thomas 1973: 175.
[26] Cameron 1980: 317.
[27] Cameron 1987: 324.
[28] Evans 1964: v.2, pt.1:277.
[29] Evans 1964: 3:457-458.

Evans comments upon women's important role in Minoan society, in general terms, throughout his work *The Palace of Minos*. One lengthy such commentary follows his description of the two miniature frescoes from Knossos (so-called because the human figures are anywhere from 6 to 10cm in height): the Temple, also called the Grandstand Fresco, and the Sacred Grove and Dance Fresco. Evans believed that they both illustrated 'festal celebrations in honour of the Minoan Goddess.'[30] He dated the miniature frescoes to MM IIIB, c. 1640-1600 BC. Archaeologist and fresco expert Sara A. Immerwahr believes instead they may be LM IA, c. 1580-1480 BC. Cameron agrees with Evans.

In the Temple or Grandstand Fresco, which measures one foot high and three feet wide, a tripartite shrine is featured in the center of the composition, on either side of which are grandstands. On the upper levels of the stands, figures of women, both seated and standing, are drawn in detail. On the lower level of the stands, crowds of women and men appear, drawn in a kind of shorthand. Evans thought they were gathered to watch the 'sports of the bull-ring in the area beyond.'[31] Commenting upon the fresco and the difference in the size between the female and male figures, and the way in which the women and men are drawn, Evans says:

> It is clear that, though the male spectators were the most numerous, the artist's attention was really concentrated on the female figures. The men are treated in the most summary way . . . . In the case of the women, on the other hand, their complete figures are reproduced, whether seated or standing, their eyes moreover are duly outlined, and full details are given of their brightly colored robes.[32]

Evans then goes on to say about the women in the Grandstand Fresco:

> Women among the Minoans, as is well illustrated by their occupation of all the front seats of the Grand Stands, took the higher rank in society, just as their great Goddess took the place later assigned to Zeus.[33]

Evans continues to make important observations about the role of women in Minoan Crete in his analysis of the Temple or Grand Stand Fresco:

> The women, as we have seen, take the front seats in these shows and the non-admission of male spectators among them may well, as suggested, be a sign of female predominance characteristic of the matriarchal stage.[34]

He goes on to remark that it may have been the fact that women were predominant in Minoan society that thus they felt free to mix with the men in the scene portrayed in the fresco. Evans observes that even in the fresco fragments where women are in the upper grandstand looking on, one does not get a sense that they were forced to sit separately from the men in some sort of seclusion. Indeed, he finds 'the most significant feature of the whole composition is the way in which they rub shoulders with the men in the Court below.'[35]

---

[30] Evans 1964: 3:31.
[31] Evans 1964: 3:31.
[32] Evans 1964: 3:49.
[33] Evans 1964: 3:227.
[34] Evans 1964: 3:58-59.
[35] Evans 1964: 3:58-59.

The Sacred Grove and Dance Fresco is twice as high as the Grandstand Fresco, but less broad. It portrays standing men and seated women looking down from under olive-trees on women 'performing what seems to be a ceremonial dance.'[36] Unfortunately, the lower left of the fresco was destroyed. This is the place to which the eyes of all the spectators and dancers are turned. Evans hypothesizes, on the basis of comparison with the Isopata ring (which shows four women in dress and stance similar to those of the dancers of Sacred Dance and Grove Fresco, and a female divinity descending from the sky), that an epiphany of the Goddess is taking place in the Sacred Dance and Grove Fresco.[37] He notes in his description that, 'On this, as in the companion piece described above, the women occupy the front places.'[38]

Although he assigned them a high rank in society, Evans still concluded that the throne at Knossos was meant for the 'priest-king' Minos, and, as Lucia Nixon has pointed out, he still assigned women less living space in the 'palaces.'[39] Evans's view, that a priest-king must have ruled in Bronze Age Crete, has dominated the literature with few exceptions. I shall return to the important question of a male ruler in the next chapter.

Evans's understanding, based on the art, that women played a prominent or preeminent role in Minoan society has been taken up by generations of scholars. Writing in 1968, archaeologist Jacquetta Hawkes notes that in the Knossian frescoes, 'the interest is predominantly with the women.'[40] She also makes the point, a very important, if subtle one, that women would not feel free to dress as they did (bare breasted) if they did not occupy a high rank in society. 'The way in which Cretan men and women dressed themselves is particularly appropriate to the high status of women in Minoan society, to their uninhibited liveliness in public and the freedom with which they mingled with men.'[41]

In 1969 classicist R. F. Willetts wrote, 'We have noticed some evidence [frescoes] suggesting the freedom enjoyed by women in Minoan society.'[42] He continues: 'This evidence, supported by later customs and traditions, has led some scholars to the conclusion that the Minoan civilization could have been based upon matriarchal institutions.'[43] The 'latter customs and traditions' that Willetts refers to are to be found in or inferred from the Law Code of Gortyn, dating from the fifth century BC. Willetts holds that,

> Rules of marriage appear to have derived from long-standing matriarchal customs. . . . There are very special regulations in the Gortyn Code concerning the marriage of an heiress and disposal of her property. They further emphasize the relatively high social position of women and prove that they not infrequently had control of property and land.[44]

I shall return to the Law Code of Gortyn below.

---

[36] Evans 1964: 3:67.
[37] Evans 1964: 3:68.
[38] Evans 1964: 3:67.
[39] Nixon 1994: 10.
[40] Hawkes 1968: 117.
[41] Hawkes 1968: 110.
[42] Willetts 1969: 139.
[43] Willetts 1969: 139.
[44] Willetts 1969: 141, 143.

In her classic 1977 article 'Women in Transition: Crete and Sumer,' anthropologist Ruby Rohrlich-Leavitt noted the religious prominence of women and the absence of portrayals of powerful male rulers in Minoan art. Like Evans, she first stressed Minoan women's importance in the religious life of the society. 'It was above all their roles in religion, the institution that integrated Bronze Age life, that attested to the predominance of women in Minoan Crete.'[45]

However, Rohrlich-Leavitt also details the other important roles women played that contributed to their preeminence. Basing her arguments on her interpretation of rings, seals, gold cups, figurines, and comparisons to contemporary ancient societies such as Sumer, she argues that women were navigators and merchants carrying on long distance trade; played a major role in agricultural production, something they had done since the Neolithic; served as midwives and 'doctors;' and were potters as well as hunters.

To substantiate her argument that women were navigators and merchants carrying on long distance trade, she cites several rings and seal impressions that show women steering a ship, particularly the Ring of Minos. As for women's role in agriculture, Rohrlich-Leavitt refers to Willetts who notes that because of the geographical conditions of the island of Crete, garden tillage and the hoe, rather than field tillage and the cattle-drawn plough remained the preferred form of agriculture in the Minoan period. As a result, the work of agriculture remained in the hands of women and matrilineal descent remained the tradition.[46] Willetts argues that this view is supported by myth. 'For Demeter [the Goddess who in Greek mythology gave agriculture to humankind] is said to have reached Greece from Crete.'[47]

Regarding women doctors and midwives, Rohrlich-Leavitt points out that in Minoan iconography the Goddess and her female attendants are associated with the poppy, iris, lily, and crocus, all plants known for their healing properties. Indeed, as we have seen in the previous chapter, these are all sacred symbols of the Goddess. Rohrlich-Leavitt's argument for women's primary role in health and medical care is given further support, I believe, in a 2002 article by Paul Rehak discussed in detail below.[48]

A statue of a woman potter, dating from *c.* 2000 BC, indicates to Rohrlich-Leavitt that 'Minoan women probably had equal access to professional status in the arts and crafts, particularly as potters, an occupation they developed in Neolithic times.'[49] As for the assertion that women were hunters, Rohrlich-Leavitt points to the Vapheio Cups *c.* 1500 BC, found in a tomb near Laconia (the southern Greek mainland but of Minoan origin) where a woman is shown attempting to bring down a bull by its horns to keep the animal from further attacking a fallen man. She adds this to the images of women bull-leapers in Crete and asserts: 'Women and men together, entrusting their lives to one another, hunted the wild bull with staves and nooses and played a most dangerous game, that of bull grappling or bull leaping, in public arenas.'[50] Ultimately, though, it is the pervasiveness of the Minoan Goddess and the fact that 'she or her priestesses or votaries were pictured in almost every aspect of the natural and social

---

[45] Rohrlich-Leavitt 1977: 49.
[46] Willetts 1962: 20.
[47] Willetts 1962: 20.
[48] Rehak 2002: 34-59.
[49] Rohrlich-Leavitt 1977: 48.
[50] Rohrlich-Leavitt 1977: 48.

ambience of Crete,'[51] coupled with 'the absence of portrayals of an all-powerful male ruler,'[52] that leads Rohrlich-Leavitt to conclude that 'Crete was matriarchal, a theocracy ruled by a queen-priestess.'[53]

C. G. Thomas's 1973 article, 'Patriarchy in Early Greece: Bronze and Dark Ages,' also tackles the issue of the importance of women in Minoan society. She approaches it by focusing upon the three crucial factors which she believes must be present in order for a society to be considered matriarchal: property ownership by women; a major role for women in the religious worldview of the society; and a privileged social status for women.[54]

Like her colleagues, Thomas begins her work by noting Minoan women's prominence in religious life and in all aspects of life as represented by the art. Minoan women, according to Thomas

> are represented frequently in all categories of artifacts with the exception of painted pottery where human representation of any sort is unusual . . . both the manner of depiction as well as the situations implied in the representations suggest a social prominence and degree of freedom possessed by Cretan women during the Bronze Age.[55]

Minoan women's significance in the religious life of their society is abundantly clear to Thomas. 'Not only are women shown in conspicuous roles at religious ceremonies, but also it appears virtually certain that Minoan religion centered around the worship of a supreme mother-goddess.'[56]

In support of her contention of women's social prominence and freedom, Thomas cites not only the Toreador, Grandstand, and Sacred Grove and Dance Frescoes, but the Camp-stool Fresco, the Corridor of the Procession Fresco, the 'Dancing Girl' Fresco from the Queen's Megaron,[57] and the woman kneeling in the flowers to the left of the Goddess in the Ayia Triadha fresco (discussed in Chapter 5). Thomas notes that on several of the frescoes, 'men are treated in a summary fashion while the women are represented more carefully.'[58]

Thomas believes that it is important when attempting to deduce women's social status from the frescoes to take note not only of the women's actual presence in the frescoes, but of the occasions in which Minoan women are present. She believes that all of the frescoes she has detailed have 'religious import.'[59] Moreover, the Procession Fresco gives an instance of a

---

[51] Rohrlich-Leavitt 1977: 49.
[52] Rohrlich-Leavitt 1977: 49.
[53] Rohrlich-Leavitt 1977: 49.
[54] Thomas 1973: 174.
[55] Thomas 1973: 175.
[56] Thomas 1973: 175.
[57] This fresco portrays a single woman, similar in dress and body position to the women dancers in the Sacred Grove Fresco. Evans believed she was to be interpreted as 'an individual dancer inspired with ecstatic motion' (Evans 1964: 3:70). Evans emphasized that her jacket, like those of the dancers in the Sacred Grove Fresco, was saffron color, which he believed had religious associations based on the fact that 'sacred saffron-flowers' (Evans 1964: 1:506) were found as decorations on the clay models of votive dresses buried with the Snake Goddesses. He dated the fresco to 1500 BC (Evans 1964: 3:70).
[58] Thomas 1973: 176.
[59] Thomas 1973: 176.

ceremonial occasion that required the presence of a woman.[60] Thomas hypothesizes that the Sacred Grove and Dance Fresco, the Dancing Girl Fresco from the Queen's Megaron, and the kneeling woman in the Ayia Triadha fresco, in addition to being of religious import, may be also concerned with portraying women in their natural surroundings.[61] Thomas notes that the frescoes show that women 'could and did attend public performances,' unlike their Athenian counterparts a thousand years later. The Toreador Fresco, 'in addition to pointing out, once again, the religious role of Minoan women, . . . tells us that the physical training necessary for this event included both men and women.'[62]

Thomas finds the social independence of Minoan women further verified in the architectural context of the frescoes.

> Frescoes depicting women are not confined to the residential quarters of the palace. . . The bull-leaping scene, for example, was located at the north end of the Central Court at Knossos.[63]

Ultimately, though, Thomas believes the 'high social position' held by women in Minoan Crete was due to 'the Minoan religious view.' Not only is the divinity a female, but women figure 'in an equally high position as celebrants'[64] as evidenced in the frescoes, rings, seals, and the Ayia Triadha sarcophagus, which shows women as well as men making offerings to the Goddess.

In addition to Minoan art, Thomas also looks to the mythology of Classical Greece, which centers on female heroines, to further substantiate her claims for the important role of Minoan women in social and political life: 'Britomartis, Dictynna, Ariadne and Europa may well have been names for Minoan goddesses whose status declined to that of heroines during the course of the Dark Age when the Olympian gods rose to prominence even in the still largely non-Hellenic island of Crete.'[65] This same view is expressed by Nilsson[66] and archaeologist Andonis Vasilakis, among others.

I pointed out earlier that Thomas's goal in this article is to argue that Crete was a matriarchal society, which she defines as a society in which 'women enjoy recognizable economic, social and religious privileges which, in sum, give them greater authority than men.'[67] The previous discussion has shown that women played the primary roles in the religious worldview of Minoan society and that they enjoyed 'a privileged social status.' Using the Law Code of Gortyn, Thomas argues that they also possessed the right to own property, thus fulfilling the prerequisites for her definition of a matriarchal society.

Before continuing with the evidence in the iconography that substantiates the hypothesis that women were preeminent in Minoan society, I would like to pause here to pursue two important

---

[60] Thomas 1973: 176.
[61] Thomas 1973: 176.
[62] Thomas 1973: 176.
[63] Thomas 1973: 176.
[64] Thomas 1973: 177.
[65] Thomas 1973: 176.
[66] Nilsson 1949: 510-529.
[67] Thomas 1973: 173.

topics that are raised in Thomas's work: mythology, and the Law Code of Gortyn, to see what they can reveal about the position of women in Minoan society.

Mythology and the position of women in Minoan society

In an article entitled 'Women in the Bronze Age,' Professor of Art History at Sweet Briar College, Christopher L. C. E. Witcombe, looks at Goddesses and heroines of the Bronze Age to substantiate his claim that Minoan Crete was a matrilineal society.[68] While Witcombe is interested in matriliny rather than matriarchy, his evidence is pertinent to this discussion.

Witcombe argues that since fully half of the plays of Classical (5th century BC) Greece feature extremely powerful women: Helen, Clytemnestra, Antigone, Iphigenia, Hecuba, Andromache, Penelope, Medea, Alcestis, and Elektra; and for a 'Greek theatre audience to accept the fact that women . . . could indeed threaten patriarchal social order or alter the course of history;'[69] the role of women in the Bronze Age must have been drastically different, and matrilineality must have had some basis in historical reality. Citing the Indo-European invasions of Greece during the Dark Ages (1200-900 BC), Witcombe writes:

> By the time the Bronze Age myths and legends began to be written down, starting in the 8th century BCE with Homer, the patriarchal Greek culture which had by then established itself on the mainland wished to see reflected in them its own social value system. Yet, despite the patriarchal adjustments made to the stories, retained within them, are clues which indicated that the original cultural context within which these stories were composed was a matrilineal one.[70]

What are the clues indicating that 'the original cultural context within which these stories were composed [was] a matrilineal one'? The first clue is the fact that in many of the legends the husband goes to live at the wife's residence. Such a practice is not found in patriarchal societies. Thus, for example, Menelaos goes to Sparta when he marries Helen, and through marriage becomes king of her land, even though Helen has two brothers. Amphitryon goes to Mycenae, to the home of his wife Alkmene, where they both rule, despite the fact that Alkmene also has a brother.

> Over and over among the legends, particularly those associated with southern Greece and Crete, we hear of influential daughters, daughters who inherit thrones, and sons who go away or are barely mentioned.[71]

In the story of Helen and Menelaos, the throne passes to a daughter, not to Menelaos's sons. Thus when Helen dies her daughter, Hermione, becomes the next ruler of Sparta. Then there is the story of Penelope who, 'following the departure of Odysseus, appears to have been regarded as the heiress-queen of Ithaka whose hand was sought by the suitors hoping thereby to be made king.'[72] Princess Nausikaa in the *Odyssey* invites Odysseus to marry her and live with

---

[68] In 'Matriliny in the Aegean Bronze Age,' Christopher Witcombe notes that much of his discussion is drawn from Atchity and Barber 1987: 15-37.
[69] Witcombe 2000.
[70] Witcombe 2000.
[71] Atchity and Barber 1987: 16.
[72] Witcombe 2000.

her in her family's home. Moreover, she tells Odysseus to pay homage not to the king, but to Queen Arete, 'who will determine Odysseus's eligibility to marry the heiress-princess Nausikaa and thereby become king.'[73] Witcombe lists other stories which illustrate succession to the throne via the women—Atalanta, Hippodamia, and Jocasta.

Finally, Greek myths are filled with children whose mother is a mortal princess, for example Helen and her mother Leda, but whose father is a god; in Helen's case, Zeus. Witcombe remarks that patriarchal sensibilities scoffed at a society in which sex with more than one partner was possible and even encouraged for women, thus a mythological father, a god, was named for those children whose mother had had more than one partner.

Witcombe concludes, 'These and other clues embedded in Bronze Age myths and legends indicate patterns of marriage and inheritance which suggest that matriliny was to be found among pre-Greek Aegean cultures.'[74]

Kenneth Atchity and E. J. W. Barber, upon whose work Witcombe has based much of his argument, point to yet another factor in the matriliny argument which is illustrated in the myths: a two sided economy based, on the one hand on horticulture, and on the other on trade. They conclude:

> If we suppose . . . that women were pivotal in the indigenous marriage, inheritance, and subsistence systems when the Greeks began to infiltrate from the north, we get a picture not inconsistent with the content of many of our myths and explanatory of many of their strange details, a picture of the patrilineal Greek 'nobles,' and chieftains attempting to intermarry with the matrilineal Aegean princesses—presumably as a bid to get control of their lands.[75]

The Law Code of Gortyn and the position of women in Minoan and post-Minoan society

My second excursus here is a discussion of the Law Code of Gortyn (fifth century BC), important because in it we can find traces of a society in which women wielded economic and social power. The Gortyn Law Code figures prominently in the question of whether or not Bronze Age Crete was a matriarchal society. Both Thomas and Gimbutas cite the Code in support of their arguments in favor of matriarchy and matrilineality in Minoan Crete. Thomas predicates matriarchy (in part) on the right of women to own property, on which subject the Code is quite clear; and Gimbutas uses the Code's provisions as evidence of matrilineal customs in ancient Crete: property ownership, the avunculate, and the right to divorce at will. I believe the Code reveals, to paraphrase Thomas, 'matriarchal tendencies in a subtle form.'[76] Thus the Code is vital to my argument as well.

Unfortunately, to date, we have no written, decipherable law documents from Bronze Age Crete. If one is attempting to understand women's economic rights: their ability to own property, or more importantly, to control the handling and distribution of basic goods, and

---

[73] Witcombe 2000.
[74] Witcombe 2000.
[75] Atchity and Barber 1987: 19.
[76] Thomas 1973: 174.

to inherit land through the motherline; to understand their relationships with men, and with the fathers of their children; and to understand the role of their brothers--all key elements in at least one definition of matriarchy that is being considered here; one is forced to use post-Bronze Age evidence to try to understand the Bronze Age.

The Law Code of Gortyn is 'a tabulation of statutory enactments amending prior written law on various topics and also modifying even earlier custom—the first European law-code and the only complete code to have survived from ancient Greece.'[77] Excavated in the late nineteenth century, the massive walls at the town of Gortyn, in south-central Crete, which contained the Code, are thought to have once been part of a law court. The Code, 600 lines long, inscribed in stone, is considered to be complete, and is the best example to have survived of laws that were inscribed on public buildings in ancient times. It dates to the fifth century BC, probably to 480-460 BC.

In his introduction to the Law Code of Gortyn, classicist Ronald F. Willetts, who translated the Code and wrote a commentary about it in 1967, notes: 'Since law is . . . notoriously conservative, it is readily accepted that the Code contains many traces of older usages than its actual date of formulation.'[78] Indeed Willetts believes the code was compiled much earlier and was transmitted orally for hundreds of years until it was finally written down.

There are numerous passages in the Code which show that property, including land, must often have been at the disposal of women; that both husbands and wives had the right of divorce 'at their pleasure;'[79] and that the woman's brother was important in the raising of his sister's children, indicating what can be termed, an avunculate, that is 'the vesting of matrilineal authority in the hands of the mother's brother.'[80]

I will look first at the provisions regarding women and property. Certainly the sections regarding divorce confirm the statement that property was often at the disposal of women in ancient Gortyn. Thus the Code states that:

> And if a husband and wife should be divorced, she is to have her own property which she came to her husband and half of the produce, if there be any from her own property, and half of whatever she has woven within, whatever there may be, plus five stators if the husband be the cause of the divorce. . . . And if she should carry away anything else belonging to the husband, she shall pay five staters and whatever she may carry away; and let her restore whatever she may have filched.[81]

Willetts makes an interesting observation here on how the Code reveals matriarchal tendencies:

> Both in the case of divorce and death, only the wife is envisaged as likely to take away more than her share of what is due. The explanation is presumably that the law and the

---

[77] Willetts 1977: 164.
[78] Willetts 1967: 8.
[79] Willetts 1967: 29.
[80] Thomas 1973: 174.
[81] Willetts 1977: 217.

state were taking the offensive against the surviving tradition of matrilocal custom and matriarchal tenure of property.[82]

Mention of divorce in the above provision also highlights Willetts's statement that husbands and wives had the right of divorce 'at their pleasure.' Willetts assumes that divorce could not have been unusual. Indeed, while divorce is often referred to in the Code, nowhere is anything said about why or how one would divorce. Women's right to divorce at their pleasure could reflect an earlier matriarchal social order.

The case of widowhood or the death of a wife further elucidates women's rights as regards property.

> If a man die leaving children, should the wife so desire, she may marry, holding her own property and whatever her husband might have given her according to what is written. . . . And if he should leave her childless, she is to have her own property and half of whatever she has woven within and obtain her portion of the produce that is in the house along with the lawful heirs as well as whatever her husband may have given her as is written; but if she should take away anything else, that becomes a matter for trial. And if a woman should die childless (the husband), is to return her property to the lawful heirs and half of what she has woven within and half of the produce, if it be from her own property.
> If a female serf be separated from a male serf while he is alive or in case of his death, she is to have her own property; but if she should carry away anything else, that becomes a matter for a trial.[83]

Regarding these last several lines on the right of a female serf to retain her property in divorce or upon the death of the husband, Willetts again finds echoes of the matriarchal past:

> It is remarkable that the property rights of the husband are not mentioned, either in case of divorce, or death of his wife; and we can assume that we have here further indication that the serf community, in obedience to the 'laws of Minos', preserved to a greater extent than the free citizens, ancient forms of property rights associated with matrilineal descent.[84]

The Code prohibits husbands from selling, mortgaging, or pledging the wife's property or possessions. Similar prohibitions are placed on the son.[85] Willetts believes that the penalties laid down for the infringement of these prohibitions are indicative of an earlier time when property was controlled by the women of the tribe:

> Abuses against women's rights of tenure must have been markedly on the increase. The whole weight of the legislation here is defensive. The intention is to try to limit the extent of encroachment upon [women's] collective rights, particularly by limiting the

---

[82] Willetts 1967: 20.
[83] Willetts 1977: 217-218.
[84] Willetts 1977: 93.
[85] Willetts 1977: 219.

powers of individual action by the males. Trespasses against the property of the heiress met with similar penalties.[86]

Further evidence of women's rights to own and dispose of their own property is apparent in the laws governing heiresses. Thomas observes that within these provisions there is reflected 'an earlier period when the laws of inheritance were based on the principle of female succession.'[87]

Also within these provisions we learn that the avunculate still operated in 5th century Gortyn, Crete. The Code stipulates that if an 'heiress,' is too young to marry and her mother is deceased, she is to be raised by her mother's brothers.[88]

Regarding the avunculate, Willetts adds:

> If the mother is alive, nothing is said about the administration of the property: it is taken for granted that this will be done by the mother. . . . Similarly, if there is no mother, that it will be done by the mother's brothers. The importance of the mother's brother, indicated here, is a survival of earlier matriarchal institutions.[89]

Thomas notes that 'The avunculate is shown in the provision that a motherless heiress was to be raised by her maternal uncles. At the same time, however, her property was to be administered by her paternal uncles.'[90] In Goettner-Abendroth's definition of matriarchy, the matriarchal social order is characterized by brothers as the supporters of women. Maternal uncles in a matriarchy

> regard their nephews and nieces as 'their children,' whom they take care of and take collective responsibility for raising. In that sense, the men have the role of 'social fathers' for their sisters' children.[91]

Despite the fact that women enjoyed the right to own and maintain control over their own property, the Code states limits on how much a father might will to his daughter. A daughter's share of the inheritance was to be one half as much as the son's. Willetts again sees this as a strike against the older, matriarchal order, or, in his words, 'a further stage in the encroachment of males upon the old established rights of tenure of females.'[92]

The comments of Willetts and Thomas make clear how one can use the Code of Gortyn to infer an earlier matriarchal or matrilocal society in Crete, although admittedly, the case is far from unequivocal, as Thomas herself points out. In order to truly appreciate the uniqueness of the Law Code of Gortyn, especially in regards to women's property rights, and to understand why one might regard it as a remnant of an earlier matriarchal/matrilocal society and legal system, it is instructive to compare the Law Code of Gortyn to a contemporaneous law code, that of

---

[86] Willetts 1967: 21.
[87] Thomas 1973: 178.
[88] Willetts 1955: 76-77.
[89] Willetts 1955: 77.
[90] Thomas 1973: 178.
[91] Goettner-Abendroth 2007: 9.
[92] Willetts 1967: 21.

Athens in 450 BC. Comparing the two law codes, as regards the property rights of women, Professor of History at the University of California at Berkeley, Raphael Sealey writes:

> In Athens the dowry, though intended for the woman's support, was administered by the husband and his discretionary power was large. . . . In Gortyn, on the other hand, the law recognized the woman's property as fully hers and safeguarded it against embezzlement.[93]

Moreover, Athenian law recognized only her dowry as the property of the woman and even that only 'in the minimal sense that others were not supposed to encroach on it.'[94] The Gortyn Law Code, on the other hand, recognized that in addition to what she brought to the marriage, the woman owned half of what she had 'woven' during the marriage, and half of what she had produced. 'The laws [of Gortyn] even provide judicial procedures to resolve disputes about the estate of the women's property.'[95]

Women's preeminence in Minoan art

Returning now to those scholars who argue for the prominence or preeminence of women in Minoan society, I turn to the work of archaeologist Helen Waterhouse. Following on the heels of Thomas's work, Waterhouse, the following year, in 1974, critically looked at Evans's priest-king. In debunking the priest-king and attempting to show instead that ancient Crete was a theacracy, ruled by a Goddess and a priestess-queen, who was the representative of the Goddess, Waterhouse also looks to portrayals of Minoan women in art to make her case. In doing so, she reiterates what other archaeologists, classicists, and anthropologists have noted:

> Though scenes of ceremony are common in Minoan art, no kingly figure takes part in or presides over any of them. In contrast, there is massive pictorial evidence, from the miniature frescoes onwards, for the predominant position of women in such scenes and in Minoan culture as a whole.[96]

Waterhouse begins by noting that 'the possible pictorial evidence for Priest-Kings is inconclusive'[97] and, as we shall see, she is supported in this conclusion by Ellen N. Davis and many other, although not all, archaeologists currently working in the field. Waterhouse states that:

> Evans's own awareness of this [the inconclusiveness of the pictorial evidence for a priest-king] is expressed in many passages in the *Palace of Minos*, though these are contradicted by the general tenor of that work. Helga Reusch has demonstrated that the throne at Knossos can only have been occupied by the goddess in the person of her priestess.[98]

---

[93] Sealey 1990: 80.
[94] Seeley 1990: 77.
[95] Seeley 1990: 78.
[96] Waterhouse 1974: 153.
[97] Waterhouse 1974: 153.
[98] Waterhouse 1974: 153. Waterhouse is here referring to an article by Reusch 1958: 334-356. For a more recent analysis of the iconography of the Throne Room see Galanakis, Tsitsa, and Gunkel-Maschek 2017: 47-98.

In this work Reusch argues, based on the fresco paintings adorning the throne room at the temple-palace of Knossos—a frieze of split rosettes, which are identical to the Hittite hieroglyph for the word 'deity,' and the two griffins flanking the throne, griffins are only associated with deities of the female gender in Bronze Age Crete—that the throne at Knossos could only have belonged to a female deity and to the female priestess who represented her on the earthly plane. Since 1958, when Reusch's article was published, numerous other scholars have pointed out that the palm trees, which appear in the fresco behind the throne, (and were restored to the fresco in the 1970s), are another symbol only associated with female deities, thus reinforcing Reusch's thesis. This interpretation, that a woman sat on the throne at Knossos, has been widely accepted by Aegeanists.

Suggesting that the Minoan Palaces were temple-palaces, an argument that has been taken up by others since Waterhouse wrote, and that 'the hierarchy living in them consisted chiefly of priestesses for they alone could enact the epiphany of the goddess,'[99] Waterhouse posits that Minoan Crete was a theacracy: 'An extension from religious to civil leadership would follow from their sole ability to speak for the divine and thus to guide the state in all its actions.'[100] I believe Waterhouse has made an extremely important point here—one that has not been made by others in quite this way. If the main deity of the Minoans was a Mother Goddess, as I have argued, and if women were her main celebrants and embodied her on the earthly plane, then it seems quite probable that they might 'guide the state in all its actions,' in other words, wield considerable and preeminent political power.

Writing in 1981, Aegean archaeologist and fresco expert Sara A. Immerwahr suggested that, based on the Grandstand Fresco and the Sacred Grove and Dance Fresco (executed between 1600-1450 BC), Minoan society exhibited a 'female bias.'

> The two compositions are best viewed together as illustrations of large gatherings at the palace, or in its vicinity, to witness some event, presumably of a religious nature. Clearly the crowds, shown in short-hand perspective, represent more than the immediate palace residents (Evans' estimate was 600 for the 'Temple,' 1400 for the 'Sacred Grove'). In both, women are emphasized at the expense of men in fullness of portrayal and in position. . . . The Minoan palace culture, as seen at Knossos, emphasizes the role of women over that of men; but this may reflect the dominance of a female divinity and her priestesses as well as the importance of the palace as a religious centre.[101]

In her 1990 classic *Aegean Painting in the Bronze Age*, Immerwahr again considered what the frescoes could reveal about women's status in Minoan society. She observes that in the first phase of Aegean wall painting, MM IIIB to LM IA, c. 1640-1480 BC, 'female figures seem to predominate.'[102] Comparing male and female figures in the frescoes, she notes

> On the whole, in Minoan painting, the male figures seem subordinate to the female and are depicted as ministrants (offering-bearers) in the service of a female divinity, or performing ritual sports, probably also in her honor. [Frescoes of females present]

---

[99] Waterhouse 1974: 153.
[100] Waterhouse 1974: 153.
[101] Immerwahr 1983: 145, 149.
[102] Immerwahr 1990: 40.

a somewhat different picture. They are not only more numerous, occurring at almost every site touched by Minoan culture, but they also show more clearly the impact of the religious life and the court dress of the palace at Knossos.[103]

Marija Gimbutas reiterates the important points that have been made above as regards what we can deduce about women's role in Minoan Crete based on their portrayal in the art, in her 1991 work *The Civilization of the Goddess*. There she notes how Minoan women are shown 'mixing freely with men in festivals, riding in chariots driven by female charioteers, and participating as athletes during ritual bull games.'[104] To Gimbutas, the art of the Minoans leaves no doubt that women were central in religious life until at least the Mycenaean era, and the throne at Knossos was occupied by a woman in her role as 'highest representative of the Goddess.'[105]

Nanno Marinatos's ideas about what Minoan art, and especially the frescoes and seals, can tell us about women in Minoan society are developed in her 1993 book *Minoan Religion*. Although the purpose of the book is not to discuss the role of women in Bronze Age Crete, in her analysis of the religious iconography, Marinatos does offer some conclusions as to the role of women, especially in the ritual/religious sphere.

In *Minoan Religion* Marinatos devotes a large section of the Chapter entitled 'The Palaces as Cult Centers' to a discussion of the frescoes at Knossos. Before turning to that discussion, I would mention again that many of the frescoes, especially those from Knossos, are difficult to date. As Immerwahr says of Knossos, 'it is difficult to distinguish decoration that may have been put on the walls as early as LM I [1580-1450 BC] and that added comparatively later in the history of the LM II/IIIA [1450-1375 BC] palace.'[106] This matters because by LM II, *c.* 1450 BC, and on, there is probably a Mycenaean presence at Knossos, although there is controversy among archaeologists as to what that presence actually means. However, I return again to what Cameron says, and Immerwahr emphasizes and Evely reiterates: even though the dates assigned to the frescoes under discussion cover several centuries, there was an 'essential conservation of imagery and purpose that survived the Mycenaean take-over at Knossos.'[107] Part of the reason that Cameron, Immerwahr, and others can make this statement with such assurance is the fact that Cameron, who spent his whole career studying the fresco fragments, drawing them, and piecing fragments together, found evidence for earlier versions of the same subject matter in close proximity to the later frescoes.[108]

Marinatos begins her discussion with the west wing frescoes, which include four key scenes. In the Procession Fresco, the central figure is a female, who is receiving some sort of tribute in the form of cult vessels. Marinatos asks if this is a 'worship ceremony or preparation for a festival?'[109] The Throne Room Fresco, displays griffins (they only flank female divinities), palms (they are only used in ritual activity, and they are most often associated with the Goddess), and incurved altars (pieces of cult equipment). Marinatos notes that it has been proposed, and generally accepted by experts, that the person occupying the throne was a woman, a high

---

[103] Immerwahr 1990: 53.
[104] Gimbutas 1991: 346.
[105] Gimbutas 1991: 346.
[106] Immerwahr 1990: 8.
[107] Evely 1999: 66.
[108] Evely 1999: 66.
[109] Marinatos 1993: 53.

Figure 14. Clanmother, Priestess, or Goddess ('La Parisienne') from the Campstool Fresco. LM IIIA/B, c. 1450-1300 BC, fresco, found in west wing, Temple-Palace of Knossos. Heraklion Museum, Crete. Photograph by author.

priestess impersonating the Goddess.[110] The Campstool Fresco is dominated by a female figure, probably two of them, filling two registers of the fresco. Marinatos points out that the women in that fresco 'preside' over the ceremony portrayed there, and she concludes that the women in the Campstool Fresco represent either the high priestess or the Minoan Goddess.[111] Marinatos declares, overall, speaking of the frescoes from the west wing of the temple-palace of Knossos, that 'the ritual role of a woman or group of women is just about certain.'[112]

Turning to the north wing of the temple-palace and the Sacred Grove and Dance and the Grandstand Frescoes, Marinatos says that what is depicted is a festival where 'women seem to be the protagonists.'[113] Like other archaeologists, Marinatos remarks that 'women only are on the stands.'[114] At another point she says: women 'undoubtedly had powerful positions derived from their involvement in, and control of, certain rituals.'[115] She concludes from the Grandstand Fresco and Sacred Grove and Dance Fresco that 'the palace played a central role in the organization of public festivals and that the cultic role of women was accentuated.'[116]

However, while Marinatos recognizes the powerful role of women, derived, as she states, from their centrality in the religious practices of Minoan society, Marinatos has reconstructed the Sacred Grove and Dance Fresco to include a scene of men holding javelins, and she labels these men warriors and protagonists.[117] Evans's restoration of this miniature fresco did not include the 'men with javelins.' He believed the fragmentary images of men with javelins belonged to an entirely different wall decoration depicting perhaps a beleaguered city. In arguing for her reconstruction, Marinatos writes that the fragments of the 'men with javelins,' which she

---

[110] Marinatos 1993: 54. Marinatos's use of the term 'impersonator' is taken from Mark Cameron. It is my understanding that Cameron did not use the term in a pejorative sense.
[111] Marinatos 1993: 56.
[112] Marinatos 1993: 58.
[113] Marinatos 1993: 58.
[114] Marinatos 1993: 60.
[115] Marinatos 1993: 61.
[116] Marinatos 1993: 61.
[117] Marinatos 1993: 59.

would reconstruct as part of the Sacred Grove and Dance Fresco, were found in the same heap as the fragments Evans used for his reconstruction. Moreover, Marinatos believes the 'men with javelins' can be comfortably associated with the theme of the Sacred Grove and Dance Fresco. She writes, 'Parade of arms in the context of state festivals is not unusual, as we know from other cultures, notably Classical Greece.'[118] I would posit that if one insists upon adding the 'men with javelins' to this fresco, one might argue they are participating in an athletic contest which is being held as part of the festival in honor of the Goddess. Such an occurrence in the context of a religious festival is also not unusual, as we know from Classical Greece. It remains an open question whether or not the men with javelins should be included in the Sacred Grove and Dance Fresco.

In her discussion of the Grandstand Fresco, also known as the Temple Fresco, Marinatos observes that women of different ages are depicted. She comes to this determination on the basis of the differentiation in their hairstyles and breasts.[119] I would posit that the fact that the Grandstand Fresco portrays women of different ages argues for a society in which women of all ages, not just women in the prime of life, are valued. Especially interesting is the fact that older, mature women are represented. Such valuation of women would probably not be found in a patriarchal society.[120]

Also from the north wing of the temple-palace, from what is termed the 'NW Fresco Heap,' come fragments of female garments decorated with sphinxes, griffins, and bulls' heads. Since the animals are sacred ones, Marinatos concludes that such clothing could only have been worn by a priestess or a Goddess.[121]

The Blue Monkey Fresco, again from the north wing, also displays an animal sacred to the Goddess, the monkey, as well as one of the sacred symbols closely associated with the Goddess, the crocus. 'One can see . . . that monkeys play an important role in Minoan iconography of ritual, especially as gatherers of plants and servants of the deity.'[122]

From the east wing and the monumental East Hall of the temple-palace of Knossos, come fragments of relief frescoes that depicted bulls; women, including the well-known and, according to Marinatos, over-restored 'Ladies in Blue' fresco; a fragment of a man holding a bull's horns; a horned crown (an item which looks like the horns of bulls tied together, usually shown in seals crowning a Goddess); and griffins flanking something, perhaps a Goddess. There are also fragments of male limbs. Marinatos concludes that the East Hall had something to do with bulls and sacrificial ritual. She also points out that the symbols found in the East Hall are the very same symbols which decorated the garments she attributes to a Goddess found in the NW Heap.

Moving to the so-called 'domestic quarter' of the east wing of the temple-palace, one of the frescoes depicts a procession of men and figure-eight-shaped shields—which Marinatos asserts were paraphernalia of the cult.[123] Marinatos is at pains to point out that the shields do

---

[118] Marinatos 1993: 60.
[119] Marinatos 1993: 59.
[120] I am indebted to Tiffany Boyd for pointing this out to me.
[121] Marinatos 1993: 63.
[122] Marinatos 1993: 63.
[123] Marinatos 1993: 66.

Figure 15. Fresco of Goddess descending from the sky. LM IA, c. 1600/1580-1480, or LM IB, c. 1480-1425 BC, fresco, found in east wing Temple-Palace of Knossos. Heraklion Museum, Crete. Photograph by author.

not necessarily have a connection with militarism. I agree with Marinatos, and am convinced by Rehak's argument that it is mainly women who appear with figure-eight shields in Minoan religious iconography in rings, sealings, plaques, and figurines. 'It is likely that the figure eight shield is associated with epiphanies, presumably of female divinities.'[124] Rehak notes that 'the few friezes on seals with male figures carrying shields appear . . . in LM IIIA.'[125] Panagiotaki has noted that the figure-eight shield has been interpreted as a religious symbol by a number of archaeologists, Evans, Nilsson, and Rutkowski among them.[126] According to Panagiotaki, representations of figure-eight shields were found in the Temple Repositories deposits, and she seems to favor an interpretation of them as a symbol of life and the renewal of life.[127] Gimbutas classifies the figure of eight shields with the 'power of two' family of symbols which in Old Europe expressed the concept of abundance.[128]

Also in this east wing were found the Toreador Fresco as well as fresco fragments with a bull's forefoot, the horn and ear of a bull, ivory figurines of bull-leapers, and a faience bull's head. Also from this section of the palace came the fresco of a torso of a woman, Evans termed her a 'dancing lady,'[129] perhaps she was rather a Goddess descending from the sky.[130] Here too was found a delightful fresco of dolphins swimming. All Marinatos will say about this part of the palace and its frescoes is that 'the bull seems to have played an important role in the iconography of the East wing.'[131] I would posit that once again women, as the female bull-leapers (in the Toreador fresco), and women, in the form of the Goddess, predominate in this wing, as they have in the others.

---

[124] Rehak 2009: 12.
[125] Rehak 2009: 12.
[126] Panagiotaki 1999: 90.
[127] Panagiotaki 1999: 90.
[128] Gimbutas1989: 163.
[129] Marinatos 1993: 67.
[130] Marinatos 1993: 67.
[131] Marinatos 1993: 68.

When she comes to the south wing of Knossos, Marinatos turns her attention to males in the frescoes. For Marinatos, this is a wing dominated by male figures. She argues that the south wing, where the Palanquin Fresco (restored by Evans as one man being carried in a palanquin by four men) was found, indicates that men played as important a role as women in Minoan society. Marinatos has reconstructed the Palanquin Fresco based on fragments which Evan left out of his reconstruction. In her reconstruction two men stand behind a wooden railing watching a procession or receiving tribute. They are surrounded by other men, some seated, some standing. Comparing her restored Palanquin Fresco, in which men predominate, to the Grandstand Fresco, in which women are the main actors, Marinatos concludes that the sexes were segregated in ritual, and that 'the predominance of women in ceremonial scenes is not as striking as one might think at first.'[132]

Mark Cameron also restored the Palanquin Fresco. His restoration differs from both Evans's and Marinatos's. In his reconstruction a figure (a priest?) is seated in a shrine.[133] What is also different about Cameron's reconstruction is that he associated the Palanquin Fresco with a chariot frieze which he restored from fragments Evans had found, along with the addition of new fragments recovered in 1955 during the consolidation of a wall at Knossos. In his reconstruction of the Charioteer Fresco, the charioteer is leading a bull, perhaps to the bull-leaping games, or perhaps to sacrifice, thus the chariot is of a ritual, not military nature. It should be noted that both the Palanquin and Charioteer Frescoes are dated by experts to LM II and are considered 'Probably 'Mycenaean' work of LM II [1490 BC or later].'[134]

Finally, Marinatos notes that the Prince of the Lilies Fresco, the figure which Evans termed a priest-king, but which Marinatos thinks may have actually been a representation of a god, was found near the Palanquin Fresco.[135] The restoration and interpretation of the Prince of the Lilies Fresco is contested and controversial, and it is discussed in Chapter 7.

To sum up, Marinatos, based on the frescoes, will only grant women a separate, but balanced role with men in the ritual or religious sphere of Minoan life. She says nothing about what the frescoes might intimate about women's social, economic, or political roles. By omitting any commentary in that regard, I believe she is implying that women had no important social, economic, or political roles in Minoan Crete, except perhaps as priestesses or 'impersonators' of the Goddess. On the basis of one fresco, the Palanquin Fresco, whose restoration is not agreed upon, she wishes to negate what all the other frescoes at Knossos have demonstrated or inferred about the position, power, and authority of Minoan women. I believe she is mistaken. It seems to me that women, in their role as celebrants and embodiments of the Goddess, and as personages of importance, judged by their size, the detail with which they are drawn, their position in the fresco composition, and their central importance in the action being portrayed in the fresco, outweigh men in importance in the frescoes at Knossos and thus in Minoan life. Even if the Prince of the Lilies is indeed a male and a prince, and even if men are portrayed in the Palanquin Fresco, there still remains the main female figure in the Procession Fresco, the two larger than life-size female figures in the Campstool Fresco, the prominence of the women in the Grandstand and the Sacred Grove and Dance Frescoes, the women bull-leapers in the

---

[132] Marinatos 1993: 71.
[133] Immerwahr 1990: 94.
[134] Hood 2005: 70.
[135] Marinatos 1993: 73.

Toreador Frescoes (and the women bull-leapers in the fragments of two more bull-leaping frescoes that have not been fully restored), and the fact that a female in all probability sat on the throne embodying the Goddess at Knossos.

Approaching the issue of the role of women in Minoan society through a different lens, the lens of motherhood, is archaeologist Barbara A. Olsen. In a fascinating article entitled 'Women, Children and the Family in the Late Aegean Bronze Age: Differences in Minoan and Mycenaean Constructions of Gender' published in 1998, Olsen argues that contrary to contemporary societies of the time, Minoan iconography associates women with power and status. Women portray the Minoan Mother Goddess, or they are high ranking public officials or priestesses 'whose social status is suggested by their jewelry, costume or administrative regalia.'[136]

In attempting to prove this point, Olsen relies not only on Linear B tablets, but on Aegean art as well. Olsen notes that when one analyzes the art, one finds that

> Minoan society does not invest in idealizing women as mothers. It seems instead to place them in capacities other than those associated with the care of infants. We see in Minoan iconography images of women in more public contexts: occupying prominent spatial positions in outdoor assemblies and processions, interacting with each other either in conversation or in dance, and acting in religious contexts either as individual worshippers or as officials involved in sacrificial rituals. Above all, emphasis is on the social rather than the biological, the public rather than the domestic.[137]

In 1999 the Museum of Cycladic Art in Athens hosted an exhibit of Mark Cameron's drawings of the frescoes of Knossos. In the catalog accompanying this exhibit, entitled *Fresco: A Passport into the Past Minoan Crete through the Eyes of Mark Cameron*, archaeologist Doniert Evely commented upon the role of women in Minoan society based on the frescoes.

> The presence of females in a central role in ritual activity as depicted on frescoes seems indisputable. Similar patterns of prominence are seen in the religious scenes on the gold signet rings and sealings, and in the faience figurines from the Temple Repositories and other statuettes of clay. In some cases the authority they wield is made manifest by posture and the possession of a staff or wand 'of power.' In such instances they are either depicted alone or with an apparently 'subservient' male or animals in attendance. These find their counterpart . . . in fresco scenes such as that from Pseira . . . and at Aghia Triadha.
> Other scenes depict groups of women. Those on fresco—by virtue of the space available—give better information than some of the scenes on the signet rings. The evidence, however, is consistent. These women are always part of a solemn and ritual event. . . . When active, they dance or process, when passive they sit and watch. Even in the last case, their important status is shown by their larger size and the often extra details of their rendition. . . . they often provide a focal pivot to events.
> It is reasonable therefore to accept that women played a prominent part in the workings of the higher levels of Minoan culture and society.[138]

---

[136] Olsen 1998: 383.
[137] Olsen 1998: 390.
[138] Evely 1999: 88-89.

J. Lesley Fitton, writing in 2002, expresses the idea prevalent in much of current archaeological literature when she says:

> The presence, indeed the importance of women in Minoan iconography cannot be denied. The goddess or goddesses of Crete had female acolytes, and women are shown in privileged positions along side men in large-scale gatherings that were probably for religious festivals. It would be simplistic to extrapolate from this a society in which women held social and political sway, though it may well be that women in the Greek Bronze Age enjoyed a higher status in society than they were accorded, for example, in the world of Classical Athens.[139]

Also writing in 2002, Paul Rehak in an article entitled 'Imag(in)ing a Women's World in Bronze Age Greece: The Frescoes from Xeste 3 at Akrotiri, Thera,' not only expands upon an idea raised by Marinatos and myself above, but presents a unique interpretation of the frescoes from Akrotiri's Xeste 3 which lends further support to my argument that women were central in Bronze Age Crete.

Marinatos and I noted above that Minoan frescoes portray women in all stages/ages of life. Looking at all of the wall paintings from Xeste 3, especially room 3, Rehak posits that the theme of the frescoes is 'female rites of passage in all stages of a woman's life.'[140] Indeed Rehak believes that it was mainly women who used Xeste 3 as a house of religious ceremony.

Rehak begins by reiterating what the authorities I have cited previously have said about women in Minoan art: they 'are usually shown on a larger scale, in more central positions, and they perform more important acts.'[141] He focuses first on the often-reproduced fresco of the three young women which is painted on the walls of the lustral basin in Xeste 3. This fresco shows one young woman swinging a necklace, another sitting on the ground holding her foot from which drops of blood trickle, and a third young woman covered by a yellow veil. They are portrayed in front of a shrine which is topped with horns of consecration. Rehak's detailed analysis of the girls' figures, clothing, hairstyles, ornaments, and the environment in which they are found, especially the abundant crocus iconography, indicate to him that that the 'wounded girl' has been 'dressed and bejeweled deliberately, probably by other women, for a particular ritual occasion.'[142] Rehak, like Marinatos,[143] maintains that the occasion is the celebration of menstruation. He adds

> If this is so, it is important to note that the event is being celebrated with rich garments and adornment with special jewelry, not marginalized or stigmatized. The ritualization of the event is suggested as well by the shrine façade on the adjacent wall and by the location of the paintings in a lustral basin, a special architectural area.[144]

Rehak then goes on to describe and interpret the rest of the frescoes in Xeste 3. In another ground floor room located near the lustral basin is a fresco that shows four males; three carry

---

[139] Fitton 2002: 178.
[140] Rehak 2002: 37.
[141] Rehak 2002: 37.
[142] Rehak 2002: 41.
[143] Marinatos 1984: 61-84.
[144] Rehak 2002: 42.

metal vessels and one, a piece of cloth. Like the women, they represent four distinct age groups. Only one of the three male figures is clothed and none of them wears any jewelry, 'indicating they all are of relatively low status or a different class.'[145] Of the fresco of the males, Rehak writes, 'they appear in a separate room and are apparently of lesser status.'[146]

Rehak then proceeds to discuss the Crocus Gatherers Fresco from Thera where four young girls gather crocus blossoms and present them to a seated Goddess who is flanked by a monkey and a griffin (discussed earlier in Chapter 5). According to Rehak, the Goddess of the Crocus Gatherers Fresco is a *Potnia Theron*, Mistress of the Animals, and he likens her to the Goddess Artemis of historical times: 'she incorporates some of the functions of the later historical Artemis.'[147]

Also on the upper floor, where the Crocus Gatherers Fresco is located, were found three other frescoes. One depicts a marsh scene with reeds, ducks, and dragonflies. Another 'shows a file of mature women with full breasts and hair tied in snoods.'[148] The mature women, like the younger women, wear clothing that is saffron yellow and decorated with crocuses with stigma, or lilies. 'These matrons could be the mothers of the crocus-gathering girls'[149](described above). A third fresco displays white lilies against a red background.

Looking at all the frescoes in Xeste 3 as an entire wall program, as Cameron would have done, Rehak says that women in four stages of life are depicted. His understanding of the figures' ages is based on analysis of hair styles, stages of breast development, and clothing, especially the length of the skirts. Thus pre-pubescence is exemplified by the flower-gathering girls; advanced pre-pubescence is represented by the veiled girl; full puberty is represented by the girl with the bleeding foot; and finally full adulthood is exemplified by 'the matronly processional women.' His hypothesis is that:

> The frescoes are outlining the importance in Aegean society of successive rituals of maturation for women at all ages with reference to a specific goddess [the seated Goddess in the Crocus Gatherers Fresco], localizing each stage within a more inclusive society of women. Moreover, references to saffron abound for all these women, whatever their age and status, within this homosocial sisterhood.[150]

Rehak does not stop there. He points out the importance of saffron and crocuses to the frescoes: they appear in the landscape, on the women's clothing, jewelry and facial decoration, and saffron-rich crocuses are being gathered and offered to the Goddess. He then details the medical properties of saffron. It is a digestive, stimulant, aphrodisiac, narcotic, emmenagogue, and can induce abortion. Moreover, it is an important source of vitamin A and B and carotenoids, 'all of which are lacking from most of the foods we know were consumed in the Bronze Age Aegean, where the diet consisted largely of grains, legumes, oil, figs, grapes and wine.'[151]

---

[145] Rehak 2002: 41.
[146] Rehak 2002: 47.
[147] Rehak 2002: 46.
[148] Rehak 2002: 46.
[149] Rehak 2002: 46.
[150] Rehak 2002: 48.
[151] Rehak 2002: 48.

Building on the work of Ellen N. Davis, who noted light blue streaks in the eyes of some of the fresco figures in Xeste 3, Rehak notes that the Goddess and young girls in the Crocus Gatherers Fresco, along with all of the women depicted in the lustral basin fresco, and the youngest boy in the fresco of the four males, have blue-streaked corneas. The matrons all have plain white corneas. The youthful males and the one adult man have red-streaked eyes. Red-streaks in the eyes are a symptom of vitamin A or riboflavin deficiency.

Rehak concludes that women controlled the cultivation, harvest, and distribution of saffron, apparently denying it to males, judging by the red eyes of all but the youngest male in the Xeste 3 frescoes.[152]

> The women of Thera must have had a detailed experiential knowledge of the medicinal properties of saffron, a knowledge that should also have been an important source of women's power and ability to experience a personal control of their bodies and thus their lives. The frescoes from Xeste 3 thus document Aegean women's extraordinary awareness of, and attention to, their body, its development, and its maintenance. In this female homosocial world . . . men are obviously of lesser status and [apparently] deprived of access to a source of nutrition that gave power instead to women.[153]

Archaeologist Gerald Cadogan tackled the question of the role of women in Minoan society in his 2005 article 'Gender Metaphors of Social Stratigraphy in Pre-Linear B Crete or Is 'Minoan Gynaecocracy' (Still) Credible?' In that work he makes an important argument in favor of the predominance of women that has not been mentioned by others: the general absence of erotic depictions in Minoan art. His point is that

> erotic depictions were a male phenomenon in the ancient world. . . . Their wholesale lack—and the lack of even signs of affection—in Palatial Crete form one of the most extraordinary, and underestimated, aspects of Minoan culture, something that could fit well with a 'female-dominated society.'[154]

In a conference in October 2011 in Chicago entitled 'Thera, Knossos and Egypt 1500 BCE,' sponsored by the University of Chicago's Oriental Institute and the University of Illinois at Chicago, some additional important points in regard to the role of women in the Minoan world were made. Particularly pertinent in this regard was the lecture entitled 'Theran Frescoes' by Andreas Vlachopoulous of the University of Ioannina, Greece. In his presentation, Vlachopoulous expressed the idea that Xeste 3, the largest, most important building in Akrotiri, was used for rituals preparatory to initiation, marriage, and fertility, and that the frescoes of Xeste 3 reflect the building's ritual purpose. He argued that this portrayal of 'customary ritual cycles' was a common theme throughout the Aegean, one that even the Egyptians would have been familiar with. In all the frescoes of Xeste 3, 'women are the protagonists.'[155] This is further affirmation of women's primary importance in the ritual life of the Minoans.

---

[152] Rehak 2002: 50.
[153] Rehak 2002: 50.
[154] Cadogan 2009: 229.
[155] Vlachopoulous, 'Theran Frescoes,' (lecture, Oriental Institute of Chicago, October 22, 2010).

Vlachopoulous also discussed the continuing restoration of the frescoes on the top floor of Xeste 3. The top floor contains two large spaces. One of them—directly above rooms 3 and 4, the rooms containing the Crocus Gatherers Fresco as well as a fresco of a marshy landscape, and a fresco of mature women in procession (see Chapter 5 above)—had walls which were painted red. They served as the background for a sophisticated and complex geometric pattern of white and blue spirals, which literally filled the space. Vlachopoulous theorizes that the red room with the blue and white spirals could have held large numbers of people, and that it was probably a gathering space people came to, after the rituals on the lower levels were completed. It seems very appropriate that after celebrating rituals honoring initiation, marriage, and fertility, people would gather within the spiral walls. Gimbutas has argued that spirals were symbols of life-giving and regeneration, of energy and unfolding.[156] Marinatos, speaking of the newly restored frescoes on the third floor of Xeste 3 argues that the 'spiral murals', as she calls them, symbolize 'the power of the Great Goddess to generate life.'[157]

It seems to me that Vlachopoulous's argument that women are the protagonists in the frescoes portraying initiation, marriage, and fertility which decorate the walls of the largest building in Akrotiri, a building for sacred ritual, ritual related to the lives of women and the honoring of the Goddess (as in the Crocus Gatherers Fresco), lends yet more support for the argument that women as mortal women and as representatives of the Goddess were preeminent in Minoan Crete.

I have concentrated on frescoes in my discussion of the iconography because they provide the largest canvas by which to view the role of women in Minoan society. However, seals, sealings, the impressions made on clay by seals, and signet rings also provide a picture of women in Bronze Age Crete, and it is to them that I now turn.

Glyptic art and what it reveals about women in Minoan society

Sealstones of various shapes are known in Crete from EM II, c. 2600-2300 BC, onwards. Early sealstones are made of soft materials such as ivory, stone, and bone, and although they contain various designs, spirals seem to predominate. The traditional view has been that 'originally the lumps of clay sealed jars, boxes or doors in the homes of individuals.'[158] In other words, seals were probably used to mark ownership. However, current research is questioning whether that is so, or if the seals, as well as the gold rings of the Neopalatial period, might rather signify some sort of group affiliation.[159] They may also have been religious amulets.

By the end of MM IA, c. 1950 BC, seals began to assume a larger role. 'Goods in palace store-rooms could be controlled by seals on the doors or on containers, and there is evidence that broken sealings were kept and counted to keep basic records.'[160] At the temple-palace of Phaistos, over six thousand sealings from more than 300 seals were found in Protopalatial strata c. 2100-1700 BC.

---

[156] Gimbutas 1989: xxii-xxiii.
[157] Marinatos 2018: 77.
[158] Fitton 2002: 66.
[159] Jusseret, Driessen, and Letesson, 'Minoan Lands?' sec. 2. Previous research and aspects of Minoan societal make-up, para. 4.
[160] Fitton 2002: 88.

During the Protopalatial period, sealstones started to be made from hard stones, including red and green jasper, rock-crystal, amethyst, agate, and carnelian; and new techniques of engraving were adopted, using drills and cutting wheels. Seal surfaces began to be convex to allow a cleaner impression to be made on the clay sealing.

> Pictorial motifs, which had been rare in the Early Bronze Age, became common on protopalatial seals. Human figures appear, as do a wide range of animals, insects and birds. Sphinxes and griffins enter the repertoire.[161]

By this time, in addition to being used to indicate ownership and seal items, seals were also worn. Attached to the neck or wrist, they functioned as adornment or jewelry, and perhaps also as good-luck charms.[162]

The use of hard semi-precious stones for seals that had begun in the Protopalatial period continued in Neopalatial Crete, c. 1700-1450 BC, as did the designs which showed humans engaged in activities such as hunting or ritual action, and animal figures: bulls, lions, goats, and deer, individually or in group compositions. This period also saw the introduction of gold signet rings which often bear elaborate ritual scenes. Archaeologists hypothesize that these rings were symbols of office or authority. The standard of workmanship on all forms of seals and rings was extremely high, and seal use was widespread during the Neopalatial period.

In the Postpalatial period, c. 1400-1070 BC, the use of hard stones for seals declines and the iconographic repertoire of seals contracts; cult scenes especially seem to be absent. Fitton remarks that this phenomenon may be attributed to the collapse of Neopalatial society.[163] Seal ownership and use seem to have declined in this period. It is at this point that seal use is re-introduced into mainland Greece from Crete. Seals had not been used on the mainland since the Early Bronze Age and they first make their reappearance in the Mycenaean Shaft Graves, c. 1500 BC. It is seals of Cretan origin that are found in the Mycenaean Shaft Graves of the Late Bronze Age. Fitton notes that some of the seals found in Mycenae come from Crete, and some were locally made, probably by Cretan craftspersons or by locals trained by Cretan artisans. 'Distinguishing Minoan and mainland fine seals is often impossible.'[164]

The above quote from Fitton brings up an extremely important point: the dating of the seals and rings. Unless they are found in well-stratified contexts, which often they are not, it is only possible to date them on stylistic grounds. This is why one often finds a wide date range given for a particular seal, sealing, or ring, and why one finds differences of opinion on the dates of a particular seal or ring. For example, the Pylos Ring, discussed below, is given a possible date range of 1450-1200 BC by C. D. Cain,[165] and one of 1600-1450 BC by Marinatos.[166] Moreover, because specific dates cannot be known, scholars lump together and discuss seals that may vary in date by as much as one to three hundred years. Thus, Marinatos in her book *Minoan Religion*, discusses seals and rings and makes interpretations about priests, priestesses, male gods, the Goddess, and religious scenes, from the period 1600-1450, without more explicit

---

[161] Fitton 2002: 93.
[162] Fitton 2002: 93.
[163] Fitton 2002: 188.
[164] Fitton 2002: 188.
[165] Cain 2001: 34.
[166] Marinatos 1993: 173.

reference to the date of each seal under consideration, if such a date is even known. Although this is common practice, it can lead to a great deal of uncertainty. Most importantly, it can make a huge difference in how the ring is interpreted, and in the conclusions that are drawn about Minoan society from those interpretations. This will become especially apparent in the discussion in the following chapter on the images of a male ruler in Crete and the seal known as the Master Impression. Suffice to say here that one would expect to find more examples of male gods or a male ruler in the iconography of seals and rings once the Mycenaeans make their presence felt in Crete, which is usually dated to *c.* 1450 BC.[167]

Another problem in working with Aegean Bronze Age iconography on seals must be pointed out here as well: 'there are often only a few examples of very important iconographical detail and sometimes [there is] only one [example of an important iconographical detail].'[168] Thus, I as well as other Aegeanists must draw conclusions from a very limited pool of evidence.

On the issue of imagery, one scholar of Minoan glyptic imagery has pointed out that the current methodology, such as it is, 'consists largely of a body of unformulated rules to be distilled from the writings of the masters, a process bound to create clones, not independent scholars.'[169] In the debate regarding how the scenes on seals and rings are to be interpreted, there is no agreement on methodology.

Sealstones are the most plentiful works of representational art that come to us from the Bronze Age Aegean, especially from the period 2000-1100 BC.

> Over 4,500 seals, clay seal impressions (sealings), and signet rings bearing imagery of some sort are known from the Bronze Age Aegean. It has been calculated that only 15% of this corpus (ca. 675 pieces) depicts the human figure.[170]

About one-third of these representations of the human figure, 225 pieces, are engraved on metal rings, most of them gold, which were produced during the period 1600-1400 BC.[171] Author Marianna Vardinoyannis estimates that 44 percent of the seals represent women, and 48 percent men.[172] All the seals, sealings, and rings under consideration here date from the period 1600-1200 BC, with the exception of one.[173]

In all the glyptic art of Minoan Crete, when women are portrayed they are portrayed almost exclusively in what have been interpreted by archaeologists as cult or religious scenes. Women appear as priestesses, votaries, adorants, or attendants of the Goddess, or as the divinity herself.

---

[167] However, this picture is further confused by the fact that scholars are not agreed about the date of the Mycenaean presence in Crete, with some even arguing that it should be assigned to the proposed new date for the Thera eruption *c.* 1628 (Moss 2005: 3).

[168] Crowley 1995: 2:488.

[169] Wedde 1995: 273. Wedde proposes the cluster approach, grouping related pictorial data together for consideration. Within such clusters there will be seals, sealings, and/or rings that match the master or the canonical copy, some that can be classified as variants of it, and others that can only be argued to be marginally related to the cluster by virtue of the fact that they invoke the essence of the master copy. Using this approach, a scholar would never make an interpretation based on only one extant seal, sealing, or ring.

[170] Cain 2001: 27.

[171] Cain 2001: 27.

[172] Vardinoyannis 2010: 238.

[173] The one exception is a seal dated to the Old Palace Period, *c.* 2100-1700 BC, portraying a male and female figure holding hands. It has been interpreted as a scene of a sacred marriage. (Marinatos 1993: 189).

Figure 16. Isopata ring: Epiphany of the Goddess witnessed by female worshippers. Dated to c. 1575-1450 BC on stylistic grounds, 2.25cm long and 1.16cm wide, gold seal ring, found in a chamber–tomb at Isopata, near Knossos, Crete. Heraklion Museum, Crete. Photograph by Dr. Mara Lynn Keller. Reprinted with permission.

While such scenes are numerous, scenes such as those depicted in the miniature frescoes, the Grandstand and the Sacred Grove and Dance Frescoes, are non-existent. One does not find scenes of female and male spectators. One does not find seals with spectators at all. This may simply be a function of the fact that the surfaces of seals or rings are too small to allow an artist to portray such a scene.

While it is not the purpose of this work to analyze all the seals, sealings, and rings which contain female figures, I propose to discuss some of the more well-known among them to detail what the seals, sealings, and rings can tell us about the role of women in Minoan society.

One of the best known of the Minoan sealings, dating to LM IIIA1, c. 1400-1370 BC,[174] the Mountain Mother, portraying a female figure on a mountaintop flanked by lions and a male adorant, was discussed in Chapter 5. There it was argued that this female figure was a representation of the Minoan Mother Goddess.

From a slightly earlier period, c. 1575-1450 BC, come other famous sealings. One is the Isopata ring, thus named because it was found in a chamber tomb at Isopata, near Knossos.

This ring has been interpreted as an epiphany of the Goddess, who is shown twice, once descending from the sky and a second time on the ground, witnessed by several female worshippers who acknowledge her presence through various gestures of adoration.[175] Yet another famous sealing of this period is the Lost Ring of Mochlos, dated to c. 1500 BC ('lost'

---

[174] The strata in which the Mountain Mother sealings were found were dated to LM IIIA1, however, the seal may well have been in use before that time. See Krattenmaker 1995: 49-50n2.

[175] It must be pointed out that the diminutive deity descending from the sky in this ring, the Isopata ring, is identified as a female because of her skirts. From a later time period, 1450-1200, at least seven other rings also show a diminutive deity descending from the sky toward worshippers of either the male and female sex. In two of these seven rings, the deities descending are considered to be female: the Zakros ring and the Kandia ring; while the other five rings portray deities considered to be male: Knossos, Pylos, Elateia, unknown provenance, and Mycenae Ramp House ring. These descending males are identified as males because of their cod pieces, or because they are naked. It is important to note, however, that the authenticity of one of the rings, the one of unknown provenance, depicting a male deity is not absolutely certain. Moreover, at least two of the rings, the Pylos and Elateia rings, are dated to a time when a Mycenaean presence in Crete is certain. Finally it must also be noted that Paul Rehak has questioned whether these diminutive figures are indeed gods appearing to their adorants or merely figures far in the background (Rehak 2000: 269-276). If Rehak is correct, all small descending divinities would have to be reconsidered. The five representations of gods and two of a Goddess might have to be re-interpreted.

because the actual ring, which was placed in the Heraklion Museum early in the twentieth century, had been lost) which portrays a Goddess arriving to her shrine by boat, which is shaped like a dragon, with a sacred tree on board. Above her float several items which have been identified as a chrysalis, an eye, and a sheaf or constellation. In another seal from Makrygialos, dated to the LM IB period, c. 1480-1425 BC, a woman standing in a boat with her fist to her chest before an altar and a tree, has been interpreted as a priestess or worshiper. From a shrine in the settlement of Kommos comes a sealing of a Bird Goddess, an image that is frequently depicted on Minoan seals, that dates from LM IA-LM IIIA1, c. 1580-1370 BC. From MM III to LM I, c. 1700-1450 BC, comes a seal made of rock crystal from the Idaean Cave. Pictured in the seal is a female blowing into a conch shell, 'with a schematized tree behind her, and an incurved altar decorated with foliage and a pair of horns of consecration.[176] She is usually identified as a priestess. However, Kate McK. Elderkin identifies the female figure holding the conch shell as the Goddess Aphrodite.[177]

Marinatos in *Minoan Religion* gives numerous examples of seals, sealings, and rings dating from between 1650-1450 BC which portray the Goddess in a great variety of ways: interacting with nature (smelling a lily, in a field surrounded by flowers); commanding authority; feeding and interacting with animals: riding a griffin or a lion; flanked by griffins or lions; in the person of the Bird Goddess; holding a dolphin; receiving offerings from female adorants; wearing the horned crown; descending from the sky (Isopata); arriving in a boat (Mochlos); seated on tripartite platforms and being brought offerings; and seated under a palm tree, being worshipped by both humans and animals.

Marinatos has also identified priestesses in the seals, sealings, and rings from the period 1650-1450 BC: women in flounced skirts, sometimes characterized by a slightly larger size than the other women in the seal; or with their hands at their waist; women who appear carrying the double axe, or a piece of ritual clothing, perhaps to adorn another priestess who will be representing the Goddess. Priestesses also appear to wear distinctive dress and sometimes the sacral knot. Marinatos has remarked that the priestesses' most important function was to portray the Goddess; therefore it is often difficult to separate a priestess from the Goddess in the iconography.[178]

Sometimes priestesses appear with figures who are dressed in hide skirts of the type worn on the Ayia Triadha sarcophagus. Marinatos has suggested that the figures in hide skirts are probably male priests. There does not appear to be consensus on this identification among Aegean archaeologists. The seals in which the two sexes appear together as priestesses and priests give no indication of which, if any, of the figures is more important than another. Marinatos suggests through her tone and language that the priests are more important. But as Hawkes writes:

> As for the part played by women in religious offices, the testimony of the Hagia Triada sarcophagus is plain enough; at least in some ceremonies, the priestesses were set above the priests. If this was still true in the fourteenth century its prevalence in earlier days must be as nearly as possible certain. It is supported by one section of the figures in the

---

[176] Moss 2005: 124.
[177] Elderkin 1925: 54.
[178] Marinatos 1993: 184.

great Corridor at Knossos where a woman, more likely to be a priestess or queen than a goddess, stands at the centre between two approaching lines of men—presumably bearing tribute.[179]

In addition to priests and priestesses appearing together on seals, Marinatos has identified seals in which male priests alone are portrayed. When priests do appear alone, they do not appear to be engaged in any kind of ritual activity. At most they are shown with their insignia of office, an axe (not the double axe, however, which is only associated with females in the iconography), or mallet, signifying perhaps their role in sacrifice. This is in stark contrast to the activity that takes place in seals which center on a priestess. Thus, for example, in the Archanes ring (from Central Crete), the female figure in the center, usually identified as a priestess or high priestess, is larger than any other figure in the scene and dressed in a flounced skirt. To her left is a male hugging a baetyl, and to her right is a male pulling at a tree shrine. These themes are echoed in Minoan-like scenes from the Greek mainland. In the gold ring from Vapheio, Laconia (the southern Greek mainland), again a high priestess is in the center of the composition (and dressed in a flounced skirt) while a male to her left pulls at a tree in a tree shrine; to her right is a shield with a garment draped over it, and above hovers a double axe. In a gold ring from Mycenae a high priestess in a flounced dress stands in the middle while to her left a male figure engages in a 'tree shaking ritual;'[180] to the right a woman bends over a table.

In the Archanes, Vapheio, and Mycenae rings, an epiphany of the Goddess seems to be taking place. The 'high priestess' is a very important part of the action. She is leading the ritual, perhaps representing the Goddess, in an action that will lead to an ecstatic vision of the Goddess. Marinatos has hypothesized that the high priestess controlled and directed ritual. She has further hypothesized that those rituals that involved the shaking of trees, and the bending over baetyls or stones or pithoi, and the witnessing of the epiphany of the Goddess, 'were of a most important and perhaps even mystical character.'[181] Male priests are not shown directing any such rituals. The seals, in my opinion, portray a role for priestesses that is far more important than that of priests. And if Marinatos is correct in her assumption that the priesthood (including both priestesses and priests) was 'in charge of organizing festivals,' and 'took care of the administration and economy of the district they were allotted,'[182] then women in their role as priestesses played a major role in organizing the social, economic and religious life of the country. From this evidence, Hawkes proposed that, 'the pre-eminence of the priestesses may be of more significance than the dominion of the Goddess herself.'[183]

In my discussion above I have already briefly touched upon male figures on seals. I return to them now. In addition to those seals that portray what have been identified by some as priests, there are seals which have been interpreted as portraying a male god. The most famous of those seals is the so-called Master Impression from Chania, LM IB/LM II, c. 1480/1425-1425/1380 BC, which shows a male figure standing on the central tower of a city, one arm outstretched with a staff or spear in his hand.

---

[179] Hawkes 1968: 153.
[180] Marinatos 1993: 185.
[181] Marinatos 1993: 188.
[182] Marinatos 1993: 146.
[183] Hawkes 1968: 153.

There is great controversy over whether this figure is a god or a king. In arguing for the interpretation of him as a god, Marinatos writes that the god here is the protector of the town.[184] She believes the ring portrays an epiphany of the god above his shrine. The Master-Impression will be fully discussed in the next chapter where I take up the question of images of a possible male ruler in Minoan Crete.

In a note above I mentioned five rings in which a male figure, identified as a god, descends from the sky to a sacred/ritual area where worshippers await. In at least one of those scenes, a ring from Knossos, now at Oxford, England, the male figure's position, one arm outstretched with a spear or staff, is similar to that of the 'god' in the Master Impression. He descends in the presence of a female votary or priestess in a flounced skirt and a shrine. In another ring of unknown provenance and uncertain authenticity, a male figure holding a bow in his outstretched arm, descends between a large female figure in a flounced skirt (a high priestess?) and a female figure (wearing what appears to be a sacral knot) bending over a pithos. Two of the rings with similar iconography come from the south of Greece. In the Ramp House ring from Mycenae, a descending male with a figure-eight shield, appears as three women present flowers to a Goddess seated under a tree. In a ring from Pylos, and dated relatively late, 1450-1200 BC,[185] a male votary 'salutes' a male god as he makes his appearance on a mountain top. In another ring, contemporary with the Pylos ring but from Elateia (central Greece), a floating male appears to have both arms raised to his chest. He makes his appearance to three figures, two men and a woman. I noted above that Rehak has argued that the small, descending figures in Minoan glyptic art, rather than representing gods, may perhaps merely represent 'figures in the far background.'[186] It has mainly been Marinatos and W. D. Niemeier who have argued that the tiny, descending figures should be considered divinities.[187] If one adopts Rehak's stance, at least five examples of 'Minoan gods' (and two Goddesses), can be eliminated from the repertoire. Moreover, the very late date of the Pylos ring and its contemporary, from the period of Mycenaean take-over of Crete, and the dubious authenticity of the ring of unknown provenance, in my opinion, do not make them strong candidates for representatives of the Minoan god.

In addition to the descending male figures, Marinatos identifies as gods, those male figures on seals, sealings, or rings, that hold or are flanked by two lions, two bulls, two mastiffs, a winged goat and a demon; or are simply accompanied by one animal, usually a lion. Rehak and Younger, however, declare that only those seals that depict 'men who stand between two rampant lions or who hold griffins on a leash' can be considered to be representations that 'depict what could be male divinities.'[188] Moreover, they emphasize that there are far fewer representations of male divinities than there are of female divinities.[189]

Some seals that show a male figure with a usually larger, more prominent female, have been interpreted as scenes of sacred marriage, and thus both the female and male figures in the seal have been interpreted as divinities. How is this interpretation arrived at? Marinatos points out that it is only natural to project human sexuality onto the gods and that such

[184] Marinatos 1993: 172.
[185] Cain 2001: 34.
[186] Rehak 2000: 274.
[187] Rehak 2000: 274.
[188] Younger and Rehak 2008: 179.
[189] Younger and Rehak 2008: 179.

beliefs, projecting what is called a sacred marriage or *hieros gamos*, were widespread among the Minoans' neighboring civilizations.[190] So, too, the Minoans also must have envisioned a marriage between the Goddess and the god.

Because the Goddess is usually portrayed in Minoan iconography as receiving gifts from female worshippers, when a male is portrayed with a female, Marinatos thinks the scholar might rightly ask 'whether some sexual intimation is hinted at.'[191] This is perhaps a clue that a *hieros gamos* might be portrayed. The second clue is body language—the male moving toward the female.[192] Marinatos identifies a seal from the Old Palace period and four from the New Palace Period as scenes of sacred marriage. She argues that the female figure, the Goddess, is larger in each of these scenes because her role in reproduction is emphasized.[193] I posit she is larger because she is the most important figure, and not only because she symbolizes reproduction, but more importantly because she is the mediator between this world and the next, and it is she who has power within all nature. It must also be remembered that in the interpretation of Aegean iconography, a larger size is generally agreed to mean more importance.

Taken all together, what can the seals tell us about the role of women in Minoan society? On the whole there are far more seals depicting the Goddess than there are seals depicting a male god. Nilsson, writing in 1949 about seals said,

> A male god appears surprisingly seldom,—the goddesses are dominant, and there is only one certain instance in which he is represented full size, the nude figure standing between the horns of consecration on a gem from the neighourhood of Kydonia.[194]

Marinatos argues that Nilsson is wrong in his assessment about the appearance of gods in Minoan iconography, however, she does note that the predominance of Goddesses is 'indisputable,'[195] and that there are fewer representations of gods in Minoan iconography than of the Goddess.[196] In arguing nevertheless for a greater importance for the Minoan gods than the Minoan Goddess, Marinatos posits that the Goddess merely feeds or tends animals, while the god controls them.[197] I would argue that the seals depict the Goddess not only nurturing nature, but controlling nature as well. If she did not control nature as well as nurture it, we would not find the Minoan Goddess flanked by lions, holding birds by their necks, carrying a dolphin, flying with a griffin, or flanked by griffins.

Younger and Rehak referring to Minoan iconography, seals as well as frescoes, have argued that:

> More women than men . . . appear in powerful roles, at a larger relative scale, and their importance seems assured by the number of them who sit on camp stools, stools like hassocks, and thrones. . . . Besides the throne at Knossos, several other stone seats have

---

[190] Marinatos 1993: 189.
[191] Marinatos 1993: 189.
[192] Marinatos 1993: 189.
[193] Marinatos 1993: 192.
[194] Nilsson 1949: 354.
[195] Marinatos 1993: 167.
[196] Marinatos 1993: 174.
[197] Marinatos 1993: 174.

also survived; Evans made the interesting comment that the tops of these seats have been hollowed to suit a woman comfortably.[198]

Younger and Rehak go on to say that the throne room at Knossos faced a lustral basin and was flanked by benches. 'Perhaps we can imagine a powerful woman on the throne at Knossos flanked by male counselors, and similar arrangements at the secondary centers.'[199] They wonder if the benches in Room 4 of Ayia Triadha, which can seat more than twenty-five people, might also be the meeting place of the Queen's council. The authors point out that next to the room with the benches at Ayia Triadha is a shrine, discussed above in Chapter 5, which features two female figures in a luxuriant landscape. One of the figures, standing in front of a platform, is generally understood to be a Goddess, the other a votary.

Helen Waterhouse, whose work was cited above, has argued that if women enacted the epiphany of the Goddess and sat on the throne as representative of the Goddess, it follows that they led civil government as well.

I believe the seals portray priestesses to be far more important than priests. If the priesthood was 'in charge of organizing festivals,' and 'took care of the administration and economy of the district they were allotted,'[200] it follows that the priestesses who enacted the epiphany of the Goddess, and who directed ritual of the most important and mystical character would have the major role in such organization and administration.

Marinatos has written that it is difficult to tell the difference between a god and a king in the iconography of Minoan Crete, and that the two are probably interchangeable.[201] If that is true, if it is difficult to determine, for example, whether the Master Impression portrays a king or a god, why cannot the same be said of the Mountain Mother seal? Is she a Goddess or a 'Queen'? I agree with Hawkes when she writes:

> If it were not for the tradition of King Minos, and the corresponding absence of any recorded memories of Cretan queens, and perhaps also certain strong if unconscious assumptions among Classical scholars, it seems that the archaeological evidence would have been read as favouring a woman on the ritual throne at Knossos.[202]

Indeed, there are no enthroned males on the seals. As Hawkes says, 'In the scenes from the seal-stones, not only is the Goddess always the central figure being served and honoured in a variety of ways; she is sometimes shown seated on a throne.'[203] Perhaps this is key: we do not see an enthroned male being served and honored in Minoan iconography. Rehak has remarked that seated males are only found in frescoes at Knossos and Pylos (on the Greek mainland) in the role of banqueters, and in clay models from peak sanctuaries and funerary contexts;

---

[198] Younger and Rehak 2008: 182.
[199] Younger and Rehak 2008: 182.
[200] Marinatos 1993: 146.
[201] Marinatos 2010: 30.
[202] Hawkes 1968: 154-155.
[203] Hawkes 1968: 154-155.

'otherwise the evidence for seated male figures is virtually nonexistent.'[204] On the other hand, 'nearly all the seated figures of identifiable sex in Aegean art are women.'[205]

Seated or enthroned women are found in Neopalatial frescoes: the Grandstand Fresco, the Sacred Grove and Dance Fresco, the Ladies in Blue and the Lady in Red Frescoes; and fragments from other frescoes may indicate seated women as well. Rehak points out that 'only four Aegean figures are represented using footstools, and all these are women.'[206] One ring which was referred to above which features a 'sacred conversation' between a large seated woman and a smaller man standing before her, shows the woman seated on what Rehak calls a throne: 'the curved supports of her seat recall the carving of the Knossos throne'[207] Architectural platforms are another form of seating or enthronement, and the most famous example of a woman seated on such a platform is the Goddess in the Xeste 3 Fresco, the Crocus Gatherers, which was discussed above. Finally women in Minoan art are depicted seated on rocky outcrops, another form of seat or enthronement.

Younger and Rehak have concluded, 'The prominence of females in Neopalatial art, important mortal women and goddesses . . . , makes it possible to imagine that women dominated Neopalatial society, perhaps even politics.'[208] In a matriarchal society as defined by Goettner-Abendroth, women would not 'dominate politics' in Minoan Crete, but rather they would be the leaders in consensus building for their regional, clan, village, and tribal councils. Perhaps it was for such councils of consensus that the benches at Knossos and Ayia Triadha were built. However, before coming to a final conclusion, I turn in the next chapter to those pieces of evidence in the iconography that have been used to argue that Minoan Crete was ruled by a priest-king.

---

[204] Rehak 1995: 97.
[205] Rehak 1995: 97.
[206] Rehak 1995: 103.
[207] Rehak 1995: 104.
[208] Younger and Rehak 2008: 180.

Chapter 7

Models of Rulership: The Paucity of Images of Male Rulers; the Images of Female Rulers

Despite the fact that '*not a single* Minoan object shows males clearly outranking females,'[1] ever since the days of Sir Arthur Evans it has been assumed by most scholars that a king or priest-king ruled Crete. How can it be that this interpretation, that Crete must have had a priest-king, continues to dominate scholarly and popular thinking? Marymay Downing, in her 1985 article, 'Prehistoric Goddesses: The Cretan Challenge' provides a clear answer: there prevails 'the tendency in mainstream scholarship to make androcentric assumptions about political and cultural structures regardless of gynocentric religious symbolism.'[2] However, as I will discuss below, I share the view that 'Though scenes of ceremony are common in Minoan art, no kingly figure takes part in or presides over any of them.'[3]

Possible candidates for the title of Priest-King

In 1995 Ellen N. Davis addressed the lack of a priest-king figure in Minoan iconography in 'Art and Politics in the Aegean: The Missing Ruler' at a panel discussion addressing the 'Role of the Ruler' in the Aegean Bronze Age. Though 'the idea of kingship is inherent in the very name [Minoan] we use for the civilization of Crete in the Bronze Age,'[4] Davis, like Waterhouse and other scholars, finds no images to which to attach the title of king. Like Waterhouse, she accuses Evans of beginning his excavations with preconceived notions of a priest-king 'derived not from Greek tradition but from his prior studies of Egypt.'[5]

Davis discusses each of the images in Minoan iconography that have been considered by scholars to be possible candidates for the priest-king title. The first is the fragmentary fresco variously called the 'Priest-King,' 'Lily Prince,' or 'Prince with the Feather.' Davis notes that current reconsiderations, in 1979 and 1990, by French physician Jean Coulomb, and in 1987 and 1988 by archaeologist W. D. Niemeier, of the fragments originally reconstructed by Evans in the early twentieth century, have shown that the torso part of the 'prince' does not belong with the rest of the fragments. Moreover, it is now understood that the torso is white, not red as Evans thought. As I established earlier, it is agreed among Aegean archaeologists that sex identification in Minoan art depends upon skin color: white indicates a female, red a male.[6] How is it possible that Evans believed the fragments of the prince's torso were red and thus the figure was a prince and not a princess or queen? Davis notes that 'fresco fragments are frequently found with red stains on the surface, either from ochre in the soil or from the red pigment of fragments buried next to them.'[7] Evans might also have mistaken the torso

---

[1] Letesson and Driessen 2020: 11.
[2] Downing 1985: 9.
[3] Waterhouse 1974: 153.
[4] Davis 1995: 11.
[5] Davis 1995: 11.
[6] Davis 1995: 12.
[7] Davis 1995: 13.

for that of a prince because of the muscular nature of the torso. Davis points out that 'such a physiognomy, however, is closely matched by one of the white, and therefore female, bull-leapers from the Knossos Toreador Frescoes.'[8] Finally there is the matter of the headdress the prince is wearing. 'There is no evidence in Aegean art for a male wearing the headdress. Sphinxes, who in the Aegean are female, wear them, and so do priestesses.'[9] Davis notes that this analysis seems to have settled the question. However, as I shall discuss below, the matter of the Priest-King fresco has been re-opened by archaeologist Maria Shaw.

As for the second candidate for a possible male ruler in the iconography, the major figure on the Chieftain Cup from Ayia Triadha, current scholarship has reinterpreted this one as well. Again according to Davis, 'The slender youthful figures have always seemed unsatisfactory as images of Minoan royal and military power as Evans saw them.'[10] Davis favors the interpretation of archaeologist Robert Koehl who views the figures on the cup as youths conducting a rite of passage.[11] Koehl came to this conclusion based on the work of the ancient author Strabo, who, quoting the Cretan author Philochorus (fourth century BC), spoke of a Cretan practice in which a noble youth (designated as the lover) selected a younger youth whom he abducted and took to the country for a two month period of hunting and feasting. At the end of the period 'the younger youth was given three gifts: military garb, an ox and a drinking cup.'[12] Excavations at Kato Syme in southern Crete have uncovered large numbers of cups in the shape of the Chieftain Cup—which is a rare cup form. The context in which they were found—the site was a special cult place—gives support to Koehl's theory. So does the fact that a bronze statuette of a youth holding out a cup of the Chieftain Cup type and a double statuette of two youths with arms linked were also found at Kato Syme.[13]

Of the third candidate for the image of a prince or king—the males on the Ayia Triadha Sarcophagus—Davis says:

> Minoan architectural decorations appear to be confined to scenes of nature that exhibit the life of the goddess or scenes of more general ritual such as bull-leaping or procession. Whenever there is any indication of dominance, it is women who appear to be the main figures. The Ayia Triadha Sarcophagus has been cited as an exception. Yet the dominance of women can be observed here as well.[14]

The dominance of women on this sarcophagus is also the interpretation of archaeologist Jacquetta Hawkes in her description of the sarcophagus:

> The scenes are also of particular significance here because they prove quite conclusively the dominant role played by the women celebrants—even in the burial of a man.

---

[8] Davis 1995: 13.
[9] Davis 1995: 13.
[10] Davis 1995: 13.
[11] Koehl 1986: 99-110.
[12] Davis 1995: 14.
[13] Rehak has written:

> The fact that women and monkeys handle swords and sheaths [a monkey in the Xeste 3 Monkey frieze from Thera, and a woman on a sealstone from Knossos] as well as men suggests that the identification of these implements on the Chieftain Cup as elements of gift exchange specific to a male homosexual courting ritual is too restrictive (Rehak 1999: 3:708).

[14] Davis 1995:14.

Whether they be priestesses or court ladies or princesses, it is they who carry out the sacred acts of the libation, the sacrifice, the offerings at the altar. The men (wearing skirts) merely carry the heavier offerings and provide the musical accompaniment.[15]

Rehak, agreeing with both Davis and Hawkes, has written of the Sarcophagus that women seem to be 'the main protagonists' in the scenes on both of the long sides.[16] He also makes the interesting observation that in the libation and the sacrifice scenes on the Sarcophagus there is only one man in each, a musician with a harp or flute respectively. Rehak goes on to say,

I do not believe it has been noted that only men are musicians in Aegean art. In Egypt and Mesopotamia, by contrast, musicians are often women portrayed as erotic subjects. We regard the civilizations of the ancient Near East as patriarchal, and female musicians as marginal. Could the reverse be true in the Aegean, with men making music for empowered women?[17]

It is important to point out that the Ayia Triadha Sarcophagus, like the 'Master Impression,' discussed below, is dated to the mid-fifteenth century BC, and may reflect the influence of the Mycenaean interlopers who brought with them patriarchal customs. It may be one of their warlord-kings who is buried in the sarcophagus.

Other candidates for images of a priest-king are 'priest' figures wearing 'spirally-wound garments.'[18] They are found primarily on seals. According to Davis, Evans considered them the prime candidates for ruler images. While Davis agrees with Evans that they are priests, she has found the unusual garment worn by a number of males, not just one king. 'It was therefore not exclusive to a king and not enough to designate a king.'[19] Moreover, since these figures are not found on iconography from the mainland, we can assume that the Mycenaeans did not regard them as royal images, or they would have used them for their own representations.[20] Nevertheless, Davis leaves the door open:

I conclude that if these, the most prominent male figures in Minoan art, were the kings of Crete, they were not represented as figures of secular power, but rather as functionaries in the religious sphere.[21]

Of the fifth and final candidate for the image of a Minoan king, the so-called Khania 'Master Impression,' a sealing dated to LM IB, *c.* 1480-1425 BC, Davis determines that the figure on the 'Master Impression' is a young god, not a king. Davis bases that conclusion on the large size of the male figure compared with the architecture, and her interpretation of the architecture on the seal not as a single complex, but as a town with a shrine in front of it. Interpreted in this way, Davis believes it follows that the 'master' holds a staff rather than a spear. She sees the point of the so-called spear as part of the artist's attempt 'to undercut the relief level

[15] Hawkes 1968: 146.
[16] Rehak 1998: 196.
[17] Rehak 1998: 196.
[18] Davis 1995: 15.
[19] Davis 1995: 15.
[20] Davis 1995: 17.
[21] Davis 1995: 17

beneath.'[22] An even more recent study by archaeologists Gunter Kopcke and Eleni Drakaki argues that the god/king on the 'Master Impression' is 'unMinoan' and that it is the work of the Mycenaeans who overthrew Crete's traditional government.[23] The debate over the Master Impression has continued since Davis wrote and is discussed at length below.

Having effectively argued that none of the iconography that has yet been discovered in Crete could represent a priest-king, Davis, to this reader's utter amazement, concludes:

> Minoan art appears to be lacking in ruler iconography. 'Minos' whether king or Priest-King is missing from the picture. Does this mean that there was no king of Crete? . . . I find it difficult to conceive a major civilization in the Mediterranean Bronze Age without a male ruler or rulers.[24]

Perhaps if Davis and other archaeologists could view Bronze Age Crete through the more multidisciplinary lens of archaeomythology and consider the possibility that Crete was matristic, matrilineal, and/or matriarchal, relatively egalitarian, and peaceful, the lack of male ruler iconography would not be so difficult to comprehend. There may be hope, for at the end of her article Davis says:

> If one views ancient art as propaganda, . . . then it is difficult to conceive how Minoan art served a king. . . . In this respect, Minoan art appears to be unique in the Eastern Mediterranean of the Bronze Age. Its unique character must reflect a unique society. It seems to me it is one that we have yet to understand.[25]

Although Davis has dismissed these five candidates for the role of priest-king, not all archaeologists would agree with her conclusions. Koehl's arguments seem to have silenced those who would call the youth on the Chieftain Cup a symbol of a king or of a deity.[26] And few scholars any longer point to the armless male on the Ayia Triadha Sarcophagus as a king, he is generally thought of as the deceased.[27] The figures of the Lily Prince, Master Impression, and the males with the spirally wound garments are still hotly contested, however, and the arguments rage on. I will now summarize the most important of those below, as well as other arguments in favor of Evans's interpretation of the fresco fragments from Knossos as the priest-king.

---

[22] Davis 1995: 18.

[23] Kopcke and Drakaki 1999: 2:341-342.

[24] Davis 1995: 18.

[25] Davis 1995: 19.

[26] Marinatos has interpreted the more richly dressed youth holding out the staff as a young god or 'man in the guise of the god.' Since she argues that divinities and rulers in Crete are interchangeable, she would see him as a ruler as well (Marinatos 1993: 134). Niemeier also argues he is a god (Niemeier 1988: 242).

[27] Marinatos's more recent book, published in 2010, is an exception. She believes that portrayed on the sarcophagus is the narrative of a festival, similar to a festival of the storm god performed by the Hittites, with the royal couple, the king and queen, acting in their roles as high priestess and high priest. She also argues, again based on Hittite texts describing worship of the storm god, that the armless figure on the sarcophagus, usually identified as the deceased, is actually a divinized king (Marinatos 2010: 40-46).

The Lily Prince

Evans's reconstruction of the Lily Prince had long been subject to debate, authorities arguing, as did Davis above, that the limbs and torso belong to separate figures, that the figure is white not red and therefore female, and that plumed headdresses are only associated with females: sphinxes or priestesses in Minoan art. In the 1970s Coulomb argued that the torso of the Lily Prince was actually that of a boxer. Indeed, Evans had originally believed that the fragments he had found and which he used to reconstruct his priest-king had belonged to three different figures, the torso to that of a boxer, and reconstructed it as such. In the mid-1980s, Niemeier, inspired by Coulomb's work as well as Hallager's recently discovered Master Impression, reconstructed the Lily Prince, minus the crowned head, which he attributed to a priestess or a sphinx, and with the left arm stretched out in front of him, as Coulomb had demonstrated it must be, and termed him a god. Niemeier argues that his restored figure is a god because his 'commanding stance or gesture' is like those of nine other figures in Minoan iconography, seven of which have been identified by archaeologists as deities.[28] Niemeier suggests that the two other figures in the 'commanding gesture' in the Minoan repertory, the Master Impression and the Chieftain Cup, should not be considered exceptions to the rule that the 'commanding gesture' signifies a deity.[29] They are deities, according to Niemeier. Interestingly, and not insignificantly, Niemeier does admit that 'a reconstruction of the figure to which our torso belonged as a worshipper cannot be entirely excluded.'[30]

Niemeier's arguments seemed to have been accepted for a time; however in 2004, archaeologist Maria Shaw challenged Niemeier's reconstruction, arguing that Evans's had been right all along. Declaring that Coulomb and Niemeier made a 'tactical error' because they consulted a modern replica of the Lily Prince made by Evans's restorers rather than examining the restorers' final restoration, she writes that after carefully re-examining the restored fresco in the Heraklion Museum in Crete, she found 'no sign of the black color [depicting hair] that one would expect had the head been originally facing left (viewer's right), as proposed by Coulomb and Niemeier.'[31] Shaw concludes there is no longer any 'compelling reason' to separate the torso from the crowned head.

> Indeed the fragments were found together in a small area, and because the lilies appear in both crown and necklace on the torso, there is good support for their association. . . . Overall, there are few changes I would suggest to the original restoration.[32]

Having concluded that Evans's restoration is correct, Shaw asks who this 'priest-king' is. Taking into account Mark Cameron's hypothesis that the figure is a female bull-leaper, because of the white skin, associated with females; but also the cod piece, necklace, and long hair, which

---

[28] These examples are the Mountain Mother sealing from Knossos, a gold ring from Knossos now in Oxford, the Chieftain Cup, a seal from Naxos, a gold ring in Berlin, a lentoid in the Athens Numismatic Collection and a gold ring from the Harbor Town of Knossos. Niemeier would also add to this category of gods shown in the position of a commanding gesture the Master Impression and the Chieftain Cup (Niemeier 1998: 241).

[29] Wedde has forcefully argued that scholars interpreting gestures such as the 'commanding gesture' of the master on the Master Impression are not using a sound methodological approach, but rather giving 'impressionistic readings contaminated by preconceived notions and the needs of scholarly narrative' (Wedde 1999: 3: 918, 912). Wedde is at work developing a methodology that systematizes the study of Minoan gesture.

[30] Niemeier 1998: 240.

[31] Shaw 2004: 72.

[32] Shaw 2004: 72.

were features associated with bull-leaping; Shaw posits that the figure is a young male bull-leaper, arguing that white can no longer with assurance be associated only with females in Aegean art. And what of the crown on this figure? Because recent excavations at Tell el-Dab'a in the Nile Delta exposed frescoes, rendered by presumed Minoan artists, depicting tumblers wearing simplified lily crowns, Shaw believes that the lily crown is linked to athletic activity and that this reinforces her argument that the figure is a bull-leaper.

> It does not take too great a leap of the imagination to picture our Priest-King as the top athlete, a kind of present-day 'gold medalist,' parading at the head of a procession in a place of honor in the closing ceremonies. . . . The 'athlete of the year' might have been given permanent quarters, treated like a prince, perhaps targeted as a possible future ruler. Could the Priest-King still be 'our missing Minoan ruler'?[33]

I believe one must question the assumption that just because a simplified lily crown is associated with a male acrobat in a fresco found in Tell el-Dab'a, Egypt, that it must mean lily crowns are to be associated with male bull-leapers in Minoan Crete. Indeed, in her critique of Shaw's thesis, archaeologist Judith Weingarten calls the lily crown worn by the male acrobat at Tell el-Dab'a a 'lily cap.'[34] Moreover, in using the Egyptian fresco to make her case, Shaw glosses over the controversy among Aegeanists regarding the creators of and meaning of the Minoan-style frescoes at Tell el-Da'ba.[35] I would also question Shaw's statement that white no longer signifies a female in Aegean art. Aegeanists are divided over this issue. Shaw's view is not the majority view. The question of the Lily Prince, or Priest-King as he is often called, is returned to below.

Shared rulership

Nanno Marinatos deals with the candidates for the title of priest-king not only in her work *Minoan Religion*, where she agrees with Niemeier who reconstructed the 'Lily Prince' as a god, his arm extended and holding a staff of authority, but also in a 1995 article entitled 'Divine Kingship in Minoan Crete,' and in her recent book *Minoan Kingship and the Solar Goddess* published in 2010. In the 'Divine Kingship' article her goal is not so much to prove that one or the other of Davis's five candidates is the true priest-king, as to advance an argument for shared female/male rulership, which she argues is 'manifested in a variety of iconographical sources.'[36] One of those iconographical sources is the miniature wall paintings of the West House at Akrotiri, Thera which show what Marinatos interprets as 'a ruler and his wife who have both religious and political authority.'[37] Marinatos hints at matriliny: 'There may have been a union between the Priest King and the goddess or her mortal counterpart, the Priestess Queen. Perhaps the line of descent went through the queen; she legitimized the ruler's position.'[38] Marinatos believes that one can use iconography from Thera to help one understand Cretan iconography

---

[33] Shaw 2004: 81.
[34] Weingarten 2012.
[35] The literature on this subject is large. Some important works include Bietak 2008: 110-118; Bietak, Marinatos, and Palivou 2007; Bietak 2000: 165-208; Bietak and Marinatos 2000: 40-45; Bietak and Marinatos 1995: 49-59; Cline 1998: 199-219; Marinatos 1998: 63-99; Morgan 1995: 29-52; and Shaw 1995: 91-115.
[36] Marinatos 1995: 47.
[37] Marinatos 1995: 40.
[38] Marinatos 1995: 46.

because this is the period of 'Minoan empire.' By the New Palace period, 'The Minoans had extended their cultural and economic sphere throughout the Aegean.'[39]

Regarding Crete, Marinatos argues that we lack much ruler iconography because Crete was a theocracy, and so rulers and deities were interchangeable. She goes on to state that 'the images of the deities are modeled on real performances enacted by a Priestess Queen or Priest King.'[40] She is referring to the 'performances' that are shown on seals, sealings, rings and frescoes. I argued in the previous chapter that priests are not shown directing ritual, in contrast to priestesses, who usually are.

In Marinatos's discussion of performances in this article she concentrates on the throne room at Knossos. Here, according to Niemeier, who has hypothesized and written about the process by which the 'Priestess-Queen' (Marinatos's words) became the Goddess,[41] the Queen would

> first appear in the doorway leading to the throne room from the interior of the palace. She would be seen dressed in a splendid costume and flanked by the painted griffins on the walls. Next she would seat herself on the throne where she would once more be flanked by her sacred guardian animals.[42]

Here she would also be flanked by a frieze imitating an incurved altar. Marinatos points out that an incurved seat is what the Goddess of Xeste 3 sits upon at Thera, and that actual incurved bases were found at the 'palatial building' at Archanes.[43] Marinatos believes that like her Egyptian counterpart the pharaoh, when the priestess-queen sat on the throne at Knossos, she was divinized.[44] Again, if Marinatos is correct in her thinking that the iconography reflects actual performance, and if the ritual of assuming her place on the throne transformed the priestess-queen into the Mother Goddess, we have yet another argument for a priestess-queen, not a priest-king. There are no enthroned male images in the iconography of Minoan Crete. I believe an enthroned, divinized priestess-queen could be a strong candidate for the role of the leader of Minoan Crete.

To return to Marinatos's' article, in support of her argument that Crete was a theocracy and the rulers and deities were interchangeable, Marinatos points first to the Priest-King Fresco. Whether one restores him as a mortal ruler, as Evans did, or as a god, as Niemeier did in his revised restoration, it does not matter, for both are correct in Marinatos's view.

The Chieftain Cup from Ayia Triadha is another example, Marinatos thinks, of this interchangeability of ruler and god. Evans believed a youthful priest was the chieftain on the cup. Marinatos argues that the prince or chieftain of the cup is 'amazingly similar to the young Minoan god.'[45] As we saw above, Koehl's assessment of the cup is that it portrays mortals

---

[39] Marinatos 1995: 38.
[40] Marinatos 1995: 41.
[41] Niemeier 1987: 163-168.
[42] Marinatos 1995: 43.
[43] Marinatos 1995: 43.
[44] Marinatos 1995: 43. Marinatos refers to the work of Egyptologist Lanny Bell who has proposed that in Luxor temple a ritual took place in which the pharaoh was divinized. The pharaoh entered an inner shrine, (somewhat like the throne room at Knossos?) was united with his divine *ka* and emerged transformed into a divinity (Bell 1985: 251-294).
[45] Marinatos 1995: 43.

involved in a ritual rite of passage. Marinatos believes that the 'mundane surroundings' of the chieftain on the Chieftain Cup, merely confirm her supposition that 'he is mortal but imitating the god.'[46]

Marinatos's third example of the interchangeability of ruler and god is the sealing known as the Master Impression. Like Davis, Marinatos believes the figure on the sealing is a god. The excavator, Erik Hallager argues that he could be interpreted as either god or ruler. Again Marinatos sees this as an affirmation of her hypothesis that god and king are interchangeable. Marinatos's thoughts on the Master Impression are discussed further below.

Archaeologists may forever disagree about whether it is a god or a man who is portrayed in the Lily Prince fresco, the Chieftain cup, and the Khania Master Impression, but for Marinatos there can be no disagreement for he is both. 'The distinction god or king is not possible to make, for the two are completely identical in the iconography.'[47] She writes,

> Minoan rulers claimed divine heritage and were considered the representatives of gods. Their ultimate authority depended on the special relationship they claimed to have had with the deities and . . . this authority was reinforced by their costume, appearance, and their ultimate control of rituals.[48]

Although she speaks of the 'duality' of Minoan rulership in this article, Marinatos vacillates between considering the priestess-queen an actual ruler, or just the symbol of the divinity through whom the male ruler receives his power. Nevertheless, Marinatos emphasizes the male element and entitles her article 'Divine Kingship,' thus indicating her male-oriented bias. This bias is found in other aspects of her interpretation of Cretan artifacts, for example her interpretation of the Toreador fresco. Marinatos also emphasizes that Minoan culture must be understood 'in the context of its Near Eastern neighbors.'[49] This argument she takes to an extreme in her 2010 book *Minoan Kingship and the Solar Goddess*, discussed below.

Before continuing to Marinatos's recent work, I wish to look at Robert Koehl's 1995 work 'The Nature of Minoan Kingship,' which, like Marinatos's 1992 article, appears to argue for shared rulership in Minoan Crete. However, like Marinatos's, Koehl's bias is evident right from the start. Reviewing the iconography, he will concede only that 'women were prominently involved at least in the religious life of Knossos.'[50] While he begins his article singing the praises of Helen Waterhouse, and by implication her views, Koehl soon qualifies his support with the statement that matriarchy does not take into account the 'uniqueness of Minoan society.'[51] He himself never offers any critique of matriarchy. Instead he quotes feminist classicist Sarah Pomeroy, 'who concluded that Crete was neither a matriarchy nor a patriarchy.'[52] This is Koehl's conclusion as well. He theorizes that Crete was governed through shared rulership. His notion of a system of shared power includes a royal couple who shared political and religious authority, with the male being the more important of the two.

---

[46] Marinatos 1995: 42.
[47] Marinatos 1995: 42.
[48] Marinatos 1995: 47.
[49] Marinatos 1995: 37.
[50] Koehl 1995: 25.
[51] Koehl 1995: 26.
[52] Koehl 1995: 26.

Koehl begins his discussion of shared rulership by arguing, on the basis of anthropological theory and archaeological evidence, that Bronze Age Crete was 'divided into numerous autonomous political units of varying sizes, of which the major palaces were the largest.'[53] He believes each unit had its own civic, ceremonial, religious, economic, and industrial quarter, though not necessarily a palace.[54] If this is the case, then each unit might also have had 'its own internal hierarchy, dominated by a local aristocracy.'[55] Koehl believes that each of these local hierarchies was dominated by a priest-shaman-medicine man. Examining the iconography depicting these priests (and here he is looking at the same material that Ellen N. Davis examined: the men wearing spirally wound garments), he concludes that because some of these figures carry an ax, they are also 'kings or chiefs of the Minoan city-states.'[56]

Since most archaeologists, including Koehl, are agreed that the 'throne room' at Knossos belonged to a priestess or priestess-queen, Koehl cannot claim that his priest-shaman-medicine man-king ruled alone, even if he were not disposed to 'shared-rulership.' He tries to bolster his argument for shared rulership by linking his priest-king-shaman with the Throne Room at Knossos:

> It may be of significance . . . that Evans found traces of a bull's hoof painted on the left wall of the anteroom to the Throne Room, as well as a wooden throne placed against its right wall. Might not the image of the bull allude to a male figure, the consort of the Priestess Queen?[57]

In the language of the Goddess, it would allude to regeneration and rebirth. Perhaps it is symbolic of both.

Koehl acknowledges that Crete appears to be a relatively egalitarian society where, even in Late Minoan days, LM I, 1580-1450 BC, 'wealth was still widely distributed.'[58] He never tries to refute matriarchy, or the argument that the Throne Room at Knossos belonged to a queen, and he has no trouble believing that Minoan women participated in public initiation rites. However, he seems unaware of his bias in favor of a male ruler, and he continually emphasizes the male aspect of 'shared rulership,' calling his article 'The Nature of Minoan Kingship.' The tone of his work makes the queen/female aspect of the shared rulership less significant than the male. His conclusion contains no mention of shared rulership. If Koehl truly believes that shared rulership was the way Crete was governed, his viewpoint would not be so different from Marija Gimbutas's, who called Minoan Crete a *gylany*, a partnership society of women and men.

A Hittite storm god as representative of the Minoan king?

I return now to Marinatos's recent work which is highly relevant to the discussion of rulership in Minoan Crete: *Minoan Kingship and the Solar Goddess*. Here Marinatos revises some of her earlier opinions and carries arguments that she has made in earlier works to, what one may argue, are extreme conclusions. In this book, Marinatos reassesses the Lily Prince fresco and

---

[53] Koehl 1995: 27.
[54] Koehl 1995: 28.
[55] Koehl 1995: 28.
[56] Koehl 1995: 31.
[57] Koehl 1995: 32.
[58] Koehl 1995: 34.

argues that the reconstruction by Evans is correct and the Lily Prince is indeed an example of a Minoan king, in the pose of a Hittite king or prince.[59] In citing this comparison, of the pose of the Lily Prince to that of the pose of a Hittite king, I am highlighting one of the major flaws in the work, Marinatos's comparison of iconography from vastly different periods. It is Judith Weingarten who makes this important point in her review of Marinatos's book. Noting that the Lily Prince and the Hittite king differ in a number of important ways, for example, the Hittite king is heavily armed, the Lily Prince is not; she adds, 'Not least, the Hittite rock carving is dated to the imperial period, hundreds of years later than the Minoan image.'[60]

The subtitle of Marinatos's book is key to understanding her approach here: '*A Near Eastern Koine.*' In this work she draws upon iconography and written sources from the Hittites, Syria, Palestine, Mesopotamia, and Egypt to make her argument that Minoan Crete was a theocracy ruled by a king who received his power from the solar Goddess.

> My hypothesis is that Minoan society and religion may be better understood with the help of data derived from Egypt, Syria, the Levant, Anatolia and, to a lesser extent, Mesopotamia.[61]

Employing that data and ignoring evidence which does not support her thesis, Marinatos contends that a king, ruling through the benevolence of a solar Goddess, governed Crete from 1600-1390 BC.

Before continuing with a discussion of this book, I must say at the outset that I do not agree with Marinatos and that I find her arguments unconvincing. My main criticism is that while she acknowledges that there were queens and priestesses in Minoan Crete, she downplays their roles and ignores much of the female imagery, focusing instead upon male imagery, and viewing the female imagery only through her focus on a presumably shared Minoan/Near Eastern koine which places a male in the role of ruler. Marinatos expects to see the female in service to the male, and that is what she finds in the iconography. Like most of the Aegeanists, with the exception of Waterhouse, Rehak, and Younger, she seems biased by her insistence that there must be a male ruler in Minoan Crete. Indeed, like Davis, Marinatos finds it difficult to conceive of a major civilization in the Mediterranean Bronze Age without a male ruler or rulers.[62]

Beginning her work with the Lily Prince and the plumed crown associated with him, Marinatos argues that the plumed crown, such as the type attributed to the Lily Prince, is always linked with gods, sphinxes, or royalty. Here she does not follow the traditional interpretation of Aegean archaeologists, that the crown is associated only with the female sex. Instead, she also links it to male gods and kings. She posits that the woman with the plumed crown on the Ayia Triadha Sarcophagus is a high priestess and queen, because she is wearing the plumed crown, which Marinatos believes is a mark of royalty, and because high priestesses are always queens *ex officio* in Near Eastern iconography.[63] Having acknowledged that the queen-high priestess

---

[59] Marinatos 2010: 18.
[60] Weingarten 2012.
[61] Marinatos 2010: 7.
[62] Davis 1995: 18.
[63] Marinatos 2010: 16.

on the Ayia Triadha Sarcophagus wears the plumed crown, Marinatos does not discuss queens further, but instead uses the plumed crown and its link with royalty via the priestess-queen as a factor in support of the argument that the Lily Prince is a representative of the king. He is wearing a plumed crown, therefore, he must be royalty.

Judith Weingarten, in her review of Marinatos's book in the online journal *Aegeus*, has specifically addressed this issue of associating the plumed crown with male royalty in Minoan Crete. Looking at the two examples Marinatos has presented of males wearing plumed crowns: the fragment of the tumbler from Tell el-Dab'a with the waz-lily ornament on his head, the figure that Shaw has used to bolster her argument that the Lily Prince is wearing a plumed crown, as well as Marinatos's other supposed example of a male wearing a lily crown—a seal impression from Knossos (which is not well preserved at the top) showing, according to Marinatos, a 'God wearing a plumed crown and flanked by beasts,' Weingarten remarks that these figures may or may not be wearing head ornaments. Weingarten posits that at most the figures are wearing no more than 'lily caps,' and 'neither is compelling evidence for an elaborate crown.'[64] Weingarten concludes that neither example is a 'sound basis on which to postulate a crowned king.'[65]

Another piece of iconography, the sphinx, Marinatos also links with males rather than with females, as has traditionally been done in Aegean archaeology. She argues that in Egypt and Syria sphinxes are associated with a king, and that such an association can be made for Crete as well. Moreover, since sphinxes are associated with the solar Goddess in Near Eastern art, they link the king to the solar Goddess in Minoan art as well.

Turning to what Davis referred to as 'spirally wound garments' and what Marinatos calls a 'long fringed mantle with bulging seams,' Marinatos argues that the men wearing them on Minoan seals are not priests, as she had argued in *Minoan Religion*, or as Davis argues in the 'Missing Ruler,' but rather they distinguish the Minoan king from ordinary individuals. Such garments are worn by royal figures in Mesopotamian, Syrian, Anatolian, and Levantine art. 'If the fringed mantle is a sign of royalty in Mesopotamia, Syria, and Palestine, why should Crete be an exception?'[66] Marinatos reinterprets the mace carried by some of these figures not as a sign of the priesthood, but rather as a sign of temporal power. Portrait seals, which she identified in *Minoan Religion* as being portraits of priests, she reinterprets as portraits of kings because she believes they imitate the masks of the Mycenaean Shaft Graves, and because she finds it impossible to believe that priests would be portrayed in the iconography, but not the king.

As she has re-identified the plumed crown and the sphinx with males, Marinatos re-identifies other symbols as well, saying that in addition to the plumed crown and sphinxes, rosettes, earrings, and chariots also denote a king.

Marinatos reiterates a point she has made in many of her previous works, mainly that the iconography of kingship mirrors the iconography of the gods, and that this was done deliberately. According to Marinatos, it is this mirroring of the iconography that has had

---

[64] Weingarten 2012.
[65] Weingarten 2012.
[66] Marinatos 2010: 19.

authorities confused all these years. There is an iconography of kingship in Minoan Crete, it just has not been recognized.

Marinatos argues that the king and queen were the *only* legitimate intermediaries between human and divine worlds in Minoan Crete.[67] She qualifies the role of the queen, however, she is the wife of the king, and mother of the heir to the throne, not a ruler in her own right! Marinatos offers no evidence for this claim. Further on, however, she admits that the queen also wielded authority in her own right, and compares the Minoan queens to the Hittite queens who held the cult title *tawannana*. 'Having access to ritual and financial means, the *tawannana* was a force with which to be reckoned and even received her own cult after death.'[68] But Marinatos does not elaborate on what powers the Minoan queen might have wielded, other than to say that the Minoan queen was a high priestess and like the king, divinized after death. Instead she seems mainly concerned here to show that 'the queens of Egypt, Syria, and Anatolia in the second half of the second millennium were high priestesses of the sun goddess.'[69]

Agreeing with Reusch and other Aegeanists that the throne at Knossos belonged to the Goddess, Marinatos uses the similarity in the physical layout of the Palace of Mari in Mesopotamia, and a Hittite text about the festival of the storm god, to argue that the Minoan king sat on the Knossian throne of the female deity, thus confirming his relationship to her as her mythical son.[70] The Goddess to whom the throne at Knossos belonged, according to Marinatos, was the solar Goddess, for her symbols, based on Syrian glyptic, Ugaritic seals, and Levantine and Egyptian iconography are griffins and palms—exactly the symbols surrounding the throne at Knossos. 'The notion that a high priestess sat on the throne is not quite adequate as a social model,'[71] states the author. For Marinatos the queen and high priestess are interchangeable, but she does not put the queen/high priestess on the throne as ruler and representative of the Goddess. Ignoring seals, frescoes, and figurines which could be interpreted as portraying females as rulers, and basing her conclusions on Middle Eastern models of a male ruler in service to a solar Goddess, she writes 'If we include Minoan Crete within the cultural horizon of the Near East, a solar goddess who would protect the king is hardly an anomaly.'[72]

Marinatos has determined that 'the chief deity of Minoan religion is the solar goddess of kingship.' How does she arrive at a solar Goddess?[73] At first the existence and preeminence of such a Goddess is argued mainly on the basis of two pieces of iconography: palms and griffins, which adjoin the throne at Knossos, 'both of which are related to solar worship in Syria-Palestine, Egypt, and Anatolia.'[74] Later in the book Marinatos adds to the iconography of the solar Goddess the double axe, the sun disc, and the split rosette. Determining that the Mother Goddess of Minoan Crete is a solar Goddess does not totally eliminate a Minoan Goddess of

---

[67] Marinatos 2010: 32.
[68] Marinatos 2010: 47.
[69] Marinatos 2010: 47.
[70] Marinatos 2010: 54.
[71] Marinatos 2010: 65.
[72] Marinatos 2010: 65.
[73] Marinatos acknowledges that archaeologist Lucy Goodison was the first to hypothesize a solar Goddess for Minoan Crete. Goodison believes she was supplanted during the Iron Age by a solar god and unlike Marinatos, Goodison does not link a solar Goddess with the king of Crete, nor argue that he derived his power through her. Marinatos writes: 'Despite the divergence of approaches, it must be stressed that Goodison was the first to recognize the existence of a solar goddess in Minoan religion.' (Marinatos 2010: 166).
[74] Marinatos 2010: 166.

Fertility (which she postulated in her book *Minoan Religion*), in Marinatos's mind, for, she says, the sun is responsible for life, plant growth, and regeneration;[75] nor does it contradict Evans's idea of a Cretan Mother Goddess. Evans was right, Crete had a Mother Goddess, but, according to Marinatos, who bases her conclusion on the mythology of the Near East, the solar Goddess's foremost function was in the role of protector of her divine son and his human counterpart, the king.

Marinatos finds iconographical evidence of the solar Goddess protecting and advising her son, the king, in half a dozen seals and rings, most of which were discussed in my Chapter 6: the enthroned Goddess on a ring from Mycenae (Greece) holding a griffin by a leash; another ring from Mycenae (Greece) in which the Goddess, who is seated, and a god are engaged in conversation; the seal now in Geneva (Switzerland) which depicts a Goddess, god, and their (?) child; and a ring from Thebes (Greece) in which the Goddess is seated on her throne facing a younger male. In my discussion of them, those rings that depicted the Goddess and a male were interpreted as scenes related to the *hieros gamos*. The other two seals were cited as examples of the importance of the Minoan Mother Goddess.

According to Marinatos, in these rings the Goddess is shown not with her partner, in the pose of the 'sacred marriage,' as some Aegean authorities, including Marinatos herself in her 1993 work *Minoan Religion,* have interpreted them, but rather, the Goddess is interpreted as portrayed in mythic terms, with a son, a figure to whom she is giving instructions. 'In social paradigmatic terms, the seated deity is the queen mother and the standing male is the king.'[76] Marinatos comes to this conclusion based on standard interpretations of Syrian and Anatolian iconography. In such interpretations the seated deity is a major deity of the pantheon, often the sun Goddess, and the standing male she is facing is the king, as well as 'his double,' the storm god. 'If the male god mirrors the role of the king and the seated goddess that of the queen mother, this shows that queens and queen mothers had an elevated social position in Crete.'[77] What that elevated social position really meant, Marinatos does not venture to discuss, and she totally ignores the important implications of her suggestion.

Turning from the iconography to the mythology of the Near East, mainly that of Babylon and Ugarit, Marinatos argues that using a Near Eastern mythological lens the Minoan iconography of the rings cited above can further be interpreted as follows:

> The seated goddess appoint[s] her standing son in a position of authority and endors[es] his power . . . the iconographical similarities between the god and king are deliberate, resulting not in confusion but in intended ambiguity. It is from this ambiguity that the royal paradigm derives its force.[78]

Marinatos emphasizes again that a solar Goddess for Minoan Crete as being the major female deity is indicated by the palm, griffins, double axe, the sun disc, and the split rosette that appears in much of the iconography. 'The principal female deity of the Minoan pantheon is a

---

[75] Marinatos 2010: 166.
[76] Marinatos 2010: 155.
[77] Marinatos 2010: 157.
[78] Marinatos 2010: 160.

sun goddess.'[79] Marinatos suggests that her Minoan name may have been *Asasara*. She attributes to the solar Goddess the epithet of mistress and queen of heaven. 'She was also a goddess of the underworld, a dragon tamer and . . . mother of the Storm God and the king alike.'[80] But though she ascribes enormous powers to the solar Goddess, rather than hypothesize that a female represented her, sitting on her throne at Knossos, and ruling Crete as the priestess-queen through her identification with the solar Goddess, Marinatos says it was a king who sat on that throne as her son and ruler.

Concluding her book, Marinatos turns her attention to the male gods of the Minoans. She argues that Evans was wrong in labeling the major male god of the Minoans a boy-god. She states that based on the 'Master Impression,' the Palaikastro kouros, and several recently discovered rings from Poros, he must be understood rather as a 'bright star in the constellation of Minoan deities.'[81]

As she did with the Goddess, so in order to understand the god of the Minoans, Marainatos compares Minoan iconography to that of the Near East, then uses the mythology of the Near East to interpret Minoan iconography. Based on the supposed koine, Marinatos hypothesizes that several Minoan rings reflect lost Minoan myths and that 'the mythical persona of the Storm God' is 'behind many of the narratives depicted on gold rings.'[82] Analyzing a ring from Palaikastro of a hunting scene, a ring impression from Ayia Triadha which shows a male grabbing his adversary by the hair, a ring impression from Khania and one from Athens which show a male figure dragging bound prisoners behind him, a ring impression from Knossos showing a monster attacking a man in a boat, a ring from Crete (now in Berlin) which shows a male and female holding a bow, and a ring impression from Zakros in which one male prostrates himself to another male, she concludes that all these rings illustrate the mythology of the storm god, that the Minoans had a storm god at the head of their pantheon, and that the storm god also served as a representation of the Minoan king. In the final pages of the book she writes:

> I would suggest that it is unlikely that the Minoans alone did not possess a Storm God and a Solar Mother Goddess. This statement is made on grounds of *historical plausibility* rather than *iconographical analysis*. And since until now the main method has been the latter, the two methods . . . converge fully.[83]

I said earlier that my main criticism of Marinatos's work was that while she acknowledges that there were queens and priestesses in Minoan Crete, she downplays their roles and ignores much of the female imagery, emphasizing instead male imagery and viewing the female imagery only through her pre-conceived notion of a Minoan/Near Eastern koine. I believe that Marinatos uses circumstantial evidence borrowed from other, even later cultures, but does not consider sufficiently the direct evidence found in Crete. I am not the only critic who feels this way.

---

[79] Marinatos 2010: 161.
[80] Marinatos 2010: 166.
[81] Marinatos 2010: 167.
[82] Marinatos 2010: 173.
[83] Marinatos 2010: 191.

Reviewing Marinatos's book in the *American Historical Review*, Quentin Letesson of the Université Catholique de Louvain writes: 'The major problem with the book is that notions of theocracy and kingship are firmly assumed from the introduction rather than being critically assessed.'[84] Archaeologist Colin Renfrew makes a similar observation in his review of *Minoan Kingship*: 'One could argue that the concepts of 'king' and 'kingship' are not newly problematized in Marinatos's work as perhaps they ought to be.'[85] I too think that Marinatos argued for a pre-conceived conclusion.

I have other major criticisms as well. In the discussion of the Minoan seal rings as they relate to the Near Eastern mythology of the storm god, Marinatos gives no dates for the rings. As Weingarten points out in her review of *Minoan Kingship and the Solar Goddess*, Marinatos has a propensity to 'erase time and place.'[86]

When gender is undeterminable in a seal or other form of iconography, Marinatos automatically assumes the figure is male. Her work covers the period 1600-1390, yet she treats the period as though it were one unit. It was not. At some point during the period covered by her book, perhaps as early as 1600 or as late as 1400—the date is the subject of a huge controversy among archaeologists—the Mycenaeans become a dominant presence on Crete. Their presence would certainly find expression in the iconography of the time, as my discussion of Kopcke and Drakaki's work below will illustrate. Throughout the work, Marinatos's insistence on kingship is based on historical plausibility—there must have been kings. The Near Eastern lens she uses to understand Minoan Crete is the lens of the Indo-European civilizations that had risen to prominence there during the early Bronze Age. If Minoan Crete was indeed a pre-Indo-European or Old European civilization, as Gimbutas argued it was, one cannot apply such a lens. Finally, just because the civilizations of the Near East were interacting with each other during the Bronze Age, must they have shared the same political and religious systems? Was there really so comprehensive a Near Eastern koine as she insists? As Colin Renfrew remarked, Marinatos too readily adopts 'simplistic unifying equations,' and needs to be more cautious about 'equating what happened in early Mesopotamia or Egypt with the prehistoric cultures of Greece and Crete on the basis of some assumed cultural unity.'[87]

Male figures in spirally wound garments

I would like now to turn to a more thorough and specific discussion of the three most important and viable candidates for the role of 'priest-king,' discussed in Davis's article: the male figures with spirally wound garments, the Lily-Prince, and the Master Impression. I consider first the male figures with spirally wound garments, which are referred to alternately as male figures with long fringed mantels or robes, or male figures with Syrian robes, or male figures with long robes with diagonal bands worn obliquely over the shoulder.

We have seen that Evans identified men wearing such garments as representations of the priest-king. Marinatos, in *Minoan Religion,* refers to the figures only as priests. But in her 2010

---

[84] Letesson 2011: 498.
[85] Renfrew 2011: 28.
[86] Weingarten 2012.
[87] Renfrew 2011: 28.

book she calls them images of the Minoan king/god.[88] Davis, though not convinced that they were images of the priest-king, leaves the door open, commenting that, 'I conclude that if these, the most prominent male figures in Minoan art, were the kings of Crete, they were not represented as figures of secular power, but rather as functionaries in the religious sphere.'[89] Paul Rehak writing about these figures notes that 'their exact status is still the subject of investigation and debate.' He offers the opinion that they are clearly 'authorities.'[90]

I wish to add to the debate by pointing out that the garment that Davis and others identify only with male priests, priests whom she, as well as Evans and Marinatos, identify as the possible priest-king, is also to be found on a woman: the 'young priestess' in a fresco in Akrotiri's West House. The 'young priestess' of Thera, as Marinatos labels her, graced a door between rooms 4 and 5 of the West House, a house with a pictorial program that included scenes of a festival and of a ritual. It is in connection with the conduct of a ritual that the 'young priestess' is pictured.

The 'young priestess' of the Theran West House fresco has a shaved head except for the very top of her head, where her hair is formed into the shape of a snake. Her lips and her one visible ear are painted a bright red[91] and she wears a necklace and earrings. But what is most important for this discussion is her clothing. It is Marinatos herself who makes the comparison between the clothing of the 'young priestess' and the clothing of Minoan 'priests' as depicted on various seals, the very seals in which the 'priests' wear 'spirally wound garments.' She writes that 'the characteristic feature of this costume . . . is the length of the robe and the arrangement of part of it over the shoulder.'[92] Marinatos emphatically points out that the dress of the 'young priestess' is unusual; she is not wearing the flounced skirt one has come to expect on the Minoan Goddess or Minoan priestesses enacting an epiphany of the Goddess. She emphasizes that one finds parallels to the priestess's garment in the seals

> which depict the same costume on male persons of apparently priestly status to judge from the symbols of authority which they hold. Note especially the man accompanied by a griffin who has been called by Evans a sacerdotal figure.[93]

It is my contention that if the same garment is worn by both male priests and female priestesses, the garment cannot be used as an indicator of male kingship. Perhaps we can eliminate the priests in spirally wound garments as contenders for the title of priest-king, except perhaps for the one who is associated with the griffin on the seal referred to in the above quote from Marinatos. The seal, which shows a male in a spirally wound garment leading a griffin on a leash, is from the tomb of Vapheio, Laconia (the southern Greek mainland). It may be that the griffin indicates that he is a god. The seal is dated as Late Helladic IIa, *c.* 1500-1450 BC.

Previously I noted the controversy surrounding the 'Lily Prince' as a candidate for the priest-king. Davis is adamant in her belief that he was a 'she,' and was thus inadequately reconstructed. Niemeier is equally convinced that his reconstruction of the Lily Prince as a god with a staff in

---

[88] Marinatos 2010: 19.
[89] Davis 1995: 17.
[90] Rehak 1994: 80.
[91] Jason W. Earle has theorized that the red ear symbolized auditory epiphanies, or facilitated an auditory connection to the divine. (Earle 2010: 775).
[92] Marinatos 1984: 46.
[93] Marinatos 1984: 46.

his hand, and minus the plumed crown and the griffin, is the correct one. Shaw's article brings the argument back full circle. I, however, am in agreement with Davis, Immerwahr, Cameron, Rehak and others that the white torso indicates a female and it therefore cannot be the torso of Evans's priest-king. To quote Immerwahr, 'The so-called 'Priest–King' is a misleading designation, for the relief may equally well have represented a victorious taureador, possible female, or even a boxer.'[94] Cameron remarks,

> Might we have here a crowned 'Princess of the Bull-ring' leading a bull into the ring (? the Central Court), rather than a white-skinned male figure leading a griffin . . . for which the Fresco presents no supporting evidence?[95]

Rehak makes an especially important point. Agreeing with Davis that 'the torso was white, and should therefore belong to an athletic young female figure, probably a bull leaper,' he goes on to say that the question is crucial to our understanding of the Minoan 'palace' and society,

> because large-scale scenes of bulls and bull-leaping—including these white figures— decorated the palace's major entrances. If the white figures are indeed young women, then they form an integral part of the 'official' iconography that greeted all visitors to the complex.[96]

Unlike Shaw, I do not believe that the lily crown should, just in this particular instance, be associated with a male figure, nor do I believe that one can argue that because a fresco in Egypt portrays a simplified lily cap on a male, we can therefore now associate it with males in Minoan Crete to designate kingship.

The Master Impression

I would like to return now to the last of the artifacts cited by Davis as a candidate for the Minoan priest-king, the Master Impression, because the male figure in this artifact is for many experts the most likely candidate of all for Evans's priest-king. The sealing known as the Master Impression is dated to LM IB/LM II, *c.* 1480-1390 BC, and was found in Khania in western Crete by Swedish archaeologist Erik Hallager. In 1983 Hallager and his Greek-Swedish team unearthed part of a town that had been destroyed in a conflagration of LM IB, the same conflagration in which most Minoan temple-palaces and settlements burned to the ground. The team uncovered the remains of two streets, one small square, and four houses. The sealing was unearthed in a dump created in LM II which contained the remains of the LM IB destruction level. Sherds from LM II were also found in the dump.

The Master Impression is a sealing made from either a ring or ring stone, which was approximately 2.7 centimeters in height and 2 centimeters in width, depicting a male in what has come to be seen as typical Minoan dress: bare-chested, belt around his narrow waist, kilt, and booted feet. He stands atop what appears to be a gated city or palace[97] with the sea below. His right arm is outstretched in the 'commanding gesture,' and he holds in his outstretched arm

---

[94] Immerwahr 1990: 60.
[95] Cameron 1970: 165.
[96] Rehak 1998: 152.
[97] Krattenmaker 1995: 57.

a long staff with its tip-point facing downward between what have been identified variously as crenellations, horns of consecration, or granaries. His left arm is bent with his hand at his waist. Four unidentifiable floating symbols appear on either side of him.

We have seen that Davis argues that the male in the Master Impression is a god. She bases her argument on the 'super-human scale of the figure compared with the architecture,' and on her reconstruction of the architecture in the sealing: the figure is not standing atop a town, according to Davis, but rather he is 'standing on a shrine atop a mountain above the sea. He is presented, symbolically, in front of the town that venerates him.'[98]

Marinatos, who agrees with Davis that he is a god, says of the ring, 'never before was a male god shown in such glory.'[99] In *Minoan Religion* she interprets him as a protector of the town. 'The subject of the ring is his epiphany on top of the town and right above his shrine.'[100] In her 1995 article 'Divine Kingship in Minoan Crete,' Marinatos argues that the 'master' was a god on several grounds: the figure is oversized, he is given a very prominent position in the sealing, he is standing above a shrine with a false door, and 'most important,' 'the stance and attribute of the figure completely match those of descending gods who come from afar to visit their votaries.'[101]

Marinatos revisits the Master Impression in her recent work *Minoan Kingship and the Solar Goddess* in the chapter entitled 'House of God.' Here she again puts forward her argument that he is a god, and that the god and king are interchangeable in Minoan iconography. Archaeologists have found no temples in Minoan Crete because the 'house of god' is not an independent structure, but 'a complex integrated within a larger building.'[102] She interprets the city portrayed on the ring, not as the literal city of Khania, as some experts have, but as the 'house of god' and 'an interpretation of reality.'[103] Yet, the god in the ring is more important than the image of the city itself, according to Marinatos.

> The city of god mirrors the human city that belongs to the king; the god is like the ruler and the ruler is like a god. Mythical and ideological manifestations converge on this representation.[104]

Thus, in line with her reasoning in *Minoan Kingship and the Solar Goddess*, the male in the Master Impression is god and king at the same time because that is how god and kingship were portrayed in the Near Eastern koine.

While Marinatos may interpret the male figure as both a king and a god, other Aegean authorities do not, and they seem almost evenly divided over the issue of whether he is a god or a human ruler. Hallager, in his concluding remarks on the sealing in his 1985 book entitled *The Master Impression*, presented arguments on both sides and gave no final judgment or opinion as to whether the male figure is a god or king.

---

[98] Davis 1995: 18.
[99] Marinatos 2010: 75.
[100] Marinatos 1993: 172.
[101] Marinatos 1995: 41.
[102] Marinatos 2010: 76.
[103] Marinatos 2010: 76.
[104] Marinatos 2010: 76.

In favor of the argument that the Master Impression depicts a mortal/king, Hallager notes his resemblance to the prominent male on the Chieftain Cup. Writing several years prior to the publication of Koehl's article on the Chieftain Cup, Hallager maintains that the 'master' is a close parallel to the 'prince' on the Chieftain Cup 'who is almost without exception accepted as a mortal and who is also generally understood to be a 'Prince' or Minoan ruler.'[105] However, as discussed earlier, Koehl argued that the prince on the Chieftain cup was no prince or ruler, but rather a youth engaged in a kind of initiation ritual.

Hallager also finds parallels to the Master Impression in a male figure on a ring (of unknown provenance and date, now in Berlin); to a lesser extent in the leader of the enemy fleet from a fresco from Thera; and in a supposed leader on a fresco fragment from Tylissos.[106] If the master is understood to be a mortal, says Hallager, then the scene on the Master Impression could be interpreted in one of three ways: (1) as a secular one in which

> we would see a fortified town . . . provided with crenellations . . . and depicted with a conqueror or ruler on top; [(2) as] a ruler or sovereign protecting his settlement; [or (3) finally] that the whole scene was intended to demonstrate the religious significance of the Minoan King.[107]

Hallager also notes that the master can be interpreted as a god, the two most obvious parallels for that interpretation being the Mountain Mother sealing from Knossos dated to LM IIIA1, c. 1400-1370 BC, (discussed at length in my Chapter 5), and the ring he terms the 'Epiphany Ring,' which portrays a small male figure, his right arm outstretched, and holding a staff, descending from the sky in front of a sacred enclosure and a woman votary.

> The poses of these two deities are exactly the same as that found on the Khania sealing and they are the only known parallels for figures depicted in exactly this way—also holding a 'staff' in their outstretched hands.[108]

The downward pointed staff, argues Hallager, might actually be a lance[109] and if this is the case, then the master has Syrian parallels. He can be compared to the god Ba'al, who is depicted with such a lance in his role as god of fertility.[110]

Hallager concludes by noting that,

---

[105] Hallager 1985: 31. In a discussion session at the conference *The Function of the Minoan Palaces*, Hallager indicated that the superhuman size of the master moved him in favor of the theory he is a god, but the similarity of the master to the prince on the Chieftain Cup kept him from embracing that conclusion (Tzedakis and Hallager 1987: 120). That conference, which eventually produced the volume that was entitled *The Function of the Minoan Palaces*, took place in 1984. Koehl's article was published in 1986. One wonders if Hallager agrees with Koehl's interpretation of the Chieftain Cup, and if so, if he is now in favor of the interpretation that the master is a mortal.

[106] Hallager 1985: 31.

[107] Hallager 1985: 31-32.

[108] Hallager 1985: 33.

[109] Krattenmaker argues that the staff is in reality a scepter (Krattenmaker 1995: 56).

[110] Hallager 1985: 33.

on present evidence, none of the hypotheses or possibilities pointed out above can be proved and the final interpretation of the impression will probably be a matter of how one approaches the complex structure of Minoan society.[111]

If, as Hallager suggests, one interprets the artifact on the basis of 'the complex structure of Minoan society,' one must take into account the date of the sealing, what was happening in Crete at the time the sealing was in use, and the tenor of the design. Two authors who have done that are Kopcke and Drakaki in their 1999 article 'Male Iconography on Some Late Minoan Signets.' There they remark that the reading of the Master Impression 'might allow for more possibilities than hitherto considered.'[112]

Discussing the Master Impression, as well as motifs from sealings belonging to the 'archive' of Odos Katre, Khania (this archive of sealings was found about 140 meters from the Master Impression and is contemporary with it), Kopcke and Drakaki say that one finds a 'starkly militaristic tenor, quite close to and quite typical of, mainland surroundings – Mycenae, but also different; whether substantially or superficially so is the question.'[113] The authors note that the physicality of the 'lord' in the Master Impression 'is unparalleled, as is the composition and vertical orientation of the signet, the mise-en-scene of his appearance.'[114]

> 'Minoan' or 'un-Minoan' is the question, the latter possibility apparently not having been considered for two reasons: because we rather desperately have been looking for precisely the sort of 'Minos,' or priest-king that we think the Master Impression renders; and for want of a plausible alternative – what else could be represented?[115]

Rather than Evans's priest-king or Marinatos's god/king son of the solar Goddess, Kopcke and Drakaki see the male on the Master Impression as 'a concottière, a military man, leader of mercenary forces, having himself – and usurped powers – recorded this way. Not even claim to kingship need be implied, just egregious presumption.'[116]

In order to make their case more forceful, Kopcke and Drakaki discuss sealings from Odos Katre, which, as noted, are contemporary with the Master Impression. The motifs of the Odos Katre sealings include various forms of hunting, especially deer hunting. The conclusions drawn about this sealing archive are used to bolster the authors' evaluation of the Master Impression as 'un-Minoan.' Kopcke and Drakaki call the poses on the Odos Katre sealings 'fresh,' they are not 'reproductions of received ideas.'[117] Again the authors assess the tenor of the sealings. They believe the fact that often the sealings portray only the expiring deer in his death throes, but not the actual spear that was used to kill the deer, is of great importance. They intimate that the Minoans would not have depicted the deer hunt in this way. In portraying the hunt and kill thusly, they believe, the Odos Katre sealings celebrate the work of a 'professional killer.'[118]

---

[111] Hallager 1985: 33.
[112] Kopcke and Drakaki 1999: 2:341-346.
[113] Kopcke and Drakaki 1999: 2:341.
[114] Kopcke and Drakaki 1999: 2:341.
[115] Kopcke and Drakaki 1999: 2:341-342.
[116] Kopcke and Drakaki 1999: 2:342.
[117] Kopcke and Drakaki 1999: 2:343.
[118] Kopcke and Drakaki 1999: 2:343.

This kind of hunt, according to the authors, is more mainland in character. They ask, 'who but military men would choose such a subject? Could this be a sign of mainland presence?'[119]

Analyzing a sealing from the archive which portrays, not a deer hunt, but a man restraining a fierce dog, the authors compare it to the design on a signet ring from Palaikastro in which a hunter is shown throwing a 'Zeus-like,' thunderbolt-shaped weapon as he runs alongside a large agrimi being attacked by dogs. 'Is this masculinity Minoan?'[120] they ask. Their answer is a slightly veiled no. 'Driessen and MacDonald believe that "Mycenaeans" were on Crete before the critical events of the final destruction. Perhaps so.'[121] Minoan art, according to Kopcke and Drakaki, does not emphasize individual power and courage, rather, they believe the art and the ethos of Crete is one partial to the collective.

While Kopcke and Drakaki emphasize that their conclusions are tentative, they do say that, 'Seen against the background known to us, some of the sealings are odd, exceptional, the Master Impression included, praising force, brutal pride in ways that others do not.'[122]

This summary of Kopcke and Drakaki's article shows that a good argument can be made for the 'un-Minoan' tenor of the Master Impression sealing. What of their claim that the Mycenaeans were already in Crete at this time? And that the male in the sealing is a 'concottière, a military man, leader of mercenary forces.'[123] That would certainly bolster the argument that the sealing is 'un-Minoan,' and that the figure on the sealing cannot represent the Minoan priest-king.

Kopcke and Drakaki refer to Driessen and MacDonald's 1997 work *The Troubled Island* for the argument that Mycenaeans were already in Crete in LM IB. In that work the authors posit that the Mycenaeans arrived in Crete in LM IB-II, c. 1480-1425/1425-1390 BC. They base this argument on their supposition that by that point in time, LM IB-II, Minoan Crete had reached a crisis stage characterized by, among other things, famine or food storages, depopulation, and abandonment of sites. What had caused such a crisis? The authors believe that earthquakes of LM IA, and the Santorini eruption and subsequent tsunami are to blame.

> Our thesis is that the archaeological evidence suggests a severe economic dislocation triggered by the Santorini eruption and gradually building up in the Mature LM I period. Moreover, a combination of a general feeling of uncertainty caused by the eruption and its accompanying effects, the destructions caused by earthquakes, the need for rebuilding and the re-establishment of normal economic life, may have heralded the end of the system. . . . Because of problems with food production and distribution, the network which had existed, disintegrated. . . . That Mycenaeans from Mainland Greece arrived at some stage on the island during the Late Bronze Age is clear. When they arrived is a matter of fierce debate . . . but the crisis years of Late Minoan IB-II appear as the most opportune moments.[124]

---

[119] Kopcke and Drakaki 1999: 2:343
[120] Kopcke and Drakaki 1999: 2:342.
[121] Kopcke and Drakaki 1999: 2:344. The reference is to Driessen and MacDonald 1997.
[122] Kopcke and Drakaki 1999: 2:345.
[123] Kopcke and Drakaki 1999: 2:342.
[124] Driessen and MacDonald 1997: 117-118.

While not all authorities agree with Driessen and MacDonald's thesis, there seems to be some agreement among Aegeanists that there is a Mycenaean presence in Crete in LM IB, *c.* 1480-1425 BC. Their arrival, either as conquerors, mercenaries, or invited guests could well explain the existence of the 'un-Minoan' 'Master Impression.'

Another hypothesis may also strengthen Kopcke and Drakaki's view of the Master Impression as 'un-Minoan.' In a 1997 article entitled 'Horns of Consecration or Rooftop Granaries? Another Look at the Master Impression,' archaeologist Thomas F. Strasser makes a case for identifying the crenellations on the tops of the buildings depicted in the Master Impression not as horns of consecration, as they often are, but as granaries instead. Strasser argues that horns of consecration would be depicted more realistically by an artist of the caliber of the creator of the Master Impression, that is 'with more angular lines and joined at the base'; that 'there are parallels for domed rooftop granaries from Egypt, Mesopotamia and possibly the Aegean that have a striking similarity to these structures'; and that rooftop granaries are eminently practical. Strasser posits that such conclusions have 'significant ramifications on how one interprets the architectural scene on the Master Impression.'[125]

If one were to view the crenellations in the Master Impression as rooftop granaries, the ensuing architectural scene would make, in my opinion, the perfect backdrop for a Mycenaean interloper to be pictured. Driessen and MacDonald believe that following the Thera eruption the Minoans, faced with food shortages, were forced to trade their riches to the Mycenaeans in exchange for the needed food. The authors think it was during this period of supplying the Minoans with the food they so desperately needed that the Mycenaean palace state emerged.[126] Having made their fortunes on the misfortunes that befell the people of the Aegean islands after the Thera eruption, through the importation of grain, and having arrived either as conquerors, mercenaries, or invited 'guests' in the wake of the social, economic and political disintegration caused by the eruption, the domed granaries as a backdrop to the 'master' are an appropriate way to iconographically depict the Mycenaean victory. And that victory need not have been accomplished through warfare alone, or perhaps at all. As Kopcke so aptly put it, 'not even claim to kingship need be implied, just egregious presumption.'[127]

Minoan art shows no male ruler, but rather, important women, priestesses or Goddesses

I have attempted above to present arguments to refute the claims of those who would put forward the Master Impression, the Lily Prince, and the priests with spirally wound garments as iconographical representations of the Minoan priest-king. Earlier in my discussion I also indicated why I think Marinatos's unique hypothesis, that a king ruled Minoan Crete through his association with a solar Goddess, is in error. In reviewing the evidence one must also keep in mind the conclusion drawn by a panel of distinguished Aegeanists at the annual Archaeological Institute of America Conference in 1992. The central theme of the papers presented at that panel discussion and subsequently published under the title *The Role of the*

---

[125] Strasser 1997a: 1:202.

[126] Driessen and MacDonald 1997: 115. The emergence of the Mycenaean palace state was also aided by the decline of Minoan influence in the Cyclades and Kythera.

[127] Kopcke and Drakaki 1999: 2:342.

Ruler in the Prehistoric Aegean[128] is that Minoan art shows no male ruler, but rather important women. My Chapter 6 was devoted to a discussion of those important women.

Why is it so difficult for archaeologists to give up the idea that there was a king of Crete and accept the possibility of a priestess-queen? Do they think in doing so they might also have to admit that Crete was a matriarchy? Rodney Castleden, a geologist and the author of several books on Minoan Crete, believes the resistance to acknowledging a priestess-queen ruler is based on the strength of Mycenaean tradition.[129] In other words, if the Mycenaeans had a king (wanax), the Minoans must have also! Leaving aside the fact that Indo-European Mycenaean civilization was vastly different than that of Minoan Crete, some scholars have argued that even the Mycenaeans had powerful queens as well as kings and some system of shared rulership. Archaeologist Paul Rehak is one such scholar.

Rehak points out in his 1995 article 'Enthroned Figures in Aegean Art and the Function of the Mycenean Megaron' that 'it is rare for Aegean iconography of any period to show seated males.'[130] On the other hand, the Linear B tablets from Pylos and Knossos indicate that the wanax (king) was the most important official in the Mycenaean state in late Mycenaean times. Rehak suggests, based on iconographic and architectural evidence, that 'Mycenaean society was much more complex than we have imagined.'[131] He postulates, based on the Linear B tablets, that Mycenaean society had several interrelated figures of authority—including a woman who held the secular title of Potnia.

> We may lack the image of a single, enthroned male ruler, not because the Mycenaeans refused to borrow or could not create such an image, but rather because the concept of an enthroned figure was not, in Mycenaean society, that of a man but that of a woman.[132]

John Younger shares somewhat similar views:

> What has not . . . been sufficiently stressed for the Late Bronze Age is the role of the female entitled 'po-ti-ni-ja' in Linear B—since she appears in texts that also mention divinities, Potnia is almost always considered to be a goddess. But in several texts, she also appears alongside the Wanax, and in a couple of brief but illuminating texts, she is paired with the Wanax.[133]

While all the experts are not unanimously agreed, it can be argued as above, that 'the strength of Greek tradition' points not to simply a priest-king, but to a system of joint rulership or *gylany*, a female-male partnership. Thus even in patriarchal Mycenaean society, women's position of authority survived.

As a way of concluding this chapter I refer to a work of Paul Rehak's entitled 'The Construction of Gender in Late Bronze Age Aegean Art: a Prolegomenon.' In that work, whose purpose is to

---

[128] Paul Rehak edited that volume.
[129] Castleden 1990: 117.
[130] Rehak 1995: 96. For an alternative view of enthroned figures, see Poole 2020: 151-152.
[131] Rehak 1995: 116.
[132] Rehak 1995: 117.
[133] J.G. Younger, email to Aegeanet mailing list March 11, 1996, http://umich.edu/classics/archives/aegeanet/aegeanet.960311.02 No longer accessible.

identify areas in Aegean archaeology that require further study, Rehak makes some important points as regards the role of women and men in Minoan society, and male images that appear in Minoan iconography.

One of the major points Rehak makes, and this is clear from my discussion of archaeologists' attempts to find a king Minos in the iconography as well, is that 'rulers are hard to identify.'[134] Discussing the scale, position, and pose of figures in Minoan iconography he writes:

> Outsized male figures are rare in the Aegean, except for the Master Impression. Instead, Aegean art sometimes shows us groups of women that are bigger than groups of men, as in the two miniature frescoes from Knossos, the Grandstand and Sacred Grove and Dance. Unlike the men, the larger women are also differentiated from one another, and have more elaborate costumes and jewellery. In both scenes, the men are mostly spectators. The Campstool Fresco, of slightly later date, also shows women at a larger scale than the men.[135]

Rehak points out the 'commanding gesture,' one of the gestures that is used to argue that the Master Impression is either a god or a ruler, is done by both men and women. That fact tends to be under-emphasized by most Aegeanists. I have found no archaeologist who argues that the images of women in the 'commanding gesture' are images of the Minoan priestess-queen.[136] This would point to a double-standard in some researchers.

What can one conclude from the evidence presented here? In this chapter I have attempted to show that while Aegeanists since the time of Sir Arthur Evans have looked for an image of a male ruler, there is a paucity of male ruler iconography in Minoan Crete. Ellen Davis tackled the issue head on in her 1995 article. Looking at the five major iconographical candidates for the missing ruler at that time: the Lily Prince, the Chieftain Cup, the man on the Ayia Triadha Sarcophagus, the males in the spirally wound garments, and the Master Impression, she analyzed and then dismissed each one, concluding that none, except perhaps for the males in the spirally wound garments, could be considered the missing ruler. She further concluded that Minoan Crete was a unique society among all the societies of the eastern Mediterranean at the time of the Bronze Age. It was a society that Aegeanists had yet to understand.

However, the search for the missing male ruler did not stop with Davis's article. Since her work, arguments have continued to come forth supporting the Lily Prince, the males in spirally wound garments, and the Master in the Master Impression as the missing ruler.

I have argued that Shaw's latest defense of Evans's reconstructed Lily Prince as the missing ruler is not sound for several reasons: the color white, despite her claim to the contrary, is still associated with women in Minoan art, and plumed crowns are still mainly associated with females. Moreover, although a male acrobat wearing a 'simplified lily crown' in a Minoan-style fresco was found in the Nile Delta, it does not necessarily follow that Evans's Lily Prince is a

---

[134] Rehak 1998: 191.

[135] Rehak 1998: 195.

[136] The several representations of women in Minoan iconography who stand in the pose of the 'commanding gesture' are usually thought of as representations of the Goddess. Rehak makes an important observation when he says 'if every important female figure is automatically a goddess, we diminish the possible existence of powerful women by removing them from the human sphere' (Rehak 1998: 192).

top athlete and heir apparent in Minoan Crete. I am much more persuaded by the arguments of Immerwahr and Cameron that he is a she and she is a female toreador or a 'Princess of the Bullring.'

As for the men in the spirally wound garments, I think the fact that a similar garment can be found on a priestess in a Theran fresco, argues for scholars continuing to regard humans dressed in spirally wound garments as priests and priestesses.

As concerns the Master Impression, I hope I have illustrated that based on the analyses of Kopcke and Drakaki, Driessen and MacDonald, and Strasser, it is likely that the master represents a Mycenaean interloper. Perhaps he is a ruler of some sort, but I do not believe he is a Minoan one.

Marinatos's work *Minoan Kingship and the Solar Goddess* and its unique reassessment of Minoan ruler iconography is not convincing either. It falters mainly on account of Marinatos's adamant insistence that Crete was part of a Near Eastern koine, and on Marinatos's unacknowledged bias that Crete must have had a male ruler.

Indeed, underlying all the arguments for a male as the missing ruler is the unacknowledged bias of all but a few archaeologists. Most believe, without bothering to make their belief explicit, that only males can rule, that no ancient society could function without a ruler, and that that ruler must have been a male king.

Even when Koehl or Marinatos argue for 'shared rulership,' they do so for what I consider to be the wrong reasons. They simply cannot avoid taking into account the overwhelming evidence for the importance of women in the iconography. Therefore they must include women, albeit in a supporting role only.

However, if one can overcome the culturally, deeply ingrained bias in favor of a male, one can then acknowledge, as the panel of archaeologists at the AIA conference in 1992 did, that a male ruler is indeed missing, instead there are only important women. If rulers are hard to identify, and if there are only important women in the iconography, might this not be seen as indicative of the type of society Goettner-Abendroth, Sanday, Du, Eisler or Gimbutas has described? It is to those descriptions and how they might apply to Minoan society that I turn in the next chapter.

Chapter 8

Was Bronze Age Crete a Matriarchy?

I said in my introduction that the aim of this work was to determine whether Bronze Age Crete was a matristic, matrilineal, matriarchal, *gylanic,* egalitarian, gender diarchic, or a patriarchal society. I further noted that the debate over whether or not Bronze Age Crete was a matriarchal society continues to be heated and unresolved and that it was the intention of this study to advance the discussion toward a more complex, detailed, and certain conclusion. Scholars discussing Bronze Age Crete do not seem to be aware of alternatives to the traditional definition of matriarchy, nor the terms *gylany* or gender equal.

I started with the hypothesis that Bronze Age Crete was a matriarchal society based either on Goettner-Abendroth's or Sanday's definition. However, I also realized that my research might prove that Bronze Age Crete was not a matriarchy, and thus I also considered the terms and definitions of Eisler, Gimbutas, and Du, as well as the possibility Minoan Crete was a patriarchal society.

Having considered the issue very carefully, I believe I have a plausible and highly probable case for arguing that Bronze Age Crete was a matriarchal society, based on Goettner-Abendroth's definition. In this chapter I detail why I believe this is so.

However, before beginning that discussion, I would like briefly to review Sanday's, Eisler's, Gimbutas's, Du's, and Lerner's terms and definitions to assess how they might also apply to the society of Minoan Crete as I have described it in the chapters of this book.

Does a definition of patriarchy apply to Minoan Crete?

Regarding Lerner's definition of patriarchy, 'the manifestation and institutionalization of male dominance over women and children in the family and the extension of male dominance over women in society and in general,'[1] and its possible application to Crete, I believe that my discussion of the role of women in Bronze Age Cretan society in Chapter 6, and the evidence I presented there for Minoan Crete as a woman-centered society, as well as the information I presented in Chapter 7 on the lack of male ruler iconography, and the archaeological evidence in this chapter for matrilineality, matrilocality, a balanced economy, and decision making organized along kinship lines, makes any argument for a patriarchal Minoan Crete highly untenable. Indeed, all the evidence presented in this book describes a society that is in direct contrast to one in which 'the men hold power in all the important institutions of society and the women are deprived of access to such power.'[2]

---

[1] Lerner 1986: 239.
[2] Lerner 1986: 239.

Sanday's, Eisler's, Gimbutas's, and Du's definitions and their application to Minoan Crete

My description of the preeminence of the Goddess in Minoan religious iconography and the role of women in Bronze Age Cretan society, in Chapters 5 and 6, indicates that the definition of matriarchy provided by Sanday can plausibly be applied to Minoan society. In defining matriarchy, Sanday writes that one may speak of matriarchy when the cosmological and the social orders are linked by a Mother Goddess (or primordial founding ancestress or archetypal queen) and when women are involved in activities that regenerate and authenticate the social order.[3] Sanday continues:

> In a strongly tradition-based society ultimate authority does not rest in political roles but in a cosmological order. If this cosmological order pivots around female oriented symbols and if this order is upheld by ritual acts coordinated by women whose social salience is also grounded in this order we can speak of matriarchy.[4]

In her work *Women at the Center*, published in 2002, Sanday expands upon her definition proposing that matriarchy can be defined as the 'cultural symbols and practices associating the maternal with the origin and center of the growth processes necessary for social and individual life.'[5]

I think there can be little doubt, given the evidence I presented above, that a Mother Goddess was at the center of Cretan Bronze Age religion, and that one can speak of a cosmological order in ancient Crete that pivoted around a Mother Goddess and around female oriented symbols. I further believe that Minoan Crete was a woman-centered society, as I illustrated in Chapter 6. Women appear preeminent in every aspect of Minoan life, and most especially in the ritual aspects of Minoan life. This provides evidence that women in Minoan Crete regenerated and authenticated the social order. That Minoan Crete exhibited 'cultural symbols and practices associating the maternal with the origin and center of the growth processes necessary for social and individual life' follows from their worship of a Mother Goddess whose symbols are present on the preponderance of the surviving artifacts of that culture (Chapters 4 and 5), symbols that represent, for the most part, the natural growth and regeneration of plant, animal and human life.

Turning to Eisler's work on cultural history, I noted in the introductory chapter that she proposed the use of the term *partnership model* for Crete rather than *matriarchy*, which she believes has negative connotations. In Eisler's vision the term partnership model can be used to describe a society in which social relations are primarily based on the principle of linking rather than ranking. *Gylany* is the term she coined for this more egalitarian relationship.[6]

Eisler characterizes partnership or *gylanic* societies as exhibiting democratic organization at all levels; equally valuing men, women, and stereotypically feminine values (such as caring and nonviolence) whether they are embodied in women or men; and living a less violent or

---

[3] Sanday 1998: 1.
[4] Sanday 1998: 7.
[5] Sanday 2003: 236.
[6] Eisler 1987: 105.

nonviolent way of life, as violence will no longer be needed to maintain hierarchies.[7] Eisler includes Minoan Crete in her books as an example of a partnership society. Certainly the evidence I have presented in the body of this work justifies that inclusion. A section of this study deals extensively with the probable democratic organization of Minoan society. The iconography of Minoan Crete, which has been extensively dealt with in Chapters 4, 5, and 6, certainly upholds a view of Minoan life as nonviolent, and as equally valuing men and women and feminine values, whether they are embodied in men or women.

The archaeologist Marija Gimbutas, who like Eisler preferred to avoid the term *matriarchy* because of its negative connotations, referred to the civilizations of Old Europe and Anatolia, to which Minoan Crete was connected, as matrilineal and matristic, and she employed Eisler's term *gylany* as well to describe those societies. Gimbutas defined matrilineal as 'a social structure in which ancestral descent and inheritance is traced through the female line,'[8] and matristic as 'a matrilineal "partnership" society in which women are honored but do not subjugate men.'[9] We have seen that, based on the Law Code of Gortyn, as well as on mythology, a matrilineal Crete is certainly plausible. Later in this chapter I will review the archaeological evidence for a matrilineal/matrilocal social structure in Minoan Crete. This evidence makes the existence of a matrilineal/matrilocal Crete an even more distinct possibility. As for the second aspect of Gimbutas's definition, 'women are honored but do not subjugate men,' the evidence presented in this work, especially as regards the iconography of the frescoes, seals, sealings, and rings, shows that this statement is plausible for Minoan Crete as well.

Shanshan Du's anthropological work offers definitions for several categories of gender equal societies with potential applicability to Minoan Crete. The one that seems most pertinent is the one she defines as *maternal centrality*. According to Du, maternal centrality is

> associated with societies that are characterized by matrilineal descendant rule and matrilocal residence pattern, . . . the symbolism of this model tends to elevate the female principle over its male counterpart. . . . The principle value of this framework is placed on the characteristics that are commonly associated with maternity, such as life-giving, nurturance, connection, and harmony.[10]

Du stresses that despite the fact that in such a system the mother is favored, this does not mean that the male is subordinate to the female.

It seems to me that Du's maternal centrality category of gender equality has much in common with Sanday's definition of matriarchy in its emphasis on maternity and the feminine principle. In its inclusion of matrilineality and matrilocality, Du's definition also shares some common ground with Gimbutas's definition of Old European/Anatolian Crete as matrilineal and matristic. As I noted in discussing Sanday's definition, the evidence I have presented in Chapters 4 and 5 can leave little doubt that Minoan Crete worshipped a Mother Goddess as its central and primary deity, and in that sense 'elevated the female principle over its male counterpart.' The Law Code of Gortyn, analyzed in Chapter 6, and the interpretation of certain

---

[7] Eisler 2008: 44-45.
[8] Gimbutas 1991: 433.
[9] Gimbutas 1991: 433.
[10] Du 2009: 257.

myths, recounted in Chapters 4, 5, and 6, as well as the archaeological evidence I will present later in this chapter, make a plausible case for a matrilineal and matrilocal Crete as well.

I believe I have presented substantial evidence in this book to show that Sanday's, Eisler's, Gimbutas's, and Du's definitions can all be argued to be applicable to Minoan Crete. However, I have concluded that the definition of matriarchy offered by Goettner-Abendroth is the most appropriate as regards Bronze Age Crete. In addition, it is the most thorough, far-reaching, and encompassing. Like the others, it is a plausible characterization of the society, and furthermore, it has the advantage of including them all, and going further, giving the scholar a much richer, deeper definition upon which to build a theory of matriarchal society and a new field of knowledge. I would like now to turn to a discussion of Goettner-Abendroth's deep structure of matriarchal societies, her definition of matriarchy, to see how each of the four levels of her definition—the economic, political/decision-making, social patterns, and culture/worldview/ spirituality can be applied in Bronze Age Crete.

Goettner-Abendroth's definition of matriarchy at the economic level and its application to Minoan Crete

We saw in the Introduction that, according to Goettner-Abendroth, at the level of economics, matriarchal societies are usually, but not always, agricultural societies.

> [They] practice a subsistence economy that achieves local and regional self-reliance. Land and houses belong to the clan in the sense of usage rights, while private ownership of property and territorial claims are unknown concepts. There is a vivid circulation of goods along the lines of kinship and marriage customs. The system of circulation prevents the accumulation of goods by one individual or clan, as the ideal is distribution rather than accumulation. . . . In economic terms, matriarchies are known for their perfectly balanced reciprocity. For that reason I define them as **societies of economic reciprocity**.[emphasis in original][11]

As regards the 'inner economy of the clan,' Goettner-Abendroth writes,

> All goods acquired by clan members are given to the women of the clan. So the women . . . *hold all the goods in their hands;* [emphasis in original] they are responsible for the sustenance and the protection of all clan members.[12]

In her 2012 work, *Matriarchal Societies*, Goettner-Abendroth stresses that for a society to be considered a matriarchy, the power of economic distribution must be held by women. The other 'necessary condition' of matriarchy is that

> mothers are at the center of society, as manifested by matrilinearity; . . . both [the power of economic distribution and matrilinearity, must be] in the context of gender equality. If these conditions are fulfilled in an actual society, we can call it matriarchal.[13]

---

[11] Goettner-Abendroth 2007: 3-4.
[12] Goettner-Abendroth 2007: 13.
[13] Goettner-Abendroth 2012: xxvi.

Goettner-Abendroth goes on to say that matriarchal societies

> at the economic level are societies creating a balanced economy, in which women distribute goods, always seeking economic mutuality; such an economy has characteristics in common with a 'gift economy.' Therefore, I define them as societies of economic mutuality based on the circulation of gifts.[14]

Was Minoan Crete a balanced economy in which women distributed goods, always seeking economic mutuality based on the circulation of gifts? In order to answer that question I want to first look at how archaeologists perceive the Minoan economy.

Neolithic Crete is generally described by archaeologists as an egalitarian society in economic as well as social and political terms. Its largely communal structures are thought to be bound by cooperation. Watrous writes that Crete was sparsely settled until the Final Neolithic and those early settlers from Anatolia brought their continental economy with them: a rich agricultural economy of cereals, vines, oils, and herds.[15] Vasilakis notes that women in the Neolithic Aegean 'were responsible for storing the farm produce and controlling access to it.'[16] That last phrase sounds very much like women controlled the distribution of goods.

In thinking about the economy of Crete during the Bronze Age, it is important, I believe, to keep in mind this quote from archaeologist Oliver Dickinson:

> All pre-industrial societies had as their essential basis the successful exploitation of the land. In the case of the Aegean B[ronze] A[ge], it may be suggested that this was even more dominant than in the contemporary Near East, in that the Aegean societies remained basically small-scale throughout their history, and the total proportion of their populations not directly involved in some form of farming was insignificant; ... Of course there were craft specialists, but ... most of these will have practiced their craft part-time and also worked land, as specialized pastoralists are likely to have done, to judge from modern parallels.[17]

When writing about Crete in the Early Minoan era, archaeologists tend to agree, as I wrote in Chapter 5, that the period was one in which a relatively equalitarian society existed, as evidenced in the communal tombs of the period, and in the settlement of Myrtos, whose layout indicates a communal social organization during the Early Bronze Age. The 'E[arly] M[inoan] period tend[s] to be viewed in similar terms to the Neolithic as simple, village-based/non-urban, conservative and lacking craft specialization.'[18] The special role of women in this early period, however, is indicated by Driessen who stated, based on burials and the analysis of skeletons at Myrtos, that there is 'some scant evidence' to suggest that 'women received a more preferential treatment ... than men.'[19] He also notes that 'our two published studies of Prepalatial skeletal material, [at] Archanes and Zakros, suggest: . . . that women

---

[14] Goettner-Abendroth 2012: xxv.
[15] Watrous 1994: 700.
[16] Vasilakis 2001: 76.
[17] O. T. P. K. Dickinson 1994: 45.
[18] Schoep and Tomkins 2012: 2.
[19] Driessen 2011: 111.

outnumber men and had better conditions.'[20] By better conditions Driessen is referring to dietary conditions. Driessen also remarks that 'It may be telling that, during the Prepalatial period, the most valuable grave offerings consisted of gold diadems, a means of adornment for women.'[21] Driessen goes on to argue, in other articles to be discussed below, that Early Minoan Crete was organized along clan/kinship lines, and that descent was matrilineal, and habitation matrilocal.

As one moves into the Old Palace period of the Middle Bronze Age, the archaeological literature no longer speaks of a relatively equalitarian society, economically, socially, and politically, but is concerned to account for the rise of the Minoan palaces.[22] It has been generally accepted, until as recently as only fifteen years ago, that the emergence of the first 'palaces' on Crete, c. 2100-1900 BC, represented the first state to develop in the Aegean. Thus archaeologists believed, and some still believe, that the 'palaces' represent 'the centralized mobilization of a labor force, materials, craft specialists, and the emergence of a new form of socio-political complexity centered upon these monumental buildings.'[23] The 'palaces' are also held to testify to 'the existence of central persons operating from central places.'[24]

Because 'palaces,' dating to the Old Palace Period, have been unearthed at Knossos, Phaistos, Malia, and Petras, it is further theorized that each was a kind of proto-state which controlled the area surrounding it. Thus, in the Old Palace Period, Crete is seen as being made up of a number of independent states with the 'palaces' as their main base of power; moreover, as regards economics, the 'palaces' were believed to be centralized economic entities with tight control over their 'hinterlands,' hinterlands meaning the territory surrounding the 'palaces' (although how large that territory really was is rarely defined). During the Late Bronze Age, with the building of the new temple-palaces, it was argued that Knossos became the ruling center of the island, led by a priest-king, and supported by a group of aristocrats who occupied the so-called 'villas.' Knossos ruled not only the island of Crete, but its supposed overseas colonies as well.

Implicit or explicit in all this as regards economics is a stratified society, a ruling class and a ruled class, and wealth in the hands of a few. Indeed archaeologist Philip Betancourt refers to Minoan society as 'feudal or semi-feudal.'[25] Vasilakis writes of the economy in the Old Palace Period that there was 'bureaucratic control of production, foreign trade was controlled by the palaces, and products were stored in the palaces.'[26] The implication, in regard to the storage of products in the 'palaces,' is that the faceless rulers of Knossos, Malia, and Phaistos exacted

---

[20] Driessen 2011: 112.
[21] Driessen 2011: 112. Driessen bases his statement that gold diadems were a means of adornment for women on the work of Costis Davaras, one of the excavators of Mochlos. Davaras has argued, based on comparisons with contemporary head-dresses from Ur and Mycenae, that the gold diadems found at Mochlos were feminine in nature and must have belonged to women. Davaras writes, 'Moreover, the high position held by women in Minoan society, which would justify the use of such precious jewels, is well established.' (Davaras 1975: 114).
[22] In the following discussion I revert to the use of the term palaces, rather than my preferred term of temple-palaces. I do so to match the usage by other scholars writing about the political role of the palaces. However, because in my understanding they ignore or underestimate the religious function of the temple-palaces, I place the word 'palace' in quotation marks.
[23] Schoep 2002a: 101.
[24] Schoep 2002a: 101.
[25] Betancourt 2002: 211.
[26] Vasilakis 2001: 118.

goods in the form of tribute or tax and then controlled the distribution of goods from the 'palace' to the populace.

I intimated above that the traditional view of the 'palaces' and state formation has changed in the past ten to fifteen years. I want to discuss how some, but not all, Aegeanists are currently looking at the economy of Crete in the Bronze Age, and how incorporating some of their arguments, along with my own interpretation of the evidence, might well lead to the conclusion that, in parallel with Goettner-Abendroth's definition of the economic aspect of matriarchy, women in Minoan Crete did distribute goods, and the society of Bronze Age Crete was a society of economic mutuality based on the circulation of gifts. In discussing economics, I will also be delving into the political and social aspects of Minoan society as they are intimately intertwined with the economic.

The first major revision to the traditional view of the 'palaces' I want to consider is the notion that the 'palaces' were centralized economic entities. Belgian archaeologist Ilse Schoep has noted that the interpretation of the 'palaces' (especially in the Protopalatial period) 'as economic centres controlling the production and circulation of goods has repeatedly been called into question.'[27] Schoep bases this assertion on several different factors. First is the fact that recent petrographic analysis of Kamares Ware pottery has shown that it was produced in south-central Crete, and not in the Knossos workshops as previously assumed by archaeologists.[28] This indicates to Schoep that Knossos was a consumer not a producer, as has always been theorized, and as one would expect if the palace exercised control over the production of goods.

Secondly, 'the role of the *koulouras* as large-scale grain storage receptacles has been questioned.'[29] This is an extremely important point. Archaeologist Thomas Strasser has convincingly argued, based on ethnographic parallels, classical sources, and archaeological evidence—including the lack of grain residue in the *koulouras*, the fact that no traces of a plaster lining (essential to make them waterproof) remain, and the fact that above-ground grain storage devices were the rule in the ancient Near East and Mediterranean—that the underground *koulouras* of the West Courts of Knossos and Phaistos were not grain storage devises, but rather drywells, or even more likely, tree-pits. Thus the actual storage space at the disposal of the 'palaces' was not as great as previously assumed; and as a result, not only is the model of the 'palace' as the economic center of the region undermined, but the 'social storage hypothesis' as an explanation for a redistributive economy leading to the formation of an elite class, and then the formation of the Minoan state is undermined as well.[30] Because of Strasser's findings, archaeologists are now embracing the view that the 'palaces' did not mainly function as re-distributive centers on a large scale.

In conjunction with their supposed role as redistributive centers, the 'palaces' have also traditionally been seen as the centers of, and exercising tight control over a wider hinterland. In a number of articles, archaeologists have posited that the model of the 'palace' as the economic

---

[27] Schoep 2002b: 19.
[28] Schoep 2002b: 20.
[29] Schoep 2002b: 20.
[30] Strasser 1997b: 73-100.

and political center of a wider hinterland needs to be reconsidered.[31] Their arguments are based not only on the discovery that Kamares pottery was not a product of the Knossian workshops, and that the *koulouras* were not grain storage devices, but on an assessment of architecture, settlement patterns, and administration in the hinterlands of several of the 'palaces.' The research of these scholars indicates that there was a great deal of regional independence and autonomy.

While archaeologists seem to concur that the centralized economic role of the Minoan 'palaces' needs to be revised, they have not yet embraced the view that the 'palaces' were not centralized political centers. In opposition to this traditional view of the Minoan political system, Schoep proposes another: that in Early Minoan, Protopalatial, and Neopalatial Crete, ideological, economic, and political power was not concentrated in the 'court-centered buildings' or 'Minoan Court Buildings,' as she prefers to call the 'palaces,' but that 'power relations were more subtle and complex.'[32] Basing her argument on her extensive study of the architecture, settlement patterns, and sealings of the territory of the western Mesara, including the 'palace' of Phaistos and the 'villa' of Ayia Triadha, Schoep states that neither Phaistos nor Ayia Triadha dominated the area. She proposes as an alternative theory that power was 'shared across different groups and sectors of society.'[33] Specifically what Schoep posits is that there existed a heterarchical structure, one in which 'each element is either unranked relative to other elements, or possesses the potential for being ranked in a number of ways';[34] and factional competition: 'factions can be defined as structurally and functionally similar groups which, by virtue of their similarity, compete for resources and positions of power and prestige.'[35]

Schoep develops her ideas further in articles that focus on the 'palace' of Malia and its environs. Here, in support of her argument for an Early Minoan, Protopalatial, and Neopalatial heterarchical society made up of competing factions, Schoep notes first that an analysis of the 'palace' of Malia reveals that its most important function was to allow for ceremonial activities involving the community at large. Schoep concludes this on the basis of the layout of the 'palace,' especially the central court and the ceremonial rooms that flank it, which are at the very heart of the 'palace.' Schoep further states that the 'early Court Buildings were a result of communal effort by large communities.'[36] Here she is discussing all the Court Buildings in general, not just Malia.

> Minoan Court Buildings [are] increasingly being understood as structures performing a ceremonial function for a wider community, . . . not least because of their usually prominent location and the presence of gathering spaces for large crowds of people.[37]

A third important point in regard to the Minoan 'palaces' that Schoep makes is that they were 'redolent with meaning.'[38] The histories of the 'palaces,' at least at Knossos and Phaistos,

---

[31] Schoep summarizes some of these arguments in Schoep 2002a: 103-105.
[32] Schoep 2002b: 21.
[33] Schoep 2002b: 33.
[34] Schoep 2002a: 106.
[35] Schoep 2002a: 106-107.
[36] Schoep 2012: 415.
[37] Schoep 2012: 415.
[38] Schoep 2012: 407.

stretched far back to the Neolithic, and their actual sites were, even during the Neolithic, areas of ritual focus.

For Schoep the fact that the 'palaces' most important function was to allow for ceremonial activity involving the whole community, that they were the result of communal effort, and were 'redolent with meaning,' makes them the perfect arena in which factions could play themselves off against each other. I would argue those same criteria made the 'palaces' the perfect place for gift-giving and economic exchange, as well as for the meeting of regional clan representatives to reach consensus on regional and/or island-wide issues. More will be said about this below.

Schoep finds further evidence in support of her argument for factional competition in 'conspicuous consumption which is an important strategy in the building of alliances and promoting group cohesion.'[39] According to Schoep, conspicuous consumption in Minoan Crete involved primarily eating and drinking ceremonies. Evidence of such ceremonies can be found at all the Minoan 'palaces.' Schoep believes that factions vying for power within towns, as well as in regions adjacent to the 'palaces' at Archanes, Nirou Chani, Amnisos, Kastelli Pediadas, Poros Katasmabas, Sklavokambos, Ayia Triadha, Tylissos, and others, used the court compounds for feasting and drinking and attempting to win adherents. Interestingly, she points out that there is a 'strong communal (i.e. aimed at inclusion at a communal scale) aspect to consumption in the Court Buildings.'[40] Glossing over the implications of that statement, she focuses her attention instead on what might be viewed as evidence of hierarchy within the activity of conspicuous consumption. Schoep writes that differences in the quality and quantity of tableware from, for example, the MM IIA 'Royal Pottery Stores' at Knossos, indicate 'social differences and hierarchies' within corporate groups.[41] I will argue below that conspicuous consumption, as Schoep terms it, can also be seen as evidence of mutuality, reciprocal gift-giving, and of celebration as well.

Factions and factional competition as an explanation for Bronze Age Cretan political, social, and economic structure is further developed by archaeologist Yannis Hamilakis. Hamilakis' thesis is that archaeological evidence indicates that 'the social and political organization during the neopalatial period might have resembled the model of competing factions that is known from other archaeological and ethnographic contexts.'[42] Whereas Schoep focused on the Early Minoan and Protopalatial period, Hamilakis' focus is on the New Palace period. He argues that one can identify factions in the archaeological landscape on the basis of a number of criteria: 1) abundance and elaboration of material culture; 2) common stylistic vocabulary; 3) frequent and elaborate symbolic displays; 4) evidence for intensifying feasting and associated changes in material culture; 5) monumentality; 6) presence of non-local goods in non-elite contexts; 7) a lack of evidence for rigid social, political, and administrative hierarchies; and 8) fragmentation of political, administrative structures and diversification of administrative technologies.[43] Hamilakis admits that 'many of the above criteria could indicate a range of phenomena and not necessarily factionalism.'[44] Indeed I believe a number of his identifiers

---

[39] Schoep 2002a: 118.
[40] Schoep 2012: 413.
[41] Schoep 2012: 413.
[42] Hamilakis 2002: 188.
[43] Hamilakis 2002: 187.
[44] Hamilakis 2002: 187.

could signal a matrilineal, matrilocal, gender equal society based on consensus and a gift economy—which I will argue below. Nevertheless, he thinks that 'seen in combination they can give reasonably reliable pointers'[45] to factional competition. Hamilakis chooses to focus on the combination of four factors: monumentality; conspicuous consumption; inter-site and intra-site organization of space and architecture; and record keeping.

Hamilakis defines monumentality as having space for public gatherings and 'imposing architectural features such as ashlar masonry.'[46] He notes that the fact there were many 'palaces,' as well as other buildings that exhibited monumentality, is evidence for the existence of factions, because he believes only the elite members of factions could build and maintain such structures. But it was Schoep who wrote that 'early Court Buildings [palaces] were a result of communal effort by large communities.'[47] If communal effort could build and maintain the 'palaces,' or Court Buildings, so it could build and maintain additional structures for use by the community for political, economic and social purposes—as I will propose below.

The fact that 'monumental' buildings were often clustered together and there was not 'an allocation of functional roles amongst [them],'[48] as well as the fact that the 'palaces' and other monumental buildings were open, and 'there are no clear spatial boundaries between elite "palatial buildings" and "commoners" residences,'[49] are further evidence for Hamilakis of the existence of factions: 'political boundaries might have been fluid and shifting, any political authority at the local or regional level short-lived and contested, and power more fragmented than we thought.'[50] But I would posit that Hamilakis' evidence could also be employed to argue that the monumental buildings, which were the result of community effort, were built for the use of various 'communities'—clans, villages, even larger groupings, all of whom who engaged in governing by consensus building, and in the distribution of resources. The fact that such buildings were not walled off or separated from the communities they served could be an indication that they were meant to be used by all in the community as meeting places, places of ceremony, and perhaps places where women distributed resources. If Minoan society was based on matrilineal/matrilocal clans governed by consensus, and existing through a gift economy, as I will argue below, there would be no need for walls of protection or separation. The openness and lack of boundaries that Hamilakis notes could also indicate communal ownership of property, and point to a society based in peace. This last is a very important point. I will return to communal ownership of property and to the question of peace below.

As for record keeping, it is illustrative of the activity of factions, according to Hamilakis, because it was widely distributed among the palaces, villas, and other monumental buildings rather than concentrated in one place: the 'palace.' He understands this wide distribution of record keeping to mean that there were a variety of authorities and no one to 'lay down the law.'[51] If instead, as I hypothesize, families, clans, villages, and regions lived by consensus decision making, what need would there be for someone to 'lay down the law'? Moreover, if the monumental buildings were community buildings, and if, as seems likely, the Minoan

---

[45] Hamilakis 2002: 187.
[46] Hamilakis 2002: 194.
[47] Schoep 2012: 415.
[48] Hamilakis 2002: 190.
[49] Hamilakis 2002: 191.
[50] Hamilakis 2002: 193.
[51] Hamilakis 2002: 194.

economy was a grid-work of local and regional self-reliance, it makes more sense for record keeping to have been done at many locations at the village and/or regional level.

Finally, 'the enormous scale of production and consumption of pottery and other crafts (including . . . frescoes), and the organization of often large-scale ceremonies of feasting/ drinking,'[52] are evidence for Hamilakis of the conspicuous consumption carried on by factions as part of the competition among them. I will argue below that feasting may also be evidence for a gift-based economy when it is taken in conjunction with other factors.

In sum, in opposition to the traditional view of Minoan Crete as a state ruled by a central authority, a priest-king residing in his 'palace,' surrounded by an aristocracy, and controlling the production and circulation of goods, Hamilakis offers the hypothesis that Neopalatial Crete is likely to have been politically, socially, and economically organized along the lines of competing factions on the local, regional, and inter-regional level. The competition and conflict among these groups were played out mainly through 'material culture and large-scale feasting and drinking ceremonies,'[53] and may also have involved 'claims to supernatural links, to ancestral power, . . . and cosmological knowledge.'[54]

I am not in accord with the long-standing, traditional view of the centralized economic, political, and social make-up of Bronze Age Crete, nor with the view of the proponents of factionalism. I have included the arguments of the proponents of factions here because I believe they offer a valid critique of the traditional view of a centralized Minoan society, though not a valid alternative, and because they have highlighted archaeological evidence that can be used, not to argue for factions, but, more profitably, to argue in favor of a Minoan Bronze Age matriarchal society that correlates with the definition of Goettner-Abendroth.

In the early twenty-first century, Aegeanists are looking for alternative models to the traditional view of a centralized Minoan Crete. Schoep, Hamilakis, and others are attempting to supply that alternative model with their factions hypothesis. Hamilakis has made the interesting comment that 'the debate on political and social dynamics in Bronze Age Crete is still influenced by the stereotypes of a high European civilization with strong hierarchical structure, monarchies and aristocracy.'[55] Those looking to competing factions in place of a central authority and a 'palace' to explain the economic, political, and social conditions of Bronze Age Crete may be guilty of something similar. I think the proponents of factionalism are influenced by the male-dominated scholarship which argues that matriarchal societies have never existed. I believe Goettner-Abendroth's definition of a matriarchal society can provide a much more satisfactory alternative to the traditional view of a centralized Minoan Crete, based on the evidence now available to us, than the proponents of factionalism propose.

The new position that the 'palaces' were not the loci of an economic hinterland, nor centers controlling the production and circulation of goods, is very important in terms of Goettner-Abendroth's economic definition of matriarchy, for it leaves room for one to consider the idea that the Minoan economy 'was a balanced economy, in which women distributed goods,

---

[52] Hamilakis 2002: 194.
[53] Hamilakis 2002: 188.
[54] Hamilakis 2002: 188.
[55] Hamilakis 2002: 185.

always seeking economic mutuality.'[56] What evidence is there for this? First of all, as will be discussed below, an argument can be made for a matrilocal/matrilineal Crete. In such a society, it is likely that women would be in charge of distributing goods, as Vasilakis noted they were for the Neolithic. We saw in Chapter 6 that in the Law Code of Gortyn there are numerous passages which show that property, including land, must often have been at the disposal of women. Was this a hold-over from an earlier time when women distributed goods and held usage rights to the land? As for the other aspects of the definition: 'a balanced economy . . . seeking economic mutuality,' I believe some of the discussion which follows, and which will interweave the political with the economic, will make this scenario plausible.

In her definition of the economic aspect of matriarchy in her work entitled *A Way into an Egalitarian Society: Principles and Practice of a Matriarchal Politics*, Goettner-Abendroth states that in a matriarchal society 'private ownership of property and territorial claims are unknown concepts.'[57] She defines 'clan' property by saying:

> In matriarchal societies, necessities of life such as land, housing, and food are clan property; as such they are in the hands of women, who manage these goods and pass them on in the female bloodline. Women's economic strength serves the greater well-being of the community.[58]

Goettner-Abendroth also notes that in matriarchal societies, there is the right to cultivate the land, but there is no right to private ownership of land.[59] She further states that 'As the central authority, the clan mother is the custodian of the clan's property: the entire harvest and income from clan members' labor is handed over to her.'[60]

The lack of fortifications around 'palaces,' villas, towns, and villages, for which Minoan Crete is justly famous, would argue, I believe, for communal use of land and its products. The lack of fortifications would also argue against factions. Hamilakis' observation that 'there are no clear spatial boundaries between elite "palatial buildings" and "commoners" residences'[61] might be another indicator of the lack of territorial claims and defensive property claims. The assumption by Aegeanists that private property (in place of clan property) must have existed early in the history of Minoan Crete seems to me to be yet another of those stereotypes Hamilakis alluded to above. Because Crete is often seen as the first European civilization, it is assumed that not only did it have a 'strong hierarchical structure, monarchies, and aristocracy,'[62] but it must have had 'private property' as well. I define the term private property as land or other objects that are held by individuals as part of their personal wealth, and which they manage as they please to the exclusion of others and to the exclusion of society's control.[63] I would argue that there is not sufficient archaeological evidence to prove the existence of 'private property' in Minoan Crete especially as regards the land and its fruits.[64]

---

[56] Goettner-Abendroth 2012: xxv.
[57] Goettner-Abendroth 2007: 4.
[58] Goettner-Abendroth 2012: 470.
[59] Goettner-Abendroth 2012: 472.
[60] Goettner-Abendroth 2012: 63.
[61] Hamilakis 2002: 191.
[62] Hamilakis 2002: 185.
[63] *Collins Dictionary of Economics*, s.v. 'private property,' accessed February 21, 2013, http://www.collinsdictionary.com/dictionary/english/private-property?
[64] For an alternative viewpoint see Apostalaki 2020: 112.

Archaeologists J. Driessen, S. Jusseret, and Q. Letesson have made some very important points in regard to the private ownership of land in Minoan Crete, noting that there is a 'remarkable absence or scarcity of traditional indicators of land ownership . . . field boundaries, rock art, agricultural terraces or clear natural borders coinciding with differences in material culture.'[65] The authors caution against approaching the subject of Minoan land ownership with preconceived modern notions, and they refer to archaeologist/architect Clairy Palyvou who has written: 'We have no access to the notion of ownership in the Creto-Mycenaean world. . . . Use of land can be traced in the archaeological record but not ownership of land.'[66]

Driessen, Jusseret, and Letesson do not rule out the possibility of some type of ownership. They wonder if a 'particular type of ownership'[67] is indicated by the distance of Minoan tombs from the settlements they serve. Do the tombs mark the boundaries of the settlements? If so, the authors ask, 'for whom is this a signal? Other communities or the ancestors themselves?'[68] They also wonder why some buildings are found with raw materials like obsidian in them, and other buildings not. Does this imply that only certain segments of society had access to and control of raw materials?[69] The authors admit that 'in the case of Minoan Crete more questions exist than can be answered on the basis of the present data set.'[70]

If the successful exploitation of land was the essential basis of pre-industrial society, and if nearly all the population of the Bronze Age Aegean was directly involved in some form of farming,[71] I believe it is extremely revealing of the economic, social, and political makeup of Minoan Crete, that the resource which was of the utmost importance in the sustenance of life itself—land—does not seem to have been privately held, but held by clans. This is an important realization, because the absence of private property is a key component of Goettner-Abendroth's economic definition of matriarchy.

Regarding smaller items such as artisan's tools, women's jewelry, or children's toys, I do not know if in Minoan Crete such items were regarded as private property or not. As regards the use of seals to mark personal property, Driessen, Jusseret, and Letesson note that current research is questioning whether seals and gold rings were used by individuals to mark ownership, as has traditionally been assumed by Aegeanists, or if seals might signify 'group affiliation identifiers.'[72] I wonder if they could be indicators of clan membership, or of some sort of regional affiliation, such as the identifier of a delegate to a village, regional, or inter-regional council. As noted before, these could be, in addition it seems, some kind of amulet with religious significance. Perhaps they are indicators of something or someone blessed by the deity or imbued with spiritual significance.[73]

---

[65] Jusseret, Driessen, and Letesson, 'Minoan Lands?,' sec. 2. Previous research and aspects of Minoan societal make-up, para 3.

[66] Palyvou 2004: 208.

[67] Jusseret, Driessen, and Letesson, 'Minoan Lands?,' sec. 3.4. Land marking, para 1.

[68] Jusseret, Driessen, and Letesson, 'Minoan Lands?,' sec. 3.4. Land marking, para 1.

[69] Jusseret, Driessen, and Letesson, 'Minoan Lands?,' sec. 3.4. Land marking, para 1. sec .3.5. Intra-settlement architectural studies: an example from Late Bronze Age Palaikastro, para 2.

[70] Jusseret, Driessen, and Letesson, 'Minoan Lands?,' sec. 3.4. Land marking, para 1. sec. 4. Conclusion, para 1.

[71] O. T. P. K. Dickinson 1994: 45.

[72] Jusseret, Driessen, and Letesson,'Minoan Lands?' sec. 2. Previous research and aspects of Minoan societal make-up, para. 3.

[73] It was Dr. Susan Gail Carter who made this last observation.

As for jewelry, Driessen has posited that the gold jewelry found in the Prepalatial tombs at Mochlos, was placed there not at the time of burial, but later, when secondary internments were made, and that the jewelry was 'intended for a general category of ancestors rather than a venerated individual.'[74] Could that general category of ancestors have been the clan mothers? We need further studies at other locations to address this issue.

Yet another factor that might point to a Minoan 'society of economic mutuality' is the new evidence which shows that the so-called villas were surrounded by settlements, and that they carried out administrative, manufacturing, and religious/ceremonial functions. This has only been understood in the last twenty years or so owing to continued excavations, and to the large numbers of field surveys that have been undertaken. Despite the fact that a major symposium was devoted to the Minoan villa, no agreement has been reached among Aegeanists as to how the term 'villa' is to be defined.[75] Archaeologist Gerald Cadogan, writing in 1980, likened the villa's place in Minoan society 'to that held by country houses in, say, non-industrial England.'[76] Greek archaeologists Eleni Mantzourani and Giorgos Vavouranakis, writing in 2005, placed villas in 'a category of edifices of exceptional architectural elaboration, which is assumed to represent second-tier centres of socio-political power and hierarchy, immediately below the so-called 'palaces.''[77] I would argue that they could be viewed as centers where clans and/or villages kept records of goods produced, stored any surpluses, and manufactured goods for exchange or gift-giving. Perhaps smaller festivals of gift-giving took place at the villas—thus the ceremonial function and an explanation for evidence of feasting at some of them. In the political realm they may also have been meeting places for regional level decision making. We saw in Chapter 6 that Rehak and Younger wondered if the benches in Room 4 of Ayia Triadha (one of the villas) might be the meeting place of the Queen's council.[78] In place of a Queen's council, I propose a regional council, led by a clan mother or a consortium of clan mothers.

Some of the larger towns may have functioned in a way similar to the villas. For example, Schoep noted evidence for ceremonies, administration, and manufacturing in various locations within the town of Malia,[79] and Carl Knappett has argued that some of the buildings in the town of Malia functioned as clan dwellings.[80] Driessen and MacGillivray found evidence for clan dwellings in Palaikastro.[81] Driessen has written that each one of the major Minoan towns 'should be understood as a holistic entity in which the main circulation arteries developed almost entirely in connection with rituals that went on within the court centres and where ceremonial routes connected the countryside to the city core.'[82] He has hypothesized that the plan and layout of many Minoan towns was dictated by the fact that they were 'inter-regional meeting places for residents and non-residents.'[83] If such surmises are correct, then record keeping, and festivals of gift-giving, as well as inter-regional political meetings could have been held in the towns.

---

[74] Jussert, Driessen, and Letesson. 'Minoan Lands?' sec. 2. Previous research and aspects of Minoan societal make-up, Para 2.
[75] See the essays in Hägg 1997a.
[76] Cadogan 1980: 135.
[77] Mantzourani and Vavouranakis 2005: 99.
[78] Younger and Rehak 2008: 182.
[79] Schoep 2002a: 101-132.
[80] Knappett 2009: 21.
[81] Driessen and MacGillivray 1989: 99-110.
[82] Driessen 2009: 51.
[83] Driessen 2009: 45.

I believe the largest scale gift-giving festivals were a function of the 'palaces.' If the temple-palaces were not the focus of political, economic, and religious centralization, what was their function? Schoep and others have argued that the 'palaces' were above all important centers for ceremonial activity, and communal gathering places. As Schoep said of the 'palace' of Malia, it was in the first place a communal building, serving the community at large.[84] Driessen has written that 'the so-called Minoan "palaces" were largely used by non-resident groups for integrative ritual action.'[85] Driessen, like Schoep, believes the 'palaces' have very ancient roots, and that the ground on which they were built was a place of meeting long before the 'palaces' themselves and their central courts were constructed.[86]

If Driessen and Schoep are correct and the 'palaces' were primarily communal buildings serving the whole community, and gathering places for visitors coming from a wider region, I would argue that in the economic sphere, the 'palaces' could have been the places which served the function of the distribution of goods or the gifting of goods to share wealth among the clans, an economic function of major importance in Goettner-Abendroth's definition of a matriarchal society. She writes:

> Due to varying harvests and more or less successful outcomes in trading over the course of the year, economic differences may arise between the clans in any village or city. In this situation the clans follow the principle of circulation of all goods . . . in order to prevent accumulation at any given point. The goods, as well as the nurturing, care, and cultural creativity in ritual events all circulate as gifts. This takes place in the festivals, which are at the core of these cultures and which drive their economies.[87]

The Minoan 'palaces' would have been the perfect sites to hold such festivals of gift-giving or circulation of all goods given their location, history, and *raison d'etre*. The 'conspicuous consumption' for which Schoep and Hamilakis find evidence in the 'palaces,' the eating and drinking which they perceive as evidence of factional competition, could instead be seen as evidence of festivals of matriarchal gift-giving; the eating and drinking being either an aspect of dispersal itself, the dispersal of food and beverages, or simply the material evidence of a celebration of the general recirculation of goods of all types.[88]

In a matrilineal and matrilocal society, women would be in charge of celebrations of gift-giving and recirculation of goods. In Minoan Crete evidence for women's important role in these festivals is indicated in at least one fresco. Author Marianna Vardinayannis notes 'it has been suggested women managed eating and drinking ceremonies which seem to have dominated the life of Prepalatial and later communities.'[89] It was the late Paul Rehak who made the point, in discussing the Campstool Fresco, dated to the Third Palace Period, c. 1450-1300 BC, that seated women are associated with festivities involving drinking and pouring.[90] Rehak suggested that the woman, (or women, there is a fragment of a second woman of similar size to the first), in

---

[84] Schoep 2002b: 21.
[85] Driessen 2009: 45.
[86] Driessen 2009: 51.
[87] Goettner-Abendroth 2007: 14.
[88] Such festivals of gift-giving are to be found among the matriarchal clans of the North American Indians, such as the Iroquois. See Goettner-Abendroth 2012: 313-314.
[89] Vardinayannis 2010: 86.
[90] Rehak 1995: 112.

the Campstool Fresco held an important ceremonial role.[91] This important fresco deserves a better name, one that reflects the presiding female presence, such as Clan Mother or Priestess Leading Toasting Ceremony.[92]

Although Rehak is specifically dealing with a fresco dating to the period when Minoan Crete was under Mycenaean domination, I do not believe the date of the fresco rules out an interpretation of it as illustrative of women's central role in gift-giving. Rather, I believe it provides evidence for female leadership in ceremony despite the Mycenaean domination. Just as the remnants of matriarchal societies still exist today, so too Mycenaean dominance did not immediately put an end to women's central role in the social and religious life of Minoan Crete.

I hypothesize that if a woman or women elders of the clan(s) oversaw the festivals of gift-giving that I believe took place at the 'palaces,' as well as elsewhere, an instance of one such festival may be preserved in the Campstool Fresco. Might not the Campstool Fresco be commemorating women's role as distributor of goods, manager of the economy, and organizer of the festivals of gift-giving that drove the economy? As I said in Chapter 6, authorities agree that in general, the frescoes illustrate the importance of women in all aspects of Minoan society. Could this fresco be illustrating women's and the Mother Goddess's ceremonial and celebratory centrality in the matriarchal economy? I think it is.

Goettner-Abendroth's definition of matriarchy at the political level and its application to Minoan Crete

Turning now to the political aspect of Goettner-Abendroth's definition of matriarchy, in her 2007 work, *The Way into an Egalitarian Society: Principles of a Matriarchal Politics*, she defines the political organizational pattern of a traditional matriarchal society as one in which decision making is organized along kinship lines. According to Goettner-Abendroth, in such a society, decision making starts in the individual clan house, where women and men make decisions, then moves to the village level and finally to the regional level. At each level a consensus, meaning unanimity, is reached. Thus delegates move back and forth between individual clan houses and the village council, and then between the village and regional councils until consensus occurs.

> It is quite evident that such a society cannot develop hierarchies or classes, and neither can a power gap between the genders or generations develop. There, on the political level I define matriarchies as egalitarian societies of consensus.[93]

This lack of hierarchies or entrenched power structures that Goettner-Abendroth describes is something most Aegean archaeologists find incomprehensible. I believe that is why they prefer to remain committed to the monarchist view of Minoan Crete, or to turn to factions as a way to make sense of the evidence.

I indicated in my discussion of the economic system of Minoan Crete that there is evidence for clan houses, especially in Malia and Palaikastro, as well as evidence that certain buildings

---

[91] Rehak 1995: 112.
[92] Because of the size of the female figures, it could be argued they are Goddesses.
[93] Goettner-Abendroth 2007: 5. A contemporary example of this is the Kuna Indians of the Kuna Yala in Panama.

within towns and villas served some special function or functions. I hypothesize that some of them would have been the meeting places of delegates working to reach consensus on various issues of importance to the population. I said above that the villas could very well have been the meeting places for regional level meetings and consensus making. That political function, in addition to their economic function, could explain the archaeological evidence found in them for administration, record keeping, and ceremony. It should be remembered that Rehak and Younger proposed the existence of a 'Queen's council' based on the benches unearthed at one of the villas.

As for the political function of the towns, one must keep in mind that Driessen posited that the layout of many Minoan towns, especially those containing temple-palaces, was dictated by the fact that they were inter-regional meeting places.[94] Hamilakis observed of Crete in the Neopalatial period that there was 'a lack of evidence for rigid social, political, and administrative hierarchies.'[95] His observation that there were no walls or spatial separation between monumental buildings and 'commoner's' residences[96] would be further evidence in support for a government of consensus, as would the wide distribution of recordkeeping, which in the eyes of archaeologists, is evidence for the wide distribution of authority.

As for the temple-palaces, I would posit they were not the seat of an all powerful priest-king, nor the location where factions vied for power, but rather the place where regional representatives met to reach consensus on issues of importance to the whole island—plausibly, foreign trade would be an example of the type of issues decided at this level. The long history and importance of the temple-palaces as sacred, ritual centers that I detailed above, would make them ideally suited for this role. Perhaps some of the archaeological evidence for feasting, drinking, and toasting found in the temple-palaces might be explained in terms of simple celebrations after having reached consensus on important decisions. In Chapter 6, I noted that Rehak and Younger, discussing the role of women in Minoan society, pointed out that benches flanked the lustral basin in the Throne Rooms at Knossos.[97] They wondered if 'a powerful woman on the throne at Knossos [was] flanked by male counselors.'[98] I would argue that the woman on the throne at Knossos was an elder clan mother who was an inter-regional leader, and that the benches adjacent to the lustral basin were for regional delegates coming to Knossos to report on what their clans, villages, and regions had decided. With the help of the elder clan mother[s], the delegates would work to reach a consensus at the island-wide level.

Both Peter Warren and Philip Betancourt[99] in defending their traditional, centralized power view of Minoan society have argued that the lack of fortifications is strong evidence for a central authority. I would maintain that the lack of fortifications, and the generally acknowledged peacefulness of Bronze Age Crete, could argue at least as well for the model Goettner-Abendroth has provided. For in a society based on consensus, what need is there of fortifications? And indeed, the lack of fortifications, as well as the lack of military/warfare scenes in Minoan art would also argue against intense struggles between competing factions—thus seriously calling into question both Schoep's and Hamilakis' hypothesis.

---

[94] Driessen 2009: 51.
[95] Hamilakis 2002: 187.
[96] Hamilakis 2002: 191.
[97] Younger and Rehak 2008: 182.
[98] Younger and Rehak 2008: 182.
[99] Betancourt 2002: 207-211; Warren 2002: 201-205.

My analysis of the Minoan temple-palaces in their political role receives support from archaeologist Jan Driessen. I find that some of his thinking and hypothesizing about the purpose of 'Minoan court compounds,' the term he prefers to palaces or temple-palaces (discussed below) is in line with Goettner-Abendroth's vision of how matriarchal societies are organized politically.

In his paper '"The King Must Die." Some Observations on the Use of Minoan Court Compounds,' in the 2002 publication, *Monuments of Minos: Rethinking the Minoan Palaces*, Driessen ostensibly is tackling the problem of the missing Minoan ruler. Observing that male images that could be construed as royal figures in pre-LM IB Crete are extremely rare[100] (he does not discuss or even seem to consider female ones), Driessen argues that the absence of such iconography argues for the absence of royalty as well. As supporting evidence for his claim that there was no Minoan 'royalty,' Driessen points to the fact that in none of the Minoan 'court compounds,' do circulation patterns lead to a 'chamber of audience,' rather they lead to the central court. Another piece of supporting evidence is the fact that no royal burials have been found before those at Archanes from the Third Palace, or Creto-Mycenaean era. By *royal burial* Driessen means 'that a single internment received so much attention in the way of energy investment in the tomb construction and offerings that set him or her apart from his or her contemporaries.'[101]

Driessen goes on to ask if the well-known definition of a Minoan palace as a 'combination of residential, political, religious and public functions and usually an important economic function ... is really the case.'[102] His answer is no. Rather he views the 'court compounds' as 'communal buildings without a primary political and residential function but still serving as the main political arena, erected by a community for the fulfilling of religious and ritual tasks.'[103] Ultimately Driessen argues that Minoan Crete has a 'corporate' orientation. Rather than being controlled by a few high-ranking individuals, 'decisions are made in assemblies made up of the constituent groups of a society whereas resolutions are implemented by a specialized, nondurative administrative staff, selected or chosen according to personal qualities.'[104]

Driessen goes on to develop some of these ideas further in 'A Matrilocal House Society in Pre- and Protopalatial Crete?' which is discussed below.

Reading Driessen I find myself comparing his understanding of the function of the 'court compound' or temple-palace to Goettner-Abendroth's definition of a matriarchal society in its political aspect. While in 'The King Must Die' Driessen certainly does not claim that Crete was a matriarchy, and indeed ignores possible representations of important women, his discussion of the function of 'court compounds' begins to approach Goettner-Abendroth's definition of matriarchal organizational patterns at the level of politics. The 'court compounds' Driessen describes seem to me to be the ideal location for inter-regional or regional meetings of clan representatives to discuss any differences until a consensus can be reached, and their decisions implemented.

---

[100] Driessen 2002: 6.
[101] Driessen 2002: 5.
[102] Driessen 2002: 6.
[103] Driessen 2002: 13.
[104] Driessen 2002: 11.

The preceding paragraphs have argued that a plausible case can be made to validate the hypothesis that Bronze Age Crete was a matriarchal society based on the economic and political levels of Goettner-Abendroth's definition of matriarchy. I want now to turn to the social aspect of her definition.

Goettner-Abendroth's definition of matriarchy at the social level and its application to Minoan Crete

Goettner-Abendroth's definition of matriarchal societies at the social level is that they are: 'based on matrilinear kinship, whose characteristics are matrilinearity and matrilocality within the framework of gender equality. Therefore I defined them as non-hierarchical horizontal societies of matrilineal kinship.'[105]

I indicated in Chapter 6 that the Law Code of Gortyn has been interpreted to include the possibility that a matrilineal/matrilocal Crete existed on the basis of a woman's right to own and dispose of property, and the importance placed on a woman's brother in the raising of her children, referred to as an avunculate. The ease with which women could divorce is interpreted as another indication that at one time Crete was a matrilineal/matrilocal society.

In a recent paper entitled, 'A Matrilocal House Society in Pre-and Protopalatial Crete?' Driessen describes a social organization not so far different from the definition that Goettner-Abendroth has offered. He argues that Pre-and Proto-palatial Crete (the period covering c. 2600 BC to c. 1700 BC) was organized along matrilocal lines. Driessen grounds his argument in a number of factors. He first establishes, based on both archaeological and anthropological data, that 'groups that were intergenerationally focusing on spatially fixed loci in the landscape formed the main social component of Minoan society during the Pre-and Protopalatial periods.'[106] Driessen calls these groups 'established houses.' The house should not be understood merely as an architectural structure, but rather it refers, as Driessen uses the term, to 'an enduring social group that is materially represented by a physical structure and the objects that go with it – furnishings, curated heirlooms and graves – within a designated locus in the landscape.'[107] This last part of the definition, that 'established houses,' have a 'designated locus in the landscape' refers to the fact that they have very strong ties to the land and locality. It is this tie to the land and locality which contributes to a sense of kinship among members of the 'established house'. 'Established houses' are always multigenerational.

Driessen acknowledges that archaeologists are hesitant to ask how such groups were organized internally, 'because kinship is not material in nature.'[108] Nevertheless, he believes it is important to ask the question and attempt some answers. When Driessen looks at the material record of Minoan Crete, he finds there is evidence which gives us some ideas about descent and that that evidence points to matrilocality and matrilineality.

The first indication of a matrilineal and matrilocal Minoan Crete is dwelling size. Driessen examines archaeological evidence noting that matrilocal societies have significantly larger

---

[105] Goettner-Abendroth 2012: xxv.
[106] Driessen, 'Matrilocal House Society?', sec. The Established House, para. 6.
[107] Driessen, 'Matrilocal House Society?', sec. The Established House, para. 6. para 1.
[108] Driessen, 'Matrilocal House Society?', sec. The Established House, para. 6.

dwellings than patrilocal ones.[109] Dwellings larger than sixty meters in total floor space are a hallmark of Minoan settlements, according to Driessen. A second indicator of a matrilineal society is that they are characterized by horticulture and trade. Patrilineal groups, on the other hand, tend to be characterized by agriculture and pastoralism. 'In the Minoan case, the matrilineal descent principle would agree with the archaeological evidence for mixed farming with a relatively low number of livestock, which consisted mostly of sheep.'[110] The absence of intra-regional warfare also indicates to Driessen that Minoan Crete was a matrilocal and matrilineal society. This is because in such societies 'incoming males are usually from closer areas, hence resulting in regional cohesion.'[111] A third factor cited by Driessen as pointing to a matrilineal and matrilocal Minoan Crete, and a very important one for this study, are representations of the Minoan Mother Goddess and the portrayal of women in Minoan art.

> The so-called "goddess" figurines from EM IIB Fournou Korifi, the female rhyta from the Mesara tombs (Koumasa) and the Trapeza Cave or the EM III Mochlos and Malia examples can perhaps be used to corroborate the present hypothesis since they underline a female aspect that fits this scenario as do the Knossian miniature frescoes in which "women are emphasized at the expense of men in fullness of portrayal and in position."[112]

With Driessen's work we have come a long way from priest-kings, and have found an implicit acknowledgement of the preeminence of the Goddess and of women in Pre-and Protopalatial Crete. Although Driessen makes no claims for matriarchy, he does assert that in a society such as the type he has described for Pre-and Protopalatial Minoan Crete, 'there is no real arena in which men can build [political] power bases.'[113] And most importantly for Goettner-Abendroth's definition, Driessen has provided archaeological evidence to show that a good case can be made for considering Bronze Age Crete a matrilineal/matrilocal society in the Pre-and Protopalatial periods.

Driessen first broached the subject of clans and larger kinship groups in a 2011 article authored in conjunction with Hubert Fiasse, '"Burning Down the House," Defining the Household of Quartier Nu at Malia Using GIS.' Here Driessen and his colleague discuss in detail the building designated as Quartier Nu, in the town adjacent to the temple-palace of Malia in north-eastern Crete. Excavated by the French Archaeological School between 1988 and 1993, Quartier Nu is approximately twenty by thirty-two meters in size and organized around a central court. It was occupied for approximately five hundred years from MM II, c. 1900-1700 BC to LM IIIA2, c. 1450-1340/30 BC when it was destroyed by an earthquake. It was reoccupied from LM IIIB, c. 1340/30 until 1190 BC.

---

[109] Driessen here refers to a work by Cutting 2006: 225-246, and writes 'Where domestic scale is concerned, Cutting . . . has stated that whenever a structure exceeds 70 m, its residents probably were an extended family. She insists that, rather than wealth, the size of the structure reflects the size of the group occupying it' (Driessen, 'Matrilocal House Society?' sec. Was the Minoan established house matrilineal and matrilocal?, para.1). Driessen goes on to say that 'Halstead and Whitelaw independently also consider 70 m as a relevant maximum size for basic households, but many Minoan residential complexes have a much larger surface' (Driessen, 'Matrilocal House Society?' sec. Was the Minoan established house matrilineal and matrilocal?, para.1). The works he is referring to are Halstead 1999: 77-95 and Whitelaw 2001b: 15-37 and 2001a: 174-179.

[110] Driessen, 'Matrilocal House Society?' sec. Was the Minoan established house matrilineal, and matrilocal? para. 3.

[111] Driessen, 'Matrilocal House Society?' sec. Was the Minoan established house matrilineal, and matrilocal? para. 3.

[112] Driessen, 'Matrilocal House Society?' sec. Was the Minoan established house matrilineal, and matrilocal? para. 4.

[113] Driessen, 'Matrilocal House Society?' sec. Was the Minoan established house matrilineal, and matrilocal? para. 3.

Using Geographic Information Software, as well as ArcView Software, Driessen and Fiasse looked at the location, elevation, and material/type/shape of movable objects found within the building. Based on this information, and the architecture itself, they concluded that Quartier Nu was 'the archaeological reflection of a house group—a *stratos* or clan building consisting of two or three *oikoi*.'[114] Elaborating, they write,

> The close relationship between the different units, the sharing of communal space, especially the presence of a single central ritual area and pits that clearly served as *favissae* [ritual deposits] for the entire complex, as well as a single kitchen linked to a major grinding installation, . . . also corroborates this hypothesis.[115]

In sum, the evidence at Quartier Nu suggests to Driessen and Fiasse

> that the complex was occupied by a single extended household with different family units, perhaps with some gender and or status differentiation among members, but with sufficient parental links to share a single complex with a single kitchen and a single court used for ceremonies.[116]

Driessen and Fiasse also make the important point in this article that excavations in recent years have revealed that for the Postpalatial LM IIIA2-B, the subsequent Dark Ages, and historical Crete, 'larger compounds with interrelated units' and extensive complexes can be 'best interpreted' as 'extended family or clan buildings.'[117] Thus there is archaeological evidence for clans from the Early Minoan period to that of historical Crete. While in this article Driessen and Fiasse do not make the claim that Quartier Nu was the home of a matrilineal/matrilocal clan, nevertheless I think it is significant that the two have argued for the existence of a clan dwelling at all, for the more usual or typical way of looking at Neopalatial Minoan social structure is to see it formed of nuclear families with the unspoken assumption that the nuclear families had patriarchs at their heads and there was a corresponding patriarchal organization.[118]

Archaeologist Carl Knappett supports Driessen's argument for the existence of clan houses, writing of the town of Palaikastro in eastern Crete, which averages houses of 215 meters in the Neopalatial period, that

> It seems possible . . . that the greater scale could represent a higher level social unit, such as an extended family, with these large households for extended family groups scaling up into 'clan' house blocks.[119]

---

[114] Driessen and Fiasse 2011: 296.
[115] Driessen and Fiasse 2011: 295.
[116] Driessen and Fiasse 2011: 295.
[117] Driessen and Fiasse 2011: 296. Those sites include: Kavousi, Vronda, Chalasmenos, Vasiliki Kephala, Azoria and Smari for the Dark Ages and historical period, and Amnisos, Gouves, Kephali Choudrou and Palaikastro for the Postminoan period (Driessen and Fiasse 2011: 286).
[118] For example, in the same volume, Murphy writes of south-central Crete that settlements were clearly divided into individual household units which could only accommodate nuclear families (Murphy 2011: 112-126). Whitelaw has argued for nuclear families at Fournou Korifi (Myrtos) in eastern Crete (Whitelaw 2001b: 15-37).
[119] Knappett 2009: 21.

Knappett also asks if the large deposits of drinking cups found in some of these large households 'might have been used in ceremonies for cementing intra-family relations within the extended family and clan groupings.'[120] This is a significant point in opposition to the Schoep/Hamilakis factions hypothesis.

While the evidence is not yet conclusive, I find it encouraging that some archaeologists are now reconsidering the assumption that Crete must have had nuclear, patriarchal households during the Neopalatial period. I believe that the archaeological evidence that does exist for extended families, or clans and matrilinearlity and matrilocality in Minoan Crete, along with the provisions in the Gortyn Code; the wealth of iconographic evidence Driessen mentions above and which I discussed in Chapter 5; and the mythology regarding Goddesses and heroines that I detailed in Chapter 6; as well as the mythology around Cretan Zeus detailed in Chapter 4; along with the economic and political evidence presented in this chapter, makes the social level of Goettner-Abendroth's definition of matriarchy entirely plausible for Bronze Age Crete.

Goettner-Abendroth's definition of matriarchy at the spiritual level and its application to Minoan Crete

It now remains to look at the final aspect of Goettner-Abendroth's definition: the spiritual:

> On the spiritual level, I define matriarchies as **sacred societies as cultures of the Goddess or Divine Feminine.**[emphasis in original] In matriarchy, divinity is immanent, for the whole world is regarded as divine—as feminine divine. This is evident in the concept of the universe as a Goddess who created everything, and as Mother Earth who brings forth everything living. And everything is endowed with divinity, each woman and man, each plant and animal. . . . In such a culture, . . . everything is spiritual. . . . There is no separation between sacred and secular; therefore all the everyday tasks . . . have at the same time ritual significance.[121]

The spiritual level is perhaps the easiest of all the aspects of Goettner-Abendroth's definition to substantiate for Minoan Crete.

In Chapter 5, I demonstrated that in Minoan Crete, from the Neolithic to the Postpalatial, *c.* 6500-1070 BC, a period spanning some five thousand years, a Goddess was worshipped as the primary deity. She was a Goddess who embodied power and protection, mediated between life, death, and rebirth, the known and the unknown, and had power within all nature. She was the Goddess in her triple aspect: Life-Giver, Death-Wielder, and Regeneratrix. We also saw in Chapter 5 that the Mother Goddess of Minoan Crete was identified with all of nature. Using Goettner-Abendroth's terms, I would suggest that this means the Minoans regarded the whole world as divine, as originating in the Feminine Divine. I believe I am corroborated in this understanding by the works of the archaeologists I cited in Chapter 4. Archaeologist Gesell called the Minoan Goddess a universal Mother or Earth Goddess, Protectress of the Sky, and chthonic deity; Marinatos emphasized the Minoan Goddess's role as a Goddess of Nature and a Nurturer of Nature; Moss, viewing the Minoan Goddess as the Many, referred to her as Bird

---

[120] Knappett 2009: 22.
[121] Goettner-Abendroth 2007: 6.

Goddess, Goddess of the Dead, Dove Goddess, Healing Goddess, Goddess of Initiation, Mountain Mother, Goddess of Renewal, Snake Goddess, Stellar Goddess, and Goddess of Vegetation/Agriculture.

I think the lack of separation between sacred and secular is evident not only in the Mother Goddess and her aspects, but in where and how the Minoans chose to worship their Mother Goddess. The Goddess was worshipped at the tomb, peak sanctuary, cave, temple-palace, and, very importantly, in the household. The fact that her worship took place virtually everywhere is one indication, I think, of the merging of the sacred and secular in Minoan life. She was all of nature, Mother Nature herself, Life-Giver, Death-Wielder, Regeneratrix; worshipped in the open air, in the town, the country, the cave, and the mountain top, and in the temple-palaces—how could she not be immanent and part of everyday life?

The seals, rings, and frescoes reinforce this sense of her worship everywhere, and they give us a sense of how she was worshipped—she was visualized in human form and presented with crocuses, or saluted; in the form of a baetyl or sacred tree she was hugged and venerated; votive offerings were left in her womb—the depths of her caves; on the tops of her mountains she was the Mountain Mother—where people came for physical and psychological healing. As Rohrlich-Leavitt has so aptly put it speaking of Crete, religion was 'the institution that integrated Bronze Age life.'[122]

Conclusion: based on Goettner-Abendroth's definition of matriarchy, Minoan Crete was a matriarchal society

This chapter has drawn together the evidence presented in this book to argue that a plausible and highly probable case can be made for Minoan Crete as a matriarchal society based on Goettner-Abendroth's definition of matriarchy. Admittedly, some aspects of that definition as they are applied to Crete are more easily substantiated than others.

That Minoan Crete fulfills the spiritual aspect of Goettner-Abendroth's definition, based on the evidence presented in Chapters 4 and 5, is the most persuasive. I think that there can be no doubt that the archaeological evidence presents us with a Mother Goddess, a Female Divine, who endowed everything with divinity.

That the social system of Minoan Crete was 'based on matrilinear kinship, whose characteristics are matrilinearity and matrilocality within the framework of gender equality,' and that it was a 'non-hierarchical horizontal society of matrilineal kinship,'[123] finds support in some of the most current archaeological literature investigating the nature of the Minoan social system, especially in the work of Jan Driessen which I discussed at length above. Support for a matrilocal and matrilinear Minoan Crete is also found in provisions of the Law Code of Gortyn, in the mythology, and in the iconography, particularly in the preeminence of women in the Minoan frescoes. This book makes a strong case for Minoan Crete as a woman-centered society, which a society must be if it is to be defined as matrilineal and matrilocal.

---

[122] Rohrlich-Leavitt 1977: 48.
[123] Goettner-Abendroth 2012: xxv.

One aspect of the social component of Goettner-Abendroth's definition must be addressed further and that is the component of gender equality. To my knowledge, no Aegeanist has used the term 'gender equality' to describe Minoan Crete. As I pointed out in Chapter 7, Aegeanists, with few exceptions, still think in terms of male rulers, and even when they posit shared rulership, the male aspect of the partnership is emphasized. In the literature patriarchy is taken for granted, and the issue of relations between genders is rarely addressed. While I have emphasized the centrality of women in Minoan society, I do not believe that that centrality precludes gender equality, but gender equality is a difficult concept to tease out of the iconography. One gets an intuition of gender equality. In my study of the iconography I do not get a sense of either women or men dominating, but at this point it seems impossible for me to say more than gender equality is plausible for Minoan Crete.[124]

In their political aspect, Goettner-Abendroth defines matriarchies as

> societies based on consensus. The clan house is the basis of decision making both locally and regionally, . . . the politics of strict consensus processes give rise not only to gender equality, but to equality in the entire society. Therefore, I define them as *egalitarian societies of consensus.* [emphasis in original][125]

I have attempted to argue, based on archaeological evidence for clan houses; de-centralized record keeping and administration; the lack of spatial separation between monumental buildings and ordinary ones; the lack of fortifications in general; the evidence of benches at Ayia Triadha and Knossos; the communal as well as sacred nature of the temple-palaces; the new understanding of the Minoan villas as the centers of settlements where manufacturing, administration, and ceremony took place, rather than as the dwelling places of the aristocracy; and the archaeological as well as mythological and iconographical evidence for matrilineality and matrilocality, that such a political system for Minoan Crete is entirely plausible, and is more plausible than the traditional view of a strong centralized hierarchical structure, monarchy and aristocracy, or the recent alternative proposed by the factions theory.

As regards the economic level of Goettner-Abendroth's four-part definition of matriarchy, I have proposed that the new studies investigating the archaeological evidence for clan dwellings; the new understanding of the Minoan villas as centers of regional manufacturing, administration, and ceremony; recent works detailing the temple-palaces as communal buildings connected to their surrounding towns and countryside by ceremonial routes; the lack of archaeological evidence for private property, especially of privately held land; the archaeological evidence for feasting, drinking, and toasting; the provisions of the Law Code of Gortyn regarding the economic role of women; current archaeological literature investigating the nature of Minoan social systems, especially matrilocality and matrilinearity; the legends, as detailed by Witcombe, that reveal the matrilocal/matrilineal roots of Minoan Crete; and the iconography, particularly the frescoes that show women managing eating and drinking ceremonies, all plausibly support the hypothesis that Minoan Crete had a balanced economy in which women distributed goods and practiced economic mutuality and gift-giving.

---

[124] For a different point of view see Poole 2020.
[125] Goettner-Abendroth 2012: xxv.

In arguing for envisioning a Minoan Crete that corresponds to Goettner-Abendroth's definition of matriarchy, I have used the term 'plausibly' because we lack the written records that might tell us, in their own words, how the Minoan economic system functioned, how they governed themselves, what relations between men and women were like, or what their Goddess meant to them. In many ways the statement Ellen Davis made twenty-five years ago about Minoan society still rings true: 'Its unique character [she was referring here to Minoan art] must reflect a unique society. It seems to me it is one that we have yet to understand.'[126] I believe that Goettner-Abendroth's definition of matriarchy allows us a greater understanding of that unique society than heretofore has been possible. At the very least, her definition, and the development of modern matriarchal studies as a discipline, allows scholars to advance the discussion, as to whether or not Minoan Crete was a matriarchal society, toward a more complex, detailed, and certain conclusion.

---

[126] Davis 1995: 19.

References

Allen, Paula Gunn. 1992. *The Sacred Hoop: Recovering the Feminine in American Indian Traditions.* Boston: Beacon Press.

Andrikou, Eleni. 1997. Thoughts and Considerations on the Mycenaeanisation of Crete Motivated by Pottery from Archanes, in Jan Driessen and Alexandre Farnoux (eds) *La Crète Mycénienne: Actes de la Table Ronde Internationale Organisée par l'École Française d'Athènes*: 9-22. Athens: École Française d'Athènes.

Apostalaki, Emmanouela. 2020. Whom the House Concerned: Land Ownership and Lines of Descent in Prehistoric Crete, in Maria Relaki and Jan Driessen (eds) *Oikos: Archaeological Approaches to House Societies in Aegean Prehistory* (*Aegis 19* Actes de Colloques): 97-120. Louvain: Presses Universitaires Louvain.

Arnott, W. Geoffrey. 1993. Bull-leaping as Initiation. *Liverpool Classical Monthly* 18: 114-116.

Atchity, Kenneth, and E. J. W. Barber. 1987. Greek Princes and Aegean Princesses: The Role of Women in the Homeric Poems, in Kenneth Atchity (ed.) *Critical Essays on Homer*: 15-37. Boston: G. K. Hall.

Bachofen, J. J. 1967. *Myth, Religion and Mother Right: The Selected Writings of J. J. Bachofen.* Ralph Manheim (trans.). Princeton (NJ): Princeton University Press.

Bachofen, J. J. 2003. *An English Translation of Bachofen's Mutterrecht (Mother Right)* (1861). David Partenheimer (trans.). Lewiston (NY): Edwin Mellen Press.

Bamberger, Joan. 1974. The Myth of Matriarchy: Why Men Rule in Primitive Society, in Michelle Rosaldo and Louise Lamphere (eds) *Woman, Culture and Society*: 263-280. Stanford (CA): Stanford University Press.

Baring, Anne, and Jules Cashford. 1991. *The Myth of the Goddess: Evolution of an Image.* London: Arkana.

Bell, Lanny. 1985. The Luxor Temple and the Cult of the Royal Ka. *Journal of Near Eastern Studies* 44: 251-294.

Betancourt, Philip. 2002. Who Was in Charge of the Palaces? in Jan Driessen, Ilse Schoep, and Robert Laffineur (eds) *Monuments of Minos: Rethinking the Minoan Palaces*, (Proceedings of the International Workshop 'Crete of the Hundred Palaces?' Université Catholique de Louvain-la-Neuve, 14-15 December 2001. *Aegaeum 23*): 1: 207-211. Liège: Université de Liège, Histoire de l'art et archéologie de la Grèce antique; Austin: University of Texas at Austin, Program in Aegean Scripts and Prehistory.

Bietak, Manfred. 2000. Rich Beyond the Dreams of Avaris: Tell el-Dab'a and the Aegean World—A Guide for the Perplexed: A Response to Eric H. Cline. *The Annual of the British School at Athens* 95: 165-208.

Bietak, Manfred. 2008. Minoan Artists at the Court of Avaris. in Joan Aruz, Kim Benzel, and Jean M. Evans (eds) *Beyond Babylon: Art, Trade and Diplomacy in the Second Millennium BC*: 110-118. New York: Metropolitan Museum of Art.

Bietak, Manfred, and Nanno Marinatos. 1995. The Minoan Wall Paintings from Avaris. *Egypt and the Levant* 5: 49-59.

Bietak, Manfred, and Nanno Marinatos. 2000. Avaris (Tell el Dab'a) and the Minoan World, in A. Karetsou (ed.) *Krete Aigyptos: Politismikoi-Desmoi Trion Chilietion*: 40-45. Athens: Kapon Editions.

Bietak, Manfred, Nanno Marinatos, and Clairy Palivou. 2007. *Taureador Scenes in Tell el Dab'a and Knossos.* (Österreichische Akademie der Wissenschaffen Denkschriften der Gesamtakademie 43). Vienna: Verlag der Österreichische Akademie der Wissenschaffen.

Branigan, Keith. 1993. *Dancing with Death: Life and Death in Southern Crete, c. 3000-2000 B.C.* Amsterdam: Adolf M. Hakkert.

Budin, Stephanie. 2003. *The Origin of Aphrodite.* Bethesda, (MD): CDL Press.

Budin, Stephanie. 2005. Minoan Asherah? in Joanne Clarke (ed.) *Archaeological Perspectives on the Transmission and Transformation of Culture in the Eastern Mediterranean:* 188-197. Oxford: Oxbow Books.

Cadogan, Gerald. 1980. *The Palaces of Minoan Crete.* London: Meuthen.

Cadogan, Gerald. 2009. Gender Metaphors of Social Stratigraphy in Pre-Linear B Crete or Is Minoan Gynaecocracy (Still) Credible? in Katerina Kopaka (ed.) *Fylo: Engendering Prehistoric 'Stratigraphies' in the Aegean and the Mediterranean* (Proceedings of an International Conference, University of Crete, Rethymno, 2-5 June 2005, *Aegaeum 30*): 225-232. Liège: Université de Liège, Histoire de l'art et archéologie de la Grèce antique; Austin: University of Texas at Austin, Program in Aegean Scripts and Prehistory.

Cain, C. D. 2001. Dancing in the Dark: Deconstructing a Narrative of Epiphany on the Isopata Ring. *American Journal of Archaeology* 105 (1): 27-49.

Cameron, M.A.S. 1970. New Restorations of Minoan Frescoes from Knossos. *The Bulletin of the Institute of Classical Studies of the University of London* 17: 163-166.

Cameron, M.A.S. 1980. Theoretical Interrelations among Theran, Cretan and Mainland Frescoes, in C. Doumas (ed.) *Thera and the Aegean World II: Papers and Proceedings of the Second International Scientific Congress, Santorini, Greece, August, 1978:* 315-317. London: Thera and the Aegean World.

Cameron, M.A.S. 1987. The 'Palatial' Thematic System in the Knossos Murals: Last Notes on the Knossos Frescoes, in Robin Hägg and Nanno Marinatos (eds) *The Function of the Minoan Palaces* (Proceedings of the Fourth International Symposium at the Swedish Institute in Athens, 10-16 June, 1984): 323-325. Stockholm: Svenska Institutet i Athen.

Carter, Susan Gail. 2001. Amaterasu-O-Mi-Kami: Past and Present. An Exploration of the Japanese Sun Goddess from a Western Feminist Perspective. PhD diss., California Institute of Integral Studies. ProQuest (3004465).

Castleden, Rodney. 1990. *The Knossos Labyrinth: A New View of the 'Palace of Minos' at Knossos.* London: Routledge.

Chapin, Anne P. 2004. Power, Privilege and Landscape in Minoan Art, in Anne P. Chapin (ed.) *Charis: Essays in Honor of Sara A. Immerwahr:* 47-64. Athens: American School of Classical Studies at Athens.

Christ, Carol P. 1987. *The Laughter of Aphrodite: Reflections on a Journey to the Goddess.* San Francisco: Harper & Row.

Christ, Carol P. 1995. *Odyssey with the Goddess: A Spiritual Quest in Crete.* New York: Continuum.

Christ, Carol P. 1997a. 'A Different World': The Challenge of the Work of Marija Gimbutas to the Dominant Worldview of Western Culture, in Joan Marler (ed.) *From the Realm of the Ancestors: An Anthology in Honor of Marija Gimbutas:* 406-415. Manchester (CT): Knowledge, Ideas & Trends.

Christ, Carol P. 1997b. *Rebirth of the Goddess: Finding Meaning in Feminist Spirituality.* Reading (MA): Addison-Wesley.

Cichon, Alexandra, K. 2016. Ariadne, Mistress of the Labyrinth: Reclaiming Ariadnian Crete, in Marion Dumont and Gayatri Devi (eds) *Myths Shattered and Restored: Proceedings of the*

Association for the Study of Women and Mythology: 78-99. Albuquerque, NM: Women and Myth Press.

Cline, Eric H. 1998. Rich Beyond the Dreams of Avaris: Tell el-Dab'a and the Aegean World—A Guide for the Perplexed. *The Annual of the British Schools at Athens* 93: 199-219.

Crowley, Janice. 1995. Images of Power in the Bronze Age Aegean, in Robert Laffineur and W-D. Niemeier (eds) *Politeia: Society and State in the Aegean Bronze Age* (Proceedings of the 5th International Aegean Conference, University of Heidelberg, Archäologisches Institut, 10-13 April 1994, *Aegaeum 12*): 475-491. Liège: Université de Liège, Histoire de l'art et archéologie de la Grèce antique; Austin: University of Texas at Austin, Program in Aegean Scripts and Prehistory.

Csapo, Eric. 2005. *Theories of Mythology*. Malden (MA): Blackwell.

Cutting, Marion. 2006. More Than One Way to Study a Building: Approaches to Prehistoric Household and Settlement Space. *Oxford Journal of Archaeology* 25: 225-246.

D'Agata, Anna Lucia. 2009. Introduction: How Many Archaeologies of Cult? in Anna Lucia D'Agata and Aleydis Van de Moortel (eds) *Archaeologies of Cult: Essays on Ritual and Cult in Crete in Honor of Geraldine C. Gesell* (Hesperia Supplement 42): 1-8. Princeton (NJ): American School of Classical Studies.

Damini Indelicato, Silvia. 1988. Were Cretan Girls Playing at Bull-leaping? *Cretan Studies* 1: 39-47.

Dashu, Max. 2000. Knocking Down Straw Dolls: A Critique of Cynthia Eller's 'The Myth of Matriarchal Prehistory: Why an Invented Past Won't Give Women a Future.' The Suppressed Histories Archives, viewed July 17, 2020, https: //www.suppressedhistories.net/articles/strawdolls.html

Davis, Ellen N. 1995. Art and Politics in the Aegean: The Missing Ruler, in Paul Rehak (ed.) *The Role of the Ruler in the Prehistoric Aegean* (Proceedings of a Panel Discussion Presented at the Annual Meeting of the Archaeological Institute of America, New Orleans, Louisiana, 28 December 1992, *Aegaeum 11*): 11-22. Liège: Université de Liège, Histoire de l'art et archéologie de la Grèce antique; Austin: University of Texas at Austin, Program in Aegean Scripts and Prehistory.

Davaras, Costis. 1975. Early Minoan Jewellery from Mochlos. *The Annual of the British School at Athens* 70: 101-114.

Davaras, Costis. 1976. *Guide to Cretan Antiquities*. Park Ridge (NJ): Noyes Press.

Day, Peter M., Louise Joyner, Vassilis Kilikoglou, and Geraldine C. Gesell. 2006. Goddesses, Snake Tubes and Plaques: Analysis of Ceramic Ritual Objects from the LM IIIC Shrine at Kavousi. *Hesperia* 75: 137-175.

Day, Peter M., and David E. Wilson. 2002. Landscapes of Memory, Craft and Power in Prepalatial and Protopalatial Knossos, in Yannis Hamilakis (ed.) *The Labyrinth Revisited: Rethinking Minoan Archaeology*: 143-166. Oxford: Oxbow Press.

Dexter, Miriam Robbins. 1990. *Whence the Goddesses: A Sourcebook*. New York: Pergamon Press.

Dickinson, O. T. P. K. 1994. *The Aegean Bronze Age*. Cambridge: Cambridge University Press.

Dickinson, S. K. 1976. 'Letter.' *Arethusa* 9: 119-120.

Dimopoulou-Rethemiotakis, Nota. 2005. The Archaeological Museum of Herakleion. John S. Latsis Public Benefit Foundation, viewed July 17, 2020, https://www.latsis-foundation.org/content/elib/book_12/heraklion_en.pdf

Doumas, Christos. 1992. *The Wall Paintings of Thera*. Athens: The Thera Foundation.

Downing, Marymay. 1985. Prehistoric Goddesses: The Cretan Challenge. *Journal of Feminist Studies in Religion* 1 (1): 7-22.

Driessen, Jan. 2002. 'The King Must Die.' Some Observations on the Use of Minoan Court Compounds, in Jan Driessen, Ilse Schoep, and Robert Laffineur (eds) *Monuments of Minos: Rethinking the Minoan Palaces* (Proceedings of the International Workshop 'Crete of the Hundred Palaces?' Université Catholique de Louvain, Louvain-la-Neuve, 14-15 December 2001, *Aegaeum 23*): 1-14. Liège: Université de Liège, Histoire de l'art et archéologie de la Grèce antique; Austin: University of Texas at Austin, Program in Aegean Scripts and Prehistory.

Driessen, Jan. 2009. Daidalos' Designs and Ariadne's Threads: Minoan Towns as Places of Interaction, in Sara Owen and Laura Preston (eds) *Inside the City in the Greek World: Studies in Urbanism from the Bronze Age to the Hellenistic Period*: 41-54. Oxford: Oxbow Books.

Driessen, Jan. 2011. The Goddess and the Skull: Some Observations on Group Identity in Prepalatial Crete, in Olga Krzyszkowska (ed.) *Cretan Offerings: Studies in Honour of Peter Warren*: 107-117. London: The British School at Athens.

Driessen, Jan. 2012. A Matrilocal House Society in Pre-and Protopalatial Crete? Academia.edu., viewed July 17, 2020. www.academia.edu/455197/A_Protopalatial_Matrilocal_Minoan_society.

Driessen, Jan, and Hubert Fiasse. 2011. 'Burning Down the House: ' Defining the Household of Quartier Nu at Malia Using GIS, in Kevin T. Glowacki and Natalia Vogelkoff-Brogan (eds) *Stega: the Archaeology of Houses and Households in Ancient Crete* (Hesperia Supplement 44): 285-296. Princeton (NJ): American School of Classical Studies at Athens.

Driessen, Jan, and Colin F. MacDonald. 1997. *The Troubled Island: Minoan Crete Before and After the Santorini Eruption* (*Aegaeum 17*) Liège: Université de Liège, Histoire de l'art et archéologie de la Grèce antique; Austin: University of Texas at Austin, Program in Aegean Scripts and Prehistory.

Driessen, Jan, and J. A. MacGillivray. 1989. The Neopalatial Period in East Crete, in Robert Laffineur (ed.) *Transition: le monde égée du bronze moyen au bronze recent* (Actes de la Deuxième Rencontre Égéen Internationale de l' Université de Liège, 18-20 April, 1988. Liège, Belgium, *Aegaeum 3*): 99-110. Liège: Université de Liège, Histoire de l'art et archéologie de la Grèce antique.

Du, Shanshan. 2002. *Chopsticks Only Work in Pairs*. New York: Columbia.

Du, Shanshan. 2009. Frameworks for Societies in Balance: A Cross-Cultural Perspective on Gender Equality, in Heide Goettner-Abendroth (ed.) *Societies of Peace: Matriarchies Past, Present, and Future*: 256-265. Toronto: Inanna Publications and Education.

Dundes, Alan. 1984. Introduction, in Alan Dundes (ed.) *Sacred Narrative: Readings in the Theory of Myth*: 1-3. Berkeley: University of California Press.

Earle, Jason W. 2010. Cosmetics and Cult Practices in the Bronze Age Aegean? A Case Study of Women with Red Ears, in Marie-Lousie Nosch and Robert Laffineur (eds) *Kosmos: Jewellery, Adornment and Textiles in the Aegean Bronze Age* (Proceedings of the 13th International Aegean Conference, 13e Rencontre Égéenne Internationale University of Copenhagen, Danish National Research Foundation's Centre for Textile Research, 21-26 April, 2010, *Aegaeum 33*): 771-778. Leuven-Liege: Peeters.

Ehrenberg, Margaret. 1989. *Women in Prehistory*. Norman: University of Oklahoma Press.

Eisler, Riane. 1987. *The Chalice and the Blade*. San Francisco: Harper & Row.

Eisler, Riane. 2008. Building Cultures of Peace: Four Cornerstones. *Off Our Backs* 38 no. 1: 44-48. Accessed February 22, 2021. http://www.jstor.org/stable/20838924.

Eisler, Riane. 2009. The Battle Over Human Possibilities, Women, Men and Cultural Transformation, in Heide Goettner-Abendroth (ed.) *Societies of Peace: Matriarchies Past, Present, and Future*: 269-282. Toronto: Inanna Publications and Education.

Elderkin, Kate McK. 1925. Aphrodite Worship on a Minoan Gem. *American Journal of Archaeology* 29: 53-58.

Eliade, Mircea. 1992. Toward a Definition of Myth, in Yves Bonnefoy (ed.) *Greek and Egyptian Mythologies*: 3-5. Chicago: University of Chicago Press.

Eller, Cynthia. 2000. *The Myth of Matriarchal Prehistory*. Boston: Beacon Press.

Engels, Friedrich. (1942) 1972. *The Origin of the Family, Private Property and the State*. New York: International Publishers.

Ergener, Resit. 1988. *Anatolia Land of Mother Goddess*. Ankara, Turkey: Hitit.

Evans, Sir Arthur. 1964. *The Palace of Minos at Knossos*. 4 vols. New York: Biblio and Tannen.

Evasdaughter, Susan. 1996. *Crete Reclaimed: A Feminist Exploration of Bronze Age Crete*. Loughborough, England: Heart of Albion Press.

Evely, Doniert. 1999. *Fresco: A Passport into the Past, Minoan Crete through the Eyes of Mark Cameron*. Athens: The British School at Athens.

Fitton, J. Lesley. 2002. *Minoans*. London: British Museum Press.

Fowden, Elizabeth. 1990. The Early Minoan Goddess: Images of Provision. *Journal of Prehistoric Religion* III-IV: 15-18.

Gadon, Elinor. 1989. *The Once and Future Goddess: A Symbol for Our Time*. San Francisco: Harper Collins.

Galankis, Yannis, Efie Tsitsa, and Ute Gunkle-Maschek. 2017. The Power of Images: Re-examining the Paintings from the Throne Room at Knossos. *The Annual of the British School at Athens* 112: 47-98.

Gesell, Geraldine C. 1985. *Town, Palace and House Cult in Minoan Crete*. (Studies in Mediterranean Archaeology 67). Göteborg, Sweden: Paul Åströms Förlag.

Gimbutas, Marija. 1974. *The Gods and Goddesses of Old Europe, 7000-3500 BC: Myths, Legends and Cult Images*. Berkeley: University of California Press.

Gimbutas, Marija. 1989. *The Language of the Goddess*. San Francisco: HarperSanFrancisco.

Gimbutas, Marija. 1991. *The Civilization of the Goddess*. San Francisco: HarperSanFrancisco.

Gimbutas, Marija. 1999. *The Living Goddesses*. Edited and Supplemented by Miriam Robbins Dexter. Berkeley: University of California Press.

Goettner-Abendroth, Heide (Göttner-Abendroth). 2007. *The Way into an Egalitarian Society: Principles and Practice of a Matriarchal Politics*. Winzer, Germany: Hagia.

Goettner-Abendroth, Heide (Göttner-Abendroth). 2009. The Deep Structure of Matriarchal Society, in Heide Goettner-Abendroth (ed.) *Societies of Peace: Matriarchies Past, Present, and Future*: 17-27. Toronto: Inanna Publications and Education.

Goettner-Abendroth, Heide (Göttner-Abendroth). 2012. *Matriarchal Societies: Studies on Indigenous Cultures Across the Globe*. New York: Peter Lang.

Goodison, Lucy. 1989. *Death, Women and the Sun: Symbolism of Regeneration in Early Aegean Religion*. (Bulletin Supplement 53). London: Institute of Classical Studies.

Goodison, Lucy. 1990. *Moving Heaven and Earth: Sexuality, Spirituality and Social Change*. London: The Women's Press.

Goodison, Lucy, and Christine Morris, 1998. Beyond the 'Great Mother': The Sacred World of the Minoans, in Lucy Goodison and Christine Morris (eds) *Ancient Goddesses: The Myth and the Evidence*: 113-132. Madison (WI): University of Wisconsin Press.

Göttner-Abendroth, Heide (Goettner-Abendroth). 1999. The Structure of Matriarchal Societies Exemplified by the Society of the Mosuo in China. *ReVision* 21 (3): 31-35.

Griffin, Wendy. 2000. Slipping Off the Sacred Lap. Review of *The Myth of Matriarchal Prehistory: Why an Invented Past Will Not Give Women a Future,* by Cynthia Eller. *The Pomegranate* 13 (Summer): 43, 48-52.

Hägg, Robin. 1997a. *The Function of the 'Minoan Villa,'* Proceedings of the Eighth International Symposium at the Swedish Institute at Athens, 6-8 June 1992. Stockholm: Paul Åströms Förlag.

Hägg, Robin. 1997b. Religious Syncretism at Knossos and in Post-Palatial Crete? in Jan Driessen and Alexandre Farnoux (eds) *La Crète Mycénienne: Actes de la Table Ronde International Organisee, par l'École Française d'Athènes, 26-28 Mars 1991 (Bulletin de Correspondance Hellenique,* Supplement 30): 163-168. Athens: École Française d'Athènes.

Hallager, Erik. 1985. *The Master Impression: A Clay Sealing from the Greek-Swedish Excavations at Kastelli, Khania* (Studies in Mediterranean Archaeology LXIV). Göteborg, Sweden: Paul Åströms Förlag.

Halstead, Paul. 1999. Neighbors from Hell? The Household in Neolithic Greece, in Paul Halstead (ed.) *Neolithic Society in Greece* (Sheffield Studies in Aegean Archaeology 2): 77-95. Sheffield: Sheffield Academic Press.

Hamilakis, Yannis. 2002. Too Many Chiefs?: Factional Competition in Neopalatial Crete, in Jan Driessen, Ilse Schoep, and Robert Laffineur (eds) *Monuments of Minos: Rethinking the Minoan Palaces* (Proceedings of the International Workshop 'Crete of the Hundred Palaces?' Université Catholique de Louvain, Louvain-la-Neuve, 14-15 December 2001, *Aegaeum 23*): 179-199. Liège: Université de Liège, Histoire de l'art et archéologie de la Grèce antique; Austin: University of Texas at Austin, Program in Aegean Scripts and Prehistory.

Hamilton, Naomi. 1996. The Personal is Political. *Cambridge Archaeological Journal* 6 (2): 282-286.

Harrison, Jane Ellen. 1913. *Themis: A Study of the Social Origins of Greek Religion.* Cambridge: Cambridge University Press.

Harrison, Jane Ellen. (1903) 1991. *Prolegomena to the Study of Greek Religion.* Princeton (NJ): Princeton University Press.

Hassan, Fekri A. 1998. The Earliest Goddesses of Egypt, in Lucy Goodison and Christine Morris (eds) *Ancient Goddesses: The Myth and the Evidence:* 98-112. Madison (WI): University of Wisconsin Press.

Hawkes, Jacquetta. 1968. *Dawn of the Gods.* New York: Random House.

Hesiod. 1977. Catalogues of Women and the Eoiae, in Hugh G. Evelyn-White (trans.) *Hesiod: The Homeric Hymns and Homerica:* 154-220. Cambridge: Harvard University Press.

Hodder, Ian. 1997. Always Momentary, Fluid and Flexible: Towards a Reflexive Excavation Methodology. *Antiquity* 71: 691-700.

Hodder, Ian. 1998. Whose Rationality? A Response to Fekri Hassan. *Antiquity* 72 (March): 213-217.

Holmström, Laurel. 2000. Review of *The Myth of Matriarchal Prehistory: Why an Invented Past Will Not Give Women a Future,* by Cynthia Eller. *The Pomegranate* 13 (Summer): 43-47.

Hood, Sinclair. 1976. The Mallia Gold Pendant. Wasps or Bees? in Frederick Emmison and Roy Stephens(eds) *Tribute to an Antiquary: Essays Presented to Marc Fitch by Some of His Friends:* 59-72. London: Leopard's Head Press.

Hood, Sinclair. 2005. Dating the Knossos Frescoes, in Lyvia Morgan (ed.) *Aegean Wall Painting: A Tribute to Mark Cameron:* 45-81. London: The British School at Athens.

Hughey, Jeffrey R., Peristera Paschou, Petros Drineas, Donald Mastropaolo, Dimitra M. Lotakis, Patrick A. Navas, Manolis Michalodimitrakis, John A. Stamatoyannopoulos, and George

Stamatoyannopoulos. 2013. A European Population in Minoan Bronze Age Crete. *Nature Communications* (May 14): 1-7. doi: 10.1038/ncomms2871

Hutton, Ronald. 1997. The Neolithic Great Goddess: A Study in Modern Tradition. *Antiquity* 71: 91-99.

Hutton, Ronald. 1999. *The Triumph of the Moon: A History of Modern Pagan Witchcraft.* Oxford: Oxford University Press.

Immerwahr, Sara A. 1983. The People in the Frescoes, in O. Krzyszkowska and L. Nixon (eds) *Minoan Society: Proceedings of the Cambridge Colloquium 1981*: 143-153. Bristol: Bristol Classical Press.

Immerwahr, Sara A. 1990. *Aegean Painting in the Bronze Age.* University Park: Pennsylvania State University Press.

Insoll, Timothy. 2004. *Archaeology, Ritual, Religion.* London: Routledge.

Jones, Bernice. 2007. A Reconsideration of the Kneeling-Figure Fresco from Hagia Triada, in Philip B. Betancourt, Michael C. Nelson, and Hector Williams (eds) *Krinoi kai Limenes: Studies in Honor of Joseph and Maria Shaw*: 151-157. Philadelphia: INSTAP Academic Press.

Jusseret, S. J. Driessen, and Q. Letesson, 2011, Minoan Lands? Some Remarks on Land Ownership on Bronze Age Crete, Academia.edu, viewed July 15, 2020, http: //www.academia. edu/798982/ Minoan_Lands_ Some_Remarks _on_Land_Ownership_on _Bronze_Age_Crete .

Keller, Mara Lynn. 1997. The Interface of Archaeology and Mythology: A Philosophical Evaluation of the Gimbutas Paradigm, in Joan Marler (ed.) *From the Realm of the Ancestors: An Anthology in Honor of Marija Gimbutas*: 381-398. Manchester (CT): Knowledge, Ideas & Trends.

Keller, Mara Lynn. 1998. Crete of the Mother Goddess: Communal Rituals and Sacred Art. *ReVision* 30 (Winter): 12-16.

Keller, Mara Lynn. n.d. Artifacts and Mysteries: Empirical and Mystical Ways of Knowing or Empiricism and Mysticism as Convergent Ways of Knowing. Work-in-progress, *The Eleusinian Mysteries: Nine Day Rite of Initiation at Athens and Eleusis*. Photocopy.

Kerenyi, Carl. 1967. *Eleusis; Archetypal Image of Mother and Daughter.* Ralph Manheim (trans.). (Bollingen Series LXV). Princeton (NJ): Princeton University Press.

King, R. J., S. S. Ozcan, T. Carter, E. Kalfoglu. S. Atasoy. C. Triantaphyllidis, A Kouvatsi, A. A. Lin, C-E. T. Chow, L. A. Zhivotovsky, M. Michalodimitrakis, and P. A. Underhill. 2008. Differential Y-chromosome: Anatolian Influences on the Greek and Cretan Neolithic. *Annals of Human Genetics* 72: 205-212.

Klein, Nancy L. 2004. The Architecture of the Late Minoan IIIC Shrine (Building G) at Vronda, Kavousi, in Leslie Preston Day, Margaret S. Mook, and James D. Muhly (eds) *Crete Beyond the Palaces: Proceedings of the Crete 2000 Conference*: 91-101. Philadelphia: INSTAP Academic Press.

Knappett, Carl. 2009. Scaling Up: From Household to State in Bronze Age Crete, in Sara Owen and Laura Preston (eds) *Inside the City in the Greek World: Studies in Urbanism from the Bronze Age to the Hellenistic Period*: 14-26. Oxford: Oxbow Books.

Koehl, Robert B. 1986. The Chieftain Cup and a Minoan Rite of Passage. *Journal of Hellenic Studies* 106: 99-110.

Koehl, Robert B. 1995. The Nature of Minoan Kingship, in Robert Laffineur, and W.-D. Niemeier (eds) *Politeia: Society and State in the Aegean Bronze Age* (Proceedings of the 5th International Aegean Conference, University of Heidelberg, Archäologisches Institut, 10-13 April 1994, *Aegaeum 12*): 1: 23-35. Liège: Université de Liège, Histoire de l'art et archéologie de la Grèce antique; Austin: University of Texas at Austin, Program in Aegean Scripts and Prehistory.

Kontorli-Papadoupoulou, Litsa. 1996. *Aegean Frescoes of Religious Character.* Göteborg, Sweden: Paul Åströms Förlag.

Kopcke, Gunter, and Eleni Drakaki. 1999. Male Iconography on Some Late Minoan Signets, in Robert Laffineur (ed.) *Polemos: le Contexte Guerrier en Egée á l'Age du Bronze* (Actes de la 7e Recontre Egéene Internationale, Université de Liège, 14-17 Avril, 1998, Liège, Belgium, *Aegaeum 19*): 2: 341-346. Liège: Université de Liège, Histoire de l'art et archéologie de la Grèce antique; Austin: University of Texas at Austin, Program in Aegean Scripts and Prehistory.

Krattenmaker, Kathleen. 1995. Palace, Peak and Sceptre: The Iconography of Legitimacy, in Paul Rehak (ed.) *The Role of the Ruler in the Prehistoric Aegean* (Proceedings of a Panel Discussion Presented at the Annual Meeting of the Archaeological Institute of America, New Orleans, Louisiana, 28 December 1992, *Aegaeum 11*): 49-62. Liège: Université de Liège, Histoire de l'art et archéologie de la Grèce antique; Austin: University of Texas at Austin, Program in Aegean Scripts and Prehistory.

Lenuzza, Valeria. 2012. Dressing Priestly Shoulders: Suggestions from the Campstool Fresco, in Marie-Lousie Nosch and Robert Laffineur (eds) *Kosmos: Jewellery, Adornment and Textiles in the Aegean Bronze Age* (Proceedings of the 13th International Aegean Conference, 13e Rencontre Égéenne Internationale University of Copenhagen, Danish National Research Foundation's Centre for Textile Research, 21-26 April, 2010, *Aegaeum 33*): 255-263. Leuven-Liege: Peeters.

Lerner, Gerda. 1986. *The Creation of Patriarchy*. New York: Oxford University Press.

Letesson, Quentin. 2011. Review of *Minoan Kingship and the Solar Goddess: A Near Eastern Koine*, by Nanno Marinatos. *American Historical Review* 116 (2): 498-499.

Letesson, Quentin and Jan Driessen. 2020. 'On the House' A Diachronic Look on the Configuration of Minoan Social Relationships, in Maria Relaki and Jan Driessen (eds) *Oikos: Archaeological Approaches to House Societies in Aegean Prehistory* (*Aegis 19* Actes de Colloques): 7-24. Louvain: Presses Universitaires Louvain.

Lincoln, Bruce. 1999. *Theorizing Myth*. Chicago: University of Chicago Press.

Long, Charlotte R. 1974. *The Ayia Triadha Sarcophagus: A Study of Late Minoan and Mycenaean Funerary Practices and Beliefs* (Studies in Mediterranean Archaeology 41). Göteborg, Sweden: P. Åström.

Mann, Barbara. 2000. *Iroquoian Women: The Gantowisas*. New York: P. Lang.

Manning, Sturt W. 2010. Chronology and Terminology, in Eric H. Cline (ed.) *The Oxford Handbook of the Bronze-Age Aegean (ca. 3000-1000 BC)*: 11-28. Oxford: Oxford University Press.

Mantzourani, Eleni, and Giorgos Vavouranakis. 2005. Achladia and Epano Zakros, A Re-Examination of the Architecture and Topography of Two Possible Minoan Villas in East Crete. *Opuscula Atheniensia* 30: 99-125.

Marinatos, Nanno. 1984. *Art and Religion in Thera: Reconstructing a Bronze Age Society*. Athens: Mathioulakis.

Marinatos, Nanno. 1989. The Bull as an Adversary: Some Observations on Bull-hunting and Bull-leaping. *Ariadne* 5: 23-32.

Marinatos, Nanno. 1993. *Minoan Religion: Ritual, Image and Symbol*. Columbia (SC): University of South Carolina Press.

Marinatos, Nanno. 1995. Divine Kingship in Minoan Crete, in Paul Rehak (ed.) *The Role of the Ruler in the Prehistoric Aegean* (Proceedings of a Panel Discussion Presented at the Annual Meeting of the Archaeological Institute of America, New Orleans, Louisiana, 28 December 1992, *Aegaeum 11*): 37-47. Liège: Université de Liège, Histoire de l'art et archéologie de la Grèce antique; Austin: University of Texas at Austin, Program in Aegean Scripts and Prehistory.

Marinatos, Nanno. 1998. The Tell el Dab'a Paintings: A Study in Pictorial Tradition. *Egypt and the Levant* 8: 63-99.

Marinatos, Nanno. 2010. *Minoan Kingship and the Solar Goddess: A Near Eastern Koine*. Urbana (IL): University of Illinois Press.

Marinatos, Nanno. 2018. The Waz Spirals of Xeste 3, Thera: Regeneration and Solar Symbolism, in Andreas G. Vlachopoulos (ed.) *Chrostires Paintbrushes: Wall-Painting and Vase-Painting of the Second Millennium BC in Dialogue* (Proceedings of the International Conference on Aegean Iconography held at Akrotiri, Thera, 24-26 May 2013): 77-86. Athens: University of Ioannina/Hellenic Ministry of Culture and Sports—Archaeological Receipts Fund.

Marler, Joan, 2006. The Myth of Universal Patriarchy: A Critical Response to Cynthia Eller's Myth of Matriarchal Prehistory. *Feminist Theology* 14: 163-187.

McLennan, John F. 1865. *Primitive Marriage: An Inquiry into the Origins of the Form of Capture in Marriage Ceremonies*. Edinburgh: Adam and Black.

Mellaart, James. 1964. A Neolithic City in Turkey. *Scientific American* 210 (April): 102-103.

Mellaart, James. 1967. *Çatal Hüyük: A Neolithic Town in Anatolia*. London: Thames and Hudson.

Miller, Donald E. 1992. *Writing and Research in Religious Studies*. Englewood Cliffs (NJ): Prentiss Hall.

Millett, Kate. 1970. *Sexual Politics*. Garden City (NY): Doubleday.

Mina, Maria. 2007. Figurines without Sex: People without Gender? in Sue Hamilton, Ruth Whitehouse, and Katherine Wright (eds) *Archaeology and Women: Ancient and Modern Issues*: 263-282. Walnut Creek (CA): Left Coast Press.

Mina, Maria. 2008a. *Anthropomorphic Figurines from the Neolithic and Early Bronze Age*. Oxford: John and Erica Hedges.

Mina, Maria. 2008b. 'Figurin' Out Cretan Neolithic Society: Anthropomorphic Figurines, Symbolism and Gender Dialectics, in Valasia Isaakidou and Peter D. Tomkins (eds) *Escaping the Labyrinth: The Cretan Neolithic in Context* (Sheffield Studies in Aegean Archaeology 8): 115-135. Oxford: Oxbow Books.

Morgan, Lyvia. 1995. Minoan Painting and Egypt: The Case of Tell el Dab'a, in W. Vivian Davies and Louise Schofield (eds) *Egypt, the Aegean and the Levant, Interconnections in the Second Millennium BC*: 29-52. London: British Museum Press.

Moss, Marina L. 2000. The 'Mountain Mother' Seal from Knossos—A Reevaluation. *Prudentia* 32 (1): 1-24.

Moss, Marina L. 2005. *The Minoan Pantheon: Towards an Understanding of its Extent and Nature* (BAR International Series 1343). Oxford: British Archaeological Reports.

Murphy, Joanne M. 2011. Individual, Household, and Community after Death in Prepalatial and Protopalatial South Central Crete, in Kevin T. Glowacki and Natalia Vogelkoff-Brogan (eds) *Stega: The Archaeology of Houses and Households in Ancient Crete* (Hesperia Supplement 44): 112-126. Princeton (NJ): American School of Classical Studies at Athens.

Niemeier, Wolf-Dietrich. 1987. On the Function of the 'Throne Room' in the Palace at Knossos, in Robin Hägg and Nanno Marinatos (eds) *The Function of the Minoan Palaces* (Proceedings of the Fourth International Symposium at the Swedish Institute in Athens, 10-16 June, 1984): 163-168. Stockholm: Svenska Institutet i Athen.

Niemeier, Wolf-Dietrich. 1988. The 'Priest-King' Fresco from Knossos: A New Reconstruction and Interpretation, in E. B. French and K. A. Wardle (eds) *Problems in Greek Prehistory: Papers Presented at the Centenary Conference at the British School of Archaeology at Athens, Manchester, April 1986*: 235-244. Bristol: Bristol Classical Press.

Nilsson, Martin P. 1949. *The Minoan-Mycenaean Religion and Its Survival in Greek Religion*. 2nd rev. ed. London: Biblio and Tannen.

Nixon, Lucia. 1994. Gender Bias in Archaeology, in Leonie J. Archer, Susan Fischler, and Maria Wyke (eds) *Women in Ancient Societies: An Illusion of the Night*: 1-23. New York: Macmillan.

Olsen, Barbara A. 1998. Women, Children and the Family in the Late Aegean Bronze Age: Differences in Minoan and Mycenaean Constructions of Gender. *World Archaeology* 29: 380-392.

Palaima, Thomas G. 2008. Mycenaean Religion, in Cynthia W. Shelmerdine (ed.) *The Cambridge Companion to the Aegean Bronze Age*: 342-361. Cambridge: Cambridge University Press.

Palyvou, Clairy. 2004. Outdoor Space in Minoan Architecture: 'Community and Privacy,' in Gerald Cadogan, Eleni Hatzaki, and Adonis Vasilakis (eds) *Knossos: Palace, City, State: Proceedings of a Conference in Heraklion organized by the British School at Athens and the 23rd Ephoreia of Prehistoric and Classical Antiquities, in Heraklion, November 2000, for the Centenary of Sir Arthur Evans's Excavations at Knossos*: 207-217. London: The British School at Athens.

Panagiotaki, Marina. 1999. *The Central Palace Sanctuary at Knossos*. London: The British School at Athens.

Papageorgiou, Irini. 2018. The Iconographic Subject of the Hunt in the Cyclades and Crete in the Second Millennium BC: Sounds and Echoes in the art of Wall-Painting and Vase-Painting, in Andreas G. Vlachopoulos (ed.) *Chrostires Paintbrushes: Wall-Painting and Vase-Painting of the Second Millennium BC in Dialogue* (Proceedings of the International Conference on Aegean Iconography held at Akrotiri, Thera, 24-26 May 2013): 301-313. Athens: University of Ioannina/Hellenic Ministry of Culture and Sports—Archaeological Receipts Fund.

Papagiannopoulou, Angelia. 1995. Xeste 3, Akrotiri, Thera: The Pottery, in Christine Morris (ed.) *KLADOS: Essays in Honour of J. N. Coldstream* (Bulletin of the Institute of Classical Studies, Supplement 63): 209-215. London: University of London Institute of Classical Studies.

Partenheimer, David. 2003. Introduction, in David Partenheimer (trans.) *An English Translation of Bachofen's Mutterrecht (Mother Right)* (1861): iii-vii. Lewiston (NY): The Edwin Mellen Press.

Patton, Laurie L. and Wendy Doniger (eds) 1996. *Myth and Method.* Charlottesville (VA): University Press of Virginia.

Plaskow, Judith. 1980. Blaming Jews for Inventing Patriarchy. *Lilith* 7: 12-14.

Platon, Nicolas. 1966. *Crete.* New York: World.

Pomeroy, Sarah B. 1973. Selected Bibliography on Women in Antiquity. *Arethusa* 6: 125-137.

Pomeroy, Sarah B. 1976. A Classical Scholar's Perspective on Matriarchy, in Berenice A. Carroll (ed.) *Liberating Women's History: Theoretical and Critical Essays*: 217-223. Urbana (IL): University of Illinois Press.

Poole, Susan E. 2020. *A Consideration of Gender Roles and Relations in the Aegean Bronze Age Interpreted from Gestures and Proxemics in Art* (UCL Institute of Archaeology PhD Series, Volume 3; BAR International Series 2980) Oxford: BAR Publishing.

Rackham, Oliver, and Jennifer Moody. 1996. *The Making of the Cretan Landscape.* Manchester, England: Manchester University Press.

Rehak, Paul. 1994. The Aegean 'Priest' on CMS I.223. *Kadmos* 33 (1): 76-84.

Rehak, Paul. 1995. Enthroned Figures in Aegean Art and the Function of the Mycenaean Megaron, in Paul Rehak (ed.) *The Role of the Ruler in the Prehistoric Aegean* (Proceedings of a Panel Discussion Presented at the Annual Meeting of the Archaeological Institute of America, New Orleans, Louisiana, 28 December 1992, *Aegaeum 11*): 95-118. Liège: Université de Liège, Histoire de l'art et archéologie de la Grèce antique; Austin: University of Texas at Austin, Program in Aegean Scripts and Prehistory.

Rehak, Paul. 1997. The Role of Religious Painting in the Function of the Minoan Villa: The Case of Ayia Triadha, in Robin Hägg (ed) *The Function of the 'Minoan Villa'* (Proceedings of the

Eighth International Symposium at the Swedish Institute at Athens, 6-8 June 1992): 163-175. Stockholm: Paul Åströms Förlag.

Rehak, Paul. 1998. The Construction of Gender in Late Bronze Age Aegean Art: A Prolegomenon, in Mary Casey, Denise Donlon, Jeanette Hope, and Sharon Wellfare (eds) *Redefining Archaeology: Feminist Perspectives*: 191-198. Canberra, Australia: ANH.

Rehak, Paul. 1999. The Monkey Frieze from Xeste 3, Room 4, in Philip Betancourt, Vassos Karageorghis, Robert Laffineur, and Wolf-Dietrich Niemeier (eds) *Meletemata: Studies in Aegean Archaeology Presented to Malcolm H. Wiener as He Enters His 65th Year* (*Aegaeum 20*): 3: 705-709. Liège: Université de Liège, Histoire de l'art et archéologie de la Grèce antique; Austin: University of Texas at Austin, Program in Aegean Scripts and Prehistory.

Rehak, Paul. 2000. The Isopata Ring and the Question of Narrative in Glyptic, in Walter Müeller (ed.) *Minoisch-Mykenische Glyptik: Stil, Ikonographie, Funktion. Internationales Siegel-Symposium Marburg, 23-25, September 1999* (Corpus der Minoischen und Mykenischen Siegel. Beiheft 6): 269-276. Berlin: Gebr. Mann Verlag.

Rehak, Paul. 2002. Imag(in)ing a Woman's World in Bronze Age Greece: The Frescoes from Xeste 3 at Akrotiri, Thera, in Nancy Sorkin Rabinowitz and Lisa Auanger (eds) *Among Women: From the Homosocial to the Homoerotic in the Ancient World*: 34-59. Austin (TX): University of Texas Press.

Rehak, Paul. 2004. Crocus Costumes in Aegean Art, in Anne P. Chapin (ed.) *Charis: Essays in Honor of Sara A. Immerwahr*: 85-100. Athens: American School of Classical Studies at Athens.

Rehak, Paul. 2009. Some Unpublished Studies by Paul Rehak on Gender in Aegean Art, in Katerina Kopaka (ed.) *Fylo: Engendering Prehistoric 'Stratigraphies' in the Aegean and the Mediterranean* (Proceedings of an International Conference, University of Crete, Rethymno 2-5 June 2005, *Aegaeum 30*): 11-17. Liège: Université de Liège, Histoire de l'art et archéologie de la Grèce antique; Austin: University of Texas at Austin, Program in Aegean Scripts and Prehistory.

Renfrew, Colin. 1985. *The Archaeology of Cult*. London: The British School of Archaeology at Athens.

Renfrew, Colin. 2011. Sun and Storm. Review of *Minoan Kingship and the Solar Goddess: A Near Eastern Koine*, by Nanno Marinatos. *Times Literary Supplement* (February 4): 28.

Renfrew, Colin. 2017. 'Marija Rediviva: DNA and Indo-European Origins.' Lecture, Oriental Institute of Chicago, November 8, 2017.

Renfrew, Colin, and Paul G. Bahn. 1996. *Archaeology: Theories, Methods and Practice*. 2nd ed. New York: Thames & Hudson.

Renfrew, Colin, and Paul G. Bahn. 2000. *Archaeology: Theories, Methods and Practice*. 3rd ed. New York: Thames & Hudson.

Renfrew, Colin, and Paul G. Bahn. 2004. *Archaeology: Theories, Methods and Practice*. 4th ed. New York: Thames & Hudson.

Reusch, Helga. 1958. Zum Wandschmuck des Thronsalles in Knossos, in E. Grumach *Minoica. Festschrift zum 80. Geburtstag von Johannes Sundwall*: 334-356. Berlin: Akademie Verlag.

Rich, Adrienne. 1976. *Of Woman Born: Motherhood as Experience and Institution*. New York: W. W. Norton.

Rohrlich-Leavitt, Ruby. 1977. Women in Transition: Crete and Sumer, in Renate Bridenthal and Claudia Koonz (eds) *Becoming Visible: Women in European History*: 36-60. Boston: Houghton Mifflin.

Roller, Lynn E. 1999. *In Search of God the Mother: The Cult of Anatolian Cybele*. Berkeley: University of California Press.

Rosaldo, Michelle Zimbalist, and Louise Lamphere. 1974a. Introduction, in Michelle Zimbalist Rosaldo and Louise Lamphere (eds) *Woman, Culture and Society*: 1-16. Stanford (CA): Stanford University Press.

Rosaldo, Michelle Zimbalist, and Louise Lamphere. 1974b. "Preface," in Michelle Zimbalist Rosaldo and Louise Lamphere (eds) *Woman, Culture and Society*: v-vi. Stanford, CA: Stanford University Press.

Ruether, Rosemary Radford. 2005. *Goddesses and the Divine Feminine: A Western Religious History*. Berkeley: University of California Press.

Rutkowski, Bogdan. 1986. *Cult Places of the Aegean*. New Haven, CT: Yale University Press.

Rutkowski, Bogdan, and Krzysztof Nowicki. 1996. *The Psychro Cave and Other Sacred Grottoes in Crete*. Warsaw, Poland: Art and Archaeology.

Rutter, Jeremy, and Dartmouth College. n.d. Akrotiri on Thera, the Santorini Volcano and the Middle and Late Cycladic Periods in the Central Aegean Islands, *Aegean Prehistoric Archaeology*, viewed July 19, 2020, http://www.dartmouth.edu/~prehistory/aegean/?page_id=775.

Sanday, Peggy Reeves. 1981. *Female Power and Male Dominance: On the Origins of Sexual Inequality*. New York: Cambridge University Press.

Sanday, Peggy Reeves. 1998. Matriarchy as a Sociocultural Form: An Old Debate in a New Light. Paper Presented at the 16th Congress of the Indo-Pacific Prehistory Association, Melaka, Malaysia, 1-7 July, 1998.

Sanday, Peggy Reeves. 2003. *Women at the Center: Life in a Modern Matriarchy*. Ithaca (NY): Cornell University Press.

Sanday, Peggy Reeves. 2008. Matriarchy, in Bonnie G. Smith (ed.) *The Oxford Encyclopedia of Women in World History*: 3: 192-195. Oxford: Oxford University Press.

Sanday, Peggy Reeves. 2009. Matriarchal Values and World Peace: The Case of the Minangkabau, in Heide Goettner-Abendroth, (ed.) *Societies of Peace: Matriarchies Past, Present, and Future*: 217-227. Toronto: Inanna Publications and Education.

Schoep, Ilse. 2002a. Social and Political Organization on Crete in the Proto-Palatial Period: The Case of Middle Minoan II Malia, *Journal of Mediterranean Archaeology* 15: 101-132.

Schoep, Ilse. 2002b. The State of the Minoan Palaces or the Minoan Palace State? in Jan Driessen, Ilse Schoep and Robert Laffineur (eds) *Monuments of Minos: Rethinking the Minoan Palaces* (Proceedings of the International Workshop 'Crete of the Hundred Palaces?' Université Catholique de Louvain, Louvain-la-Neuve, 14-15 December 2001, *Aegaeum 23*): 15-23. Liège: Université de Liège, Histoire de l'art et archéologie de la Grèce antique; Austin: University of Texas at Austin, Program in Aegean Scripts and Prehistory.

Schoep, Ilse. 2012. Bridging the Divide between the 'Prepalatial' and the 'Protopalatial' Periods? in Ilse Schoep, Peter Tomkins, and Jan Driessen (eds) *Back to the Beginning: Reassessing Social and Political Complexity on Crete during the Early and Middle Bronze Age*: 403-428. Oxford: Oxbow Books.

Schoep, Ilse, and Peter Tomkins. 2012. Back to the Beginning for the Early and Middle Bronze Age on Crete, in Ilse Schoep, Peter Tomkins, and Jan Driessen (eds) *Back to the Beginning: Reassessing Social and Political Complexity on Crete during the Early and Middle Bronze Age*: 1-31. Oxford: Oxbow Books.

Schussler Fiorenza, Elisabeth. 1984. *Bread not Stone: The Challenge of Feminist Biblical Interpretation*. Boston: Beacon Press.

Sealey, Raphael. 1990. *Women and Law in Classical Greece*. Chapel Hill (NC): University of North Carolina Press.

Shaw, Maria. 1995. Bull Leaping Frescoes at Knossos and their Influence on the Tell el Dab'a Murals. *Egypt and the Levant* 5: 91-115.

Shaw, Maria. 2004. The 'Priest-King' Fresco from Knossos: Man, Woman, Priest, King, or Someone Else? in Anne P. Chapin (ed.) *Charis: Essays in Honor of Sara A. Immerwahr*: 65-84. Athens: American School of Classical Studies at Athens.

Simandiraki, Anna. 2006. The Agrimi in Minoan Ceramic Relief, in Theochares E. Detorakes and Alexes Kalokairinos (eds) *Prepragmena Th' Diethnous Kretoilogikou Synedriou, Elounta, 1-6 Oktovriou 2001*: A3: 95-108. Herakleion: Hetaireia Kretikon Historikon Meleton.

Smith, William Stevenson. 1965. *Interconnections in the Ancient Near East: A Study of the Relationships between the Arts of Egypt, the Aegean, and Western Asia*. New Haven (CT): Yale University Press.

Strasser, Thomas F. 1997a. Horns of Consecration or Rooftop Granaries? Another Look at the Master Impression, in Robert Laffineur and Philip P. Betancourt (eds) *Texnh: Craftsmen, Craftswomen and Craftsmanship in the Aegean Bronze Age* (Proceedings of the 6th International Aegean Conference, Philadelphia, Temple University, 18-21 April, 1996, *Aegaeum 16*): 2: 201-207. Liège: Université de Liège, Histoire de l'art et archéologie de la Grèce antique; Austin: University of Texas at Austin, Program in Aegean Scripts and Prehistory.

Strasser, Thomas F. 1997b. Storage and States in Prehistoric Crete: The Function of the Koulouras in the First Minoan Palaces. *Journal of Mediterranean Archaeology* 10 (1): 73-100.

Thomas, Carol G. 1973. Matriarchy in Early Greece: The Bronze and Dark Ages. *Arethusa* 6: 173-195.

Thomas, Carol G., and Michael Wedde. 2001. Desperately Seeking Potnia, in Robert Laffineur and Robin Hägg (eds) *Potnia: Deities and Religion in the Aegean Bronze Age* (Proceedings of the 8th International Aegean Conference, Göteborg, Göteborg University, 13-15 April 2000, *Aegaeum 22*): 3-14. Liège: Université de Liège, Histoire de l'art et archéologie de la Grèce antique; Austin: University of Texas at Austin, Program in Aegean Scripts and Prehistory.

Thompson, William Irwin. 1981. *The Time Falling Bodies Take to Light: Mythology, Sexuality and the Origins of Culture*. New York: St. Martin's Press.

Tringham, Ruth, and Margaret Conkey. 1998. Rethinking Figurines: A Critical View from the Archaeology of Gimbutas, the 'Goddess' and Popular Culture, in Lucy Goodison and Christine Morris (eds) *Ancient Goddesses: The Myth and the Evidence*: 22-45. Madison (WI): University of Wisconsin Press.

Tyree, Loeta. 1974. Cretan Sacred Caves: Archaeological Evidence. PhD diss., University of Missouri, Columbia. ProQuest (7520167).

Tzedakis, Yannis, and Erik Hallager. 1987. A Clay-sealing from the Greek-Swedish Excavations at Khania, in Robin Hägg and Nanno Marinatos (eds) *The Function of the Minoan Palaces* (Proceedings of the Fourth International Symposium at the Swedish Institute in Athens, 10-16 June, 1984, Stockholm): 117-120. Stockholm: Svenska Institutet i Athen.

Ucko, Peter J. 1962. The Interpretation of Prehistoric Anthropomorphic Figurines. *Journal of the Royal Anthropological Institute* 92: 38-54.

Ucko, Peter J. 1968. *Anthropomorphic Figurines of Predynastic Egypt and Neolithic Crete with Comparative Material from the Prehistoric Near East and Mainland Greece*. London: A. Szmidla.

Vandiver, Elizabeth. 2000. *Classical Mythology, Part I, Course Guidebook*. Chantilly (VA): The Teaching Company.

Vardinoyannis, Marianna V. 2010. *Labouring with the Challenges of Female Identity: Insights into Minoan Society*. Athens: Livani.

Vasilakis, Andonis. 2001. *Minoan Crete from Myth to History*. Athens: Adams Editions.

Vasilakis, Andonis. n.d. *Visitor's Guide Herakleion Archaeological Museum*. Athens: Adam Editions.

Vlachopoulos, Andreas G. 2008. The Wall Paintings from the Xeste 3 Building at Akrotiri: Towards an Interpretation of the Iconographic Programme, in Neil Brodie, Jenny Doole, Giorgos Galavas, and Colin Renfrew (eds) *Horizon: A Colloquium on the Prehistory of the Cyclades*: 451-465. Cambridge: McDonald Institute for Archaeological Research.

Vlachopoulos, Andreas G. 2011. 'Theran Frescoes.' Lecture, Oriental Institute of Chicago, October 22, 2010.

Ward, Anne. 1968. The Cretan Bull Sports. *Antiquity* 42: 117-122.

Warren, Peter M. 1972. *Myrtos: An Early Bronze Age Settlement in Crete*. London: Thames and Hudson, British School of Archaeology at Athens.

Warren, Peter M. 1973. The Beginnings of Minoan Religion, in Doro Levi and Giovanni Rizza (eds) *Antichità Cretesi: Studi in Onore di Doro Levi*: 1: 137-147. Cantania, Italy: Università di Catania, Instituto di Archeologia.

Warren, Peter M. 2002. Political Structure in Neopalatial Crete, in Jan Driessen, Ilse Schoep and Robert Laffineur (eds) *Monuments of Minos: Rethinking the Minoan Palaces* (Proceedings of the International Workshop 'Crete of the Hundred Palaces?' Université Catholique de Louvain, Louvain-la-Neuve, 14-15 December 2001, *Aegaeum 23*): 201-205. Liège: Université de Liège, Histoire de l'art et archéologie de la Grèce antique; Austin: University of Texas at Austin, Program in Aegean Scripts and Prehistory.

Warren, Peter, and Vronwy Hankey. 1989. *Aegean Bronze Age Chronology*. Bristol: Bristol Classical Press.

Waterhouse, Helen. 1974. Priest-kings? *Bulletin of the Institute of Classical Studies of the University of London* 21: 153-155.

Watrous, Livingston V. 1984. Ayia Triada: A New Perspective on the Minoan Villa. *American Journal of Archaeology* 88 (2): 123-134.

Watrous, Livingston V. 1994. Review of Aegean Prehistory III: Crete from the Earliest Prehistory through the Protopalatial Period. *American Journal of Archaeology* 98 (4): 695-753.

Wedde, Michael. 1995. Canonical, Variant and Marginal: A Framework for Analyzing Imagery, in Walter Müller (ed.) *Sceaux Minoens et Mycéniens IVe Symposium International 10-12 Septembre 1992, Clermont-Ferrand*: 271-284. Berlin: Gebr. Mann Verlag.

Wedde, Michael. 1999. Talking Hands: A Study of Minoan and Mycenaean Ritual Gesture—Some Preliminary Notes, in Philip Betancourt, Vassos Karageorghis, Robert Laffineur, and Wolf-Dietrich Niemeier (eds) *Meletemata: Studies in Aegean Archaeology Presented to Malcolm H. Wiener as He Enters His 65th Year (Aegaeum 20)*: 3: 911-920. Liège: Université de Liège, Histoire de l'art et archéologie de la Grèce antique; Austin: University of Texas at Austin, Program in Aegean Scripts and Prehistory.

Weingarten, Judith. 2012. Review of Minoan Kingship and the Solar Goddess; a Near Eastern Koine, by Nanno Marinatos. *Aegeus—Society of Aegean Prehistory, Aegean Book Reviews*, viewed July 19, 2020, https://www.aegeussociety.org/en/book_reviews/review-of-nanno-marinatos-2010-minoan-kingship-and-the-solar-goddess-a-near-eastern-koine-urbana-university-of-illinois-press/

Whitelaw, Todd. 2001a. The Floor Area of Minoan Houses, in Keith Branigan (ed.) *Urbanism in the Aegean Bronze Age* (Sheffield Studies in Aegean Archaeology 4): 174-179. Sheffield: Sheffield Academic Press.

Whitelaw, Todd. 2001b. From Sites to Communities: Defining the Human Dimensions of Minoan Urbanism, in Keith Branigan (ed.) *Urbanism in the Aegean Bronze Age* (Sheffield Studies in Aegean Archaeology 4): 15-37. Sheffield: Sheffield Academic Press.

Willetts, R. F. 1955. *Aristocratic Society in Ancient Crete*. London: Routledge and Kegan Paul.

Willetts, R. F. 1962. *Cretan Cults and Festivals*. New York: Barnes & Noble.

Willetts, R. F. 1967. *The Law Code of Gortyn*. Berlin: Walter DeGruyter.

Willetts, R. F. 1969. *Everyday Life in Ancient Crete*. London: B.T. Batsford.

Willetts, R. F. 1977. *The Civilization of Ancient Crete*. Berkeley: University of California Press.

Witcombe, Christopher L. C. E. 2000. Matriliny in the Aegean Bronze Age. Art History Resources. Women in the Aegean. Minoan Snake Goddess, viewed July 19, 2020, http://arthistoryresources.net/snakegoddess/aegeanmatriliny.html

Yang Erche Namu, and Christine Mathieu. 2003. *Leaving Mother Lake: A Girlhood at the Edge of the World*. Boston: Little, Brown.

Younger, John G. 1995. Bronze Age Representations of Aegean Bull-Games, III, in Robert Laffineur, and W. D. Niemeier (eds) *Politeia: Society and State in the Aegean Bronze Age* (Proceedings of the 5th International Aegean Conference, University of Heidelberg, Archäologisches Institut, 10-13 April 1994, *Aegaeum 12*): 507-523. Liège: Université de Liège, Histoire de l'art et archéologie de la Grèce antique; Austin: University of Texas at Austin, Program in Aegean Scripts and Prehistory.

Younger, John G. 2016. Minoan Women, in Stephanie Lynn Budin and Jean Macintosh Terfa (eds) *Women in Antiquity. Real Women Across the Ancient World*: 573-594. New York: Routledge.

Younger, John G. 2020. Narrative in Aegean Art: A Methodology of Identification and Interpretation, in Fritz Blakolmer (ed.) *Current Approaches and New Perspectives in Aegean Iconography* (*Aegis 18* Actes de Colloques): 71-86. Louvain: Presses Universitaires de Louvain.

Younger, John G. and Paul Rehak. 2008. Minoan Culture: Religion, Burial Customs and Administration, in Cynthia Shelmerdine (ed.) *The Cambridge Companion to the Aegean Bronze Age*: 165-185. Cambridge: Cambridge University Press.